International
Orff-Schulwerk Forum
Salzburg

Texts on Theory & Practice
of Orff Schulwerk

MOVEMENT
and **DANCE** in
ORFF
SCHULWERK

Edited by

Barbara Haselbach
Verena Maschat
& Carolee Stewart

**A Series of Publications
from the
International Orff-Schulwerk
Forum Salzburg**

edited by Barbara Haselbach

International
Orff-Schulwerk Forum
Salzburg

Texts on Theory and Practice of Orff Schulwerk
Volume III

Movement and Dance
in Orff Schulwerk

edited by Barbara Haselbach,
Verena Maschat,
and Carolee Stewart

Pentatonic Press

Cover Design: Lisa Berman
Editors: Barbara Haselbach, Verena Maschat, Carolee Stewart
Design of the International Orff-Schulwerk Forum Salzburg logo tree: Hermann Regner
Book design and typesetting: Bill Holab Music
ISBN 979-8-89372-315-1

Dedicated with deep gratitude and affection to the memory of
Gunild Keetman,
whose gentle, creative nature and guidance
blended music, movement/dance, and speech into a single artistic entity,
and whose influence will be felt for generations.

I am not exaggerating when I say that without Keetman's decisive contribution, Schulwerk could never have come into being.

—Carl Orff

Photo: Hilde Zemann, with kind permission

And dedicated to all people, young and old, learners and teachers,
who joyfully move, dance, sing, and play.
May the ideas of this book help them to do so.

Contents

Verena Maschat (Austria/Spain) with Tamara Figueroa (Argentina),
Danai Gagné (Greece/USA)

Manuela Widmer (Austria) with Astrid Bosshard (Switzerland),
Katerina Sarropoulou (Greece), Natalya Shestopalova (Russia)

Barbara Haselbach (Austria), Sofía López-Ibor (Spain/USA),
Raquel Pastor Prada (Spain), Warangkana Siripachote (Thailand)

Christine Schönherr (Austria) with Françoise Grenier (Canada),
Barbara Haselbach (Austria), Christoph Maubach (Germany/New Zealand)

PART III—TARGET GROUPS

Bethany Elsworth (Australia/Canada), Nadja Kraft (Austria/UK),
Wakako Nagaoko (Japan), Soili Perkiö (Finland)

Michele Ellis (Australia/Netherlands), İlkay Nişanci (Turkey),
Victoria Redfearn Cave (USA), Michaela Reif-Schnaidt (Germany)

Peta Harper (Australia), Judith Thompson-Barthwell (USA),
Doris Valtiner-Pühringer (Austria), Michel Widmer (Austria)

Greacian Goeke (USA), Sister M. Johannita Kweon (South Korea), Insuk Lee
(South Korea/Germany), Andrea Ostertag (Austria), Christine Schönherr (Austria)

Anida Chan, Maggie Ho (Hong Kong), Isabel Galeza (Germany),
Miriam Gurbanov (Argentina), Fátima Moreno González (Spain)

Tetiana Chernous (Ukraine), Angelika Holzer (Austria), Evelyne Walser-Wohlfarter (Austria)

Insuk Lee (South Korea/Germany), Annabell Opelt (Germany), Sonja Pfennigbauer &
Vivi Tanzmeister (Austria), Paul Scheer (Austria), Manuela Widmer (Austria)

APPENDIX

Foreword

My sincere congratulations on the publication of the third volume in the series Texts on Theory and Practice of Orff-Schulwerk. Because this topic—movement and dance in Orff Schulwerk—has not received much written attention in the past, this book, with its wealth of material and teaching ideas, provides a much-needed resource to address this shortage.

Many teachers come to the Schulwerk from a background in music and are therefore less likely to be comfortable with the movement aspect of the artistic-pedagogical concept of the unity of music, movement/dance, and speech—the idea that was developed by Carl Orff, Dorothee Günther, and Gunild Keetman and that has continued to grow for decades through the work of many educators and artist-teachers around the world. This book has the power to help bring all aspects of elemental music and dance education into balance.

An impressive number of authors from many different countries and cultures have collaborated on articles that broaden our knowledge about how movement/dance can be integrated with music. They offer useful, practical examples of how movement and dance are experienced, taught, and learned in many different contexts.

The release of this book is a wonderful way to celebrate the International Orff-Schulwerk Forum Salzburg's 40th anniversary. I believe it should be in the library of every Orff Schulwerk practitioner, and I hope it will find an extensive circle of readers.

Shirley Salmon
President of the International Orff-Schulwerk Forum Salzburg
February 2024

Introduction

From movement to music, from music to dance.
—Dorothee Günther

The particular nature of the art of movement lies in the fact that all the aspects of the personality are brought into play: body, spirit, intellect, emotions.
—Joan Russell

Elemental music is never music alone but forms a unity with movement, dance and speech.
—Carl Orff

This book, the third volume of the series *Texts on Theory and Practice of Orff Schulwerk (Studientexte zu Theorie und Praxis des Orff-Schulwerks)*, is dedicated to the topic of movement and dance, an area that has been an integrated and essential component of the Schulwerk from the very beginning during the 1920s (see the article by E. C. Gray, "The Munich Günther-Schule [1924–1944]: Cradle of the Orff Schulwerk").

Since the closing of the Günther-Schule in 1944, however, various events and circumstances have prevented movement and dance from finding acceptance and recognition as equal partners in elemental music and dance education in many places. The reasons for this are:

- It is difficult to notate movement. Even in the 1932/36 *Elementare Musikübung* publications of the Günther-Schule we find many examples of music accompaniment but no description of the dances themselves.
- The post-war school radio series of the Bavarian Broadcast, which Gunild Keetman directed for many years, understandably did not allow for the inclusion of movement, except body percussion.
- Because the five volumes of *Orff-Schulwerk - Musik für Kinder* [Music for Children] published between 1950 and 1954 were largely based upon the material of the radio broadcasts, practical examples of the integration of music and movement are missing. The necessity for including movement and dance is only pointed out in the appendix.
- Because the model of the original German-language version became the model for the first international publications (Canada, England, etc.) we do not find movement examples in these subsequent books either.
- Many teachers have little dance experience themselves and therefore feel reluctant to work with it in their classes.
- It is difficult to include movement and dance in some countries and cultures where there exists a moral prejudice against dance.

This began to change with the three-volume American edition conceived by Hermann Regner[1] during the 1970s, when games, dances, and teaching examples were included. Consequently, supplements to *Music for Children* began to include examples of movement and dance as well. Orff Schulwerk teacher training courses worldwide have gradually increased the emphasis on movement/dance in their curricula. In addition, the widespread use of video and access to the internet have helped to promote movement and dance as essential to elemental music and movement education.

The influence of the Orff Institute and the International Orff-Schulwerk Forum Salzburg

During the early 1960s, when the circumstances presented themselves, Carl Orff seized the opportunity to pursue his idea of a comprehensive teacher training program and established the Orff Institute as a *Seminar und Zentrum für das Orff-Schulwerk* (Seminar and Center for the Orff-Schulwerk[2]) at the then *Akademie Mozarteum* in Salzburg. Orff and a circle of experts including Dorothee Günther and Gunild Keetman collaborated to develop a curriculum that once again included a number of dance/movement subjects. Above all, the understanding of the mutual influence of music and dance was again consciously and practically realized as well as theoretically reinforced (see the article by B. Haselbach and V. Maschat, "Movement and Dance in the Teacher Training at the Orff Institute").

It was also during this time that the first two books dealing with movement and dance in the Orff Schulwerk were published: Gunild Keetman's *Elementaria* and Barbara Haselbach's *Tanzerziehung*. Furthermore, graduates of the various degree programs and further education courses of the Orff Institute and participants in summer courses and symposia who had experienced firsthand the close connection between the sister arts of music and movement/dance, influenced the Orff Schulwerk practice at their workplaces around the world.

Nevertheless, there have been very few publications specifically about the role of movement and dance in the Orff Schulwerk and we felt it was time to address this deficit. To accomplish this, the series *Texts on Theory and Practice of Orff Schulwerk* seemed to be the right place to reach colleagues around the world. Hence, we present here a very multifaceted collection of ideas and examples from a wide international group of authors who broaden the range of target groups and expand content while emphasizing the creative aspect and cultural diversity of our contemporary world. We have deliberately dispensed with a stylistic unity in order to demonstrate all the more clearly the creative richness and diversity with which the basic ideas of the Orff Schulwerk are realized worldwide today.

Expansion of target groups

Originally, the Orff Schulwerk was intended for elementary school children, but very soon the scope of its application expanded to include both younger and older target groups. Today, in the spirit of the Orff Schulwerk philosophy, work is being done with the unborn (i.e., with pregnant mothers), with toddlers, with kindergarten and elementary school children, with teenagers, adults, seniors, people with disabilities of various kinds, in inclusive and community

[1] Hermann Regner (1928–2008) was a composer, conductor, musicologist, author, and pedagogue. As director of the Orff Institute, he was instrumental in its academic development; as chairman of the Carl Orff Foundation and the International Orff-Schulwerk Forum he was influential in the dissemination of Orff Schulwerk through countless lectures, seminars, and workshops all over the world.

[2] The Center for the Orff-Schulwerk is now known by the name International Orff-Schulwerk Forum Salzburg.

groups, in the context of museums, in the church environment, at youth clubs—even if not always under the name of Orff Schulwerk. Each group must be taught in an appropriate way and must incorporate specially selected materials and activities.

The structure of the book

The book is organized around three focal points. Part I—Historical and Theoretical Background—establishes a foundation. The second part covers various topics such as movement/dance games, traditional or improvised dances, elemental choreography, as well as the combination of movement and dance with language and the visual arts. The third part concentrates on the work done with a wide variety of target groups.

Each article in Parts II and III begins with introductory theoretical material and is followed by a section of practical examples. These examples are models, and not recipes or lesson plans. We hope they will inspire teachers to incorporate more movement/dance in their educational settings.

Suggestions for how to use this book

As is the case with the previous volumes in this series, it is not necessary to read the articles in order.

We recommend that readers first get an overview of the structure and contributions in this book. Not every article will be of interest to everyone. Familiarizing yourself with the theoretically oriented articles in Part I and selection of topics and target groups from Parts II and III that correspond to your own teaching practice can give you very specific suggestions for your work. In addition, the contributions on more specialized topics from Part II may enrich your planning of the content in your educational setting.

Acknowledgements and thanks

First, we deeply thank all our wonderful authors for the enthusiasm with which they responded to our invitation to collaborate, for their openness to discuss and consider our suggestions, and finally for their patience during the sometimes-long process of revisions and cuts. We especially thank Doug Goodkin, who once again offered to publish this book with his publishing house, Pentatonic Press in San Francisco.

May this book, with its numerous and varied suggestions and ideas, help teachers to integrate movement and dance with music in a sensitive, varied, pedagogically and artistically inspiring, and joyful way.

The editors
Barbara Haselbach (Austria)
Verena Maschat (Austria/Spain)
Carolee Stewart (USA)

PART I
Historical and Theoretical Background

The Munich Günther-Schule (1924–1944): Cradle of the Orff Schulwerk

Esther Cappon Gray (USA)

When I founded the Günther-Schule in 1924, it was my goal to find a means for restoring the natural union between music and movement—music and dance. I sought a method that was not only appropriate for a few intuitive artists, but also an educational approach that would awaken rhythmic sensitivity and capability, as well as a hunger for dance and music, in all people. (Dorothee Günther, 1935, pp. 32–35)

Innovative intellectuals and artists energized Munich during the early 1920s. Carl Orff (1895–1982) described the ferment there as a "spring storm" that captivated "enthusiastic young poets, writers, painters and musicians" (Orff, 1978, p. 7). The city became a haven for forward-looking young trailblazers, and it was an ideal place for Dorothee Günther (1896–1975) to found the legendary *Münchner Günther-Schule für Gymnastik, Rhyhmik und künstlerischen Tanz* (gymnastics, rhythmics, and artistic dance), whose movement art delighted audiences and enthused critics. Günther's emergent approach to education provided a site where Orff could develop and test his ideas for a new way of teaching music.

Günther came to the field of dance with a rich background in art, theater, and gymnastic physical exercise. She began studies in 1913 at the *Kunstgewerbeschule* (Arts and Crafts School) in Dessau. While taking figure-drawing, she also studied anatomy and art history. In 1916-1917 she was an intern producer at the *Staatstheater* in Hamburg. Memories of the contorted models she had sketched in Dessau led her to study exercise instruction in the method of Bess Mensendieck, which she completed in 1919. She spent four years publishing and teaching about Mensendieck Gymnastics in Berlin, Breslau, and Hamburg, before she met composer Carl Orff in 1923. Her courses included anatomy, movement notation, and exercise methods (Brown & Sommer, 1969, pp. 58–59; Günther, 1962, p. 220).

Like Günther, Carl Orff was also completing studies and embarking on a career. He finished his training at the *Akademie der Tonkunst* (Conservatory of Music) in Munich in 1914, and he was studying piano and enjoying his first work as a theater conductor in 1916. After he was drafted to fight in World War I in August 1917 at the age of 22, he suffered severe injuries at the front. Following his recuperation, he was unable to return to combat, and he served out his deployment as substitute theater conductor in Mannheim and Darmstadt. When he and Günther joined forces on a musical project recommended by his mentor Curt Sachs (1881–1959), the prestigious curator of the Prussian State Instrument Collection in Berlin, they discovered common interests. Sachs was an expert advisor to Orff in 1921 during his study of early music and musical theater, and would be again later, regarding instruments for the Günther-Schule. Recognizing Orff's avid enthusiasm for dramatic theater, Sachs suggested that Orff examine works of Claudio Monteverdi: "You are a born musical drama composer. Your field is the stage! Go and study with the original music dramatist!" (Orff, 2020, p. 68). Orff was profoundly impacted when he saw the score of Monteverdi's *Orfeo* and envisioned creating a modern version of the work with a German libretto.

Günther-Orff Collaboration

While seeking a librettist who could craft a modern German text, Orff became acquainted with Dorothee Günther and was delighted to discover that she was a capable translator of Italian who understood and valued early music. Also, she was interested in translating Orfeo. It became Monteverdi's work, recommended by Curt Sachs, that brought together the original Orff Schulwerk practitioners, Carl Orff and Dorothee Günther.

According to Orff, he and Günther found it easy to work collaboratively, and their Orfeo project progressed quickly. As they worked, Günther spoke often about her ambition to open a school in Munich where modern physical education and dance could be taught. Many Munich schools of movement or gymnastics narrowly emphasized the methods of particular charismatic teachers, but her school would offer varied options, enabling students to develop individualized skill sets for personal professional goals. Günther was displeased with the emphasis on drill in gymnastics schools and with the use of martial-sounding piano music in gymnastic and dance studios. She longed to offer a fresh educational experience that would bring music, rhythmic development, and movement together naturally, and she agreed with Orff's idea of approaching music instruction hand-in-hand with movement teaching (Orff, 1978, pp. 12–13).

Günther's professional reputation in Mensendieck gymnastics was strong when she founded the Günther-Schule where Orff, as music department head, would first implement his ideas for music education. He participated in 1923, when the Southern German Mensendieck Society of Diessen held a "holiday course with practical work, lectures, and discussions." Orff never forgot the day when he and Günther presented their ideas in Diessen:

> *Günther gave an excellent lecture about her ideas for a new training school and then asked me to outline my thoughts about a corresponding music training... I spoke mercilessly of the deficient or out of date musical activity that was customary in most gymnastic schools, and I gave an imaginary picture of how I would change and renew it all.* (Orff, 1978, pp. 14–15)

In September 1924 when Günther opened her academy for gymnastics and creative artistic movement, it was called the *Günther-Schule München: Bund für freie und angewandte Bewegung* (Training Center of the Society for Free and Applied Movement). There her vision of three program areas became reality: "therapy gymnastics, rhythmic-gymnastic training, and dance training... Each of the first two branches lasted two years. The dance training... could only be chosen as a third complementary year of study after successful completion of the two-year training" (Kugler, 2013, p. 37). In the beginning, the program "lacked a really leading personality for teaching dance, so the dances... were usually in the convention of the times with choreography and mime mostly in the foreground" (Orff, 1978, p. 63). During the autumn of 1924, Orff taught all music for the school: piano, piano improvisation, conducting, ensemble improvisation, harmony, and music history, with assistance from a timpanist for percussion (Kugler, 2013, p. 41).

Carl Orff and Dorothee Günther, ca. 1923
Photographer unknown, from a private collection

Many classes were held in small groups, but recorder, piano, and timpani lessons were individual. Courses in musical improvisation included technique with the percussion ensemble, with piano, and with recorder. Orff developed many kinds of exercises in his lessons: "The task that I had set myself was a regeneration of music through movement, through dance." To him: "Improvisation is the starting point for elemental music-making." In his early days at the school, he began improvisation groups with rhythm: "handclapping, finger-snapping, and stamping in forms and combinations that ranged from simple to difficult and that could be integrated, in many different ways, into the movement lessons." A technique that enabled students to create non-metric, free improvisation was the use of language: "words, series of words, and sentences," that the students would transfer... onto drums. Keyboard improvisations began with drones: simple octaves or fifths that could "wander" between a limited number of notes. "To these fundamental sounds... I improvised melodies on a second piano that served as models for the students' improvisations that followed." Other techniques included the use of rattles and jingles that students crafted from "small stones, shells, snail shells, dried fruits, nut shells, and wooden balls in all possible sizes" (Orff, 1978, pp. 17–23, 28–29).

Tough Examinations and Youthful Leadership

The challenges of school examinations illustrate the competence required in the program. Dance students could be given a specific piece of music and asked to create a solo dance. Students could be asked to demonstrate how they would lead the percussion orchestra in rehearsal of a composed piece of music. In a two-and-a-half hour written exam for those completing the music requirement, students faced tasks such as: "composing a melody to a given rhythm; composing a free melody for recorder in a prescribed key and time,... the creation of a percussion accompaniment to a movement task or arrangement of the text of a children's song" (Kugler, 2013, pp. 38–39).

Two outstanding young students became teachers at the school after their graduations. Maja Lex (1906–1986) entered the Günther-Schule in 1925, at age 19, and Gunild Keetman (1904-1990) began studies there in 1926, at age 22. Orff described both women as "instrumental in the school's development" and praised them for "giving equally to both the dance and the music a new, unmistakable [school] profile" (Orff, 1978, p. 67). Lex and Keetman completed their courses quickly; Lex became an instructor in 1927, and Keetman in 1929 (Kugler, 2013, p. 40). Glossy black and white photos from that time capture young women dancing, conducting, and playing elemental instruments. Their alert concentration is dramatic. Always seriously focused, always working together, they radiate poise and intensity (Orff, 1978, pp. 76–79, 110-113, 145–149).

The school operated in small, humble rooms in the back of a courtyard at 21 Luisenstrasse for twelve years, 1924–1936, and then for eight more years from 1936 to 1944 in a spacious setting at 16 Kaulbachstrasse, with large windows that provided bright, natural light and looked out upon their garden. Former students from each site enthusiastically described unforgettable collaboration, hard work, and satisfying success. The following five Günther-Schule eyewitness-participants, students, and teachers, provide glimpses of the activity there.

Carl Orff emphasized the unity in creating music for dances, rather than creating dances for music:

> [At the Günther-Schule,] group dances with their own rules of form and their inherent dynamics usually came before the music, according to the ideas of the choreographer; the music grew stepwise as the dance composition unfolded, forming a unity together. The sustaining melody . . . as well as purely rhythmic dance accompaniments . . . formed the foundation in sound for the dance. To this individual members of the group often contributed ideas that were tried out and evaluated by everyone together. There arose a music, that . . . had the power to intensify and direct the dance. (Orff, 1978, p. 150)

Friederike Praetorius was a student in the Kaulbachstrasse building from 1936 to 1939 and offered a perspective from the "music studio" in the basement and the rhythmic movement classes with Keetman:

> There was a parquet hall upstairs, and downstairs in the cellar was the "studio"—Keetman with her instruments. Upstairs, Lex would be working with the dance ensemble. Keetman would go up when a movement sequence had been developed, a part of a finished dance. She'd look at it, then come down to the studio and suggest, "You try this" and "Now you add something there."... And we would do it, and then the music was there! It would be considered and evaluated. It unfolded in such a close relationship—a dance—out of the mix.
>
> Keetman was a brilliant teacher; I had rhythmic movement with her. She might start with one simple little step, a rhythm, and a movement, and add another simple little step to that, and maybe a little turn, and then finally a four- or eight-measure rhythm with movement would develop. Each class we'd start with new material. (F. Praetorius, author interview, May 8, 1985)

Sieglinde Mesirca, who danced with the Günther ensemble for ten years, (1932-1942), described movement improvisation:

Mostly Lex had the ideas for the dances and planned the choreography. Sometimes we'd improvise dances in groups of two, three, or six, and Lex would use what we had invented. Sometimes Lex would formulate something, and we'd try it out and work with what she suggested. Günther didn't get involved with choreography during our rehearsals. I don't know if she discussed it with Lex. Lex would give ideas to Keetman, and Keetman would react, and that's how they collaborated. (S. Mesirca, author interview, July 22, 1985)

Maja Lex described Keetman's shy personality and brilliant talent:

I would go to her and say, "Look at this. I have this and this idea. I'm picturing this and that, and I need a kind of music of this sort, you know? Or maybe better that I say nothing to you at all – look at this movement for yourself, then you'll know what we need!" And she would look at the movement, nervous (well, we were really young, and we were also nervous) and she would say, "I can't do that," and "I don't know."

Then the next morning she would come to me and say, "Do you have a little time for me? I worked on this last night. But it's not good. It's nothing, and—well, please, just listen to it." She would agonize before the first tone sounded. I would listen to it, and every time it would be exactly what I needed. Great fortune on both sides. (M. Lex, author interview, April 26, 1985)

Gunild Keetman wrote "Memories of the Günther-Schule" and described the complexity of the collaborative creativity at the school:

[Maja Lex] developed her own, strongly rhythmic, dynamic and imaginative style. This was absorbed and adopted by her students with youthful vigour and great enthusiasm... All dancers who were not needed for a particular dance were used as musicians... Every player, whether mainly a dancer or musician, was able to react with great sensitivity to every nuance of the dance... Maja Lex would work to realise [a dance] idea with her students... We [the musicians] would then usually discuss together and decide on the most appropriate instrumentation and then work out the music for the dance... Much was tried out together, suggestions were either rejected or taken up, and then came the decisive moment: we gathered up our instruments and took them to the big hall to see and hear [the outcome]. (Keetman, 2011, pp. 56–60)

The "Orff Instruments"

In the first years of the program when rhythmic and melodic improvisation were limited to piano keyboards, body percussion, spoken or singing voices, or drums, Orff turned to Curt Sachs for advice regarding the kinds of instruments for the inventive musical activities. Sachs suggested that the most basic, essential component would be drums. After early lessons with body percussion and piano, Orff took Sachs' advice: "For my idea of developing an elemental music style, the percussion instruments, whose origins stretch back to earliest antiquity, had the most decisive significance . . . shaping form and tone color, developing a life of their own" (Orff, 1978, p. 69). A year after the school opened, the Spangenberg instrument company began to produce small, cylindrical, tunable drums that became the basis of the school percussion orchestra. Additionally, Orff's friend, Oskar Lang, an art historian, combed antique shops, "always purchasing exotica . . . in the form of new, and . . . valuable instruments: unusual rattles, little bells and on one occasion, a larger African slit drum" (Orff, 1978, p. 73).

On a visit to the school, Lang brought two Swedish sisters with him. Puppeteers, interested in music for their small theater, they said xylophones would be excellent for puppet performances and showed Orff pictures of Chinese and Javanese shadow plays and gamelan orchestras. Later, they sent Orff a large African xylophone—a marimba. Excited about the new sounds, he and Keetman experimented four-handed after lessons and often into the night. Students at the school brought percussion instruments and participated. Lex created *Stäbetanz* (Dance with Sticks) to music by Keetman (Orff, 1978, pp. 88–96).

Because the marimba was tuned to intervals smaller than a European semi-tone, Orff consulted Curt Sachs in Berlin, hoping for a way to craft xylophones with Western pitches. Sachs found it unwise to try producing a marimba with Western tuning, as the required materials (gourds for resonators) were not available in Europe. He thought Orff should use recorders rather than barred instruments for melody. Orff wanted both. While the school waited excitedly for the arrival of a set of recorders, a former student sent them a large African xylophone from Cameroon. The resonator of this instrument was a wooden box that had previously held builder's nails, demonstrating that such an instrument could be made in Europe (Orff, 1978, pp. 96–102).

The recorder was as exotic as the xylophone in Munich in the 1920s. Though there was a recorder quartet of "eccentric, elderly painters" in town who played early music enthusiastically, the basic mechanics of recorders were unknown at the school. When the long-awaited recorders arrived with neither instructions nor fingering charts, "Keetman experimented... and developed a rhythmic-dynamically emphasised way of playing," which suited the work of the school (Orff, 1978, p. 109).

Modest Public Performances to International Triumph

Günther, Orff, and the other school faculty emphasized individualized goals and training for each student. They did not drill a set repertoire of movements or dance steps to guide instrumental or movement work for their performances. From the beginning, they avoided ballet influences, symphonic music, and folk dances. They encouraged experimentation, originality, and creative inventions by students. Early on, public performances were built on musical sources like early lute music and pantomime styles of movement, but the group was looking for ways to develop more distinctive movement and music. They succeeded in inventing a style that was genuinely their own during the four years between 1926 and 1930. Orff recalled,

> We were always organising open evenings in smaller and larger halls to test our work, submit it to proof, and to make it more widely known. If on these first evenings gymnastic exercises were used as introductory material, these soon gave way to dance and music pieces, since public interest had shifted to this particular aspect of the work of the school.
> (Orff, 1978, p. 63)

They offered the first public performances before Maja Lex and Gunild Keetman had completed their studies. These included demonstrations of Mensendieck exercises, simple dances performed to early music, dances to vocal music sung by the performers, or narrative pantomime dance—outmoded styles, in contrast to the movement that later brought them fame. On their program during the 1926 season two narrative dance sequences were included. One was a pantomime dance trio to the Renaissance work, *Tre ciechi siamo* (Three Blind Men), by Giovanni Domenico da Nola, sung by the school chorus in role as bystanders. Also, that season five dancers performed a five-scene choreography by Günther to a delicate harpsichord accompaniment of Samuel Scheidt's *Passamezzo Variations,* which was a ceremonial "Dance of the Pages" around their unseen mistress (Orff, 1978, pp. 63–66).

A 1926 critic of the performance attacked them, writing: "A dance theater must produce something definite, of original dance art, positive... At the very least, one demands liveliness of dancers, also attractive attire, grace, and beautiful bodies." The reviewer criticized "dances that last too long with high repetition or similarity of movement," and denounced the use of sixteenth century music "whose interpretation is confined to dance school steps and arm movements." Though he did admire the choreographic concept of the "Dance of the Pages," he condemned their "Three Blind Men" as "hopelessly pitiful," and added, "one believed that the ecstasy and the rapture of the soloists and choir would come to a climax, but nothing came... It was all so primitive and clumsy that it raises fundamental questions about such 'dance' art" (F. K., 1926, Maja Lex papers).

Maja Lex did not like this style of dance. Just before graduating, she told Günther she wanted to leave the school dance group to join the program of acclaimed modern dancer Mary Wigman (1886–1973). "I just do not feel right performing any longer with this ensemble. I do not feel the connection between the movement elements, which are so simple, and Hertha Hackert's approach, interpreting with pantomime." Günther told her that Hackert was leaving. She added that both she and Orff were convinced that working with the Günther-Schule musicians and dancers would enable Lex to go her own way artistically, and Lex stayed to take a leadership role (M. Lex, Author interview, April 26, 1985). Similarly, Gunild Keetman gradually became the tutor for all the practical music instruction except piano (Kugler, 2013, p. 41).

The group earned a solid reputation during the years 1926 to 1930 and gave a stunning performance during the 1930 Munich Dance Congress. Carl Orff began to teach Schulwerk guest courses beyond the school (Frankfurt an der Oder, Stuttgart, Berlin) in 1931 and 1932, after Schott began to publish the Schulwerk books that he, Keetman, and their colleagues Hans Bergese and Wilhelm Twittenhoff created (Orff, 1978, p. 199). Just as the 1926 dances "Three Blind Men" and "Dance of the Pages" demonstrate the early style of dance at the school, their performance at the 1930 Munich Dance Congress illustrates their sophisticated shift to an avant-garde aesthetic. Two enthusiastic Americans wrote about the qualities that delighted them in the *Suite* presented by the Tanzgruppe Günther. John Martin, *New York Times* dance critic, wrote biting criticism of many dance performances that week. In contrast with the mediocrity he condemned, he found the Günther-Schule performance dazzling:

> *The first bright spot of the week appeared in a Barbaric Suite presented by the concert group of the Günther-Schule of Munich, under the direction of Maja Lex, with excellent music by Gunild Keetman for xylophone and percussion orchestra. Miss Lex was entirely unknown in Germany and is merely a member of the school staff. Her composition and its performance, however, would have stood out with distinction even on a good program, and it assuredly constituted one of the four real successes of the congress... Its variety of rhythms and movements met the eye with as much relish as Miss Keetman's charming music met the ear.* (Martin, 1930)

American dancer-scholar Elizabeth Selden valued examples of an ideal she called "absolute dance." Such movement art, she said, cannot be produced by mechanically combining bits of form and technique, or by dancing a narrative, but must, rather, be created when dancers can build upon "impulse" and "improvisation"; things that are only possible when a dancer is able to "listen to the impulses of motion in the body" (Selden, 1935, p. 29).

When Selden saw the Günther dancers perform at the Dance Congress in Munich, they seemed to fulfill this ideal. She remembered it vividly five years later and characterized it in superlative terms in her book, *The Dancer's Quest:* "The most perfect example of an absolute dance composition that I recall was undoubtedly Maja Lex's Barbaric Suite,... at the International Dance Congress in Munich, in 1930." Selden described their work:

> *It was in large part a direct result of improvisation to the sound of... a percussion orchestra. It was an outgrowth of the training characteristic of the Günther-Schule, in Munich, where music and dancing are not two parts of the performance, but one... Every dancer there is a musician,... and every musician is also a dancer. Thus, Gunild Keetman, the composer of that very interesting score, took part in the third dance while another dancer took her place in the orchestra.* (Selden, 1935, p. 104)

Naming every instrument on the stage, she emphasized, "The orchestra . . . is always in full view and a part of the stage picture," and concluded, "A better balanced, more perfectly disciplined work than that accomplished by Maja Lex's remarkable dance group could not be imagined" (Selden, 1935, pp. 104, 106–107).

Following the 1930 Munich triumph, in 1931 the Tanzgruppe Günther won the *Concorza della Grazia* (a gold medal and silver cup) in Florence, Italy, and in 1932 they were awarded a bronze medal and a certificate at the *Grand Concours International de la Danse* in Paris, France (Abraham & Hanft, 1986, p. 57). On January 25, 1933, the dancers offered a *Großes Wohltätigkeitsfest* (Grand Charity Festival) to benefit the *Verein Prinzessin Ludwig-Kinderheim e.V.* (Society for the Princess Ludwig Children's Home; Günther-Schule, 1933, Maja Lex papers). Five days later, January 30, Adolf Hitler seized power of the country.

Survival in Threatening Times

Days were stressful as time passed and there were examples of what it would mean to live in a country where totalitarian National Socialist guidelines impacted most aspects of life and controlled all the operations of schools and dance groups. It became a time of rumors and fears, terror, and intimidation. People of Jewish heritage lost their German citizenship; among them Orff's cherished mentor, Curt Sachs, whose papers identified him as *Volljude* (100% Jewish). Sachs was terminated from his position as curator of the Prussian State Instrument Collection, and he fled the country. Günther was warned in winter 1932-33 that her school would be placed under a new, temporary director due to its "unacceptable music education," and a friend told her in spring 1933 that the school was to be closed by the authorities. The school was her life, and she became a member of the Nazi Party in hopes of preserving the ongoing work of the program. She also enrolled Lex and Keetman in the Nazi Party. Unwilling to join the Party, Orff distanced himself from the school (Kugler, 2013, p. 41; Haselbach, pp. 50–51). Keetman continued to teach but failed to update her address and did not pick up her membership material, thus committing serious breaches that were noted by the officials. In 1937 she was stricken from the Party (Berlin Document Center, 1937).

There were unthinkable shock waves that made life unpredictable. Authors and artists could be charged with not being German enough, and this could have dire consequences. Four years after the Tanzgruppe Günther's success at the Munich Dance Congress, the 1934 *Deutsche Tanzfest* (German Dance Festival) in Berlin brought the Günther ensemble and the group of Mary Wigman to a shared stage on December 11 and 15, and newspaper critic, K. G. Grabe ominously declared that they were not German enough:

> *Neither the Tanzgruppe Günther, Munich, whose leading force is Maja Lex, nor Mary Wigman gave us valid evidence that their dance, in the deepest sense, is German... What*

did Lex bring us?... Perfect choreography, accompanied by alien, Eastern-sounding rhythms with obtrusive tones that injured the ear so badly that the eye had trouble following the sequence of the dancers. (Grabe, 1934, Maja Lex papers)

In August 1936, the Günther-Schule contributed extraordinary pageantry to the "Festival of Youth" in the opening of the Summer International Olympic Games in Berlin. Dorothee Günther choreographed movement for two segments of the ceremony: "Children at Play" for 2,500 girls and 900 boys, as well as "Maidenly Grace," for 2,300 teenage girls. The music of those performances, composed by Gunild Keetman, was exquisite and airy, played on the unusual instruments of the Günther-Schule, amplified through the arena with the latest technology. The performance included processional lines of dancers dressed in white, moving in straight and curving lines. The lines of figures flowed and became circles that turned and shifted as the young performers danced. Viewed by the 100,000 viewers in the Olympic Stadium, the lighted field was like a constantly changing kaleidoscope of white patterns (Organisationskomitee für die XI. Olympiade, 1937, p. 577).

In addition to administering the school program in Munich, Günther managed the dance ensemble's European tours, including performances in Holland, Belgium, Czechoslovakia, Austria, France, Italy, Hungary, Switzerland, and Poland (Abraham & Hanft, 1986, p. 57). When the Second World War began in 1939 the tours were downscaled because transport of the instruments became impossible. In July 1944, students and staff were devastated when the school building on Kaulbachstraße was confiscated by the Nazi authorities, and the school had to be closed. On January 7, 1945, when Munich suffered widespread bombing damage, the school was struck, and it burned. Many papers, educational materials, photos, costumes, scores, and priceless instruments were destroyed (Orff, 1978, pp. 110–111).

Postwar Epilogue

After the war, Dorothee Günther retired from teaching and devoted herself to writing about education and dance, including a comprehensive book, *Der Tanz als Bewegungsphänomen* (Dance as a Phenomenon of Movement). Maja Lex became director of the artistic dance program of the new *Deutsche Sporthochschule* (German Sport University), which was founded in 1947 in Cologne. Orff turned to composition and fostered the founding of the Orff Institute at the Mozarteum Academy in Salzburg, Austria. Keetman, always the teacher, enthusiastically taught music to the children in her village, Breitbrunn, and also to the nuns who cared for the children in a nearby orphanage (G. Keetman, Author interview, December 1984). She taught Orff Schulwerk pedagogy at the Salzburg Mozarteum; she accompanied Orff for a month of teaching and lectures in Japan in 1962; and that same year she went with him to Canada to teach at the University of Toronto, bringing the Schulwerk to North America (Orff, 1978, pp. 239–243).

In 1948, Gunild Keetman, Carl Orff, and Orff's wife, Gertrud Orff-Willert, worked together when Annemarie Schambeck, head of the school broadcasts at Bavarian Radio, heard a recording of the bright, delicate, music from the 1936 Olympics and asked, "Can you write music like this that children could play themselves? We believe that this kind of music appeals especially to them, and we are thinking of a series of broadcasts." The radio programs brought Orff Schulwerk to children and their teachers in ways that evoked national and international interest and enthusiasm. (Orff, 1978, p. 212). The progressive process these three teachers created with the children of the radio broadcasts yielded the five Music for Children volumes of sample rhythm and melody materials for experiential "learning by doing" (Köllinger, 2018, pp.

38–49). Since its origin in Central Europe, Orff Schulwerk activities with rhythms, melodies, movement, and speech have been adapted and embraced in diverse cultural settings throughout the world.

References

Abraham, A., & Hanft, K. (1986). *Maja Lex: Ein Portrait der Tänzerin, Choreographin und Pädagogin* [Maja Lex: A portrait of the dancer, choreographer, and teacher]. Düsseldorf: Grafische Werkstatt.

Berlin Document Center. (1937). *Gunild Keetman*.

Brown, M. C., & Sommer, B. K. (1969). *Movement education: Its evolution and a modern approach*. Reading, MA: Addison-Wesley.

F. K. (1926). Münchner Kammertanz Bühne [Newspaper review, Maja Lex papers, German Sport University, Cologne].

Grabe, K. G. (1934, December). Tanzgruppe Günther [Newspaper review, Maja Lex papers, German Sport University, Cologne].

Günther, D. (1935). Das Orff-Schulwerk als elementare Musikübung für Gymnastiker und Tänzer [The Orff Schulwerk as an elemental musical exercise for gymnasts and dancers]. In W. Twittenhoff, *Orff-Schulwerk: Einführung in Grundlagen und Aufbau* [Orff-Schulwerk: Introduction to basics and structure] (pp. 32-35). Mainz: Schott.

Günther, D. (1962). *Der Tanz als Bewegungsphänomen: Wesen und Werden* [Dance as a movement phenomenon: Essence and development]. Reinbek bei Hamburg: Rowohlt.

Günther-Schule. (1933, January 25). *Grosses Wohltätigkeitsfest* [Grand charity festival] [Concert program, Maja Lex papers, German Sport University, Cologne].

Haselbach, B. (2013). Dorothee Günther (M. Murray, Trans.). In M. Kugler (Ed.), *Elemental dance–Elemental music: The Munich Günther-Schule, 1924–1944* (pp. 42–55). Mainz: Schott. (German edition published in 2002).

Keetman, G. (2011). Erinnerungen an die Günther-Schule/Memories of the Günther-Schule (M. Murray, Trans.). In B. Haselbach (Ed.), *Studientexte zu Theorie und Praxis des Orff-Schulwerks, Bd. 1: Basistexte aus den Jahren 1932-2010/Texts on theory and practice of Orff-Schulwerk, Vol. 1: Basic texts from the years 1932–2010* (pp. 44–65). Mainz: Schott. (Original work published in 1978).

Köllinger, S. (2018). *Gertrud Orff-Willert: Das musikpädagogische und musiktherapeutische Werk* [Gertrud Orff-Willert: The music pedagogical and music therapeutic work]. Mainz: Schott.

Kugler, M. (2013). *Elemental dance–Elemental music: The Munich Günther School, 1924–1944* (M. Murray, Trans.). Mainz: Schott. (German edition published in 2002).

Martin, J. (1930, July 20). The dance: A futile congress. New York Times, p. 120.

Orff, C. (1978). *The Schulwerk* (M. Murray, Trans.) Mainz: Schott. (German edition published in 1976).

Orff, C. (2020). *Erinnerungen: Leben und Werk* [Memoir: Life and work]. Mainz: Schott.

Organisationskomitee für die XI. Olympiade Berlin 1936 e.V. (1937). *The XIth Olympic Games Berlin, 1936: Official report* (Vol. 1). Berlin: Wilhelm Limpert. https://www.olympic-museum.de/o-reports/olympic-games-official-report-1936.php

Selden, E. (1935). *The dancer's quest: Essays on the aesthetic of contemporary dance*. Berkeley, CA: University of California Press.

When the new recorders arrived without instructions, "Keetman experimented autodidactically and developed a rhythmic-dynamically emphasised way of playing that fitted our music style" (Orff, 1978, p. 109).

Photographer unknown; Orff Center Munich

Student conducting exercises (1930): "It was the forming of an improvisation through gesture. The music came out according to the movement. Certain rhythms were indicated... through unmistakable signs. Every beat, every rhythm... dynamics, and tempo" (Orff, 1978, p. 74).

Photo: A. A. Gulliland. Carl Orff Foundation/Archive: Orff Center Munich

"Maja Lex [front right] would work to realise [a dance] idea with her... students... We [the musicians] would then usually discuss together and decide on the most appropriate instrumentation and then work out the music for the dance" (Keetman, 2011, p. 58).

Photo: A. A. Gulliland. Orff Center Munich, Günther-Schule collection

"Timpani Dance," part of the Barbaric Suite, an international triumph of the Günther-Schule at the Munich Dance Congress, 1930.

Photo. A. A. Gulliland. Carl Orff Foundation/Archive: Orff Center Munich

"Dance with Cymbals," 1934. At the Günther-Schule, "Every dancer there is a musician... and every musician is also a dancer... The orchestra... is always in full view and a part of the stage picture" (Selden, 1935, pp. 104–105).

Photo: V. Blücher. Carl Orff Foundation/Archive: Orff Center Munich.

"Day of Defiance," ("Dem Kämpferischen Tag"). Dance by Maja Lex (front left) and the dance group of the Günther-Schule, 1935.

Photo: S. Enkelmann. Carl Orff Foundation/Archive: Orff Center Munich

Movement and Dance in the Teacher Training at the Orff Institute

Barbara Haselbach (Austria), Verena Maschat (Austria/Spain)

Introduction

This article gives an overview of 60 years of development in the area of movement and dance as an essential part of the teacher training at the Orff Institute, Mozarteum University, Salzburg. If one understands the Orff Schulwerk not only as a collection of examples of elemental music-making, but also primarily as a timeless artistic-humanistic-pedagogical concept of aesthetic education—and this is how we interpret it at the Orff Institute—then it is obvious that movement/dance plays an important role in its relationship to music and language (and to other arts). We understand movement/dance first of all in its original function as a medium of expression and communication, using a form of heightened everyday movement, not necessarily as a technical or historically standardized direction of style. The program of the Orff Institute offers a broad framework both in the training of teachers and in practical application with many different target groups.

New Beginning: *Orff-Schulwerk—Musik für Kinder*

Continuing the history of Orff Schulwerk (see the article by E. C. Gray, "The Munich Günther-Schule [1924–1944]: Cradle of the Orff Schulwerk") we start with the second phase of the Schulwerk's historical development, which began several years after the closure of the Günther-Schule by the National Socialist regime in 1944 and its subsequent destruction by bombs in 1945.

In 1948, Carl Orff was asked to write some music for children for the school broadcasts of the Bavarian Radio. However, because he was working on the completion of his Antigone, which premiered at the Salzburg Festival in the summer of 1948, he asked Gunild Keetman to plan these educational programs with him and to take over its realization. These broadcasts, led by her over several years (and later continued by Hermann Regner and Wolfgang Hartmann until 2003 with only a few years of interruption; Hartmann, 2011, pp. 42-45), represented a phase with an emphasis on music and a deficit in the field of dance. Limited by the medium of radio, movement had to be almost totally excluded except for sound gestures (now called body percussion).

Following the radio broadcasts came the publication of the five volumes, *Orff-Schulwerk—Musik für Kinder* (Orff & Keetman, 1950–1954). Because the content of the books was based mainly on the material developed during the school broadcasts, movement is found only in written indications that strongly emphasize its importance and use, but do not give examples of how to incorporate it. In addition, there was the difficulty of describing dance in writing in a generally understandable way. This same problem probably prevented the inclusion of dance in *Elementare Musikübung*, the first Schulwerk booklets by Keetman, Bergese, Twittenhoff, and

18

Orff published by Schott during the time of the Günther-Schule (1932/33). Music for dance is notated, but never the dances themselves. For a long time therefore, the impression was given that within the Schulwerk framework the role of dance, movement, and drama were complementary because it was mentioned only in footnotes that might inspire further activity.

The result of this misunderstanding is that in many places Schulwerk was, and sometimes still is, incorrectly believed to be a method of music education, realized without dance or with only very little movement like body percussion and, if at all, using some folk or children's dances. This is a fundamental misinterpretation, and it misses entirely the essence that lies at the heart of Schulwerk. Gunild Keetman's book *Elementaria - First acquaintance with Orff-Schulwerk* (1974, original German 1970), and Barbara Haselbach's *Dance Education* (1978, original German 1971) ultimately provided clear guidance and encouragement for incorporating movement and dance in children's classrooms. Other books followed.

In 1949, more than a decade before the Orff Institute was founded, Gunild Keetman was invited to teach students of *Schulmusik* (music education for primary and secondary schools) as well as children's classes at the Academy Mozarteum in Salzburg. She was assisted by Traude Schrattenecker, a former student of the Günther-Schule. Here, dance was considered again. After Keetman's retirement, Minna Lange-Ronnefeld, a Danish music teacher and former student of Keetman, continued for a few years (Ronnefeld, 2011, pp. 62–63).

It was in 1957, when a series of Schulwerk programs were shown on television (again directed by Gunild Keetman, moderated by Orff's daughter Godela) that dance-like and dramatic movement were once more included (Hartmann, 2011, p. 44). This was also the time of the collaboration between Gunild Keetman and Suse Böhm at Böhm's children's dance studio in Munich, when several new elements arose in the work with dance that were presented in many performances and two films (Sedlmayer, 2004, pp. 82–88).

Radio broadcasts and the publication of the five central volumes of *Musik für Kinder* led to a rapid dissemination of the Schulwerk, but even though these books and the instruments produced by Studio 49 were available, the results were far from what Orff and Keetman had hoped for. A central training institution for teachers became unavoidably necessary.

Movement/Dance at the Orff Institute

Thus, in 1961, with the help of Eberhard Preussner, president of the then Mozarteum Academy, and the support of the Austrian Federal Ministry for Education and the Arts, the *Orff-Institut* was founded as a *Seminar und Zentralstelle für das Orff-Schulwerk* [Seminar and Information Center for Orff Schulwerk]. In Orff's words, it was, "A training centre in which music, movement and speech should be taught with equal emphasis, and a centre that should catch and satisfy the interest and desire for information that was now world-wide" (Orff, 1978, p. 241).

During the first years of the Orff Institute's existence, it was particularly Gunild Keetman— with Dorothee Günther as an external adviser—who determined the movement training curriculum. In addition to Traude Schrattenecker and Barbara Haselbach, who was invited to begin teaching when the Institute opened in 1961, a young team of movement and dance teachers was formed, whose members, after previous training in gymnastics or dance, had completed their studies at the Orff Institute and were then taken on as members of the dynamic teaching staff. Because they had different backgrounds, they offered a variety of content and ideas that were essentially complementary. In this first phase of the Institute, during which much experimentation took place, the spectrum of topics, content, and ways of teaching expanded.

Since the very beginning, there has always been both a pedagogical and an artistic aspect to the teacher training. The pedagogical aspect concentrates on the integration of theoretical and practical training with existing material, as well instruction about how to create inspiring examples for specific target groups including, of course, the methodology of creative teaching. During the first years, the emphasis was on kindergarten and elementary schools, and therefore the students at the Institute were teachers of kindergartens and primary schools. Right from the start, students were able to observe their instructors working with these target groups, and gain experience teaching them. Based on traditional children's games, dances, and songs, a child-oriented movement repertoire was adopted, expanded, and differentiated. Rhythmic exercises with sound gestures (body percussion) or small percussion instruments were developed and transferred into dynamic movement and spatial representations as well as simple dance forms related to children's songs, to which accompaniments were improvised or developed. Dramatic representations of fables and fairy tales, picture books, poems, and other texts incorporated language into the design. Music, language, and dance activities were not separated, but emerged from each other and inspired each other.

Over the years, more and more groups came into being, offered as music and dance sessions for parents with babies, for adults and seniors, for people with different abilities in clinics and homes, for inclusive and community dance groups, classes with youth clubs, and groups associated with church activities, museums, playgrounds, etc. These participants were not students of the Orff Institute but interested guests, and the classes also served as practice teaching groups for the students. Each group needed different materials. At the beginning the teachers used examples and contexts from their own cultural backgrounds and adapted their instructional approaches to suit each group. With the growing internationalization of the Institute's students and faculty, other cultural influences became increasingly significant and enriching.

A detailed description of the study programs at the Orff Institute and their development from 1961 to 2011 can be found in the special issue of *Orff-Schulwerk Informationen: 50 Years Orff Institute* (Grüner & Haselbach, 2011, pp. 114–139). Contributors to this extensive documentation include Micaela Grüner, Wolfgang Hartmann, Barbara Haselbach, Ulrike Jungmair, Andrea Ostertag, Minna Ronnefeld, Shirley Salmon, Manuela Widmer, and others.

Orff's concept is that the educational mission is not only humanistic but also artistic. It aims at the students' own artistic development, to impact their later teaching activities as well as their own music and dance creations. The students' own technical and creative skills are furthered as they learn about rehearsals and performances of programs that include compositions and choreographies by students and teachers. Such performance opportunities apply not only to students in the bachelor's or master's studies but also to children and teenagers who, after their basic training, chose special interest groups (including dance) in which they work toward performances.

A special study opportunity, the so-called intensive week (week of alternative learning), which unfortunately was held only for a few fruitful years, enabled independent and highly concentrated work on topics suggested by individuals or groups of students, occasionally also by teachers. Often topics were chosen from the field of dance, mime, or the integration of dance with other forms of artistic expression (e.g., painting, sculpture, puppet theater, dramatization of a story book, etc.). At the end of the week the results of the various projects were shown to an audience. Occasionally, performances were presented in schools, senior homes, even on the streets of the city during festivals, and during conferences at home and abroad.

Various dance ensembles—*Musica Scenica* (directed by Barbara Haselbach); *Musik-und Tanzwerkstatt* (Helmi Vent); *Das Collectif* (founded by Susanne Rebholz, Doris Valtiner and advanced students and later directed by Irina Pauls), *Company Flitz* (see the article by S. Pfennigbauer and V. Tanzmeister, "Movement/Dance Projects with Diverse Target Groups")—have emerged over the years at the Institute. They have performed at conferences and symposia and toured in several countries (Grüner & Haselbach, 2011, pp. 142–147).

After completing all required subjects, the final examination for students who have chosen dance as their main focus includes a choreography and composition for a group with a solo by the candidate, a thesis about a freely chosen theme, and a pedagogical exam after working with a group for a semester under the mentorship of one of the teachers.

In addition to the bachelor's and master's programs that last several years, since 1969 the Orff Institute also offers part-time courses such as the one-year so-called Special Course, "Advanced Studies in Elemental Music and Dance Pedagogy-Orff-Schulwerk." While applicants must have dance experience, most are musicians or music teachers. Decades of experience with Special Course participants and knowledge of their careers after completing their studies in Salzburg have shown that the multiculturality of the groups and the longer teaching and life experiences the individual students bring with them allows them to have a different kind of understanding and perspective about what they learn in movement and dance. They can use movement and dance in their classes in an inspiring way, even though their own dance technique may not be on a high level.[1]

In the following decades, the group of teaching personalities in the field of dance/movement and therefore also the program responded to new influences from general pedagogy, art, society, and therapy according to Carl Orff's words: "Remaining alive also means to change with time and through time. Therein lies the hope and the excitement" (Orff, 1978, p. 249). All this resulted in a lively and constantly evolving curriculum.

Characteristics of the Work in the Field of Movement/Dance at the Orff Institute

In Orff Schulwerk, movement and dance are understood to be the means of expression and communication most closely related to music. Here "elemental dance" is taken to have its original meaning as a playful and/or structured form of movement that goes beyond everyday functions, but not as a trend of style that is technically and historically standardized. In this context the following aspects have their significance and complement each other:

- The spontaneous physical behavior of the individual or the group;
- The improvised and artistically created dances of individuals or groups;
- The traditional movement and dance material that is used in the social dancing of particular times or cultures and their specific segments of society.

Worldwide the elemental, universal material of dance consists of varied forms of locomotion, jumps, rotations, and gestures, that are performed with different movements of the head, trunk, hips, arms, and legs, including sound gestures and expressive moments of stillness. Of course, the execution of this basic movement material has a different character and significance in the various world cultures. Rudolf von Laban, one of the most important dance theorists of the 20th century, has given the pedagogy of contemporary dance commendable, structural help with his clear and impressive analysis of movement. This basic material is available to all

1 See *Orff-Schulwerk Informationen, 79* (2008), special edition: 25 Special Courses.

physically mobile people before they enter into differentiated dance training of a particular style and is performed in culturally specific and diverse dance contexts by individuals, couples, or groups usually (but not always) accompanied by music. (see the article by B. Haselbach and A. Wolf, "Overview of Various Applications of Movement and Dance in the Orff Schulwerk").

The starting point of dance education at the Orff Institute is this original and relatively simple movement material. Through the versatile individual exploration of time, space, and energy, and their effects on movement, through diverse content-related suggestions, and through experiences while dancing with others, rich movement material emerges. Dance creations can have a narrative character or express music in an abstract way. The character of music in all its diversity and of language with its tonal-rhythmic or content-related dramatic effects influences and inspires the movement of individuals and groups. There is also the dance without any rhythm or accompaniment from outside, directed only by the inner feeling of time and rhythm—an experience worth trying with older children.

The following list provides a rough overview of the teaching areas that are used in the Orff Institute's teacher training program as well as in work with the various target groups—certainly always adapted to the respective group. These details do not constitute specific subjects (for their titles have constantly been changed according to the respective curriculum) but outline the range of content.

Overview of the Scope of Subjects
(Grüner & Haselbach, 2011, p. 168)

- **Warmups with movement games as motivation**
  Preparing the body for dancing, sound gestures, singing, conducting, playing instruments, speech exercises, etc. needs a warmup of the muscles, an opening of the mind for the space and the other participants, and a joyful feeling of being part of the group, anticipating the next experiences. Traditional or freely invented movement games help to prepare the state of mind and the body.
- **Body awareness**
  Building up a differentiated body consciousness through sensitization exercises needs time, silence, and concentration, and should be developed when the teacher feels that the group is able to concentrate for a short while, standing still or lying on the floor. Later on, this leads to concentrating individually on the movement memory and how the movement felt by quietly reviewing short periods of movement, possibly with closed eyes, "listening" to one's body and its reactions and feelings.
- **Work on the parameters—understanding movement in theory and practice**
  This involves providing bodily experience and a richly varied practice of the individual parameters: space, time, energy (dynamics), articulation, and form, these being equally the basic elements of music as well as movement and dance. Experiencing and practicing them within the body also helps musical understanding and interpretation.
- **The acquisition of a fundamental, open, and many-sided movement/dance technique**
  Based on Laban's movement analysis, a subjective as well as an objective technique is developed. This leads from basic body activities—in a multitude of variations and combinations—to an extensive movement and dance vocabulary that can later be further developed toward a specific dance style such as Release technique and other contemporary dance forms as well as for the interpretation of specific dance steps and movements of certain traditional dances.

- **Movement accompaniment**
  Music and dance-like movement have their closest relationship in the process of mutual improvisation of a dance with music or in the interpretation of a dance with its assigned music. Movement accompaniment is directly connected to music improvisation and instrumental technique. It is performed with voice, sound gestures, all kinds of hand percussion, recorders, and barred percussion together with any available personal instruments.
- **Creative dance or the invention (improvisation) and creation (choreography) of a dance**
  This process leads from the explorative search for material through spontaneous improvisation to the worked-out and fixed choreography, in narrative or abstract, in dramatic or lyrical form, composed for soloists, duos, trios, and small or large groups. It may start with simple units like a movement ostinato or a motif and continue in question-and-answer phrases until it might grow to a longer period of movements created for a soloist, a duo, or a group.
- **Interpretation of traditional dance forms**
  This includes children's dances as well as folk dances from various regions and countries, and historical dance and current social dances up to actual hits from popular dancing. It is also understood as the reproduction and interpretation of fixed dance forms that have been worked out by others (choreographers, teachers, or other participants). Using such material should always be connected with learning about the specific culture or time period of the original dance. It should not be movement alone, it is a great help in learning about diversity, and it opens up the world beyond one's own environment.
- **Dramatic dance representation**
  In elemental music and dance theater this refers to the dramatization of original texts, stories, fairy tales, and picture books of one's own or foreign cultures. It includes the invention of new themes and texts for dramatizing. Depending on the age and experience of the participants this might be simply a nonsense rhyme interpreted with rhythmic movements and changing shapes in space or it may lead to a whole little "opera." It allows for the use of various expressive media, particularly with children.
- **Integration of the fine arts**
  This involves the combination of dance, music, and texts with pictures, sculpture, architecture, and photography. Rather than a simple addition of parts, it refers to an integrating and integrative form of expression in which reciprocal inspiration and mutual effects are recognizable.
- **Basic knowledge of physiological anatomy,** with links to movement and dance technique.
- **Dance history and dance analysis,** with links to music and cultural history and the study of form.
- **Introduction to notation,** with links to dance and music composition and the historical subjects.
  Above all, last but not least:
- **General and subject specific didactics and methodology**
  Teaching practice is offered in numerous groups in the Institute itself as well as outside in kindergartens, schools, youth clubs, homes for elderly people, inclusive groups, community dance institutions, etc. This is part of the training in every semester, until during their last semester students are entirely responsible for a group and the weekly classes, mentored by a member of the faculty.

The demands regarding content are high. Because the training at the Orff Institute is by no means thought of as only for primary school teachers but as preparation for work with target groups of different types, the content must be adapted to suit each target group. After a basic four-semester course of study, students can choose a concentration on subjects according to their interests and special gifts. In the case of a dance focus, it means an intensified study of all the practical and theoretical dance subjects, various projects, participating and directing artistic productions, and teaching different target groups with an accent on dance.

To Summarize:

- The importance of living the arts instead of learning about the arts characterizes the Schulwerk. This applies to the role of movement and dance and how it was developed at the Orff Institute for more than six decades and has radiated from there into other countries.
- Traditional material from one's own—as well as from foreign cultures—is as important as the individual and group initiative that is creating new ideas and realizing them through movement, dance, music, and other expressive media.
- Learning takes place almost exclusively in groups. There is a flowing transition from one medium to another, always taking individual needs into consideration.
- There is a special quality in the relationship between the teachers and those being taught; learning at eye level, as former students often called it.

Lecturers in the Area of Movement/Dance at the Orff Institute from 1961–2023

Margarida Amaral, Eva Bannmüller, Dagmar Bauz, Stella Blanc, Ruth Burmann, Christa Coogan, Thomas Demarmels, Johanna Deurer, Ursula Fritsch, Avon Gillespie, Katharina Grill, Barbara Haselbach, Rahel Imbach, Susanne Jankula, Gunild Keetman, Gabriele Klein, Gabriele König, Verena Maschat, Monika Mittendorfer, Kordula Möser, Helge Musial, Andrea Ostertag, Hector Palacios, Helder Parente Pessoa, Irina Pauls, Martina Peter-Bolaender, Susan Quinn, Susanne Rebholz, Petra Sachsenheimer, Barbara Schönewolf, Ursula Schorn, Traude Schrattenecker, Tomaz Simatovic, Wolfgang Tiedt, Frits Tummers, Doris Valtiner, Helmi Vent, Beatrice Vögelin, Chris Wang, Lucinda Weaver, Astrid Wegner, Adelheid Weidlich.

References

Coogan, C. (2011). Elemental composition and its didactics—Dance. *Orff-Schulwerk Informationen, 85* (special edition: *50 Jahre Orff-Institut*), 171–173. https://www.orff-schulwerk-forum-salzburg.org/magazine-osh

Grüner, M., & Haselbach, B. (Eds.). (2011). *50 Jahre Orff-Institut / 50 Years Orff Institute 1961–2011* [Special edition]. *Orff-Schulwerk Informationen, 85*. https://www.orff-schulwerk-forum-salzburg.org/magazine-osh

Hartmann, W. (2011). Orff-Schulwerk with the Bavarian Radio—a catalyst and guide for many decades. *Orff-Schulwerk Informationen, 85* (special edition: *50 Jahre Orff-Institut*), 42-45. https://www.orff-schulwerk-forum-salzburg.org/magazine-osh

Haselbach, B. (2011). Reflections on the dance educational aspects of Orff-Schulwerk (M. Murray, Trans.). In B. Haselbach, (Ed.), *Texts on theory and practice of Orff-Schulwerk, Vol 1: Basic texts from the years 1932–2010* (pp. 196-218). Mainz: Schott. (Revised version of the original work published in 1984)

Haselbach, B. (1978). *Dance education. Basic principles and models for nursery and primary school* (M. Murray, Trans.). London: Schott. (Original work published in 1971 as *Tanzerziehung. Grundlagen und Modelle für Kindergarten, Vor- und Grundschule*. Stuttgart: Klett)

Haselbach, B., Grüner, M., & Salmon, S. (Eds.). (2007). *Im Dialog - Elementare Musik und Tanzpädagogik im interdisziplinären Kontext / In Dialogue - Elemental music and dance education in interdisciplinary contexts.* Mainz: Schott.

Keetman, G. (1974). *Elementaria. First acquaintance with Orff-Schulwerk* (M. Murray, Trans.). London: Schott. (Original work published in 1970 as *Elementaria. Erster Umgang mit dem Orff-Schulwerk*, Stuttgart: Klett)

Kugler, M. (Ed.). (2013). *Elemental dance–Elemental music. The Munich Günther School 1924–1944* (M. Murray, Trans.). Mainz: Schott. (Original work published in 2002 as *Elementarer Tanz - elementare Musik. Die Günther-Schule München*)

Maschat, V. (2010). Dance as an expression of personal freedom. *Orff-Schulwerk Informationen, 83*, 62–65. https://www.orff-schulwerk-forum-salzburg.org/magazine-osh

Orff, C., & Keetman, G. (1950-1954). *Orff-Schulwerk. Musik für Kinder,* 5 Volumes. Mainz: Schott.

Orff, C. (1978). *The Schulwerk* (M. Murray, Trans.). New York: Schott. (Original work published in 1976 as *Carl Orff und sein Werk: Dokumentation, Vol 3, Schulwerk – Elementare Musik.* Tutzing: Hans Schneider)

Regner, H. (Ed.). (2002). *40 Jahre Orff-Institut 1961–2001* [40 years Orff Institute]. Institut für Musik- und Tanzpädagogik – "Orff-Institut" der Universität Mozarteum in Salzburg & Orff-Schulwerk Forum Salzburg.

Regner, H., & Ronnefeld, M. (2004). Gunild Keetman. Ein Leben für Musik und Bewegung – A life given to music and movement (M. Murray, Trans.). Mainz: Schott.

Ronnefeld, M. (2011). The launching of the Orff Institute. *Orff-Schulwerk Informationen, 85* (special edition: *50 Jahre Orff-Institut*), 62–63. https://www.orff-schulwerk-forum-salzburg.org/magazine-osh

Sedlmayer, D. (2004). Working in Suse Böhm's studio (M. Murray, Trans.). In H. Regner, & M. Ronnefeld (Eds.), *Gunild Keetman. Ein Leben für Musik und Bewegung – A life given to music and movement* (pp. 82–88). Mainz: Schott.

Widmer, M. (2011). *Die Pädagogik des Orff-Instituts in Salzburg. Entwicklung und Bedeutung einer einzigartigen kunstpädagogischen Ausbildung als Impuls für eine allgemeinpädagogische Diskussion* [The pedagogy of the Orff Institute in Salzburg. Development and significance of a unique education through the arts as an impulse for a general pedagogical discussion]. Mainz: Schott.

Widmer, M. (2011). Development of studies. *Orff-Schulwerk Informationen, 85* (special edition: *50 Jahre Orff-Institut*), 124–127. https://www.orff-schulwerk-forum-salzburg.org/magazine-osh

Children were invited to present a special person or way of walking, e.g., on a rope in
the circus, as Hans guck in die Luft, a heavy angry person, or with one leg in plaster.
Photo: Hilde Zemann, with kind permission

In front of an enlarged replica of Miro's *Carnival*, a scenic realization is worked out in the Rupertinum Museum, Salzburg.

Photo: Stefan Zenzmaier, with kind permission

After inventing graphic motives, students interpret them with a dance sequence and musical accompaniment.

Photo: Hilde Zemann, with kind permission

Four dancers in textile tubes. Their anonymity and the material intensify the plasticity of the positions.

Photo: Stefan Zenzmaier, with kind permission

Dance study on the theme "Imitation-Variation-Contrast."
Photo: Stefan Zenzmaier, with kind permission

Dancing with hands and feet.
Photo: Hilde Zemann, with kind permission

Is the sound or the gesture leading?

Photo: Hilde Zemann,
with kind permission

Preschool children improvising to rhythmic accompaniment.
Photo: Hilde Zemann, with kind permission

Sound in Movement—Music in Dance

James Harding (USA), Verena Maschat (Austria/Spain), Angelika Wolf (Austria/UK)

In this article, we explore the variety of ways that sound can support and inspire and emerge from dance in Orff Schulwerk. Who is making the sound? Is it the dancers themselves, an accompanying teacher, an ensemble of classmates, or a professional recording? What kind of sound? Is it the breath, expressive speech, singing, a portable percussion instrument, melodic instrument, piano, or ensemble? How organized is the sound? Is it exploratory, responsive, improvised, or previously composed? Which comes first? Does the sound emerge from movement, or does movement respond to the sound?

A Musician's Path to Movement
James Harding

As someone trained primarily in music, I experienced dance later in my life. Although my own enjoyment of dancing was strong as a child (I remember moving ecstatically around my family's New York apartment to "Trepak" from Tchaikovsky's *Nutcracker*), I never had the chance to study dance in school. The closest experiences were Dalcroze-inspired music and movement lessons at a young musicians' training class, which I remember enjoying very much. I soon entered into more focused musical study and left movement and dance behind for the time being. My next experience of delight in movement came in the form of Saturday night dances to recorded music at a summer camp during high school. Well-worn recordings of "Ma Navu," "Zemer Atik," and "Misirlou" (among others) provided the soundtrack for the joyful experience of moving in synchrony with my fellow campers in a circle. I felt the thrill of sharing weight with a partner as we sailed around the room in waltzes and polkas or the fun of high stepping on "Salty Dog Rag."

My first experience accompanying dance as a musician came during college, where I had the opportunity to play in a Balinese gamelan ensemble. As a classical musician accustomed to interpreting the written page, I found it compelling to play with my eyes focused outwards on the dancer, listening for the cues of the drummer leading the whole ensemble in precise support of a turn, hand gesture, or phrase-ending posture. Fresh from this experience of the interconnection of sound and movement in Balinese music and dance, I arrived at my first encounters with Orff Schulwerk.

In my Orff Schulwerk training, I learned about the historic interconnectedness of sound and movement in the development of the Schulwerk, i.e., Orff's encounters as a young composer with the "musicless" dances of Mary Wigman, the experiments of the Günther-Schule in training dancers to create their own sound through the use of portable percussion instruments, the development of the barred instrument ensemble, and the choreographies of Maja Lex and Gunild Keetman featuring percussion instruments played by the dancers.

As a musician these days, I spend a very small amount of my time behind a score, and most of my time producing sound in service of music or movement made by children. My voice is the primary instrument to accompany the youngest children in movement exploration, directing them through speech to "galloping, galloping" and "tiptoe, tiptoe" and "GI-ANT WALK-ING," "Stre-e-e-e-e-tching," etc. Congas, temple blocks, and a standing cymbal have become favorite non-verbal instigators and signal-givers to young dancers. When playing the piano, my hands work the keyboard by feel, as my attention goes outward to the group that I am accompanying. To support students' choreographic variations based on folk dance music, I prefer to play the melody of the dance on the recorder, so that I am able to respond to each group's tempo and accent with varied articulation. Recorded music also plays an important role, and ever easier access to quality dance recordings through the internet allows me to select the best performance to accompany my students' dancing. Audio technology even makes it possible to adjust the tempo of a dance recording to suit the needs of learners.

I give student musicians opportunities to accompany movement with sound throughout their years at school. This can range from following a partner's improvised movements while playing on a percussion instrument to accompanying dance as part of an ensemble. In recent years I have enjoyed employing older students as the "dance band" for their younger school-mates. In a recent example with the "Bear Polka," fifth graders danced with second graders, helping to demonstrate the dance figures, and then playing xylophones and recorders while the younger students performed the dance on their own.

Within our middle school curriculum with its themes of world music (sixth grade), classical music (seventh grade), and jazz (eighth grade), students learn to play and sing music that accompanies folk dance, historical dance, and swing dance. Technology has played a part in extending the varieties of interaction between music and movement for older students, with projects in animation and filmed shadow choreography creating elemental movement visuals to accompany performances of more challenging and less elemental musical repertoire. The accessibility of videos of dance performances through the internet made possible a recent project, where eighth grade students "accompanied" the Alvin Ailey American Dance Theater, performing a marimba arrangement of the spiritual "I've Been 'Buked and I've Been Scorned," in four-part *tremolo*, following the gorgeous, elastic phrasing of the dancers in a video of the opening choreography of *Revelations*.

My training in Orff Schulwerk opened my eyes to the intrinsic musicality of movement, and the movement classes during my training thrilled me with the discovery of the profoundly musical experiences to be had through my body, exploring space, weight, shape, and energy. As a teacher of movement in my own classes with children, I began with what felt like easier content, having students create variations using the forms of folk dances, doing exploratory work with appealing movement props, and working with concrete images from texts or interpreting visual art examples. While I enjoy all these forms of creative movement work with children and still employ them regularly, I feel a special delight in working with movement as its own language, having students create sequences of movement based on elemental parameters. I now feel comfortable using the language of Laban to inspire student movement exploration, and also to evaluate and encourage them towards more effective choreography. Working with opposites in the categories of direction, weight, speed, and flow, plus the body shape categories of arrow, wall, ball, and screw, I now feel that I can help shape movement experiences that can stand on their own, with or without accompanying sound.

In the sections that follow we approach the topic of sound in movement first through an overview of ways of working (Verena Maschat) and then a specific example of a pedagogical sequence exploring the mutual inspiration of movement and expressive technique on a specific instrument: the body-drum (Angelika Wolf).

Music in Movement and Dance
Verena Maschat

There is no dance without sound. If the sound is not music as such and the dance seems "soundless," there is always rhythmic sound made by the body and breathing, thus always musicality. In this section, we take a close look at various possibilities for movement/dance accompaniment.

The importance of live music for movement/dance activities
Music is movement in itself, it moves us, but musicians also respond to movements of dancers. There is no doubt about the mutual influence when there is live music accompanying our movement activities. We might say that a musician has to accompany a dancer, observing the tempo, dynamics, and quality of movement, but invariably the dancer is influenced by the sound of the accompanying instrument. The same happens vice versa, the dancer reacts to the sound offered by the musician who, in turn, is inspired by the resulting movement.

Singing while dancing: Traditional dances and canons
Sung dances have been documented since the 12th century in France, e.g., Carole, Farandôle, or Pavane, and later in Italy the *Balletti per Cantare, Sonare e Ballare*. Songs for dancing exist in all cultures. They can be couple dances or simple circle and line dances, often in two-part form, the A-part sung by the dancers accompanied by quiet movements, the B-part instrumental and lively.

In the regions of sub-Saharan Africa, singing is never static but always connected with rhythmic movements. The children of the world accompany their outdoor games with voice and sound gestures. In the various adaptions of Orff Schulwerk volumes, we find several traditional dance songs from different cultures.

Another resource for sung dances is Georg Götsch's *Geselliges Tanzbuch 2: Tanzkanons* (Dance canons; 1966). Polyphonic singing while moving has a special magic. Children and adults have enjoyed sharing the dance canons I have created over the years. The melody of simple three-part canons, initially learned using scat syllables and body percussion on different levels, have provided a great starting point for inventing a text for the melody and a simple choreographic version to be sung and danced simultaneously in different floor patterns (circle, semi-circle, line, etc.).

Movement accompaniment (by the teacher or the students)
Vocal (speech and melody)
The most elemental way of sound in movement is with our body as a sounding instrument. We are warming up our body and voice simultaneously copying the movement ostinato each participant proposes in turn, accompanied by the voice (spoken or sung, long-short, high-low, loud-soft sounds, etc.). Longer phrases can be created using onomatopoeias or short melodies.

An excellent didactic tool for teaching traditional dance forms is the voice of the teacher singing parts of the melody and including words for directions, etc., combined with gestures. This allows for adjusting the tempo or modulating the voice to suggest smaller or bigger movements or accents instead of the common way giving long verbal directions and counting the steps out loud.

Body percussion

In the beginning we just used four: snap, clap, patsch, and stamp. Gunild Keetman called them sound gestures and taught accompaniments in a way that the sequence would flow in a natural gesture, organic breathing included.

New movements that produce sounds followed over the years and were combined into "moved rhythm" compositions or ostinato patterns accompanying songs. Especially with teenagers or people reluctant to dance, body percussion is an excellent start to get them involved in basic movement activities.

Untuned percussion

"Listen with your feet"- Two different sounds for two feet.

To develop active listening to the accompaniment, basic patterns for locomotion can be worked by using a low and a high sound (e.g., bongos or congas) for right and left foot respectively. After preparing the different steps by listening to the rhythm played by the teacher and patsching the corresponding ostinato with right and left hands (rhythm of walk, run, skip, gallop, polka step, etc.) students dance in space, reacting to tempo changes and intensity of movement. Later they work in pairs, one with a chosen instrument, the other following, including silence/stillness.

For practicing not only pulse, rhythm, meter, phrase length, and tempo, but also dynamics and character of movement, it is vital to accompany with different instruments according to the respective exercise. The accompanist should be able to choose from instruments with different sound possibilities (e.g., skin, wood, or metal) in order to help the dancers hear and feel the specific movements. Ideally, the instruments should be on a stand so that the accompanist can swiftly change from one timbre to another (e.g., bongos, congas, tom-tom; temple blocks, woodblocks, reco-reco; hanging cymbal, chime, bells). However, in a typical classroom we usually get by with a hand drum, claves, and a triangle.

Small percussion instruments as an inspiration for improvisation

Apart from rhythm activities, the sound character of small percussion instruments provides many ideas for creative exploration, improvisation, and composition. First, we experiment in motion with a previously chosen instrument, then improvise starting on the floor moving in locomotion, and finally develop a short solo sequence where the movement evokes the sound, which then gives a new impulse to the motion. We dance with our instrument to explore its sound possibilities; to imitate shapes with our body; to mime imagining other objects; to carefully move them across the floor; to make them sound with different body parts; to let the movement needed to make them sound initiate different ways of locomotion; to interact with it in all possible ways.

Barred instruments

Our xylophones, metallophones, and glockenspiels provide us with a wide range of possibilities (even more if there is a marimba or a vibraphone available). There are many different sound effects other than just those played with the corresponding mallets in the conventional way. Observing a group in movement can suggest different techniques and sequences of sounds.

Apart from playing melodies and ostinati we can use effects such as glissando, tremolo, and cluster. Combined with speaking or singing, this allows harmonic accompaniment with a rich sound.

Other instruments (played by the teacher or a student)
If there is a piano or keyboard in the room, many teachers might use it for comfortable and versatile accompaniment. However, even students who do not play the piano can find interesting sound possibilities on an open piano in non-conventional ways, even without touching the keyboard (e.g., glissando or individual strings played with a triangle mallet; using the pedal for duration of sound; marking a rhythm with our hands on the wooden part while the strings still sound, etc.).

On special occasions, a great variety of sounds inspiring new qualities of movement can come from string or wind instruments played by the teacher or a student (even with limited technical skills). Associations for movement ideas will come from the students as they react to these new sounds.

**Dance as inspiration for musical improvisation and composition
(and vice versa)**
The ideas of the Schulwerk first developed in the Günther-Schule (see the article by E. C. Gray, "The Munich Günther-Schule (1924-1944): Cradle of the Orff Schulwerk"), where frequently the musical composition and the choreography were developed at the same time, inspiring and influencing each other mutually. The holistic understanding of the Greek word μουσική (*mousiké*, derived from the term Muses) is the expressive connection between voice/instruments, speech/drama, movement/dance, and the visual arts.

In the Orff Institute during the 1970s, I participated in a joint experimental project developed by Hermann Regner and Barbara Haselbach where dancers and musicians improvised together using a proposed theme as the starting point.

The choice of recorded music for movement improvisation and dance
Traditional dances and their respective music, vocal or instrumental, have been transmitted orally from one generation to the next. They are excellent social vehicles bringing together young and old in a joyful celebration.

It is wonderful if there is the possibility to have live music accompanying us in the classroom, but we rarely have the opportunity to hear and see musicians from different countries playing their instruments for us or singing in their own language. Of course, there is the possibility to make an arrangement for instruments that students can play while we are dancing, but we also need to find an original recording of the dance music. The quality is important, and we need to honor the respective culture where the dance and its music are from.

For movement improvisation and choreography, we can experiment with a wide range of musical styles—classic, contemporary, jazz, folk, new age, pop, and more—always searching for musical quality. The criteria for the selection are mainly the musical parameter we need in order to achieve a certain quality of movement. We might listen to a certain piece of music that inspires us to improvise and eventually create a composition, or we have a choreographical idea and are looking for a suitable musical base to develop it.

The "Drum of Wonder"
Angelika Wolf

Inspired by Soili Perkiö's song about our vibrating and sounding planet, a "Drum of Wonder," I developed an idea rooted in this special theme: to evolve from body awareness into "sound in movement," then recognizing in this process, "I am a drum of wonder!"

The start

LISTEN – it is the key word for "sound in movement." Listen not only with our ears, but also from the soles of our feet, even with our whole body. We are a "body-ear."

- Listening to our body, following its need to stretch, to open up from different body parts and…a yawn emerges, not only from the throat, but also from the heart. Yawning and stretching are a perfect match - sound in movement.
- Playfulness comes into the game. By stretching out "yawningly" into the space we start to listen to the sounds surrounding us. A sudden (imagined or real) sound attracts our ear to move into its direction. More sounds follow, and abrupt and small movements of body parts slip into the role of a listening ear reaching out into different directions in order to listen into the sounding space. An interplay of easygoing slow movements and sudden attentiveness emerges.
- We might have experienced in these first movements memories of a beginning day. Now it is time to leave our "home"—the self-space we have just discovered - in order to start the tasks of our day. More sounds emerge from a moving body. Feet release sounds on the ground in irregular rhythms—stepping, brushing, stamping, jumping, running, stumbling, slipping - or they sound from the other end of the energy scale, shuffling heavily. Again, sound in movement that is individual, but on a common journey into the new day.
- But isn't it our desire to find a rhythm throughout our day that supports us in everything we do? Maybe it begins with a moment of connecting with an image of nature, e.g., the soft wind, the endless width of the blue sky, a rainbow. Transferring the weight on the spot, swaying, swinging, sounds of our breath are joining in, balancing, and… we fall into the pulse of our day. A common pulse carries the group through space. A floating pulse, a jumping pulse, and the voice accompanies the pulsing dance in its legato and staccato manner.
- We calm down the movement until we stand on both feet, still active, and we listen to the heart, our heartbeat. Sound in movement, inside.

Touch and listen

Touching the area where we feel and hear our heartbeat, pounding like a drum, makes us aware of the connection of touching and listening. Our eardrum, being touched by sound waves enables us to listen. And even more: What we feel and hear in this moment is movement, sounding vibration.

This experience leads us into a special awareness in the next exploration. When we play with our hands on our body and later on a drum, can we open ourselves to this sensation that any touch on the instrument comes from a sensitive movement releasing the sound we listen to—with our "body-ear"?

Simultaneous imitation

As the leader of the group, I invite students in a circle to breathe and move with me and play sounds emerging from hands on the body, feet on the ground, from the mouth. Taking time for focusing on a common movement of body and breath supports the playing on the body, with the body in unison. With a gesture I pass the leading role to another student who continues fluently. Everybody has a turn, and afterwards we listen, feel the vibrations of our body, the drum. We notice that touch, movement, and sound are still present in our bodies and our imagination—a little wonder.

The verse

> I'm a drum of wonder,
> listen to the beat . . .
> of my hands
> of my mouth
> of my heart
> of my feet.
> That is all I really need!
> I'm a wonder drum indeed.

This verse expresses in its simple words the idea that we are a drum of wonder if we just listen to its magic:

> "I'm a drum of wonder, listen to the beat …."

(We play in unison—patting on our heart, playing our "finger drum" next to our ears.)

This first line serves as an invitation for everybody to play freely, improvising on their own body-drum. Explored movements and sounds from before arise spontaneously. Sounding feet might travel into space, which becomes filled with liveliness. In the beginning, I play the pulse very quietly on a drum to give a feeling of the phrase for this improvisation. Being free over a pulse can mean playing completely free-metric or improvising in relation to the pulse. Repeating the invitation line and each new improvisation over four bars sets the feeling of the phrase.

We continue. The wonder drum offers now sounds of certain parts and plays a dialogue between words and body sounds:

"Of my hands"—hand sounds
"Of my mouth"—vocal sounds
"Of my heart"—sounds on the chest
"Of my feet" —feet sounds

"That is all I really need"—a clap opening the space.
Three silent beats sound into that wide space.

"I'm a wonder drum, indeed"—finger drum.

As we experienced earlier that vibrations are still moving after the sound, our body-drum does not stand still, but is still slightly moving individually into a finishing body-drum shape.

There are so many ways to sound with hands, feet, mouth, and heart. Rudolf Laban's parameter of body, space, time, dynamics, and relationship can support further exploration.

- Which parts of your hands can sound? Where in space do your hands play? Sudden impulses, lingering sounds, soft touch, or strong impetus? Do they stay in touch (rubbing) or "fly away" quickly after the sound? In that way we support the idea that movement initiates the sound and sound moves us.
- For the "heart dialogue," I mention the idea to dance a movement that comes out naturally, just heart-felt from the moment.
- Experiments with all drum parts of the body lead to developing individually a short sequence for the dialogue part, focusing especially on interesting transitions.

Partner dance

We share our dance with a partner: Starting with the invitation rhythm in unison, sounding in the improvisation with free-flowing body movements around each other, continuing into the choreographed dialogue part directed toward the partner (and watching their individual dance) and molding into a common body shape.

A drum interlude played by the leader gives time to release the shapes and approach a new partner: *"And 1, and 2, and you know what to do!"*

Group wonder drum

All students build together one big phantasy wonder drum made of complementing body shapes. One student is invited by the group leader (by playing the invitation rhythm on their body) to dissolve the body shape (together with the group) and play their wonder drum solo freely. The following dialogue happens between the group and the soloist, who brings in their choreographed dance. A common end: *"You're a wonder drum indeed"* leads slowly again into a new group body shape.

Instruments

Students choose a portable percussion instrument or even a sounding object (paper, stone, etc.) and explore sounds from movement: from free improvisation to choosing certain sounds to create the dialogue structure by adapting the original body-drum sounds to the instrument. How can the instrument be brought into the dance of hands, mouth, heart, and feet? How can the body eventually mold into a shape together with the instrument?

Impulse and ripples

The image of a stone being thrown into the water and creating ripples serves as an image for a group improvisation bringing in the previous exploration with instruments and sensory awareness built up in this session. One student creates the center and is surrounded by several concentric circles of group members. With eyes closed they play the invitation rhythm to the group, which continues the improvisation from the inside to the outside circle (like ripples in the water) even spreading out into space. The dialogue part happens between the person in the center and the group around, who moves back fluently with the last line (*You're a wonder drum indeed!*) and brings the sound back, close to the person in the center, still eyes closed. Could they "see" and "feel" the dance of the group, just by listening with their "body-ear"?

Conclusion

Angelika Wolf's final metaphor from her lesson, the rippling of water, speaks to the exquisite sensitivity possible at the intersection of sound and movement. In Orff Schulwerk, this sensitivity should be present at all levels of practice in the pairing of music and movement experiences, from the encouragement of nuance in a child accompanying their partner's improvised movements, to the teacher's thoughtful choices of tempo and arrangement in the selection of recorded music for dance.

References and Resources

Götsch, G. (1966). *Geselliges Tanzbuch 2: Tanzkanons* [Social dance book 2: Dance canons]. Kassel: Bärenreiter.

Haselbach, B. (1978). The role of music in dance education. *Orff-Schulwerk Informationen, 22*, 5–13. https://www.orff-schulwerk-forum-salzburg.org/magazine-osh

Haselbach, B. (1991/92). Der Kassettenrecorder als deus ex machina oder Über ignoranten Musik-Konsum im Tanzunterricht [The cassette recorder as deus ex machina or about the ignorant use of music in dance classes]. *Orff-Schulwerk Informationen, 48*, 21–26. https://www.orff-schulwerk-forum-salzburg.org/magazine-osh

Keetman, G. (1974). *Elementaria. First acquaintance with Orff-Schulwerk.* (M. Murray, Trans.). London: Schott. (Original work published in 1970).

Maschat, V. (2010). Dance as an expression of personal freedom. *Orff-Schulwerk Informationen, 83*, 62–65. https://www.orff-schulwerk-forum-salzburg.org/magazine-osh

Maschat, V. (2013). Gesungene Tänze–getanzte Lieder/Dances to sing – songs to dance. *Orff-Schulwerk Informationen, 88*, 33–36. https://www.orff-schulwerk-forum-salzburg.org/magazine-osh

Schönherr, C. (2007). Stimme und Sprache im Fachbereich Bewegungsbegleitung [Speech and language in the subject area of movement accompaniment]. *Orff-Schulwerk Informationen, 78*, 34–38. https://www.orff-schulwerk-forum-salzburg.org/magazine-osh

Widmer, M. (1991/92). Vom tanzenden Klang zum klingenden Tanz [From dancing sound to sounding dance]. *Orff-Schulwerk Informationen, 48*, 18–21. https://www.orff-schulwerk-forum-salzburg.org/magazine-osh

Building Blocks of the Orff Schulwerk Pedagogy

Manuela Widmer (Austria)

Prologue

About 100 years ago, Carl Orff began to think about music education through movement. As a composer and musician, he observed specific connections between people, music, and movement at the Günther-Schule for Movement and Dance in Munich, where he was the music director. He wrote down little himself. Three essays from these early years, based on lectures he gave at advanced training courses for the first edition of the Orff Schulwerk publications—the *Elementare Musikübung*[1]—still offer us statements that can be starting points for a current consideration of building blocks of Orff Schulwerk pedagogy.

"Music begins inside human beings, and so must any instruction... The starting point is one's own stillness, listening to oneself, 'being ready for music,' listening to one's own heartbeat and breathing" (Orff, 1931/32 in Haselbach, 2011, p. 66). The topicality of this thought is confirmed by the physician, psychologist, and musician Manfred Spitzer, who writes: "Music is very intimately interwoven with us humans: It has existed for millennia, it calms us even in the womb, our memory processes make it possible and are addressed by it at the same time, and it is no different for our entire body. Anyone who makes music or dances is not simply making music or moving to music; rather, they are music" (Spitzer, 2003, p. 440).

And so we can observe that in many advanced training courses, in music lessons, in education seminars that have elemental music and movement/dance education in the sense of the Orff Schulwerk as their content, a lesson begins entirely in the spirit of Orff's as well as Spitzer's thoughts: The teacher asks the participants to close their eyes, to listen within themselves, to let their breath flow quietly, to feel their own pulse beat, and then to move through the room exactly at this individual pace. Only in a further step should everyone turn to the other people in the room, observing, in order to gradually find a common tempo. The teacher can then take it up and accompany the group on an instrument. With children, this initial situation is a little different. The teacher asks the children to move through the room at their own tempos, observes the children, and gradually picks up the most common tempo to accompany the children and synchronize their individual movements.

All over the world, children are curious and eager to learn. With their senses they want to investigate everything within their reach. Adults—first in the family environment and later in a formal one—can support them in this, challenge them appropriately, and encourage them

---

1   Ed.: *Elementare Musikübung* is the name of the first publication series of the Orff Schulwerk, which appeared in 1932–35 parallel to the earliest Schulwerk courses. The series title *Elementare Musikübung* means the quasi-artistic and pedagogical manifestation of Orff's concept of "elemental music." The term *Übung* is reminiscent of the conceptual understanding of the basso continuo era, and the title of Orff's Klavierübung echoes the famous *Klavierübung* by J. S. Bach. Here *Übung* (English: exercise, practice) means primarily the practice of musical structures and not a technical exercise in playing. Schott-Verlag Mainz published a total of 21 booklets during the years 1932–1935 (eight by Hans Bergese, eight by Gunild Keetman, four by Carl Orff, and one by Wilhelm Twittenhoff), of which only a few were reprinted after World War II (Kugler, 2019).

according to their age. Work in the sense of the Orff Schulwerk begins "in the human being" (see above). It starts with the human being and connects with human history, which provides us with evidence enough that music, speech, movement, dance, and play often form a unity to which every human being is open from birth. This general openness is independent of time, space, and culture; it begins in early childhood and can remain throughout life.

Connection Points

In the past years there have been several attempts to name the principles of Orff Schulwerk in books, book chapters, and newspaper articles. My own research in this regard is based on the one hand on my practical experience and, on the other hand, on my acquired knowledge from my studies at the Orff Institute. Parallel to my work with children, I began to offer continuing education courses and to work in the area of teacher education at conservatories. Thus, I was constantly challenged to explain and justify my teaching to colleagues in continuing education and to the students in training. In addition to my knowledge, I also intuitively built on my own subjective theories. I soon realized that this no longer satisfied me, and I began to study systematically the literature of my own field (Goodkin, Hartmann, Haselbach, Jungmair, Keller, Kugler, Nykrin, Orff, Regner, and many others). Later, I completed a degree in pedagogy and dealt with the "Pedagogy of the Orff Institute" in my dissertation (Widmer, 2011). Using an interview guide, I interviewed more than 50 former students of the Orff Institute from five decades (1961-2010). The rich material and the analysis of these expert interviews in the sense of qualitative social research then went into my research. In due brevity, I present my findings here on three levels and make them available for further discussion in professional circles:

- The first level names basic features (principles) that are terminologically located on a theoretical level and outline a general framework of thought.
- The second level formulates some didactic theses, which are derived from the framework of thought in the main features of the first level, but now refer to a concrete teaching situation.
- Finally, the third level offers personal reflections directly from teaching practice, which can also be called "personal theories" that every teacher develops in the course of their professional life, and which are often combined with scientific theories that are well supported on the basis of various studies.

Incidentally, in the scientifically based research process, the approach is often exactly the opposite: A subjective theory is reviewed; hypotheses emerge via initial classroom observations, reflections, and analyses, and are then tested in the context of research studies. As a result of the evaluation of such studies, usually some of the hypotheses can be confirmed, others may be refuted.

Basic Features of the Orff Schulwerk

The ability to change in time and space is perhaps the most central characteristic of the Orff Schulwerk in general. Orff himself emphasized this time and again: "The elemental remains a foundation that is timeless. The elemental always means a new beginning. Whatever they may be, the fashionable attributes that can and do attach themselves to all work must fall off again. Everything up to date, conditioned by time, becomes out of date. In its timelessness the elemental finds understanding all over the world. So it was not Schulwerk, about which I have written here in order to record an idea, but the idea itself that went round the world" (Orff, 1978, p. 277). One could also always hear from him how essential it was that the starting point of all music-making and dancing was one's own culture with its songs, dances, stories, poems, and instruments.

Starting from this core characteristic of mutability in time and space, I come to the following four basic features of Orff Schulwerk that will be put up for discussion here (Widmer, 2011, p. 440 ff.). These features position themselves free of any ideology and are open to adaptations in other linguistic spaces and cultural traditions. Freedom from ideology is shown above all by the rejection of a claim to general validity. The concept of "gestures of searching" (Zur Lippe, 1990/91, p. 14) characterizes the development of Orff Schulwerk pedagogy through the years, but does not mean the renunciation of providing concrete food for thought again and again in the service of this pedagogy:

First basic feature: Interdisciplinary
Relational (meaningful) connection of music, movement, dance, dramatic play, and speech are within the framework of integral music making and dance.

Second basic feature: Elemental
A body-bound "musical-dancing potency" (Keller) inherent in every human being can lead to moments of "incomprehensible experiences" (Jungmair), which nevertheless become latently effective according to individual possibilities.

Third basic feature: Artistic-pedagogical
An artistic-pedagogical approach establishes an essential relationship between the human being and the arts of music, dance, theater, and the visual arts, because: "In every human being there is hidden an artist" (Orff).

Fourth basic feature: Humanistic
The human individual with their specific needs (also determined by developmental phases) is and always will be the standard of an Orff Schulwerk pedagogy and makes it possible to this day to promote a "piece of being human" through one's own musical and dance production (from the expert interviews).

Orff Schulwerk pedagogy, as a pedagogical-artistic conception that cannot be generalized, can also be understood as a kind of musica universalis, as "radically [rootlike] human" (Keller, 1996, p. 49) and thus also promotes self-realization entirely in the sense of Orff, who speaks of "developing the whole personality" (Orff, 1961/2011, p. 154).

Didactic Theses

Based on the above four basic features, three didactic principles can be derived, which are mutually dependent and in constant interaction with each other. The work in the tradition of the Orff Schulwerk builds on the following:

- making teaching processes as well as the communication between teachers and learners *person-centered and therefore based on partnership and individualization;*
- providing *spaces for play, improvisation, and development* in the planning and implementation of lessons; and furthermore,
- not losing sight of the importance of a *workshop, model, and building block character.*

In summary, these principles lead to the following five didactic theses:

1. Intrapersonal learning arises from the strong challenging character of the versatile tasks (and the wide range of materials) in the context of self-determined improvisation and the promotion of a constructive working attitude.
2. The interpersonal peer group situation has a supporting effect, because the group plays a central role in the Orff Schulwerk pedagogy.
3. The variety of tasks and materials provides the ideal basis for internal differentiation, also in the sense of "discover what is inside you."
4. Liveliness and emotional quality are pursued in the lessons through a cooperative, authentic, and appreciative orientation of the teachers.
5. The Orff Schulwerk pedagogy understands its various models, which have developed over the decades, as "material for the creative expressive will" of the individual. Teachers, as artistic role models, create free spaces (workshops) so that the individual's own creativity can emerge.

My Personal Building Blocks as Food for Thought for Orff Schulwerk Practitioners

Ideal building blocks
Before we enter a room to teach a group of young or older people in the spirit of the Orff Schulwerk, we have usually completed one or more educational trainings. We have learned to sing, make music, and dance, and we have heard about lesson structure, methods, and child development. We have built up a repertoire of songs, dances, instrumental and speech pieces, and a mentor has guided us in the first practical steps of teaching. We know a lot and are excited finally to be able to stand in front of a group on our own and get started.

But something that even the best and most comprehensive training can only hint at, but never guarantee, remains a lifelong challenge for each of us: With what image of humanity do I meet my students? How well do I succeed in adapting to the many different individuals with my choice of content, my methodological tools, my own behavior (such as my body language), my choice of words, and my comprehensive empathy, in picking them up where they are, meeting their needs, and perhaps accompanying and supporting them attentively for many years without losing them?

Techniques are hardly useful for this task, for that I need ideals, visions, hopes, dreams, faith, love. Too big words? Our personal idealistic efforts cannot be big enough. We draw the impetus for this from our work with our students, if we are always willing to open our senses wide and are prepared to reflect consciously at the end of each day whether our teaching has been enthusiastically accepted, politely completed, or disappointedly rejected. We may rejoice with pride in good days and must equally admit with shame when we have failed. If we share our joys and sorrows with our students, they experience us as a caring person who takes interest in them. "Moved by love and guided by knowledge is good living" says British philosopher Bertrand Russel, and that applies to good teaching as well.

Didactic building blocks
This is about our tools of the trade. For us teachers of music and movement in the spirit of Orff Schulwerk, "Jack-of-all-trades" is a good friend. Whether it is about the selection of lesson content, methods, or social learning forms, for the most part the little word "and" plays a central role. It starts with our subject title: We are teachers of music AND movement/dance AND speech AND play/theater and, and, and... We do not just sing the song; we invent a

dance or a game to go with it and enrich the creation with costumes or appropriate props. Already during the learning of a song, but also during its repetition in the next lesson, we use small visual aids, such as hand signs, picture cards, small objects, and we set no limits to our didactic imagination. We know about the importance of space, its different areas, its paths, its appropriate equipment. We strive for an appealing design, enough space for roomy activities, but also cozy corners.

Above all, we are aware that group teaching requires special preparation, well-considered methods, versatile use of social forms, and our utmost attention and presence. The individual wants to be noticed, but also looks forward to meeting others in the group. The younger our students are, the more limited the group contact. Four- to five-year-olds initially seek the teacher's attention, then readily turn to one or at most two other children, and gradually begin to accept and eventually enjoy large group play and movement as well. The older the students get, the easier it is for them to make group contacts. They are now able to accomplish clearly defined tasks largely independently in small groups of up to five children and to move with increasing coordination in circle dances or other spatial formations.

Because we want to stimulate creative experience and learning processes, our work also demands content and methods that open up spaces for discovery and play, but at the same time also offer structures that provide our students of all ages with security and orientation that allow creativity to flow.

Material building blocks
Carl Orff and Gunild Keetman, in addition to their proposals and models of elemental music education, which is never just music education alone, but always connected with movement, dance, and speech, gave us another incomparable gift: the elemental instrumentarium. Don't worry, it is still not out of fashion, despite computer games, music apps, and composition programs. YES, we can use the new media in a profitable way, especially if we know them well and are able to use them creatively and in a way that promotes contact. And NO, these new media do not replace the drum, the xylophone, not even an inconspicuous rattle or even a big gong! A peaceful and meaningful coexistence is called for. There is a vast collection of literature—besides the classic five Orff Schulwerk volumes—with new pieces for the Orff instruments as well as new elemental instruments such as *Boomwhackers* or plucked string instruments that can be used helpfully in ensemble playing, just like self-made instruments.

All dedicated Orff Schulwerk teachers usually have an extra closet (or even a whole room) at home in which they store materials, objects, costumes, and masks and bring them to class in baskets, bags, and suitcases. In addition, self-made instruments, sounding materials, props, headdresses, cloths of all colors, and much more for such things as Chinese or Spanish fan dances, jungle trees, waterfalls, royal polonaises, and animal performances of all kinds are in this personal reserve, which grows throughout a teacher's life.

All this makes our lessons so personal and so unforgettable for generations of children who enter our rooms day after day, year after year, all over the world, and are greeted by us—tirelessly—with a smile.

Conclusion

The following graphic is intended to show the interrelationships of the various principles, basic features, theses, and building blocks listed above, and also to make us aware of the different levels between which we often unconsciously move back and forth in the exchange of experiences and in professional discourse, and which is why misunderstandings often arise.

- The construction "Orff Schulwerk pedagogy" is fragile, in limbo, in motion, overlapping, i.e., the workshops and the models are designed individually, depending on my interests and possibilities as well as the wishes and possibilities of the participants.
- All building blocks are interwoven, interdependent AND independent, i.e., as a teacher, despite my commitment to interdisciplinarity, I may well set content priorities in phases, and a performance project may be motivated more artistically than pedagogically, yet I still offer the participants individual leeway.
- In all periods of culture and time, Orff Schulwerk teachers have striven and strive for an appropriate balance of basic principles, didactic theses, and subjective theories.

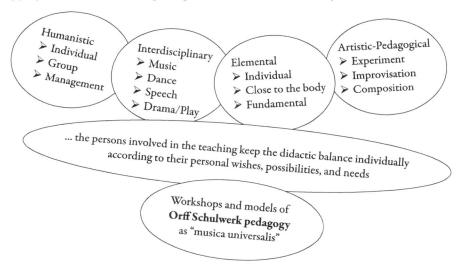

References and Resources

Haselbach, B. (Ed.) (2011). *Studientexte zu Theorie und Praxis des Orff-Schulwerks, Bd. 1: Basistexte aus den Jahren 1932–2010 / Texts on theory and practice of Orff-Schulwerk, Vol. 1: Basic texts from the years 1932–2010*. Mainz: Schott.

Haselbach, B., & Stewart, C. (Eds.) (2021). *Texts on theory and practice of Orff Schulwerk, Vol. 2: Orff Schulwerk in diverse cultures–An idea that went round the world*. San Francisco: Pentatonic Press.

Keller, W. (1996). *Musikalische Lebenshilfe. Ausgewählte Berichte über sozial- und heilpädagogische Versuche mit dem Orff-Schulwerk* [Music - a life enrichment. Selected reports on social and remedial educational approaches with Orff Schulwerk]. Mainz: Schott.

Kugler, M. (2019). *Online-Lexikon der Orff-Schulwerk Gesellschaft Deutschland*. https://orff-schulwerk.de/lexikon/

Orff, C. (2011). Orff-Schulwerk: Past & Future (M. Murray, Trans.). In B. Haselbach (Ed.), *Studientexte zu Theorie und Praxis des Orff-Schulwerks, Bd. 1: Basistexte aus den Jahren 1932–2010/Texts on theory and practice of Orff-Schulwerk, Vol. 1: Basic texts from the years 1932–2010* (pp. 134–159). Mainz: Schott. (Original work published in 1964)

Orff, C. (1978). *The Schulwerk* (M. Murray, Trans.). New York: Schott. (Original work published in 1976 as Vol. 3 of Carl Orff und sein Werk. Dokumentation. Band III: Schulwerk–Elementare Musik. Tutzing: Schneider.)

Spitzer, M. (2003). *Musik im Kopf. Hören, Musizieren, Verstehen und Erleben im neuronalen Netzwerk.* [Music in the head. Listening, making music, understanding, and experiencing in the neural network]. Stuttgart/New York: Schattauer.

Widmer, M. (2011). *Die Pädagogik des Orff-Instituts. Entwicklung und Bedeutung einer einzigartigen kunstpädagogischen Ausbildung* [The pedagogy of the Orff Institute. Development and significance of a unique arts education program]. Mainz: Schott.

Zur Lippe, R. (1990). Hermeneutik des Erbens. Überlegungen, den Fortsetzern des Orff-Schulwerks gewidmet [Hermeneutics of inheritance. Reflections, dedicated to the continuators of the Orff Schulwerk]. *Orff-Schulwerk Informationen, 46*, 11–15. https://www.orff-schulwerk-forum-salzburg.org/magazine-osh

A Culture of Collaboration

Sofía López-Ibor (Spain/USA)

Introduction

Orff Schulwerk emphasizes collaborative and active learning through music-making and dancing, using language and poetry as well as other artistic media. If elemental music and dance classes are part of a school's program, it needs very versatile teachers. If a project takes place encompassing a new and unfamiliar context and environment, a multifaceted leader is sought after. However, because it is rare that a single teacher is trained in multiple areas, the best and most productive solution would be a cooperation of colleagues who plan and implement the theme together from different focal points. Too often music programs operate in silos, with teachers working in solitude. And yet, there are other possibilities through collaboration.

Three Examples

Example 1 (a school production)

At The San Francisco School, a group of 7th grade middle school students is preparing to perform Shakespeare's *A Midsummer Night's Dream*. In the Orff Schulwerk class, they explore the plot of the comedy and the intricate love stories while improvising the dramatic scenes in modern language. They also learn dance repertoire from *The English Dancing Master* by John Playford (1975/1651). They improvise movement, create mini-studies, and compose music for the magic forest where the mighty Oberon and Titania rule. They watch videos and listen to and analyze the great works of Henry Purcell (*The Fairy Queen*), Felix Mendelssohn-Bartholdy, Benjamin Britten, Thomas Hodges (*A Midsummer Night's Dream*), and Michael Tippett (*The Midsummer Marriage*). They create puppet shows to depict short scenes, and they create animations of broken hearts and an enchanted garden. In visual arts class, they design costumes for the mischievous Puck, the mythical fairies, and other magical creatures. They design sets and three-dimensional trees. They also use technology to get acquainted with the Shakespearian language making an "insult generator" both with computer coding and playing with a Makey Makey kit, an invention kit using electrical circuits to connect everyday objects to the computer. At last, the students are eager to face the original text by Shakespeare, which they do in language arts class. Students end up acting, playing music, dancing, creating art, doing theater tech, and much more. In a period of approximately four weeks, we are ready to raise the curtain. Interdisciplinary teaching is an approach that integrates multiple areas of knowledge in the curriculum and recognizes that subjects are not isolated one from another. This is a collaborative model in which many teachers are working with the students in their individual classes toward a common goal.

Example 2 (a theme approached from multiple perspectives)
Another group of students at the school is immersed in a unit of study about Ghanaian music and dance. Apart from learning the basic rhythms and choreography of a *Bobobo* dance, the students explore the meanings of the *Adinkra* symbols. These ideograms are used extensively, not only in textiles but also in jewelry, architecture, and daily life objects of Ghana and many other communities of the African diaspora. In music class they have experience with the shape, form, size, and appearance of symmetrical or asymmetrical symbols, working with different senses in movement games, using language, guessing the meaning, drawing new versions of them, and more. The visual arts teacher and the music teacher together might share information by looking at Ghanaian textiles and leading a discussion about how and where we can find these symbols used by communities in our own cities. In art class, the students make their own stamps and collaborate to create a textile design. In language arts class the students use the meaning of the symbols to write poetry. In this model of collaboration, the music and art teachers prepare the sessions together and do some co-teaching.

Example 3 (preparing the teachers)
Music teacher colleague James Harding and I, decided to embark on a project in which we wanted to explore the Orff Schulwerk principles in relation to the Bauhaus, as we celebrated its 100th anniversary. We took an online course together, organized by the National Museum Thyssen-Bornemisza in Madrid. After the children left the school, we listened to the lectures together, took notes, created art pieces, read articles, and discussed how the different topics could be brought to life with the children. This is an example of how teachers can learn together, inspiring each other. A self-managed team, in which we took our own responsibility to do the work and were accountable for each other. We then collaborated on creating a presentation for the International Orff-Schulwerk Forum Salzburg that served as a celebration and self-reflection at the same time.

Impact of Collaborative Teaching

The previous examples suggest the power of interdisciplinary collaboration that leads to authentic learning for students and adults who have the chance to thrive when they cooperate with others. Schulwerk teachers are used to working with concepts in an integrative way that connects music, movement, language, fine arts, culture, and more.

Teacher collaboration is a key component of a wonderful school experience and environment. Everyone wins when teachers work together, design interesting and aligned programs and curricula, and evaluate teaching practices. The benefit is not only for the students, but also for the adults who seek inspiration and professional growth. When the collaboration is between different subject areas, the students become motivated, see the relationship between concepts, and enhance their critical thinking.

Why is it Important to Promote a Culture of Collaboration in Our Schools?

Schools that promote collaboration have the potential to offer a more memorable, engaging, and comprehensive learning experience for the students. When we create opportunities to work together, we foster positive relationships and teamwork, thus preparing students for the future. Being able to work in a team is defined in education as a critical 21st century skill. Teamwork is a compelling experience because we can combine the experience, ideas, and skills of several individuals who contribute their unique perspectives. In the real world, people need to interact with others who have different backgrounds, points of view, training, and experiences. It is never too early to start developing an open attitude, communication skills, respect for each other, and working together towards a common goal.

What Are the Structures We Can Create to Support Collaboration?

Most of the collaboration projects that we see in schools are project-based, which means the team will not continue working together when the project is over. In most situations, schools have departments organized by subject area, teachers' divisions, and other team structures that suggest collaborative work. It is crucial that the schools allow and design opportunities for people to meet, share, dream, and plan. It is clear that teachers working in the arts, in the sciences, or in language subjects teach in similar ways, and are therefore better prepared to collaborate. But teams can be formed by adults who come from completely different subject areas, and who can contribute to the final goal.

There are at least two forms of implementing cooperative teaching. In both, planning and goal setting must be done jointly by the teachers involved. In one case, two teachers of different subjects teach together, present an idea or a topic from different angles, e.g., change from graphic to musical/dance motifs, and finally lead the resulting solutions into a joint performance. However, this practice of joint teaching usually has its difficulties of implementation due to the different timetables and workloads of the partners. The second form takes place, so to speak, in parallel lessons on the same topic but in different subject areas (see the example of A Midsummer Night's Dream above). In this case, one can delve more into the respective subject-specific details, but the immediacy of expression when switching from one medium to the other is less instantaneous.

Preparing a Collaborative Team

Another important aspect of creating a culture of collaboration is thinking about the skills, competencies, and attitudes that one needs to work in a team. There can be situations in which the teamwork does not 'flow' or where there is no 'chemistry.' And there are certain conditions and qualities that everybody appears to appreciate in teamwork, i.e., the ability to communicate ideas clearly, to be an active listener, to share ideas, and to give constructive feedback. Also important is the potential to be flexible, adaptable, and ready to learn new skills. To have initiative and to be responsible are a must. Most articles in this book have been written in a collaborative manner. Sometimes the collaborator-authors were living in separate continents and time zones, spoke different languages, and worked in different settings. In my opinion, one of the most important things in team building is trust—the ability to rely on and appreciate each other. Teachers who fulfil this role are, beyond their professional leadership, important examples of cooperative behavior worthy of emulation by their students.

References

Playford, J. (1975). *The English dancing master.* New York: Dance Horizons. (Original work published in 1651)

University of California Television. (2010, December 10). *A midsummer night's dream* [Video]. Original music composed by Thomas Hodges. YouTube. https://www.youtube.com/watch?v=bzHu2LUWaso

Influences of Embodiment and Cognitive Neuroscience Research on Dance Pedagogy

Robyn Staveley (Australia)

Translating research into classroom practice is important for discovering how new information can improve teaching and learning. Embodiment research suggests that cognition is tightly integrated with the action by the body in the world and is reflected in the motor, sensory, and reward systems in the brain. This combined cognitive and neuroscience research informs pedagogy of the centrality of the body in learning. While many of the topics discussed here may seem intuitive for dance teachers, the aim of this article is to provide neuroscientific support, terminology, and description so that teachers can consider how their practice aligns with and is informed by cognitive neuroscience, and how to communicate this with others.

Embodied Cognition

The art of dance is embodied. When someone is described as the embodiment of their art, we imagine that everything about them, the way they look, act, what they say, how they sound, is entirely apparent through perceiving them. It is IN their body, and this is what embodiment truly is. Embodied cognition describes the brain, body, and world as a unified system, and grounds all cognition, thinking, and learning in sensory and motor activity (Anderson, Richardson, & Chemero, 2012).

I think of my body as my brain, as the boundary between what my brain does and what my body does is indiscernible. I think with my body. For example, when I am "looking" to find my keys in my bag, it is my fingers that DO the thinking for me through touch, and they find the keys. In fact, I think of the world as being my brain as well, as what experience would my brain/body have without being and interacting in the world? However, when we experience the world and things in it, such as nature, tools, and especially people, and develop memories, we can imagine those experiences, build upon them, manipulate them, and conceive other possibilities. This is *abstract* thought, the origins of which lie in those initial interactions and experiences in the brain-body-world system. When we recall those experiences, networks in the sensory, motor, and reward systems in the brain involved in that experience are triggered, so that it is as if we are reliving those events. Experiences build conceptual knowledge of the world (Macrine & Fugate, 2022), and become the grounding building blocks for creative thought.

The development of embodied cognition is a personalized journey through a lifetime. Everyone's journey is different and changed through every action and experience, every person and social context, and every place where it occurred. Embodied knowledge has emotional, psychological, biological, and developmental trajectories that deeply impact every memory and influence cognition (Glenberg, 2015). Each student has their own personalized set of memories.

When students use action and movement to demonstrate their knowledge, this demonstrates their embodied understanding. Teachers can then actually see something of what students have learned from the past, build upon it, and develop further scaffolding for learning in the future.

Movement is at the Core of All Learning

Movement shapes cognition. Experience, action/interaction, making, and moving are all words associated with embodiment, because at the core of embodiment is movement. Without movement, nothing happens. Movement can be the action we use to express how we perceive a sound or how we interpret music, art, emotion, or a story. It can be how we guide sound through dance expression and use gesture to create, enhance, or emphasize meaning.

"The key concept of embodied cognition is that our mind is shaped by our body and the way it interacts with the world around us. We are not passive recipients of sensory information; perception is shaped by how we move in the world" (Evan Thompson in an interview with Campbell, 2012, p. 28 transcript).

Movement can be the turning of the head to gain a different perspective of the world, or the rhythm of breath that punctuates the marrying of the body with the music. It can be the turning of a thought to link one idea to another. It can be how our brain changes as a result of experience.[1]

We are designed to manage and make sense of the world through our action in it. All thinking is grounded in movement. As my body moves, it thinks for me. For example, when improvising in dance, as each movement unfolds, it drives my thinking onward, into the next moment and next movement. Moving is thinking in motion.

We also think through moving with others. In joint sensorimotor integration,[2] the sensing/acting self and others are moving together to the same intention, gaining meaning through each other, creating cognition. This is an important aspect of movement and dance behavior, where we become as one as we express our artistic inner life with others, to an audience, or simply for the joy of experiencing being part of the unified whole.

Prediction:[3] The Way the Brain Saves Cognitive Overload

The brain is a prediction-making machine (Anderson, 2016). It stores models of the world so that every time we encounter something we have experienced before in some way, we do not have to relearn or recreate it in our minds. The brain recognizes the model, and what it notices most is what it does not expect, what is different, what it can build from the real-time event taking place. Real-world behavior is time-pressured, so we only really act upon the unexpected as it occurs (Wilson, 2002). We do not have to think of the expected, because it is there. "It turns out to be better to use the world as its own model" (Brooks, 1991, p. 140). We use the world (place, people, things in the world) to remember, make memory, and develop skills because that saves cognitive space. The brain is always looking for the easiest and most efficient use of its resources, through prediction (Anderson, 2010).

Take as an example, learning to perform a rotation jump. To learn to do this, should we watch someone, talk about it, or just do it? Possibly all of those would contribute to knowing how to perform a rotation jump, but until our own bodies do it, we do not fully understand how to do it. When we do it, our body and brain form a system with the world to enable us to adjust, respond, explore, experiment, test, and so on until we become skillful. And every time the world throws up a different set of time-pressured unforeseen challenges, in real-time, the body/brain system interacts with the world to solve it, such as when we are performing with a partner, or at a faster pace. We do not have time to consider the "model." The model is held

1 Neuroplasticity—neural changes in response to learning or experience (Martin, 2015).
2 Joint sensorimotor integration—where the sensory and motor integration is shared between two or more people.
3 Prediction—an interpretation of the world based on past experience and held as a model in memory.

in the body as it interacts with the world, and this saves cognitive overload, so that we do not have to overthink.

If we try to remember a previously learned dance before doing it, it would be time-consuming and cognitive-heavy. Just doing the dance allows it to unfold out of the body as it occurs through time. The body holds the memory and triggers systems that fire synchronously in a pattern of activity that results in the performance. Maybe we will not remember the exact movements as they had occurred before, but that can be a good opportunity for the brain/body/world system to improvise something different.

Improvisation holds powerful learning benefits. It consolidates skills and conceptual knowledge because it utilizes memories, making them transferable to new contexts. Improvisation develops memory rapidly because decisions are made quickly in real time. This time-pressured thinking therefore creates fast, efficient neural processing. And most importantly, the brain works harder when presented with something not predicted. "There are some who argue that such deviations from predictions are the very foundation for learning" (Bar, 2009, p. 1240). It is while improvising in dance that we develop problem-solving skills, artistic response, and new realizations as we delve into our personal responses and expression. Improvisation is the perfect scenario for fast, efficient processing, and this consolidates old knowledge and transfers learning. It enriches and updates predictive models.

The embodied system not only includes our own body and brain in the world. Contexts where learning occurs are important. For example, in dance, the surfaces we move on, the other people we dance with, any "things" (props, materials, tools), the spatial aspects of the environment, and so on, all affect our learning and performance. When we use things and people that become part of how we interact and learn, this is called extended cognition.

Extended Cognition

When thinking and learning are affected by tools, technology, or other people we interact with, this is described as extending our thinking into things in the world (Clark & Chalmers, 1998). Through using them, we can increase our capacities, skillfulness, or memory. This can simplify thinking and increase cognition. For example, using a smartphone or pencil and paper can increase our capacities for storing information, such as when we note phone numbers, make lists, or conceptualize an idea by writing it down. When a visually impaired person uses a white cane, their perception of the world is shaped by what they perceive through the end of the cane. It enables them to manage the world. Thinking is extended into the tool.

Physical actions on a tool simplify mental actions or thinking and reduces cognitive load (Clark, 2017). For example, if a dancer wanted to explore balances with objects, using a chair or another person might offer more possibilities for both balances and other movements. The objects become part of the cognitive system of the dancer and increase their balancing skill repertoire and capacities.

When teachers provide a world that includes many tools, teaching does not need to be explicit. The tools afford learning, and it is implicit in the action by students in exploring and trialing solutions. Tools can include repertoire (music, dances, speech pieces, poetry, stories, games, and so on), people (partners, groups, audiences, choreographers, etc.), and objects (chairs, artworks, materials, elements such as water or sand, sound sources, etc.).

The critical aspect in extending thinking outside the body is that with the tool, we achieve greater conceptual knowledge. It is the actions that are executed on or with the tool that uncover information that would be hard to compute in the head.

The Peripersonal System—Guides Movement in Relation to People and Things

The peripersonal system is an integrated system across the brain. It allows the brain to think of a tool as part of the body, a sort of virtual body part (Iriki, 2006). This includes other people or objects. In this way, the body and brain together understand and hold information about the action and capabilities of the tool. The peripersonal system manages the space around the body, so understands how far away objects are in relation to self, and in the case of a tool, how far things are from or around a tool. The more the tool is used, the better the system is in measuring, using, and synchronizing with sensorimotor systems in using this tool. For example, when a dancer moves with an object, such as an artwork, if they treat it like another body part, the brain considers it as part of the body space so the dancer can skillfully move with it.

The peripersonal system is also implicated in social understanding, joint action,[1] joint attention,[2] and attunement,[3] and it guides our movements in relation to objects and people (Graziano, 2018, p. 8). It helps us synchronize our actions, intentions, and emotions with others. The more we socialize and interact with other people, the more attuned the system will be in interacting with others. These are important aspects of successful dance performance and have implications for dance pedagogy.

When I am observing my students engage together, I am looking to see how attuned they are to each other as they work together. Can they "read" the other's body well enough to coordinate their movements and respond in kind? Do they cooperate with each other? Are they paying close attention to each other's movements so they can perform empathetically? Can they synchronize their movements accurately together? These questions all relate to the peripersonal system's action.

Like any other system in the brain, the more it is used, the better it gets. Partnering with lots of different dancers, learning to respond to a variety of expressions, copying, being the leader, or following the guidance of others, all improves the individual's ability to "read" others. However, sometimes we truly match some people better than others, and teachers can guide students in recognizing this affinity. Synchronizing behavior and using tools successfully is in some part the action of the peripersonal system.

Integration: The Brain's Way of Making Highly Complex Processes Look Easy

One of the defining features about how the brain works is integration. Nothing is ever processed just in one place in the brain. Everything connects, and processes overlap and integrate to make knowledge holistic and deep. Integration means we have multiple ways of memory retrieval.

---

1 Joint action—coordination of action or behavior between two or more individuals (Keller, Novembre, & Hove, 2014, p. 1). In movement and dance, joint action promotes coordinated and synchronous movements, heightened awareness of others, understanding of the goal of actions and mutual motor capabilities and the unity of being "as one."

2 Joint attention—coupling of two or more minds to a unified goal or focus. JA can be initiated in several ways, such as a gaze, gesture such as pointing, posture, breath, facial expression, or through physical interaction during a task.

3 Attunement—the ability to share perspectives and think as one. This involves empathy, shared intentions, and emotional states.

An old tale, "The Blind Men and the Elephant" describes an ancient wisdom, verified in neuroscience, about the way the brain organizes experiences and knowledge into holistic structures. The tale tells the story of a group of blind people who are introduced to an elephant, an animal they have never come across before. Each blind person touches and explores just one area of the elephant, such as the leg, the ear, the trunk, or the tusk. When asked later what an elephant is, they all have quite different ideas because they have only explored one small part of the elephant, and not one of the people has the whole picture of the elephant. There are many slightly varied versions of this tale and the related moral, but in terms of this discussion, the story reveals that knowledge that is derived from many views provides a fuller, richer, and more holistic structure or model in the brain.

Prediction relies on these models for us to successfully manage the world. Integrated models are more useful than separate, unrelated models because there are more parts to trigger retrieval. Small models, such as one part of the "elephant," have few memory triggers. In terms of pedagogy, the idea from this understanding of how the brain organizes knowledge, is that we need to make experiences for our students as multisensory, multimodal, and sensorimotor as possible, to create rich, neural models.

Multisensory[1] Integration

Multisensory integration occurs when all the sensory systems—peripheral (sight, taste, touch, etc.), haptic, vestibular, and proprioceptive—integrate or combine to create a holistic sensory picture. Multisensory engagement cross references knowledge from one sense to another, to develop a deeper understanding of an experience (Zimmerman & Lahav, 2012). It also develops understanding of how parts work together in a unified whole. For example, when learning a movement or dance skill, through doing the movement, our senses combine to give us the feeling of what the movement looks like, sounds like (maybe), what body parts are involved, how much energy is used, and so on.

Multimodal[2] Integration

Multimodal integration describes the combining of the many ways of behaving in a certain domain. When concepts and skills are practiced across modes, information in one modality reinforces understanding in another, making the memory multimodal. We can integrate these by practicing the same idea many different ways, or combine modes, such as sculpting a figure, painting a movement, commentating a dance.

In describing dance behavior, we might include:

- choreographing,
- notating,
- speaking (specific language and terminology that describes and engenders movement and dance ideas),
- thinking/imagining in movement[3] (abstract thought),
- improvising,

---

1 Multisensory—many senses.
2 Multimodal—many modes of behavior.
3 Abstract thought cannot be observed by others as it is an internal neural activity, but brain imaging captures that thinking about movement in dancers is processed primarily and more highly in the motor (movement) regions of the brain (Zardi, Carlotti, Pontremoli, & Morese, 2021).

- communicating non-verbally.[1]

Sensorimotor[2] Integration

Sensorimotor integration occurs when our sensory and motor systems are engaged in active experiences in a rich context, or a context that engenders this behavior (Spencer et al., 2006). These systems combine to produce skillful behavior. The key word is action, and for deep sensorimotor integration, the action must be self-produced.

For example, you can get ideas about performing a lift in dance from watching others, but until your body and brain are coupled with a partner to perform this, you will not have a fully developed sensorimotor understanding of how to lift or be lifted and maintain the movement. It is the integration of moving and the senses that produce highly skilled, sensorimotor behavior. Further, dance-producing actions affect the perception of dance performance. When watching dance performance, the dancer's brain fires more in the motor regions associated with dance movements than non-dancers.

Dance pedagogy creates holistic predictive models when students engage in multisensory, multimodal, and sensorimotor activity. Dance experiences are active, self-produced, embodied, engage all the senses, many modes of dance-like behavior, and tightly-couple action and perception. Thinking is extended into the world through the use of tools and other people. This increases skillful dance behavior, capacities, and cognition.

The Mirror System and Its Role in Pedagogy

When teachers understand the role of the mirror system, it can change their teaching techniques. When appropriate, and especially in initial learning, using imitation instead of descriptive language can make learning faster, meaning more accurate, and it can resonate more in the brains of their students. The body, and specifically the face and hands, are so important in the learning process. The way the teacher uses their body, expresses their feelings through facial expressions, and uses language are all processed through the mirror system.

Mirror neurons are nerve cells in the brain that fire both when an action is perceived and when it is performed (Rizzolatti & Sinigaglia, 2016). When we see someone do something, in our brains it is as if we are doing it ourselves. The same areas in the brain that are involved in that action fire both when we do it and when we see others do it. The more expertise we have, the more sensitive we are to others' actions, we recognize finer detail, and are better in identifying the outcome of actions.

The mirror mechanism is strongly implicated in social cognition and learning through imitation. In social cognition, mirror neurons map the facial expressions of others onto our own mirror system. All the motor, sensory and emotion networks involved in the facial expression fire in our brains so that we understand what the facial expression means. We literally feel the expression. This is called empathy. For example, if disgust was expressed by someone on tasting food, we would probably not want to taste the food because we are literally feeling their disgust. The ability to respond to facial expressions makes us successful in interpreting the intention of others' behavior and appropriately respond.

The mirror system makes us expert in reading body language, and this ability allows us to manage social situations. Face and hands have great meaning in the mirror system as they

---

1 Non-verbal communication is clearly involved in many areas of life; however, dance could be characterized by NV communication whereas maybe accounting would not.

2 Sensorimotor = sensory + motor (movement).

strongly indicate what is going on in the social world. They let us know if we are safe, connected, make us knowledgeable about situations and appropriate behavior, and so on. Processing of social information in the mirror system is extremely swift and unconscious because it "resonates" in the motor, sensory, and emotion centers of the perceiver. This is the way the brain has evolved to make interpretation of the world and learning easier.

Actions are also processed through the mirror system, so that we understand the intention of others' behavior. For example, if we see someone reaching for food, we expect that they will eat it, because if we were doing those actions, that is what we would do. Our mirror systems make predictions about the intention of others' actions based on our own past actions.

Copying others' actions is one of the primary ways we initially learn. From birth, our brains are primed to learn through imitation. The mirror system makes imitation of others' actions quick and almost irresistible, because of the way our own brains fire when we observe others' actions.

All language is grounded in the actions and context in which we learned it. When we speak, the motor regions of the brain are activated, not only because we are using jaw, tongue, muscles, and so on to produce speech, but because the words all map back to the action of learning them. Verbs strongly resound as action in the brain. If you say, "jump," in the listener's brain, they jump. All the motor areas of the brain involved in jumping light up. This is why "Simon says" games work so well. In this game, the leader calls out an instruction, such as "clap hands," but unless it is preceded by "Simon says" the action must not be performed. This game works because as soon as we hear an action word, it maps back to the action of doing it, and we find it difficult to resist doing it.

Understanding the neural effect of hearing action words, teachers need to use language and words wisely for effective teaching. If you say, "Stop jumping," you have instructed two conflicting actions: stopping and jumping. In the first milliseconds upon hearing this, students are confused. Language is a powerful learning tool for expression and understanding, and when we understand the way it is processed in the brain, we can use it more effectively.

Research by Mina Johnson-Glenberg (2014; 2017; 2016) looked at the effect of learning through: (a) direct instruction (teacher telling the information), (b) embodiment (students physically engaging with learning), and (c) embodiment plus virtual reality (VR) (physical engagement plus engagement in VR). Testing after the learning phase showed equal results amongst the three groups. Post-testing three and six months later showed not only more retention of knowledge in the embodied and VR groups (b & c), but more usability of knowledge; meaning, they understood how to use their knowledge because it was mapped to their motor and sensory systems and created strong predictive models of the world. This tells teachers that it is the physical engagement in learning that develops deep knowledge structures.

Understanding the mirror system provides insights for pedagogy, in dance as well as all areas.

1. Action is understood and processed through the mirror system, and maps back to and fires all the sensory, motor, and emotion systems involved in that conceptual knowledge. Therefore, an active dance teacher modelling the idea activates the neural systems of the student through imitative learning. It is swift and efficient, and a good starting point for learning.
2. Language needs to be used carefully in teaching. Leave the "telling" until after the action so that the learner can generate their own language to describe their learning (consolidation). The teacher can provide specific terminology of dance to represent the idea and add deeper meaning.
3. The actions of learning build cognition.

4. Facial expressions are powerful in conveying the meaning behind the expression because we are hard-wired to notice and gain meaning from these.

Final Words

Pedagogy based on embodied cognition acknowledges the centrality of the body in learning. Place, people, and tools all contribute to the development of cognition and predictive models. We use prediction to make sense and meaning and to save cognitive load, focusing on what is different and what we need to know. We can also save cognitive load by off-loading our thinking into using tools to help us build knowledge and increase skillfulness. Social learning, through joint action and attention, develops attunement and understanding of others' movement intentions. This is processed through the peripersonal and mirror systems in the brain. Seeing others move stimulates learning and activates action-based knowledge. Thinking and imagining actions can engender action-based knowledge and develop abstract thought, and gestures and words represent action-based cognition.

Dance is an embodied activity, and pedagogy in dance can capitalize on understanding neuroscience research that underpins an embodied practice.

References

Anderson, M. L. (2010). Neural reuse: A fundamental organizational principle of the brain. *Behavioral and Brain Sciences, 33*(4), 245–313. https://doi.org/10.1017/S0140525X10000853

Anderson, M. L. (2016). Précis of after phrenology: Neural reuse and the interactive brain. *Behavioral and Brain Sciences, 39*, 1–45. https://doi.org/10.1017/S0140525X15000631

Anderson, M. L., Richardson, M. J., & Chemero, A. (2012). Eroding the boundaries of cognition: Implications of embodiment. Topics in Cognitive Science, 4(4), 717–730. https://doi.org/10.1111/j.1756-8765.2012.01211.x

Bar, M. (2009). The proactive brain: Memory for predictions. *Philosophical Transactions of the Royal Society B: Biological Sciences, 364*(1521), 1235–1243. https://doi.org/10.1098/rstb.2008.0310

Brooks, R. A. (1991). Intelligence without representation. *Artificial Intelligence, 47*(1), 139–159. https://doi.org/10.1016/0004-3702(91)90053-M

Campbell, G. (Host). (2012, October 3). "Mind in Life" with Evan Thompson (BPS 89) [Audio podcast episode]. In *Brain Science.* https://brainsciencepodcast.com/bsp/mind-in-life-with-evan-thompson-bsp-89.html

Clark, A. (2017). Busting out: Predictive brains, embodied minds, and the puzzle of the evidentiary veil. *Noûs, 51*(4), 727–753. https://doi.org/10.1111/nous.12140

Clark, A., & Chalmers, D. (1998). The extended mind. *Analysis, 58*(1), 7.

Glenberg, A. M. (2015). Few believe the world is flat: How embodiment is changing the scientific understanding of cognition. *Canadian Journal of Experimental Psychology/Revue canadienne de psychologie expérimentale, 69*(2), 165–171. https://doi.org/10.1037/cep0000056

Graziano, M. S. A. (2018, January 5). Our primal need for personal space. Why do we need buffer zones? Over the decades, scientists have delved into the evolution, psychology and neuroscience of personal space. *Wall Street Journal.* https://www.wsj.com/articles/our-primal-need-for-personal-space-1515174455

Iriki, A. (2006). The neural origins and implications of imitation, mirror neurons and tool use. *Current Opinion in Neurobiology, 16*(6), 660–667. https://doi.org/10.1016/j.conb.2006.10.008

Johnson-Glenberg, M. C., Birchfield, D. A., Tolentino, L., & Koziupa, T. (2014). Collaborative embodied learning in mixed reality motion-capture environments: Two science studies. *Journal of Educational Psychology, 106*(1), 86–104. https://doi.org/10.1037/a0034008

Johnson-Glenberg, M. C., & Megowan-Romanowicz, C. (2017). Embodied science and mixed reality: How gesture and motion capture affect physics education. *Cognitive Research, 2*(1), 24. https://doi.org/10.1186/s41235-017-0060-9

Johnson-Glenberg, M. C., Megowan-Romanowicz, C., Birchfield, D. A., & Savio-Ramos, C. (2016). Effects of embodied learning and digital platform on the retention of physics content: Centripetal force. *Frontiers in Psychology, 7*, 1819. https://doi.org/10.3389/fpsyg.2016.01819

Keller, P. E., Novembre, G., & Hove, M. J. (2014). Rhythm in joint action: Psychological and neurophysiological mechanisms for real-time interpersonal coordination. Philosophical Transactions of the Royal Society B: Biological Sciences, 369(1658), 20130394. https://doi.org/10.1098/rstb.2013.0394

Macrine, S. L., & Fugate, J. M. B. (2022). *Movement matters: How embodied cognition informs teaching and learning.* Cambridge, MA: MIT Press.

Martin, E. A. (Ed.) (2015). *Concise medical dictionary* (9th ed.). Oxford: Oxford University Press.

Rizzolatti, G., & Sinigaglia, C. (2016). The mirror mechanism: A basic principle of brain function. *Nature Reviews: Neuroscience, 17*(12), 757–65.

Spencer, J. P., Clearfield, M., Corbetta, D., Ulrich, B., Buchanan, P., & Schoner, G. (2006). Moving toward a grand theory of development: In memory of Esther Thelen. *Child Development, 77*(6), 1521–1538. https://doi.org/10.1111/j.1467-8624.2006.00955.x

Wilson, M. (2002). Six views of embodied cognition. *Psychonomic Bulletin & Review, 9*(4), 625–636. https://doi.org/10.3758/BF03196322

Zardi, A., Carlotti, E. G., Pontremoli, A., & Morese, R. (2021). Dancing in your head: An interdisciplinary review. *Frontiers in Psychology, 12*, 649121. https://doi.org/10.3389/fpsyg.2021.649121

Zimmerman, E., & Lahav, A. (2012). The multisensory brain and its ability to learn music. *Annals of the New York Academy of Sciences, 1252*(1), 179–184. https://doi.org/10.1111/j.1749-6632.2012.06455.x

Overview of Various Applications of Movement and Dance in the Orff Schulwerk

Barbara Haselbach (Austria), Angelika Wolf (Austria/UK)

Introduction

Movement and dance in the context of the Orff Schulwerk are not seen as subjects for training future dancers, but they always emphasize their contribution to the development of the whole individual. They rarely stand alone; they nearly always connect with music, and often with language and other artistic forms of expression. They are not just tools to teach and learn music with more joy or to understand music better. Music, dance, and speech are primary means of expression and communication in the nature of every human being and are the basis of the Orff Schulwerk.

Therefore, movement and dance should find their application consistently and continuously in Schulwerk lessons. The following is a brief overview of the possible areas of application and tasks that can have different emphases depending on the age level and the specific objective of the group or the theme of a class.

Areas of Application

1. Movement games and warm-ups as psycho-physical-social attunement for a subsequent part of the class.
2. Training of sensory perception both in relation to one's own body and in the visual and auditory spheres as a means of experiencing oneself and others in expression and communication in terms of developing physical, emotional, social, and cognitive skills.
3. Acquisition of a basic, free, and versatile movement and dance technique as well as an understanding of a movement concept and terminology (mostly based on the movement analysis of Rudolf von Laban).
4. Physical experience and learning of parameters common to music and dance (time, space, dynamics, form, articulation).
5. Live accompaniment to movement/dance with voice, body percussion, and various instruments, alone or in a small ensemble, to deepen and practice the understanding of their mutual influence in the relationship between music and dance.
6. Creative use of movement/dance in an improvised way: alone; with partners or in a group; with or without music, text, objects, images, or other stimuli. Improvisation may be guided by the teacher or created independently by the participants.
7. Creating dance (elemental choreography) inspired by music but also from time to time without music (to strengthen the inner musical feeling), with texts, objects, or visual models for solos, duos, small or large groups.

8. Imitative learning of traditional dance forms from different cultures and historical periods, not only learning dance material and forms but also gaining insight into the historical, social, and cultural context of these dances.

9. Dramatic presentation (of songs, traditional or self-invented stories, fairy tales, picture books, rhymes, poetry, proverbs, etc.) using language, songs, instrumental music, movement, and indicated stage design.

10. Integration of other artistic media of expression (vocal and instrumental music making, dancing, speaking, performing, drawing, acting, painting, writing poetry, sculpting, modeling, etc.) that offers every participant the chance to choose their favorite way of expression as well as to learn about others with whom they are not familiar.

11. Learning to observe and remember movement and to reflect about the outcome of creative work in a personal, yet fair and objective manner.

And finally: The Orff Schulwerk does not represent a self-contained world but should lead to and create connections with different styles of "great art" in all its forms, most importantly including the art of our time. This means that from time to time reference should also be made to a variety of manifestations of dance.

For a Better Understanding of Movement

All areas of application start with an impulse to move the body as one's instrument that produces and expressively shapes movement in an extraordinary variety of ways. For this to succeed, the body must become the focus in the creative process. Perceiving, experiencing and play-oriented exploration enable the individual to establish a special relationship with themselves with others, and with the environment. This gives rise to the need to create movement and to express it as an individual language of dance.

The following explanation is partly based on Laban's creative dance concept and his movement analysis. Rudolf von Laban (born 1879 in Bratislava, then Austro-Hungarian Empire; died 1958 in Weybridge, UK) was a dancer, dance educator, and choreographer. He is famous as the founder of the German expressive dance as well as probably one of the most important dance theorists of the 20th century. His movement analysis is still used today in dance as well as in such different fields as theater, therapy, ergometry, and other areas. His work has been recognized and developed further by some of his collaborators (Lisa Ullmann, Valerie Preston-Dunlop, Irmgard Bartenieff, Joyce Boorman, and several others). In this context, it is not possible to give an accurate account of the full range of his analysis. We recommend that anyone wishing to study it in greater depth should read some of the books mentioned in the references at the end of this article.

The following diagram is intended to give the reader an overview of the essential elements that constitute and influence every movement and to help develop a versatile dance vocabulary and personal dance language. Each movement is performed by the body in space and time with a certain energy and a corresponding flow of movement. This presupposes self-awareness and a certain intention and conveys a corresponding expression and meaning. In the encounter with others a specific relationship of togetherness arises. All this ultimately shapes the form of the movement/dance action.

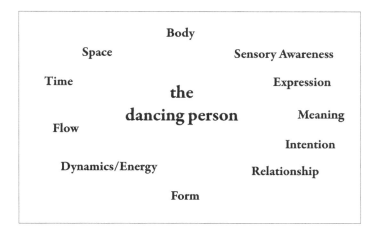

Body

Space

Time

the
dancing person

Flow

Sensory Awareness

Expression

Meaning

Intention

Dynamics/Energy

Relationship

Form

Descriptions of the Elements in Detail

Sensory awareness

Open senses serve as a basis for movement experimentation and experience in all areas that are mentioned and explained in the following paragraphs. Sensory awareness is a learning process in which perceptions are absorbed and processed through sensory stimuli. Time and a calm atmosphere will help to allow the perceptions to sink in and be stored and, if necessary, also reflected upon.

In concrete terms, kinesthetic, auditory, visual, tactile, and other stimuli are used during lessons to develop awareness of one's own body, one's own movement behavior, of contacts with other people, reactions to music, spatial conditions, and much more. Sensory awareness refines our physical, psychical, emotional, and social being and is an important and indispensable part of elemental music and movement education.

Examples:

- After an intensive period of movement, lie on the floor with closed eyes and feel how your breathing comes to rest and your limbs feel relaxed and heavy.
- Sitting in a circle with closed eyes listen to the sound of the steps created by one of the participants who is moving around the circle. Who can imitate the movement just from the auditory impression?
- Draw straight or curved lines in the air (also with different parts of the body), then watch somebody else doing their "painting" and draw what you have observed with crayons on a piece of paper.

Body

- Body parts: head, torso, pelvis, arms, and legs with their refinements (e.g., fingers, hand, lower arm, elbow, upper arm, shoulder, or toes, foot, lower leg, knee, thigh, hip).

The five basic anatomical functions of movement (bending, stretching, rotation, abduction, adduction) are components of every movement and are practiced in the context of spatial, temporal, and dynamic variations.

Example: writing letters, numbers, names, etc., with different body parts, first in a small, then in a spatially extended way, so that it develops from its functional exertion to individual expression.

- Basic body activities: locomotion, gesture, rotation, elevation, stillness, rising-sinking, and weight-shift.

The whole repertoire of movement can be described by these terms. Exploration begins with singular activities and later develops into connected basic body movements.

- *Locomotion*: Any movement leaving the spot, e.g., walk, run, leap, jump, hop, skip, gallop, crawl, creep, etc. Exploration in spatial, temporal, and dynamic variations.
- *Gesture*: Movement of different body parts that are not weight bearing that either convey a culturally specific meaning or are abstract movement.
- *Rotation*: Changing the body front on the spot or in locomotion resulting in a turn. It also refers to turning the arms or legs inward or outward.
- *Elevation*: Any movement when feet leave the floor (jump).
- *(Active) Stillness*: A conscious stopping of movement for a short or long duration in a particular position demanding conscious participation and attention.
- *Rising-sinking*: A change of position of the body in space by bending and lifting.
- *Weight-shift*: Change of weight from one supporting body part to another on any space level.

Space
Where does the body move? What spatial shape does the body take in a certain position of stillness?

- Kinesphere/General sphere
The *kinesphere* is an imaginary sphere around one's own moving body. Movements can be explored from near to the body to as far as body parts can reach.
    Example: On the spot move your arms in wide curves around you.
    The *general sphere* is all the space beyond the body's reach. The dancer moving into it always takes their kinesphere with them and gains in this way a sense of self-space in the space they share with others.
    Example: Combine arm movements while running in curves through the whole space.

- Center and extension
The lively interplay of reaching out and contracting into the body develops a focus on the tension between self and environment. Extension into space leads naturally to the experience of a "large" body, whereas coming back to center the body retreats into a small dimension.

- Level
The movement can be exerted upwards and towards the ceiling (high level). It can lead deep into the floor (low level), and it can take place between the two extremes on an intermediate level. Spatial awareness (high, medium, low) develops simultaneously with the exploration of movement in a specific area: e.g., kneeling (low), in normal upright position (medium), stretching or jumping (high).

- Direction
Forwards/backwards/right/left/up/down are the six basic directions the body can move into using different body parts and basic body activities. They serve as focus points after having

explored the vast "ocean" of the kinesphere with movements not focused in certain directions. Experiencing movement directions first in a one-dimensional way with the body in its own kinesphere prepares the progression of directions into space. After the basic directions, a step further would be to include diagonals.

• Planes
Natural movements often show the use of more dimensions. By moving an arm into space, it might describe a pattern on an imaginary plane. Three planes are distinguished: "Wheel plane" includes (like the movement of a wheel) the directions forward-backward and up-down. "Table plane" (like the movement of cleaning a table) forward-right-backward-left, and "Door plane" (like looking at the frame of a door) up-left-down-right. It is helpful to experience the three planes for a while in an isolated version, supported by imagining the three words wheel, table, and door.
  Example: A wide jump on the door-plane, traveling with rising-sinking on the wheel-plane, twisting and turning on the table-plane.

• Pathways
With straight, angular, round, curved, or twisted movements paths and patterns can be created. In locomotion, patterns such as circles, spirals, figure eights, zigzags, or meanders can be created. Similarly, different body parts can initiate aerial patterns with gestures as a clear spatial concept.

• Body shapes
Space patterns such as straight or curved lines can be expressed by the body mass itself. The body then emerges into a shape showing a linear or rounded character that can develop on the spot or move into space maintaining its shape. The four basic three-dimensional shapes are called pin, wall, ball, and screw. They can be explored with the whole body or parts of it.
  Example: Shape and move a sphere first just with one hand, later a larger sphere with both hands and let them open to a wall moving on the door plane.

Time
• Tempo and duration
Movement happens at different speeds such as slow, medium, and fast. It can continue on a constant speed-level, or it can change between the extremes of slow and fast. A regular speeding up is an *accelerando*, whereas continuous slowing down is a *ritardando*. Independent of its speed, movement can have a long or short duration. The combination of speed and duration produces a rhythmic pattern.

• Pulse/Breath
Pulse and breath originate from the liveliness of the body. The pulse has a steady beat whose speed can change but still give the feeling of regularity. Breath with its clear phases of breathing in, breathing out, and pause appears as a phrase with beginning, middle, and end. Breath is flexible and irregular, as every new breath might develop a new rhythmic phrase.

• Rhythm/Pattern
A feeling of rhythm develops when the flow of movement becomes structured. A rhythmic pattern consists of a sequence of certain sounds or note values (durations) including rests, developing on a set of beats performed in a certain speed. Rhythm patterns can be metrical when performed on the base of a regular pulse. Free-metric rhythms follow a movement flow

not based on a regular beat and are more related to the flow of the breath, but they still express the sensation of structure. Regular accents in these sets create different times like duple or triple meter. Rhythms can change between even and uneven measures or combine into irregular meters like five or seven.

Motifs as the smallest recognizable elements can evolve into phrases, which might be connected to sequences. A motif contains the potential for development and serves as a building block for composition.

Dynamics/Energy
Every movement needs energy to be performed. A loud clap or a delicate snap comes from a body that uses strength to produce them and create a dynamic. A feeling for the weight of the body evolves in sensations of heaviness and lightness. Pushing against a partner gives the feeling of being strong, while balancing a feather produces a light impression, experiences that can be transferred to instruments.

• Connection with time
Sharp and smooth energies add dynamic color to a movement. When a quick or a sustained movement also integrates a "light" weight, a dynamic quality of staccato or legato is achieved, and a movement appears like flicking or floating.

Flow
• Continuity
Any movement manifests itself by flow, which can be continuous or interrupted. After a pause the movement will go on.

• Free and bound flow qualities
A movement focusing on the image of a never-ending free flow adds quality to the dynamic of a movement. On the other side of the spectrum a movement is bound when it is controlled and can be intentionally stopped at any time. It is the interplay of both of these elements that contributes to the expression of the movement.

Relationship
• Body parts to body parts
One part of the body may dance in a dialogue with another, for instance the right hand with the left. Body parts may also move in similar or different ways, alternating or at the same time, in parallel, symmetric or asymmetric lines.

• Individual and object
An object can emphasize, prolong, or even deliberately restrict the movement of the body. Example: A scarf can become a dancing partner through impulsive movements of a hand. Or dancing and accompanying oneself with rhythm sticks may show an especially versatile performance.

• Social relationship (individual—partner—small or large group)
Dancing alone gives a feeling that is different from dancing with a partner, where one of the two might lead the movement and the other repeats or answers it, so that one has to observe and react to the other's movement ideas. Dancing in groups might happen in unison, following a leader, or independent of those close in a spatial vicinity. Different degrees of relationships between dancers would be: being aware, addressing somebody, being near, touching, supporting.

- Spatial relationship

Relationships in space can be for parts of the body but especially for dancing with a partner or a group. This can be used to describe spatial positions (near/far, over/under, above/below, alone/connected, beside/between) or activities (meeting/parting, mirroring/shadowing, gathering/scattering, around/through) or even pathways of two dancers or groups (parallel, symmetrical, or asymmetrical).

- Time relationship can be simultaneous/unison, or successive.

Simultaneous movements between two partners may be in unison, using the same movements, or in "two voices," meaning that each of the partners is performing their individual movements at the same time. A successive execution means that partners do the same sequence of movements after each other as soon as the first finished (echo), or just starting one after the other, repeating the same movement material (canon).

Intention

We have to distinguish between the intention just to move around, or to create movement that interprets a certain piece of music, a text, a specific character, or a work of visual art. The latter requires a certain purpose, imagination, and experience, as well as a decision for or against certain movements. The intention to create something in a certain way becomes stronger and more precise with increasing movement experience.

Expression

Expression means the externalization of an emotional process that in turn is the consequence of an inner mood as a result of our sensory awareness. It can be an unconscious spontaneous release, or it can be deliberately formed through one's own body (voice, facial expression, posture, and movement) for the purpose of characterizing a certain role or mood. The ability to give one's movement an intended expression develops over time from an interplay of emotional and cognitive decision-making.

Meaning

The subjective intention of the dancer may not always be clear to the observer. Therefore, a joint reflection after a presentation, which also allows for other interpretations, might often be very helpful and inspiring.

Form

Form can be understood and interpreted very differently. On the one hand, it can mean the "architecture" of the dance or movement event, i.e., the structure of the individual parts or building blocks. However, it can also mean the overall impression of a choreography in a more extensive way. Kandinsky, for example, speaks of form as expression of the inner content.

In order to structure a dance that interprets a piece of music within the framework of an elemental choreography, it is advisable to apply the basic theory forms.

- Form principles: repetition, development, variation, contrast
  A motif or a sequence may be:
    - repeated in the same way (echoed, mirrored, or shadowed),
    - developed by adding new movements,
    - varied (in at least one characteristic, for instance: focus, dimension, tempo, parts of the body, number of participants),
    - contrasted by the opposite of the original movement or by one of its characteristics.

- Compositional forms (adopted from forms in elemental music)

The most elemental structures based on the principles of sequencing, layering, developing are:

- ○ Motif: A short and concentrated movement idea.
- ○ Ostinato: Constant repetition of a motif.
- ○ Layering ostinati: Simultaneous performance of several movement motives—each complementing the other.
- ○ Question and answer that can be developed into a larger two-part form.
- ○ A, AB, ABA, ABC, Rondo: Beginners should start with a one-part form (A), then add a second contrasting part B until more parts can be remembered and executed in a rondo A-B-A-C-A, etc.
- ○ Canon: Execution in canon already presupposes being able to remember and replicate one's own sequence of movements with certainty. And next, also being able to perceive the overall sequence following individual cues and always observing the connected space pattern of all participants.
- ○ Theme and variations particularly promote expressiveness as different qualities of movement are performed in immediate succession.

- Formations in space

A varied sequence of the basic spatial forms includes circle and double circle, line and row, various positions in threes and fours, and also a carefully considered use of the spatial zones—foreground, center, background, sides—as well as the opportunities for entrance and exit (if used on a stage). The descriptions mentioned under "Spatial relationships" above can also enrich the spatial form.

Other contexts like working on a narrative dance, using movement in a dramatic presentation, or interpreting a drawing, a painting, or a sculpture with movement will need other formal solutions. Examples can be found in other articles of this book.

Summary

Dance and movement can be viewed, analyzed, and created in many different ways. The condensed selection of criteria presented in this article is intended primarily for those teachers whose focus is not especially dance and dance education. It is aimed to give them new basic insights and suggestions.

References

Boorman, J. (1971). *Creative dance in grades four to six*. Ontario: Longman.

Fritsch, U. (Ed.). (1994). *Tanzen–Ausdruck und Gestaltung* [Dancing–expression and creation] (2nd ed.). Butzbach: Afra.

Hackney, P. (2002). *Making connections. Total body integration through Bartenieff fundamentals*. London: Routledge.

Haselbach, B. (1978). *Dance education. Basic principles and models for nursery and primary school*. London: Schott.

Haselbach, B. (2000). The phenomenon of expression in aesthetic education. In S. Mattila & J. Siukonen (Eds.). *Expression in music and dance education. International Orff Schulwerk Symposium 2000*. Orivesi, Finland: JaSeSoi.

Kennedy, A. (Ed.). (2014). *Bewegtes Wissen. Laban/Bartenieff–Bewegungsstudien verstehen und erleben* [Moving knowledge. Laban/Bartenieff–understanding and experiencing movement studies] (2nd revised ed.). Berlin: Logos Verlag.

Klein, G. (Ed.). (2015). *Choreografischer Baukasten. Das Buch* [Choreographic construction kit. The book] (2nd ed.). Bielefeld: transcript Verlag.

Laban, R. (1975). *Modern educational dance* (3rd ed.). London: Macdonald & Evans.

Moore, C. (2014). *Meaning in motion. Introducing Laban movement analysis.* Denver (CO): MoveScape Center.

Newlove, J., & Dalby, J. (2004) *Laban for all.* New York: Routledge.

Preston-Dunlop, V. (1980). *A handbook for modern educational dance* (Rev. ed.). London: Macdonald & Evans.

Preston-Dunlop, V. (1998). *Looking at dances. A choreological perspective on choreography.* London: Verve.

Teaching and Learning Strategies for Creative Dance in Orff Schulwerk: Learners' Agency, Artistry, and Feedback

Christa Coogan (USA/Germany), Andrea Sangiorgio (Italy/Germany)

Introduction

This article addresses a teaching methodology[1] of working with movement and creative dance within the artistic-pedagogical framework of Orff Schulwerk. Our educational lens is one of social constructivism: Orff Schulwerk as a learner-centered, collaborative, creative approach. The main characteristics of the Orff Schulwerk process as well as main methodological considerations are elucidated. To illustrate this kind of approach, we examine a teaching unit that focuses on generating movement ideas, improvising individually and in a group, and creating a group choreography. The emphasis is on three main ideas: aspiration towards artistry, creative agency, and the power of observation and feedback.

The Theoretical Background: Social Constructivism

If we look at different learning theories to better understand the kind of creative dance processes that take place in Orff Schulwerk lessons, we find that social constructivism offers a research-based theoretical framework that can fruitfully explain and orient our teaching practice.[2] Of course, as music and dance practitioners, we do integrate behaviorist, cognitivist, or other possible approaches in our teaching, but the fundamental principles underlying our pedagogical action relate to the fact that learners actively construct their knowledge in interaction with others within a culturally situated context.

The key concepts of social constructivism can be summarized as follows:

1. Knowledge is not just transmitted and passively received, but rather learners build their skills and knowledge based on their previous experiences and pre-existing cognitive structures. Importantly, in the context of movement/dance and music education, "knowledge" or "thinking" have a strong bodily component, which is referred to as embodied knowledge and embodied cognition.
2. Learning is a dynamic experience. Learners construct meaning by actively engaging with the world around them. Further, learners are different from each other, i.e., knowledge is specific to each individual, as they have diverse personal, social, and cultural backgrounds that contribute to the ways they experience the learning activities.
3. Learning is shaped through social interaction. We learn through and with the others by collaborating and synergizing with them. Knowledge is co-constructed between teacher

---

1 The authors define methodology as a system of practices and strategies that a teacher uses to teach. In the case of Orff Schulwerk—which is not a method, but rather an approach or a pedagogical conception—methodology is based on assumptions about the nature of music and movement/dance and how they can be learned.
2 Many of these principles were already formulated within the progressive education approaches at the beginning of the 20th century (Terhart, 2003).

and learners as well as among learners themselves. Processes of shared understanding with others are essential to the formation of new cognitive structures and meanings for the individual person.

4. Learning is socially and culturally rooted in that it is subject to cultural influences of various kinds. Every learning experience is embedded in a specific cultural context—be it society at large or the learning environment in a classroom—that has an influence on the contents, the strategies, and the aims of the activity.

5. Collaborative learning—a central focus in the Schulwerk—is, at least to some extent, also a creative act as two or more learners have agency and ownership of the ideas that they jointly develop in the learning process.

Given these principles, a teaching/learning approach based on social constructivist premises includes learner-centered, experiential, problem-based, collaborative, dialogic, participatory, and inclusive forms of learning. In addition to these, Orff Schulwerk positively integrates a variety of transmission and acquisition strategies that are more traditionally based on imitation and are oriented to behaviorist views of learning. This blend of approaches—thoughtfully balanced in relation to each contingent situation and the teacher's intentions in it—is what makes the Schulwerk such a powerful educational conception. Thus, within the same lesson there might be learning processes ranging from strongly guided learning (as in imitation-based phases of work) to fully self-directed learning (as in creative group work).

An Orff Schulwerk Process

A network of relationships

The premise of relationship is at the center of an Orff Schulwerk process. Wolfgang Hartmann (2021), in defining the characteristics of an Orff Schulwerk approach, writes that the human being and the development of their personality is at the center of any learning experience. Yet, a person is not alone. Paramount to a Schulwerk process is thus the relational aspect of learning, knowing, and understanding. The artistic components comprising the idea of Orff Schulwerk (the subject matter), connecting with an individual learner, connecting with the group members as they interact with each other and as they interact with their teacher(s), encompass the dynamic of the relational trajectory.

An environment in which trust, respect, and appreciation flourish is attentively constructed by the teacher. They foster the ideas of the participants and support them as their ideas unfold. They offer manifold opportunities for the development of their self-agency, their joint agency or we-agency (Salmela & Nagatsu, 2017), and their sense of self. The teacher recognizes and articulates the strengths of the individual. Such a responsive connection to the students calls upon the observational and empathetic skills of the teacher and assures that they "assume a learning stance" (Raider-Roth, 2005, p. 157).

The harmonious interplay between art forms

An Orff Schulwerk process encompasses the interplay between the art forms of music, movement and dance, speech, and visual arts. Practicing creative agency in this artistic-educational model presupposes making foundational experiences through:

* *Imitation* (learning by reproducing a model given by a teacher or a peer),
* *Exploration* (experimenting with ideas; uncovering or discovering various facets of a certain subject),

- *Improvisation* (a process and a product in which material from a previous exploration is selected and employed in an intentional manner), and
- *Gestaltung/Composition* (a creative final forming of ideas that can be understood as a composition or a choreography and may contain improvisatory elements).

These four principles for action send impulses to each other, inform both the teacher's pedagogical choices and the student's active participation. They are the foundation of artistic and creative pathways, interacting with and energizing relationships between music, dance and movement, visual arts, and the spoken word as they are experienced by the learners as creators, as meaning-makers, and as witnesses to the artistic endeavors of their peers.

Creative dance in Orff Schulwerk

Creative, or elemental, dance begins with the experience of physical consciousness and the exploration of dance elements through clearly structured exploratory and improvisatory play. Learners are not taught a technique (as is the case of ballet, jazz, or hip-hop) or specific dances (from European folk traditions or other cultures), but rather are asked to discover individual ways of expressing ideas, thoughts, and feelings through movement[1] and thus develop a personal kinesthetic signature. Natural movements, such as running, skipping, leaping, falling, bending, twisting, and dance parameters such as tempo, size, and strength, are explored in their expressive, communicative variety.

The model that has established basic principles for movement as well as one that offers possibilities for continued learning in creative contexts is based upon the theories of Rudolf von Laban (1960, 1966) and those researchers and practitioners who developed these ideas with him and continued on after his death.[2] Laban's parameters of movement[3] offer a comprehensive, rich, and non-judgmental framework in which to understand the unique personality of an individual dancing. There are numerous ways to adapt these theories in an educational context and, specifically, in Orff Schulwerk. What follows is our conceptualization of Laban's theories based on our teaching practice with children and adults. In synthesis, Laban's elements of movement are:

- The **body**: Dance begins with the instrument of the body, with its parts (legs, arms), its actions (walking, turning, bending, stretching, gesturing). This body plays with the parameters of space, quality, relationship, and time to create form, meaning, and expression.
- The **space**: *Where* is the body in space? How is the space utilized and made apparent? We see space through the size, direction, pathway, level, or spatial relationship of movement.
- The **quality** (or dynamics): *How* does the movement take place? Is the muscular tension needed to complete a movement strong or delicate (the *weight* factor)? Is the time it takes to do a particular movement quick or sudden? Or is it rather leisurely, or continuous (the *time* factor)? Is a movement performed in a clearly aimed manner—straight and direct? Or is it a movement that meanders, that does not need to get to the point (the *space* factor)? Finally, there is the *flow* factor: Is the movement carefully and deliberately executed (*bound flow*)? Or is it movement that moves freely and easily (*free flow*)?
- The **relationship**: *With whom or with what* does the body create relationships? One creates a relationship through focus, proximity, surrounding, touch, and sharing weight. Relatedness is also shown through shadowing or mirroring, through body designs and linear patterns.

---

1   This individuality, however, is not aloof from cultural influences but arises out of them.
2   Among these: North (1973), Preston-Dunlop (1987).
3   Laban referred to the art of movement in *Modern Educational Dance* (1966).

- The **time**: The *when* of the movement. Here the familiar parameters are the beat or pulse; metered and unmetered (including time signature, ostinato pattern, accent, breath, emotional and sensed rhythm); tempo, and lastly, timing relationships such as unison, canon, before or after, faster or slower than, long or short.[1]

The connection between music and dance

An Orff Schulwerk approach values the musical, poetic body in relation to music. Such an approach is based upon the assumption that everyone can dance musically, with intention and quality. Music and musicality are intimately connected to dance, and creative dance offers a broad access in realizing this connection. Dance is not only rhythmic but also melodic; it has sweeping breath phrases and also embodies the excitement of the beat. Learners discover parallels in ideas of form and structure, be it the smallest building blocks—the motif, the phrase—or the AB form, or the extended rondo form. They draw bridges between musical and dance parameters such as tone color and movement quality, or pitch and movement levels. Music begins to be understood on an analytical level. Concepts such as legato and staccato or accents as well as qualities of movement are understood in the learners' muscles. Both children and adults react to the powerful atmospheric pull of music as well. Their senses are awakened, their imaginations are stimulated and thus music becomes internalized on emotional and associative levels. Each person learns to interpret music in their very own personal, aesthetic, and physical way.

Methodological Considerations

Enhancing the confidence of participants

It is likely that movement teachers working in Orff Schulwerk have experienced participants who feel uncomfortable with dancing, whether teachers in professional development courses or children, youth, or adults in weekly classes. Some are hesitant with improvisatory tasks; others feel inept at following a sequence of steps. What strategies can we employ to set participants at ease with dancing?

Knowing what I am doing: Being as knowledgeable as possible with the movement and dance content being taught and likewise being clear in the sequencing of the lesson are first steps. If the teacher is cognizant of their contents, strategies, and goals, the participants are more able to trust the process. The movement/dance content might begin with addressing the kinesthetic consciousness, which enables a participant to act and react more quickly, with more sensitivity, and with greater physical ease. Intention and movement quality supports the (explicit or implicit) understanding of *what* I am doing, *why* I am doing it, and *how* I am doing it. Developing a sense of phrasing in one's movements and increasing rhythmic coordination of one's body lead to more refined musical expression.

Addressing psychological needs: In this approach to creative dance making, the teacher addresses participants' needs for *autonomy* and *relatedness* (Deci & Ryan, 2000), that is, they offer opportunities in which participants can make decisions independently and are able to encounter one another through active tasks. Furthermore, having a feeling of *competence* and a sense of achievement in their doings supports self-confidence. How, as a teacher, can I recognize the individual with their strengths and their needs and yet be able to relate to the group and help

---

1   From Laban's perspective, time structures are evidenced through the combination of the weight, space, time, and flow factors. Rhythm is defined as being impulsive, with impact, swinging, percussive, vibratory, or unaccented. Adapting Laban's theories to Orff Schulwerk means also integrating established music parameters into the terminology of creative dance.

guide and fulfill group expectations? Can I give motivating, honest, and meaningful feedback that encompasses both appreciation and information?

Guiding artistic processes

An artistic process is one in which not everything is known at the beginning. Rather, it is an evolution of discovery that brings surprise, uncertainty, and delight. Relinquishing control of knowing exactly how something will develop and indeed, how it will result in a product, conveys the heart of making art and is a powerful experience for learners.

In delving into this process, can I offer sufficient possibilities and liberties for learners to explore ideas, feelings, and imaginative worlds through their bodies, leading to those powerful moments of expressivity? In what ways can perceptual habits be stretched through aesthetic experience, thus expanding attentiveness for and revelations of artistic beauty in its myriad facets?

Modeling

Modeling by the teacher is an impetus for students to generate their own ideas and thus it is an essential ingredient in creativity-oriented classes. Modeling requires the teacher to be completely present in their body, voice, and attentiveness. Some practitioners claim that modeling can have an inhibiting effect on the generation of individual ideas or lead learners to simply imitate the movements of the teacher. We argue that participants learn as they experience their teacher exploring, improvising, finding not-so-fantastic ideas and, with focus and determination, discovering more favorable ones. This model becomes then a source of inspiration, not one of inhibition. Above all, if you, the teacher, are not dancing (however untrained), then why should your students?

Setting the stage

Preparing an environment for an open process, that is, creating balance between structural guidelines and flexibility in following exploratory and improvisatory pathways, can entail a certain theatricality or *staging*. This is conducive to gaining and retaining the attention of the participants, increasing their motivation, and capturing their imaginations during a music and movement lesson. Three such compelling elements are: creating excitement, including moments of mystery in lessons, and offering opportunities to fall in love with what they are doing.

- *Excitement*: Dancing is thrilling when it becomes a challenge. For instance, it is a challenge to be completely still—without any wobbling; to jump quite high, stay up, and then land so softly that one hears only the breath of exertion.
- *Mystery*: Mystery is the fun of not knowing. It is the treasure hunt, the closed eyes, the whispering voices, the uncertainty of what will happen now, at this moment.
- *Romance*: Alfred North Whitehead (1929) referred to the "rhythm of education," in which the first stage is that of romance, "the vividness of novelty... unexplored connexions [sic] with possibilities half-disclosed by glimpses and half-concealed by the wealth of material" (p. 17). This feeling of *falling in love* captivates children as well as adults. It is the step of enticement of the sensibility for the sound of certain words and the feeling that they make in your mouth; the rumbling, swerving, leaping, lifting movements you can make in your body; tests of strength and speed; the rhythm of a sentence; the secrets to be discovered in a piece of music; the intimacy of dancing together; the magic of trust as your partner catches your weight; the depth of meaning perceived in an ever-so-small movement; or word pictures that create a world.

Feedback

Feedback that includes both recognition and task-related information is integral to learning. It can be a powerful tool to stimulate engagement, autonomous actions, and self-assessment, and can be a path to deeper learning. Feedback relates to aesthetic curiosity, expression, and to the development of creative and individual pathways of thought and action. Thus, it is particularly welcome in a Schulwerk practice. The following three strategies have informed our collaborative work:

1. Through feedback, we communicate our enthusiasm for aesthetic and compositional problem-solving. In such an environment, the joy of discovery, courage, and the will to communicate wonderful ideas are valued.
2. Feedback helps students to acquire subject matter vocabulary and to articulate their aesthetic perceptions. A prerequisite for giving differentiated feedback is the ability to make precise observations. This vocabulary, pertaining to musical or dance concepts, is addressed and developed in our classes through various tasks in which—via feedback—processes and pathways are described.
3. In structured and non-structured feedback moments, there is space and time for dialogic exchanges between teacher and students as well as between peers. Importantly, invigorating feedback arises out of non-judgmental observations (Lerman & Borstel, 2003). Observers share how they were moved by the work of their peers; the art-makers experience appreciation for what they have shown and might explain the thinking behind their work. This, in turn, gives both observers and creators an opportunity to gain valuable insights into creative processes, into principles of improvisation and composition, and into meaning making.

These methodological principles inform an Orff Schulwerk approach in creative dance. They are strategies that are flexible and responsive, helping to guide multifaceted processes that support both individual and group learning. In the following, we highlight the ways in which these strategies are applied within a particular example from our teaching practice.

The Teaching Unit: The 1234 Game

The springboard for this lesson idea is a game[1] that unfolds from exploratory actions, through group improvisational tasks, to a choreographed result. The game and its variations can be used with primary school children, teenagers, and with adults in professional development courses. It works best with eight or more people, including larger groups of 25+ participants. Learners work in groups of four or five. The development of the game is suitable for smaller spaces and is adaptable to various functions within a class plan: i.e., a warm-up game, an improvisation exercise, or an extended compositional process.

Here, we describe a 60-minute teaching unit that we led with 24 third graders with a varied multi-cultural background in a weekly Orff Schulwerk music and movement lesson that we team-teach in a primary school in Munich, Germany. Although we have different foci—dance and music—as Schulwerk teachers we share the following aims:

- To create an atmosphere in which each person feels empowered to work on challenges, musically and kinesthetically, developing a sense of phrasing and musicality as dancers-musicians.

---

1 I, Christa Coogan, took the basic structure of the activity from a workshop with Astrid Weger in the early 2000s and, realizing its potential, developed and extended it further in different ways and with various emphases.

- To guide learners to realize their own artistry through deliberation and attention to quality and intention.
- To offer possibilities for observational discernment and sensitivity, and for reflective articulation.
- To provide opportunities for participants to co-construct knowledge and skills with one another while engaging on a creative task.
- To facilitate the development of social and cultural competencies.

In the activity, children create shapes, either individually, with a partner, or with a group, according to four different movement rules or prompts. The movement shapes and their transitions can be improvised or choreographed. The rules are:

1. (the *starfish*) standing with straight legs in an open stance, arms reaching outstretched on a high diagonal, head lengthening up from the neck,
2. *sharing weight* with a partner,
3. making a shape with only *three body parts touching the floor,*
4. (in groups of four) *three people support one person* who must not touch the floor.

Sequence of the lesson
The lesson can be structured in different ways. In the following description, we make clear not only *what* we are doing, but also the *why* and the *how*.

Greeting and warm-up in a circle
- Awakening interest and activating concentration with questions and rhythmic exercises in preparation for the movement combination that is to come.
- "Follow me" warm-up imitation: Connecting rhythm with the body and movement; activating body control; reviewing movement vocabulary; honing attention towards the quality of individual movements.

Imitation—teaching a movement combination that moves through space
- Stimulating children's cardiovascular system.
- Engaging children in a combination that is complex enough to be challenging in coordinative and spatial aspects, yet possible.
- Including partner work (*relatedness*[1]), nearness, and bodily contact (in preparation for the game).
- Offering an activity that is rhythmic with a specific time structure (as a contrast to the upcoming, non-pulse-based game).

Exploration—reviewing Laban-based movement vocabulary and introducing component #1 of the 1234 game
- Employing vocabulary known by the children to support them in the generation of ideas for actions and qualities (e.g., dashing/twirling/sudden/strong), (autonomy + competence).
- Encouraging traveling actions that move throughout the space (as a contrast to the upcoming improvisation that takes place mostly on the spot).
- Modeling the body shape for #1 (the starfish).
- Dancing the game Stop-and-Go: Improvisatory movements in space alternating with sudden stops for #1.

---

1   Terms in italics refer to above mentioned concepts in the methodological section.

- Adding pulse-based music (recorded or played live) as motivating and energizing support for children's bodily engagement.

Exploration continues—rules #3, #2, and #4

- Rule #3 - guessing game (*sense of mystery*): Children close their eyes as the teacher takes a shape with three body parts touching the floor (*modeling*); children open eyes and notice the shape; the process is repeated two times with different #3 shapes; the challenge for children is to figure out the rule for #3 (excitement).
- Dancing the game Stop-and-Go with prompts given by teacher: Movement explorations in space, alternating with sudden stops for #1 and #3.
- Teacher's *feedback* to #1 includes describing children's captivating or unusual body positions (e.g., some children begin transferring the plane of #1: lay on the floor, tilt their shape to the side, bend one knee, etc.); regarding #3, teacher checks to ensure that there are only three points on the floor; the *feedback* includes acknowledging and celebrating creative ideas.
- Rule #2 - guessing game (*sense of mystery*): Children close their eyes as the teacher takes a weight-sharing position with a chosen child, for instance, leaning into each other, hand-to-hand; one holding the leg of the other; piggy-back carry (*modeling*).
- Each pair finds their own solutions to #2 (*relatedness*).
- Teacher's *feedback* includes noticing original partnering choices and encouraging children to observe the wonderful ideas of others.
- Dancing the game Stop-and-Go: Movements in space, alternating with sudden stops for #1, #2, and #3.
- Transition to #4 - children quickly make groups of 4 by the teacher's count of 4 (*challenge*).
- Explanation of #4 - in the group, three children begin to explore different ways to support one child. Children take turns at being lifted (challenge).

Improvisation in small groups with rules #1, #2, #3, #4

- All groups are spread out in the space.
- The teacher calls out a rule number with an acoustic signal (e.g., a triangle), and the children improvise a solution to that number (#1 *starfish*, #2 *weight with a partner*, #3 *three body parts on the floor*, #4 *lifting a member of your group off the floor*).
- Children must transition smoothly from one number to the next one without talking (non-verbal communication: challenge).
- Music is added to create an *artistic atmosphere* in which the children assign meaning and expressive intention to what they are doing. A gentle triple meter in a moderato tempo suggests a feeling for breath and phrasing.

Gestaltung (creative forming)

- Each group decides a sequence of the numbers, sets positions, figures, and transitions (*competence, autonomy, relatedness*). The teacher can assist with memory prompts, such as graphic notations.
- Further parameters can be added. For example, a more specific prompt for #2 is changing your partner within the group. To make #4 more challenging, each of the three holders is on a different level or the held dancer is in a round or stretched shape. A new rule #5 could be added: The children move to a new spot in space.
- Teacher observes each group, offering assistance if necessary, sharing enthusiasm for the children's concentration and their ideas (*feedback*).

Sharing, feedback, reflection

- Each small group presents its work to the whole class (*artistry*).
- Teacher prompts individual audience members to comment upon those ideas that they found inspiring, surprising, or moving (*feedback, excitement, artistic process*).
- As a preceding step, two groups could present and give feedback to each other. The feedback might include "stars" (acknowledging wonderful ideas[1]) or "wishes" [2] (what could be modified or improved upon?).
- As a concluding step, the teacher can initiate a group reflection on the significance of their experience, e.g., discovering riveting ideas, being energized by challenges, appraising the quality of their work in the group.

Conclusion

Reflecting on the opportunities for experiencing creative dance in Orff Schulwerk that this kind of teaching process offers, we organize our thoughts based on three overarching trajectories of learning.

The agency of the learners

Over the course of the learning process—be it at the microscale level of a single session or at the macroscale level of a school year—participants negotiate challenges of tasks (from body control to rhythmic accuracy, to improvisational skills) and the ensuing creative choices. They acquire a deeper sense of self-efficacy, self-awareness, and competency. They develop social skills while working with a partner and in a group, thus building trust in themselves and with each other. Importantly, they progressively take ownership and control of their own intrinsically motivated learning process.

Artistry of both learners and the teacher

A unique feature of Orff Schulwerk is the connection between pedagogy and artistry, i.e., making it possible for learners to experience a heightened state of alertness, an enlivened and deepened aesthetic perception, and a ready access to their own imagination. They gain skills in creative vocabularies, broaden their movement repertoire and, ultimately, develop their individual and shared artistic voice. The fascinating challenge for the (music) teacher lies in the opportunity to expand their own artistic-pedagogical horizon to include creative approaches to movement and dance.

The role of feedback

Given the openness of the learning process, the dialogic exchange between all participants, the non-judgmental stance, and the preciseness of the articulation are crucial to the effectiveness of the artistic and pedagogical outcomes. The teacher's own experiences of wonder and acknowledgement of the students' ideas contribute decisively to the motivational dynamics of the lesson. The interplay between doing, observing, and reflecting unleashes insights into learners' creative processes and supports further engagement in the activity.

These trajectories infuse the artistic-pedagogical approach of Orff Schulwerk with thoughtfulness, enthrallment, and a sense of community.

---

1 See Duckworth (1987).
2 Thanks to Jenny Hill for the idea of stars and wishes.

References

Boorman, J. (1971). *Creative dance in grades four to six*. Don Mills, ON: Longman Canada.

Coogan, C. (2014). Orff-Schulwerk: Fundamentals of creative/elemental dance for children in elementary school age. *JaSeSoi ry Journal, 2*, 9–10.

Davies, M. (2003). *Movement and dance in early childhood: 0–8 years*. London: Paul Chapman Publishing.

Deci, E. L., & Ryan, R. M. (2000). The "what" and "why" of goal pursuits: Human needs and the self-determination of behavior. *Psychological Inquiry, 11*(4), 227–268.

Duckworth, E. (1987). *The having of wonderful ideas*. New York: Teachers College Press.

Duncker, L. (1999). Begriff und Struktur ästhetischer Erfahrung [Concept and structure of aesthetic experience]. In N. Neuß (Ed.), *Ästhetik der Kinder* (pp. 9–19). Frankfurt/M: GEP Verlag.

Hartmann, W. (2021). *Looking at the roots. A guide to understanding Orff Schulwerk*. San Francisco, CA: Pentatonic Press.

Haselbach, B. (1994). *Improvisation, dance, movement* (M. Murray, Trans.; 2nd ed.). London: Schott. (Original work published in 1976 as Improvisation, Tanz, Bewegung, Stuttgart: Klett)

Joyce, M. (1994). *First steps in teaching creative dance to children*. Mountain View. CA: Mayfield Publishing Company.

Laban, R. (1960). *The mastery of movement* (2nd ed.). Hampshire, UK: Dance Books Ltd.

Laban, R. (1966). *Modern educational dance*. Braintree (MA): Macdonald and Evans.

Lerman, L., & Borstel, J. (2003). *Critical response process*. Takoma Park. MD: Dance Exchange.

North, M. (1973). *Movement education. Child development through body motion*. New York: Dutton.

Preston-Dunlop, V. (1987). *A handbook for dance in education* (2nd ed.). London: Longman.

Raider-Roth, M. B. (2005). *Trusting what you know: The high stakes of classroom relationships*. Hoboken, NJ: Jossey-Bass.

Salmela, M., & Nagatsu, M. (2017). How does it really feel to act together? Shared emotions and the phenomenology of we-agency. *Phenomenology and the Cognitive Sciences, 16*(3), 449–470.

Sansom, A. N. (2011). *Movement and dance in young children's lives: Crossing the divide*. New York: Peter Lang.

Terhart, E. (2003). Constructivism and teaching: A new paradigm in general didactics? *Journal of Curriculum Studies, 35*(1), 25–44.

Whitehead, A. N. (1985). *The aims of education and other essays*. New York: Free Press. (Original work published in 1929)

Online Teaching and Learning:
A Framework for Enhancing the Quality of
Kinesthetic Experiences in Movement and Music

Franziska Böhm (Germany), Christa Coogan (Germany/USA)

Introduction

> Through COVID-19 the scene has been shaken up. We see the world differently. We had to swerve, deviate, to change course seemingly in only a breath's time. Reality shifted and still is being recalibrated from one day to the next.

Prior to the COVID-19 pandemic, we—Franziska Böhm and Christa Coogan—cultivated a collaborative practice of planning, co-teaching, co-choreographing, and reflecting on our work with and for children, youth, and young adults in various situations. We situate our artistic and pedagogical work for this article within the music and movement educational framework of Orff Schulwerk. Included in Wolfgang Hartmann's definition of the teaching process of Orff Schulwerk (2022) are several fundamental principles that include: the individual is at the center of this process and is involved in creative group activities experienced through imitation, exploration, improvisation, and composition. Furthermore, one important idea of Orff Schulwerk is to connect the rhythms and phrasings of music, language, movement, and dance.

Plunging into the COVID landscape, we needed to ask ourselves unfamiliar questions, such as how can the transmitting, constructing, and receiving of embodied knowledge be possible within the small picture frame format of online platforms, and what kind of meaningful learning can take place online?

Introducing the challenge

We acknowledge that there is a great deal of qualitative loss in digital teaching: nearness, connection, contact, perceptual acuity, sound, and traditional ways of assessment. It is a long list. And yet, we decided to explore the possibilities emerging out of this challenge to find enjoyable forms of teaching online. In what ways can we work with movement, despite the absence of the familiar, e.g., a big space, a dance floor, physical contact, instruments, etc.? Unison dancing on Zoom might not work, but mirroring and shadowing exercises could very well be possible. Perhaps specific exercises to develop bodily awareness or movement accompaniment can be newly envisioned. We can create untried improvisational structures. And yes, how would it be possible to dance in a circle online?

Teachers are accustomed to adapting to the impulses of a dynamic world. We are continually improvising. However, one circumstance changed: We were not in a shared space but were working online through a screen. Recognizing the impact of this condition on our teaching practice, we had the immediate need to find other strategies and address the abovementioned questions of learning and knowing. Navigating our teaching practice in the unstable environment of the pandemic offered us the opportunity to re-examine ideas and build upon what we already knew. We propose that focusing on what can work in each specific online situation is for the teacher more important than trying to emulate a live session digitally. We have to accept and adjust to the latency realities of digital interactions and the lack of physical contact.

A phenomenological perspective is applied here as a lens to gain terminology for insights into the experience of teaching and learning online, supporting our understanding of these unanticipated ways of knowledge transmission, construction, and reception in Orff Schulwerk.

Scientific Framework

Sitting slumped in front of a screen, having tired eyes, losing attention, etc., are phenomena that we all encounter when we work online. We realized that these phenomena became heightened during the pandemic, with online teaching becoming the only medium of working together. This sparked our interest in and curiosity about thinking of our work in elemental music and dance education in relation to the field of phenomenology. What do we know and what ways of knowing are possible when we work with a screen and interact online?

Phenomenology is a field of study within philosophy that is concerned with how we perceive and know the world through our bodies and senses. It offers thought processes that are different from the Western historical way of thinking that emphasizes a Cartesian split between body and mind. Instead, phenomenologists argue that the body and mind function with each other. Here, we present a brief overview of the concepts pertaining to knowledge from four pioneering phenomenologists, and then home in on the concept of the *felt sense*, developed by psychologist Eugene Gendlin.

The philosopher Edmund Husserl was one of the first phenomenologists to initiate the turn from a universal, objective way of thinking about the world to the perspective of the subjective experience in relation to the world (2012/1913). For this notion of embodied perception, he gave the term *lived experience*. Following Husserl, the philosopher Maurice Merleau-Ponty focused on the idea of perception as being an active process, and that through active perception, knowledge in two forms—implicit and explicit—emerges (1945). Extending Merleau-Ponty's phenomenology of perception, the experimental phenomenologist and psychologist Eugene Gendlin (1997, 2003, 2018) understood that between the experience of implicit knowledge and that of explicit knowledge a process of meaning-making occurs. In this process, searching for words attempts to signify what we experience, and enhances possible meanings. Experience and language are revisited multiple times and thusly refined. He termed this process of refinement the felt sense and proposed that the nature of experiencing cannot be compared to or seen in the same way as organizing explicit knowledge through language. Gendlin suggests that the 'knowing' that is associated with the felt sense is "not like knowledge or science; it is rather like 'knowing how' to do something—perhaps how one does it cannot be explained, at least not easily" (2018, p. 48).

Michael Polanyi, a scientist-turned-philosopher whose understanding of tacit knowledge is equivalent to Gendlin's concept of implicit knowledge, argued instead that tacit knowledge is scientific knowledge (2009/1966). Although Polanyi and Gendlin had different understandings of embodied knowledge, they both agree that, as opposed to explicit knowledge, neither tacit nor implicit knowledge can be clearly formalized and put into exact words and that we know more than we can articulate (Gendlin, 2003; Polanyi, 2009/1966). Instead of defining explicit knowledge as purely cognitive and removed from the body, Polanyi and Gendlin argue that all knowledge is rooted in the body and exists on a non-hierarchical continuum from tacit to explicit. This understanding dissolves the two separate components of the Cartesian model, which is still present in Western thinking. Explicit knowledge, referring to the mind, and implicit knowledge, referring to the body, function together as embodied knowledge.

The fundamental principles of Orff Schulwerk that we referred to earlier are all aspects through which we aim to engage the body, to feel and experience our internal and our external world. This continuum of knowledge was understood and practiced before it was conceptualized in academic, scientific research. The scholar and dance educator Mollie Davies (2003), investigating the linkage between kinesthetic experience and cognitive thinking, proposes that they are inextricably linked in emotional and intellectual functioning.[1]

Being in front of the screen for a long period, forgetting to relax our shoulders and breathe, are bearings that occur unconsciously. The screen has power over our awareness and can lead us away from our bodies. From the context perspective of Gendlin's concept of the felt sense, we already know that not being able to focus does not feel good in our bodies, but we do not quite know how to say or change it yet. However, Gendlin gives value to this experience: He argues that we do know something about how we feel and that this is a form of implicit knowledge. This phenomenological perspective in general and Gendlin's *felt sense* in particular helped us to realize that we need to cultivate an awareness of how we feel in our bodies in front of the screen. The process of becoming aware needs to be practiced and refined.

In the following section, we share an example of how we aim to cultivate a sense of awareness in our bodies while working online.

A practical example

Please read through the following section, notice the specific steps. We invite you to engage in this exercise, opening your eyes and closing them when necessary. You are most likely sitting, so continue to do so.

Close your eyes.

Notice one thing about how your body feels.

And now, say what you noticed to yourself with silent words. Is there something specific that you notice about this feeling?

Open your eyes.

Look around the room in which you are sitting. If there are people in the room with you, let your eyes alight upon one person. What do you notice about that person?

If you are alone, notice something in the room. What is it that you notice?

And again, say what you notice to yourself. This saying to yourself, even silently, helps you to remember what you noticed.

Please stand up. Take a little walk around your space with normal-sized steps if possible. If not, experiment with a bigger step here and some smaller ones there.

Find the corners in the space; find the crowded parts as well as the open spaces.

As you walk, sense the openness of the throat, and make a connection between that openness and the softness at the front of the ankles. Keep walking.

Find a place to stand. Let the top of the head reach up towards the ceiling and let the body follow. Can you widen the space between your ears? And soften the space behind your eyes?

Sense the verticality of your pelvis: The tailbone hangs towards the floor as the pubic bone lifts upwards.

---

1   Recent findings of research studies in 4e cognition (Newen, de Bruin, & Gallagher, 2018), now support what we have been working on in the fields of music and dance education and Orff Schulwerk pedagogy.

Let the ribcage respond to your inhalation of breath and then the exhalation. Where do you feel the weight in the body? Where is there openness? Are your eyes opened or closed? Let them stay as they are as we repeat our noticing exercise.

Notice one thing about how your body feels. Is it the same as before? More detailed? Different?

Say what this is to yourself silently. What do you notice about this feeling?

Open your eyes if they are closed. Look around the room; notice another person or something in the room. What is it that you notice? What caught your eye this time? Is it the same as before? And again, say what you notice to yourself.

Linkage between theory and practice

The colors, textures, sounds, and the internal movements of your body while breathing that you have just noticed are all aspects of your *felt sense*. You know something particular about your relationship with yourself and your environment, and if you have not been alone, also about your relationship with others.

Our online experiences have helped us to understand that while this exercise might be a familiar one, known and practiced in certain kinds of dance classes, we often tend to forget to channel our awareness and felt sense once we sit ourselves in front of a screen. Thus, in the context of our example, exercises in which one experiences, for instance, a physical quality such as the throat opening or a sound quality such as clothes rubbing against the chair and then articulates those experiences, become part of a regular process linking both kinds of knowledge. These experiences can offer a richer perspective on the phenomena of teaching and learning online.

Guiding questions

Based on this continuum of knowledge, i.e., from tacit/implicit to explicit, we arrived at three guiding questions that inform our work online and were decisive in the development of our process-blueprint.

- What kind of meaningful learning can take place online in relation to music and dance activities?
- How can we rethink our teaching strategies in terms of knowledge transmission and knowledge construction within digital frameworks?
- How can we still teach the joyful, intimate, and strong classes that we remember from our pre-COVID times?

Anatomy of the Process-Blueprint

In this section, we examine the process-blueprint that we developed to support and encourage online teaching. The process-blueprint has three phases:

1. *From remembering to re-imagining*
2. *Shifting perspectives—cultivating an online Orff Schulwerk approach*
3. *Shaping an artistic-pedagogical teaching space*

Working foundation

This process-blueprint arose primarily out of our individual teaching work that incorporates principles of Orff Schulwerk and of creative dance, various contemporary dance techniques, and somatic practices.[1] It was developed as we worked with:

- Teenagers attending the vocational Bode Gymnastic, Sport, and Dance School in Munich;
- students studying Elemental Music Pedagogy at the University of Music and Theater, Munich;
- students studying to be schoolteachers and music teachers at the University of Potsdam; and
- music and movement/dance teachers in online professional development courses.

Although our online experience is primarily focused on youth and (young) adults, we argue that this process-blueprint is applicable for use by teachers who are working with primary school children as well.

First phase: From remembering to re-imagining

Memories are based on explicit and implicit knowledge: We do not remember only in our minds; we remember in our bodies; we remember how something feels. Through accessing these memories in our roles as teachers, we consciously build a learning environment that includes kinesthetic experiences.

Thus, we understand remembering as a transformative, embodied process that enables us to rethink our present situations and influence the connections that we make between our past experiences (in this case, in-person teaching) with present experiences (online teaching).

> I remember a situation of being with other people, standing in a circle, holding hands. Somebody is standing to my right. I remember the feeling of reaching with my whole body to grasp their hands. I remember the sense of being connected.

Remembering is a kind of portal to re-imagining, a doorway that opens possibilities to re-imagine embodied knowledge in a digital context. Drawing on the implicit memory of standing in a circle shifts, for instance, the habit of being in front of the screen towards an enlivening of attention and an intensity of intention. Awareness is heightened.

> I ask everyone to stand up and create a small amount of space in which to move. I ask them to look into each small picture frame on their screen and acknowledge each other's presence. Then, we all stretch our arms to the side, and I ask them to imagine grasping their picture-frame neighbor's hands. I ask questions that stimulate their implicit memory. "Can you feel each other's hands? Can you feel each other moving to the right? Do you have a sense of being a part of this circle?"

We apply such questions, which are adapted from phenomenological research methods, and relate to the *how* of an experience (the quality). The aim is to support both teachers and students in accessing their *lived experiences* to reimagine the present moment online.

---

[1] These include Rudolf Laban and contemporary practitioners of Laban's choreological studies of educational dance (such as Valerie Preston-Dunlop, Barbara Haselbach, Mary Joyce, Joyce Boorman), Skinner Releasing Technique, Body-Mind-Centering®, Feldenkrais, and yoga.

Second phase: Shifting perspectives—cultivating an online Orff Schulwerk approach
The moving image on a single screen (as in film or video) is an intricate and fractured representation of space and time. On Teams, Zoom, and similar video conferencing tools, these aspects are amplified by the number of participants, each of whom inhabits a single screen. In the aggregate, this produces a multiplicity of spatial representations of many screens on one screen. In addition to this, spatial fragmentation intermingles with a crucial temporal issue, i.e., the problem of latency. It is just not possible to synchronize.

In the introduction, we acknowledged that there is a great deal of qualitative loss in digital teaching. However, we do not want to be limited by the means of technology, attempting to emulate a live session digitally. We are interested, as mentioned above, to create a new list of what does work. Recognizing and accepting these latencies of both image and sound are first steps towards stimulating our curiosity and our resourcefulness to discover opportunities arising from this challenge.

> In what ways can we feel and sense vibrations of different sounds and pitches in our bodies? How might that influence the quality of our voice when we work with movement accompaniment, or with echo and call and response structures? What if we do not look for exact rhythmic synchronization because it is disturbed by latency and redirect the focus instead on the creative and interactive aspects of the activity? Through this, we leave the frontal aspect behind and use digital tools such as Breakout Rooms or the Spotlight functions. We focus on the students' unusual or surprising ideas, and we notice compositional and choreographic structures (e.g., counterpoint, unison, ABA-form, the use of space). We turn our attention to aesthetics (e.g., the use of details, elements of surprise, choices of quality, intention) and to the artistic presence (e.g., concentration, attention, being seen as musicians and dancers/performers).

Movement, which unites the *lived experience* of music making and dancing, is a means to help us shift our perspectives. In understanding movement and dance in this way, teachers can create lists of wonderful ideas, as well as inquiries and strategies that illuminate the joyful and intimate aspects of teaching an Orff Schulwerk class. Our guiding questions not only serve to develop the teachers' and students' *felt sense* and nourish observational skills, but also contribute to developing an online repertoire.

Third phase: Shaping an artistic-pedagogical space
In pre-COVID times, it was clear that the living room had a distinct usage and meaning, different from the usage and meaning of a classroom space. During the pandemic, this differentiation faltered because personal space had to become classroom space. Cultivating an online Orff Schulwerk approach enabled us to access knowledge and reimagine the uncomfortable present moment. This helped us to reframe our teaching situations in which the screen might be set up in a kitchen, which usually indicates the activity of cooking, or in a living room, in which the couch signifies relaxation.

> But what if the couch becomes a path on which to take a walk, and perhaps to stop and stand for a moment on one leg and find your balance? And then take another step and find another balance. Or the oven might become an instrument on which to create a soundscape or a rhythmic ostinato. When the class begins, the space has transformed. It is no longer just a living room. It is no longer just a classroom, but

rather it is a merging of environments for imitation, exploration, improvisation, and composition.

The conventional use of objects and their meanings shape how we relate to and interact with the world. In a music and movement/dance room, the instruments are there, enabling us to make music, and the open space can invite us to move. Where can we find possibilities in these other spaces, i.e., in the living room or the kitchen?

We find metaphors, we make associations with things that are personally important to us. Thus, personal spaces and the objects within them must become reframed with another meaning. Everyday objects and spaces mean something else in an artistic-pedagogical context. In these situations, we accordingly extend, expand, and connect the digital screen space with the three-dimensional space around us. Hence, for teachers, there is a need for a heightened sense of artistic preparation within the personal spaces. This is an act of relocating and reframing the nature of how we conceive of, plan for, and carry out our work. We understand this as a refined definition of space: An artistic-pedagogical space.

These three phases of the process-blueprint—from remembering to re-imagining; shifting perspectives – cultivating an online Orff Schulwerk approach; and shaping an artistic-pedagogical space—focus not just on the possibilities of technology and the acquirement of necessary skills to work effectively with these technologies. Our emphasis begins in relying on knowledge of embodying music, trusting what we already know via the felt sense, and of sharpening our observational capabilities.

Our Personal Manual

In this article, we have been discussing the cultivation of the *felt sense* in front of the screen. Our goal was to ensure that our online teaching could become as strong, joyful, and professional as it had been live. This manual is not a handbook to tell you how to teach or structure your classes. Rather, it is a small selection of strategies that emerged out of our work while adhering to the phases of the process-blueprint. In the following, we map activities in relation to the abovementioned Orff Schulwerk principles and we organize these into three contexts:

1. Working within the frame of the screen
2. Leaving the screen
3. Building an online archive

1. Working within the frame of the screen
Notes to ourselves:
- Warm up my body before the class in order to heighten my awareness.
- Organize placement of the camera; explore what is captured of the physical space.
- Create as much space around me as possible.
- Create a communal space. Smile while also acknowledging difficulties/discomfort to yourself; come closer to the screen; notice well to give specific, intentional, and respectful feedback. It will help to increase motivation and engage the students.
- Focus on the clarity of the gesture/action and the intention of musical expression rather than on rhythmic precision.

Imitation
A movement combination in which the participants learn a movement sequence and practice this. Alternatively, the participants can follow the teacher or a student's

movement in real-time (mirror/shadow). Despite the latency, this is possible to a good extent.

Exploration

Exploring movement accompaniment, instigating movement through sound and sound through movement (using the mute button in plenum; this is a good exercise to use also in breakout rooms, allowing participants to interact creatively in pairs or small groups).

Improvisation

The teacher gives a prompt, e.g., a 1-minute improvisation focusing on space: the connection between up and down; or body: curves and straight lines. This can be accompanied by the teacher's voice or recorded music.

From exploration to composition: A chair choreography

Explore and then decide upon 1. an extended body shape on a chair; 2. a shape behind the chair; 3. a one-legged shape standing on the chair; 4. a twisted shape on the chair. The teacher adds tempo and counts to the open-phrased sequence via a steady drumbeat. The students practice their short choreography in the center of their screen so that the teacher can see, give comments, and have an overview of all participants.

2. Leaving the screen

Notes to ourselves:

- Be playful!
- Change of environments, e.g., outside homes or buildings/in personal spaces/digital breakout rooms.
- Find new meanings in the interaction with personal spaces, e.g., making a musical composition in the kitchen/improvising in the shower or under the kitchen table.
- Can we make the uncomfortable comfortable? The comfortable uncomfortable?

Improvisation

Personal space: work with time limits, specific prompts, and places (e.g., 1.5 minutes, body shapes, under the kitchen table). Work with a reflective structure (e.g., sharing discoveries with a partner, improvising again to the same prompt, writing down experiences and sharing these with the group to create a communal feeling).

From exploration to composition

Outside or personal space (If you live with other people, include them in this assignment!): The aim is understanding the concept of symmetry and asymmetry and the connections between beginnings and endings of compositions.

1. Guided explorations (e.g., making a symmetrical still image with your body and/ or other bodies): Create a shape that is symmetrical but with a hint of asymmetry and that is in some way connected to the first shape.
2. Guided composition: Create a beginning and end shape that have a symmetrical relationship with each other.

Plenum and breakout rooms with a partner:

Plenum: Explore body percussion sounds, starts and stops, and phrase length. Then each person creates their own 8-beat body percussion sequence, repeated once (mute button on).

Breakout rooms in pairs: Teach each other your 8-beat sequence; put them together; create a form for the 32-beat sequence: AABB, ABAB, ABBA.

Plenum: Share these duets in the plenum space.

3. Building an online archive
Notes to ourselves:
- Documentation helps to create a "red thread" over a longer period.
- The archival material supports the process of memorizing, remembering, and reflecting.
- Padlet as an archiving tool is easy to access and navigate and it is aesthetically pleasing (drawings, writings, photographs, audio, and video recordings are easily uploaded and organized).
- This is a place with photos etc., to return to for compositional ideas.

Guided exploration (focus on 'seeing')
Return to a drawing that you created last week. Look at it in proximity and then from a distance; look at it in unusual ways (upside down, sideways) in the context of other things near the drawing. What is similar or different? Look at it for longer than you usually would. What kind of music can you imagine being played for the drawing?

Composition
Choose two objects from your room and three ideas from the drawing and draw your own composition. Transform the drawing into a musical score by recognizing and assigning sound qualities and rhythms. Return to your symmetrical assignment (being away from the screen) and photograph your symmetrical/asymmetrical beginning and end shapes and upload them to Padlet.

We invite you to create your own manual.

Thinking and Practicing Further: Reflections and Discoveries

We find that through this approach to teaching online, meaningful learning is fostered, knowledge transmission and construction do take place, and teaching and learning can be intimate, fun, and of high quality. We now consider future perspectives.

The pandemic compelled us to maneuver our way in and around digital spaces immediately, with little or no preparation to study and understand these new realities of teaching. Suddenly we were dependent on any previous knowledge and experience of digital techniques. Microphone and camera qualities, video making and editing, acoustic principles in digital media, audio recording, etc., are not areas of knowledge for many in the Orff Schulwerk field. Thus, we breathe a sigh of relief in acknowledgment that the state of emergency has passed, and we now can dance and play music together in the same room, in real-time.

Nevertheless, we have acquired many new skills during the pandemic that will be useful in navigating the continuing reality of digital options in education—whether through choice or necessity. The phenomenological context of the process-blueprint sharpens the significance of embodied processes experienced during online classes. We contend that the principles and methods of this empirical model developed and applied during the COVID era are also valuable resources for informing our pedagogical practices in face-to-face teaching.

There are other examples of online teaching (such as the Harvard University Project Zero online courses,[1] offered since the early 2000s; the Juilliard Extension Program[2] courses in dance, drama, music theory, and instrumental lessons, etc.). We want to further situate our approach amongst these kinds of practitioners.

In our collaborative practice, we recognize possibilities for further research, such as:

- Developing online teaching as a supplemental approach to how we work in Orff Schulwerk, initiating a dialogue between face-to-face and digital, thus maintaining a focus towards the future. This could include discovering additional ways to engage with digital technologies that are accessible (instead of waiting for improvements).
- Empowering students to engage with digital resources that are personal, allowing for self-agency and creativity.
- Investigating the relationship between experience and language; fostering an environment for constructive and stimulating dialogue; providing tools to help articulate aesthetic experiences; analyze pedagogical decisions.

The author Siri Hustvedt (2021) refers to the continually shifting borders of human dynamic experience. We conclude that the process-blueprint addresses and responds to these fluid movements inherent in our experiences. With it, we shift our attention towards future possibilities.

References

Davies, M. (2003). *Movement and dance in early childhood* (2nd ed.). London: Paul Chapman Publishing.

Gendlin, E. T. (1997). *Experiencing and the creation of meaning: A philosophical and psychological approach to the subjective.* Evanston, IL: Northwestern University Press.

Gendlin, E. T. (2003). *Focusing: How to gain direct access to your body's knowledge.* London: Rider.

Gendlin, E. T. (2018). *A process model.* Evanston, IL: Northwestern University Press.

Hartmann, W. (2021). *Looking at the roots: A guide to understanding Orff Schulwerk.* San Francisco: Pentatonic Press.

Husserl, E. (2012). *Ideas: General introduction to pure phenomenology* (W. R. Boyce Gibson, Trans.). Oxfordshire: Routledge. (Original work published in 1913)

Hustvedt, S. (2021). *Mothers, fathers, and others.* New York: Simon and Schuster.

Merleau-Ponty, M. (1945). *Phenomenology of perception.* London: Routledge and Kegan Paul.

Newen, A., de Bruin, L., & Gallagher, S. (2018). *The Oxford handbook of 4e cognition.* Oxford: Oxford University Press.

Polanyi, M. (2009). *The tacit dimension* (2nd ed.). Chicago: University of Chicago Press.

---

1 http://www.pz.harvard.edu/professional-development#link-onlinecourses (accessed 12.2.2023)
2 https://www.juilliard.edu/stage-beyond/juilliard-extension/about-juilliard-extension (accessed 12.2.2023)

PART II
Topics

Children's Games and Dances

Introduction by Doug Goodkin (USA)
Examples by Ana Rosa García del Fresno (Spain),
Kalliopi Mastrogiannopoulou (Greece), Sencer Özbay (Turkey)

INTRODUCTION

The Role of Play and Children's Games
Doug Goodkin

Musical instruction for a child does not begin in the music lesson. Playtime is the starting point. One should not come to music - it should arise of itself. What is important is that the child be allowed to play, undisturbed, expressing the internal externally. Word and sound must arise simultaneously from improvisatory, rhythmic play. (Orff, 2011/1932, p. 68)

The child at play and the artist at work share much in common. From the depths of the magical and mysterious dream-world, from the grand sweep of the unbounded imagination, the formless takes form, the shapeless takes shape, the unseen is revealed. The creative instinct that lies sleeping at the bottom of the well of each human consciousness is drawn up by the ropes and buckets of the child at play, the artist at work—and the thirsty world is refreshed.

The kind of play Carl Orff refers to here is that instinct in its pure form, the way children animate the world with their imagination. They engage with the things that surround them using the full range of their senses—exploring, experimenting, poking, and prodding as their minds roam free, unfettered by adult rules and boundaries. They find the secret song hidden inside things, coax it forward into some kind of pattern and form, expressing their "internal [world] externally."

One of the forms that emerges from the child's play instinct is children's games. The wide world of structured games created by and carried forth by children follow the blueprint of Nature's curriculum. They are intuitively designed to coordinate the rhythmic energies of the body, to develop the mind's quest to understand pattern, to serve the heart's need to learn how to play well with others. Clapping games that cross the midline to help knit together the two hemispheres of the brain, quick reaction games that spring from ancient hunter's skills of awareness and alertness necessary for survival, counting out and numerical games that codify mathematical intuitions, movement games that artfully focus the body's impulses, drama games that allow children to try on different personas—all of this and more are Nature's schooling, unencumbered by adult teachers and scheduled classes. The texts of the songs range from sheer nonsense to deep metaphor, the child's way of trying to make sense out of a chaotic, confusing, and sometimes terrifying world.

Though the games themselves naturally differ in terms of the language and the musical styles of each distinct culture, their presence and function are universal. The common types of games found everywhere include:

- partner clapping games
- stone-passing games (or other objects, including just passing claps around the circle)
- quick-reaction games
- ring plays and circle games
- rock, paper, scissors games
- counting-out games to determine who is "IT"
- elimination games
- jump rope rhymes
- hopscotch games
- fingerplays
- body awareness games
- making-up motions games
- chasing and hiding games
- guessing games (who is singing? etc.)
- blindfold games (trying to locate other players by sound)
- games that name professions and invite motions common to each
- games that tell a story and invite the children to play-act the characters

Why play these games in the music classroom? What is their role in a dynamic music and movement education? How can we use them effectively? Here are a few key points:

Preservation

Screens and adult-organized activities have diminished the presence of children's games in many parts of the world, and that has been a great loss to children's physical, intellectual, social, and musical development. The music teacher teaching them in the classroom becomes like a national treasure preserving something of great value.

Child-centered education

A cardinal rule of effective teaching is to meet the students where they are and then take them to where they have never yet been. By bringing children's games into the music classroom, the teacher enters the child's world, and that changes everything. The child feels, "You know me and understand how I love to learn."

The teacher as student

The teacher has lived longer, has a bigger body, knows more things than the children, but understands that the children are often more expressive in their body and voice, more imaginative in their thinking, more curious and open to possibility. While it is the teacher's job to lead, they understand that there are times when the child's expression and/or idea is better and should be followed. When teacher and student meet on these terms in the world of games, an exciting and fruitful conversation commences.

If the teacher is not careful, bringing the games into the classroom will taint them with the adult perspective and they will lose some of their energy and power. So, step one is to play them inside the class the way the children do outside in the playground, field, or city street.

Beware of the stiff bodies that school both creates and expects as it tries to make children into little obedient adults. Encourage the children's natural exuberance and celebrate the bounce in the body as they clap with their partner, their unbridled joy sashaying down the center of the lines with their partner, their uninhibited expressive movement as they show their motion in the middle of the circle.

Equally important is to teach the games as children often learn them from each other—just jumping in and imitating. As you play the games with them, make sure that you yourself model and embody the rhythms and fully express the gestures.

The teacher as teacher

While it is a good idea to begin from the child's world as noted above, the teacher has the tools to teach the games in ways that the children might not consider on their own. If children are having trouble absorbing the game, then sequential teaching from simple to complex, slowing the tempo as needed, simplifying the patterns, and more can be helpful.

Likewise, the teacher has the freedom to extend the game beyond its fixed version. Once the original game is mastered, simple variations cannot only make it yet more interesting, but they also help to develop the children's music, movement, and imaginative skills. They give the children the repetition needed to master the game alongside the variation that always keeps it new and fresh. Some examples:

Play the game…

- as fast as you can.
- as slow as you can; as if you are under water.
- with your eyes closed.
- inventing a new clapping pattern.
- inventing a new clapping choreography in a group of four.
- combining the thrown rock/paper/scissor shapes to make a new shape together (an idea I learned from Masumi Hasai-Smith).
- having the "winner" and the "loser" of a competitive partner game join as a team to play against two others. The "winner" and "loser" of that game then join to make a group of four to play against four others, etc. (an idea from my colleague James Harding).
- having those who get "out" in a competitive circle game choose a percussion instrument to play one of the rhythms or a xylophone to play the melody.
- changing directions, levels, tempos, energies, formation when playing movement-based games.

Here is where the Orff Schulwerk practice of asking "How else can we do this?" moves the games from a repertoire of fun activities (valuable as that is) to a higher level of musical skill, understanding, and creative interpretation. Some of these further extensions include the following suggestions:

From game to folk dance

Some games, like American play-parties, are line dances created to get around the Puritanical prohibition of dancing as sinful and the fiddle as the "Devil's instrument." Putting words to fiddle tunes and singing while moving, the dances continued disguised as children's play-parties, i.e., a "harmless little pastime" for the young ones. Simply playing them as they are adds to a folk dance repertoire common in many Orff Schulwerk programs.

Many are circle games with movements typical of many folk dances—walking to the left, to the right, towards the center, weaving in and out of raised-arm "windows," spiraling in and unravelling out. Playing a variety of such games both prepares the students for later folk dances and adds to the choreographic repertoire.

From game to choreography

This progression invites the children to take some of the motions of the game and explore them in a new context. As mentioned above, things like changing the tempo, performing them "underwater" in slow motion, transposing them to different planes and levels—higher, lower, diagonally, etc.—changing the size of the motions, makes for intriguing movement choreographies. Once in Japan, I introduced a Japanese game that students already knew, a risky choice as a foreigner bringing "coals to Newcastle." After we played it once, I gave them the challenge of choreographing a version of the game in small groups using their whole bodies. This presented a challenging movement problem to solve, and the results ranged from hilarious to aesthetically pleasing.

From simple to complex variations

In games like hopscotch, there can be different levels of movement challenges that the children pass through. This includes inventing their own challenges (jumping with eyes closed without touching the line, continuing to hop in place while picking up the stone, etc.).

From fantasy play to drama

In games in which children do motions of various professions or move in the style of different characters (a witch, a ghost, a giant, etc.), these initial explorations can be incorporated into a larger, more formal drama.

From game to percussion ensemble

Games are built on a rhythmic foundation and anything that includes handclapping, finger snapping, leg patting, or foot stamping can be transferred to percussion instruments to create some satisfying ensemble music. This is particularly effective in elimination games, where the children who are "out" choose a percussion instrument to accompany the game while the remaining children continue to play.

From game to Orff instrumental ensemble

Games that include songs invite the possibility of orchestrating melodies and accompaniments on Orff instruments. This works best when the songs fit into the developmental sequence of arranging and composing music for the Orff ensemble. A game with a pentatonic melody that can be accompanied by drone and ostinati can be a good choice for the younger children. Modal examples can supplement the study of intermediate levels and harmonic examples can be appropriate for the older children. In my own work, I have found African American children's games to be the perfect steppingstone to beginning jazz ensembles, containing in seed form the rhythmic qualities of offbeat, syncopation and swing, the short melodic phrases in blues-type scales, the harmonic I or I-IV or later I-IV-V vamps that lead to the blues. When I travel and work with high school and even college jazz bands, I have them clear the floor of chairs and music stands, put down their instruments and get into a circle to play some of these games. Afterwards, they pick up their instruments and play what we have been singing and dancing and they often testify how they felt the music deeper than reading the notes on the chart—and had more fun in the process.

This is a good reminder that games are not just for young children but help keep the child in all of us alive, awake, and happy to play. When we approach the serious arts of music and movement/dance performance from a playful foundation, we combine the mastery of the adult with the spirit of the child, and all are refreshed.

The examples that follow from Greece, Spain, and Turkey highlight the universality of some of the types of games listed above and show how an imaginative Orff Schulwerk teacher can extend them in their work with children.

PRACTICAL EXAMPLES

Overview

1. **Kalliopi Mastragiannopoulou (Greece): "Perna perna i melissa"–Greek traditional arch game**
    The Greek version of an internationally known "bridge game" leads to an improvised dance about bees and flowers with kindergarten children.

2. **Ana Rosa García del Fresno (Spain): Lou Pripet/France–Weavers' dance**
    This example, for first and second graders, is about trades from former times, recognizing them as themes that have given rise to songs, games, and dances.

3. **Sencer Özbay (Turkey): Ebe tura 123**
    This game for primary school children (8–9 years old) leads to experiencing the planes of the body as a theme for dance improvisation.

1. "Perna perna i melissa" - Greek Traditional Arch Game
Kalliopi Mastrogiannopoulou

Introduction
"Perna perna i melissa" is the Greek version of an internationally popular movement game (similar to the English "London Bridge is falling down," the German "Ziehe durch, durch die gold'ne Brücke," the Korean "Dong, Dong, Dongdaemun," and many others). Based on the original version, an improvised dance for kindergarten children is developed from it. Thus, the following suggestions can be used or varied depending on the group of children and the teacher's ideas.

The original game
To play the game, two children form an arch with their hands and all the other children walk underneath singing the song. In the more difficult Greek version, the children who form the arch clap each other's hands following the beat of the song. But for very young children starting with a simple arch is a nice idea. The "bridge children" choose two words, one for each of them (for instance: flower and bee, or something else). Then they sing the song.

Per - na per-na i me-li-ssa Me ta me-li-
Περ - νά περ-νά η μέ - λι-σσά Με τα με-λι-

sso - pou - la Ke me ta pe - do - pou - la.
σσό - που - λα και με τα παι - δό - που - λα.

(The bee passes by with the little bees and the children)

The child who is under the arch when the song is over is caught by the bridge children. They whisper the two words to the trapped child and ask them to choose one of them, and the trapped child goes behind the one whose word they chose. The song is repeated until all children have been caught. Whoever gets the most people on their team wins.

The improvised dance

As soon as two groups have been formed behind the children who form the arch, it is time to invite the children to dance. At that point the teacher should be aware that the two groups might not be equal. They ask the children from group A to be the flowers, who stay static, and group B to be the bees, who dance freely around the flowers like flying in the air. The dance is inspired by the text of the song about the bees.

The flowers (group A) will be standing or sitting spread around the space. They sing the song and accompany it by clapping or playing small percussion instruments like tambourines or claves, while the teacher plays the melody on the recorder or another instrument. They can try out different rhythmic patterns until they find one that they will play to "call the bees to dance." When playing with very young children, it might be helpful to offer, among other patterns, this one, which nicely fits to the text of the song: quarter note, quarter note, half note.

The bees (group B) could now fly around the flowers and improvise a bee dance, following the melody of the recorder and the rhythmic accompaniment of the flowers. Of course, it would be important that the teacher discusses with the children first about the way that the bees move. They should remind them that the little insects move all the time changing place until they rest on a flower. So do the little children. They can dance lower, close to the floor, or higher above the flowers. After some repetitions the teacher could offer more hints to give them more movement and space experiences making their dance more interesting. When the song is over, each child in the group of bees should end close to a flower and then, switching roles, the improvisation starts again.

When the song is over again, some duets or a trio (depending on the number of children) can be formed. Each grouping should have at least one flower and one bee. Then it is the moment when the children together can create their own little dance. Each couple can decide who will have which role and whether to keep the small percussion instruments or not. Their dance should last as long as one repetition of the song and be presented to the rest of the group while the teacher is playing the recorder and the other children are singing and accompanying. The presentation can be done by one pair separately or by several at the same time in order to reduce the excessive repetitions of the song that may tire some children. The teacher could ask the last pair to form the arch again and let the game start from the beginning with everybody singing.

Conclusion

The elements of the traditional form of the game—the bridge and the chain of the children, the choice of the roles, and especially the text of the song—offer, as a matter of course, an extension to more individual representations and the implementation of creative ideas from the children.

2. "Lou Pripet" – Weavers' Dance from France
Ana Rosa García del Fresno

Group

First and second graders from a primary school for children with special education needs (ASD). Three 90-minute lessons in consecutive weeks as part of artistic education workshops.

Objectives

- To know tasks and trades from former times and to recognize them as themes that have given rise to songs, games, and dances.
- To explore gestures and movements based on trades that can lead to dance forms.
- To approach the gestures and movements of a traditional dance.

Motivation

- A group of 1st graders have compiled a collection of stories told by their grandparents that reflect places, activities, and traditional trades nearly forgotten.[1]
- The presentation of this booklet that was expanded through texts and images made by the students themselves has provided a good starting point.

Sequencing

- Trades and work
- Motivation, presentation of the dance melody, and creation of choreographies.

> *Antón, Antón,*
> *Antón Pirulero,*
> *Cada **cual**, cada **cual***
> *At**iend**a su juego,*
> *y el que **no** lo at**iend**a*
> *pagará una **prenda**.*

Game description

Players in a circle seated on the floor. One player is the leader, all the others imagine an instrument.

When the song starts, the leader circles their fists around each other, the other children perform the gesture of playing the violin, the guitar, the piano, etc. When the leader changes the gesture to that of one of the instruments, all the players who are using this instrument gesture must change to the gesture of the leader (e.g., circling their fists). When the leader returns to circling their fists, the others resume their original instrument gestures.

The player who fails to react must hand over a small personal item (e.g., shoe, bracelet, hair band). This continues until the leader has collected several items. To recover their item, each

---

1   A selection of pages from the book *Historias de nuestros abuelos* (stories of our grandparents) can be accessed at the following link: https://drive.google.com/file/d/1_oB4R8H6Oh74VpPdnlMMq7IK4gsRNlT3/view?usp=share _link.

child must do what the leader says (e.g., run without making noise, jump on one leg, walk in slow motion).
- Repeat the game, but now the gestures of playing the instruments are replaced by gestures typical of trades and professions.
- Discuss preferred trades and list gestures used with the trades.
- Graphic representations of the agreed names of trades with pictograms of gestures.

Presentation of this traditional French melody of "Lou Pripet," a weavers' dance, distinguishing parts A and B by exploring different gestures

Rhythm of steps under the melody: Stem up = right foot; stem down = left foot

- Listen to the recording. We are going to do a dance of "trades." Choose a trade and, while listening, imagine two gestures associated with this trade.
- Perform your first gesture while the teacher sings the melody of part A. Do the same for your second gesture to the melody of part B.
- Same activity, moving around the classroom joining someone who performs similar gestures.

Elaboration of choreographies
- Grouping by trades: Agreement by groups on the gestures to be used.
- Practice with our melody.
- Presentation by the groups of their "trades" dances.
- Discussion with students about the different proposals.

Steps and coordination: process for learning the dance
- We look at pictures of looms to become familiar with the weaving tools, their function and movement (scissors, beater, etc.).
- We sing the melody with the following text (accented syllables in bold):

A Teje con su **aguj**a **t**eje,
   Teje y teje **sin pa**rar.
   Verde, azul y rojo, amarillo,
   Todo el **día** en **su t**elar.

B Tris, tris, tras, con las tijeras,
   Tris, tris, tras, cor**ta el hilo.**
   Tris, tris, tras, con las tijeras,
   Tris, tris, tras, vuelve a cortar.

Dance description
Circle, standing close to each other, hands joined.

Part A: Walking to the right, starting right foot (Variation: side-close step to the right).
Arms: Bend moving upwards on first step, back down on the second.

Part B: In place (Variation: Bar 1–4 move slightly backwards, repeat back to place).
Step: in traditional dances "scissors" step.

First two quick steps (eighth notes) on the ball of the foot, third step (quarter note) on the whole sole of the foot. The foot in the air is extended forward with little toe close to the floor. Arms: extended forward, parallel to the floor, body inclined slightly backwards.

Perform gestures related to the use of the loom elements. Imitate significant examples provided by the students.

Agreement on gestures:
Part A: patching, elbows bent, moving arms up and down alternately, imitating the movement of the beater.

Part B: arms stretched in front palm to palm, do the rhythm of the "scissors" step imitating the movement of the scissors.

Learn the dance by following this didactic sequence:
In a circle, hands joined...

1. Legs/feet only, in place: **A:** marking the pulse. **B:** "scissors" step.
2. Arms only: **A:** move arms up and down. **B:** arms in front, parallel to the floor.
3. Legs/feet only: **A:** walking steps to the right. **B:** on the spot, facing the center of the circle, "scissors" steps starting with the right foot.
4. Legs/feet and arms: **A:** walk to the right while arms move up and down. **B:** in place, facing the center. Arms in front, parallel to the floor. "Scissors" steps starting with right foot.

Finally, perform the dance with the sung melody or the recording
(https://youtu.be/KLydos4d22s).

3. "Ebe tura 123" (Turkey) - From Movement Game to Dance Improvisation
Sencer Özbay

This theme is started with one of the traditional children's movement games played in our country, which is also internationally known under various names. The idea of stopping in a frozen position is developed into a dance improvisation using the three body planes (sagittal, horizontal, and vertical) first in position, then in gesture, and finally also in locomotion.

Group
Primary school, 8–9 years old. Depending on previous experience in dance, the theme can also be developed over several lessons to understand and deal creatively with the theme of body levels. The music accompaniment may be improvised during the process, but it can also be refined later as an ensemble piece.

The original game
On one end of the movement space the group of children is waiting to move forward; on the other end "IT" is hiding their face in their bent arm and looking at the wall. "IT" is speaking the text in the following rhythm:

The other children move forward, trying to reach the opposite wall. As soon as "IT" stops and turns around everybody freezes. Whoever is still seen moving by "IT" has lost and moves to the instruments. The game is finished as soon as somebody touches the opposite wall without being seen by "IT." The winner can now take on the role of "IT" in the repetition of the game.

In the beginning, "IT" may only stop at the end of the rhyme and turn around, but later it becomes much more exciting when they can do it at any moment.

From game to dance improvisation
The three body planes
The teacher explains the three planes of the body (see the article by B. Haselbach and A. Wolf, "Overview of Various Applications of Movement and Dance in the Orff Schulwerk") and how to move within them. They may also show picture cards or photos of sculptures.

- The children experience moving in one of the planes then another until they feel secure. First, they are asked to use only frozen positions, after a while also gestures, and finally with steps in locomotion.
- They also may watch each other to see different positions and movements appropriate for the various planes used by other children.

- Now the space is divided into three sections (if necessary, with two chalk lines drawn on the floor). Whoever moves in the first section uses movements in the table (horizontal) plane, when they get into the second section they dance in door (vertical) plane, and in the third in wheel (sagittal) plane.

Music accompaniment
First the teacher plays alone in the same rhythm as the text, after a while they are joined by children who have moved through all the three sections. They choose one of the already prepared instruments and play an ostinato with the teacher's improvised melody.

Final dance
The children are divided in three groups, one is dancing, the other watching, and the third playing the music. They enter the dance space of the three sections one group after the other. The change from one section to the next happens after four (later after 8) repetitions of the text. The more experienced the children become, the longer the dancing phase in each section can become.

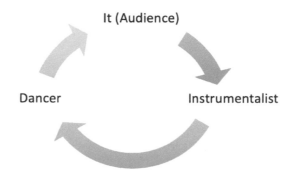

What started as a traditional game now becomes a creative exercise in music and dance.

References and Resources

Orff, C. (2011) Gedanken über Musik mit Kindern und Laien/Thoughts about music with children and non-professionals (M. Murray, Trans.). In B. Haselbach (Ed.), *Studientexte zu Theorie und Praxis des Orff-Schulwerks: Basistexte aus den Jahren 1932–2010/Texts on theory and practice of Orff-Schulwerk: Basic texts from the years 1932–2010* (pp. 66–77). Mainz: Schott. (Original work published in 1932)

The Shenanigans—Topic. (2015, October 6). *Lou Pripet* [Recording]. YouTube. https://www.youtube.com/watch?v=xzN_bKs61Dk

Various Artists—Topic. (2016, September 8). *Teppichknüpfen (Lou Pripet)* [Recording]. YouTube. https://youtu.be/KLydos4d22s

Improvisation and Elemental Choreography

Susan Kennedy (USA), Hana Novotná (Czech Republic),
Patrick Ware (USA), Angelika Wolf (Austria/UK)

Every phase of Schulwerk will always provide stimulation for new independent growth; therefore it is never conclusive and settled, but always developing, always growing, always flowing.

(Carl Orff, 2011/1964, p. 134)

INTRODUCTION

In the wide field of dance, improvisation and choreography represent those activities that do not refer to or repeat traditional dance material and dance forms but design something new. Within the framework of the Orff Schulwerk, creative moving and dancing is very often connected to other forms of expression such as singing songs, speaking texts, playing instruments, presenting people who are wearing costumes and masks, painting and performing lines and ornaments, sculpting body figures, and many others. Creating with our bodies and movement may happen spontaneously or it may be planned and developed step by step. We distinguish between two creative processes:

Improvisation means an action that is not pre-planned but develops from an inspiration or idea in the moment. It is fleeting, rarely repeatable and arises from playful experimentation based on sensory awareness. In the artistic education setting improvisation means spontaneous creation.

Elemental choreography refers to both the process and the result of creating and shaping ideas as well as movement material that make the content visible. It requires conscious planning, a clear structure of solo or group movement in space, time, and dynamics. It should be carefully rehearsed before shown to others and then reflected in its process and outcome by the performers and observers. In German (and at the Orff Institute) the term *Gestaltung* is used to mean designing or giving form to something through a creative process. It has a wider meaning than "choreography," which might sound a bit too professional in the context of Orff Schulwerk, and it can also include the musical accompaniment.

Objectives

- Affecting different human qualities: sensory–motor–individual–social–affective–cognitive–verbal.
- Individual body perception and sensitization.
- Intuitive and individual expansion of movement experience and movement repertoire.
- Non-verbal communication in the social area.
- Translating ideas and perceptions into movement as a performer and developing observational skills and interpretive understanding of movement presentations as a spectator.

Some examples (themes) for solo or group improvisations

- Themes from the field of body awareness and experience in space, time, and dynamics (variations or combinations of basic body activities, e.g., alternation between locomotion and stillness); movements of individual body parts (e.g., hands only); stability-lability; touch (also with partners); contrast of fast and slow, strong and light movements, etc.
- Music, short examples from different periods; also using instruments and the voice in movement.
- Lyrics, poems, riddles, proverbs, advertising slogans, etc.
- Dramatic ideas (fairy tales, stories).
- Metaphorical images.
- Graphic motifs, videos, photos, paintings, sculptures, styles of architecture.
- Using objects/materials in movement (e.g., ribbons, sticks, etc.) and those that inspire movement through observing and discovering their function (e.g., kaleidoscope, magnet).

Methods for improvisation guidance

Ways of introducing a theme
- Concrete introduction: Students can acquire concrete sensations by looking at or touching an object, listening to music or to a text, viewing a painting or touching a sculpture, and then expressing their individual impressions and interpretations that become embodied in the improvisational process that follows.
- Verbal introduction: Explanations (by the leader) describing the idea in a lively or a more formal way.

Exploring
- Exploration emerges directly from the chosen idea/topic: an object reveals or inspires a whole world of movement possibilities; music initiates basic movement activities; movement words become gestures, graphic lines lead to gestures or locomotion.
- Verbal tasks of the group leader inspire and guide the exploration phase. Suitable questions awaken curiosity about the movement potential hidden in the chosen theme.
- A dialogue between dancer and theme has started and can initiate a whole process that encourages body awareness in space, time, dynamics, and the awareness of partner and group.
- If improvisation experience initially arises from playful experimentation, then in the course of time and with increasing practical experience, the awareness of what is created in the moment becomes more conscious.
- Of course, we learn not only by our own practicing but also by watching others and reflecting (not in a judging way, but in a more descriptive or interpreting way) what we have seen.

At this point the development begins.

From improvisation to elemental choreography (Gestaltung)

The liveliness and creative outcomes of improvisation can be a desired result in themselves, or they may be carried on into a compositional activity. They are the basis for the *Gestaltung*—combining sound and movement elements and finding a structure that is calculated by thinking, imagining, discussing, deciding, trying out, changing, or even rejecting and looking for different possibilities until the creator or the creating team is satisfied with the results.

Each *Gestaltung* needs a theme or an idea. It may be a description or narrative of a certain event (e.g., using the image of wind or waves), or an idea that is introduced in an abstract way (creating a dance from soft to energetic movement). The movement material suitable for any idea must be developed and an appropriate spatial and temporal structure found. A refinement of the movement execution needs dynamic and rhythmic differentiation to convey the intended expressive quality. If the setting is intended for a group, then of course the division of space also plays an important role. One can start with motifs (short, characteristic movement sequences), then expand them through repetition, continuation, variation, or contrast and adjust them to the chosen music.

This process can be directed verbally by the leader or worked out through imitation. Small groups can be challenged with a specific task (e.g., how should the group formation look or how should the spatial paths be designed?).

Students undoubtedly learn more when they are given tasks that they have to solve themselves and when they reflect on what they have achieved together than when they merely imitate what is given. With more experienced participants the whole choreographic *Gestaltung* could be developed by themselves. However, it has to be taken into consideration that the time required for a whole or partly creative process is correspondingly longer. Through a short or long process an idea or a task is finally turned into a finished product. Both are equally important.

Demonstrating and reflecting

The conclusion of even simple improvisation and design processes should, if possible, be demonstration and reflection. The students, on the one hand as performers, become used to demonstrating and verbally representing what they have produced, and on the other hand as spectators they learn to describe their impressions as objectively as possible without making offending judgments.

PRACTICAL EXAMPLES

Overview
In this section four authors who work with Orff Schulwerk in different countries, languages, schools, and age groups give examples of creative dance projects designed for different ages and connected with four distinctive themes.

1. **Hana Novotná: *Swimmy*–creative movement exploration of Leo Lionni's book about life in the ocean**
   Inspired by the book *Swimmy* and the composition "Aquarium" from the Carnival of Animals by Camille Saint-Saëns, this example is meant primarily for children who are three to eight years old.
2. **Susan Kennedy: Playing with rice, improvised movement, and music score**
   Students create a flexible score that can be erased and made new with whole-body movement. For ages ten to twelve.
3. **Patrick Ware: Improvised movement from improvised music**
   Children ages nine to ten improvise movement to jazz music.
4. **Angelika Wolf: "A strange morning"–Using alienating everyday movements**
   14-to-16-year-olds play with the topic of strangeness, awkwardness, and the idea of doing things differently using themes from the book Virginia Wolf by Kio McLear.

1. *Swimmy*–Creative Movement Exploration of Leo Lionni's Book About Life in the Ocean

Hana Novotná

The theme of this example was inspired by the book *Swimmy* by Leo Lionni and the composition "Aquarium" from the *Carnival of Animals* cycle by Camille Saint-Saëns. It is meant to be applied primarily with children who are three to eight years old.

Aims
- Performing, acting, and dancing the story of Lionni's *Swimmy* to the music of Saint-Saëns' "Aquarium" in an improvised but well-prepared manner.
- Deepening and developing individual kinesthetic and spatial awareness.
- Concrete focus on movement and dance (different kinds of locomotion and body shapes in various levels) on the basis of imaginative ideas.

Motivation
First, the story is briefly narrated and then the whole book is shown to the children with Saint-Saëns' music, but without talking.

A group sound improvisation with cups and buckets of water, straws, and bottles creates the soundscape that invites students to dig into the imaginative scenery of the ocean.

Exploration
Students warm up under the teacher's guidance through exploring the movement material and focusing on movement qualities that are inspired by the book's characters, including the suggestions of:
- Jellyfish sway and float in the waves with scarfs.
  - Adding further movement ideas (shape qualities) such as opening, closing, rising, or falling enriches the movement.
- Lobster walk might resemble the "water moving machine" (Lionni, 2017, p. 10).
  - Use arms and legs to walk on the floor in all directions in different tempi and dynamics.
  - This walk could be combined with pausing in various body shapes while balancing a light flat prop (for instance a foam fish) on different body surfaces.
- Eel leads the group to explore floor patterns.
  - Several children hold hands and move one after the other through the room, following the leader.
  - Children can also draw the pathways they used, which will help them to understand what they were doing.
- Fish and the seaweeds.
  - Group A/seaweeds grow from "sugar candy rocks" (p. 14) and then sway on the spot in various body shapes using vertically low, middle, and high levels in space.
  - Group B/fish swim between the plants and examine the close space around them.
  - Both groups could switch their activities from time to time.
  - Body shapes of non-moving objects, such as stones, rocks, star fish are usually tried out first with little children.
- Children move through space close to each other in a group as one giant fish.
  - They follow a leader (who usually holds a prop, e.g., a toy fish).
  - Once an instrumental sign is given, the leader changes.

Reflection and further elaboration

Watching each other's movements and listening to the teacher's comments will help them to identify and start to name the experienced movement qualities. Later, guided by the teacher, they repeat movement motives with higher self-awareness and intensity.

To put all the scenes together and dance the whole story in a more or less improvised way, the children might need the teacher's guidance by reading or telling the whole story to the music.

When working with older students, the elaboration part of the process may be rather focused on independent group work including composing individual scenes chosen by students.

Demonstration and reflection

Finally, the *Gestaltung* featuring "water soundscape intro" and all chosen movement phrases is performed accompanied by Saint-Saëns' "Aquarium."

Afterwards, the children can sit with the teacher and talk about what they liked, what was interesting, what they learned, how the music helped them to express the characters they were portraying, etc. Such conversations should encourage them to think about their own actions and experiences. They could also be invited to draw or paint their own illustrations of the story.

2. Playing with Rice, Improvised Movement, and Music Score
Susan Kennedy

Introduction

This idea evolved from my desire to find a way to create very flexible scores, i.e., scores that could continually be erased and made anew, and that could be made with whole-body motions. I also wanted a way to have the visual score-making, the movement, and the sound constantly influence each other. I was originally inspired by the Chinese and Japanese free-style calligraphers whose brush-stroke writings come from deep within their bodies, not just from their wrists and hands.

Solo exploration

We start with a mound of rice on a square of black felt (felt is used so that the rice patterns do not shift easily). One person kneels and, using large movements that come from the back or base of the spine, pushes and pulls the rice into varying abstract patterns, continually changing them. It is a dance of sorts in the way the movements result in these graphic designs. After a short time, two students lift the four corners of the felt to meet together and "erase" the designs, returning the rice to a clean mound in the center of the black cloth. The next student takes a turn, moving the rice with large body motions, playing with light movements like sprinkling, sharper movements like dabbing or slapping, or flowing movements like sweeping, gathering, and pressing.

The movement is leading the accompaniment and the drawing.
Photo: Susan Kennedy

Layered improvisation

Once students have a feel for the sensuality of moving the rice, then, working in a small group, one student is moving the rice, and one or more other students stand behind and shadow the motions of the rice mover. Because they are standing, they can enlarge the movements. In addition, one or more students can freely accompany vocally. Simple instruments, especially ones that can be rubbed or scraped or have their tones bent, metal-barred instruments, drums and wood blocks can be grouped around the rice score for students to improvise accompaniment as the rice is being moved. With more familiarity, the sound and movement can influence what is happening with the rice designs, i.e., it will go beyond one medium simply imitating another, but will become a conversation. This improvised exploration can be a "performance" in its own right.

Composition/*Gestaltung*

The teacher chooses a stopping point when the evolving scores will be "frozen." Everyone walks around and views the scores and shares impressions of what they see in them. Then, returning to their original scores, the students play with and solidify a movement and/or sound interpretation of their score. Each group performs for the rest of the class. Performers and viewers describe what connections they see between the scores and the movement/sound studies.

Observing the outcome. Photos: Susan Kennedy

3. Improvised Movement from Improvised Music
Patrick Ware

This example describes a lesson with a school class of nine-to-ten-year-olds that can also be adapted in a similar way with any group, regardless of age.

Exploration
There must be exploration before improvisation with the intent of building vocabulary. Dancers explore locomotor movement, react to prompts from the teacher such as hop, skip, spiral, and dart, as well as explore non-locomotor movement, such as, twist, bend, shudder, and dissolve. Next, we pair that exploration with music. The music in this example is jazz. Because the rhythmic elements and the feel of jazz differ from that of classical music the dancer and therefore the movement vocabulary may take a bit more time to develop.

Choosing the music
The selected music used in a movement exploration is often determined by the desired outcome. What should the dance look like? What type of energy should the dance have? Because the jazz style is foreign to many it is beneficial to play various examples first. For initial explorations it may be prudent to use recordings of instrumental jazz arrangements. When dancers are asked to describe what they hear attention can be drawn to the syncopation, the phrasing, and the rhythmic feel. If a dancer has a foundation in another style this discussion can take the form of compare and contrast. It helps to create a list of descriptive words that can later be referred to by dancers.

In a live jazz improvisation, the combination of ideas used by the musicians may come together for the first time in that moment, however many, if not all, of the ideas and phrases have been worked out in prior practice sessions. What does that look like for the dancer?

Selecting movement motifs to work on
As one is moving their own hands as if shadowing the other, gliding on a diagonal may become a favorite movement during exploration. That movement combined with a shift of weight and descent to the floor becomes a favorite idea, an idea to be used later or what is in jazz called a "lick." Returning to the piece of music chosen, the dancer can now put together a series of licks to create a dance sequence.

After dancers have listened to the music they return to the dance with a new sense of rhythm, and a new sense of intention. A re-exploration begins with creating licks from the prior explorations. The objective is to obtain a look that matches the feel. Consider the question, when one listens to a piece of music with eyes closed what is the dance they see? So, in our exploration we ask, when one closes their ears and watches a dance, what is the music they hear? Can they see the feel?

Once the feel has been established in self-space the dancer can expand the use of the body into shared space. In moving across the floor, is the feel still present? Do the qualities of movement mirror the qualities of the music? Does the movement have the syncopation, anticipation, tension, and release? Can I see the music in the movement?

Creating a dance together
Dancers are tasked with working together to create a dance that begins with a unified statement (let us call it part A) by the group. Like the music that is being played, each dancer is seemingly in concert with the others in the group yet wholly an individual. In a contrasting section (part

B) the dance and dancers reflect the spirit of jazz. Each dancer using the collective vocabulary creates an improvisation in shared space. Finally, part A may be repeated.

Learning through reflection
There is constant evaluation and discussion during the process. After the groups finish the students alternate between the roles of performer and audience member. After each performance we use the "I noticed...," "I valued...," "I wonder..." sentence starters to give feedback and prompt self-exploration for each dancer.

When dancing to jazz music, dancers may exhibit a greater use of improvisation. Each performance of the dance is somewhat different. Due to the nature of jazz music, the constant improvisations made throughout the dance should be not only acceptable but expected.

4. "A Strange Morning"—Using Alienating Everyday Movements
Angelika Wolf

This idea evolved from a book called *Virginia Wolf* by Kio McLear. The main character Virginia wakes up one morning "feeling wolfish and doing strange things." Strangeness, awkwardness, the idea of doing things differently is the topic of a session for 14-16-year-olds taking part in a regular movement improvisation course in a musical, dance, or theater-based setting.

Learning objectives
Students discover the everyday as a stimulus for movement; they recognize space, time, and weight as "creativity-boosters" using varied and challenging movement with different expression. By trying to express different moods and ideas, they come to understand that this can be represented by particular spatial, temporal, and energetic execution and changes of movement.

Motivation and introduction to the theme
- Body awareness with "Shape change":
  Students lie on the floor, scattered around the room. The teacher directs them verbally and encourages them to respond in movement that is inspired by morning routines focusing on the sensation of the changing body shape. In stretching out, the shape follows personal body needs. Imaginative suggestions encourage the body to adapt to other shapes.
  "You put on your much too tight trousers and your baggy shirt and leave the house. Walk into space."
- Everyday gestures: Verbal comments interrupt the walk and invite gestures such as

  "Wave at somebody standing far away."
  "Give a high five to a person next to you."
  "Write a text message."
  "What else would you like to do?"

Exploration
The teacher suggests that this morning is a "strange" morning. Suddenly gestures are done high up in the air or deep down at the ground. One student gives a "low five," another one is lying on their back with feet running in the air, and another one writes a slow-motion text message to the sun on tiptoes. "This is funny!" "And why?" "It is fun to do things the other way round!"

"Can we reverse a gesture?" Handshakes, wiping off sweat are done repeatedly in "the other way round" manner.

Now the group is brain-storming some more movements from everyday life. Students find possibilities to exchange body parts: e.g., shrugging with knees, chewing with the belly, clapping with thighs. Some movements are performed with high, some with low energy.

Reflecting: Students recognize that movement from everyday life can open up a whole new world when they become aware of it. They notice that becoming bigger, quicker, stronger requires more energy, and that energy-use on the other end of the scale makes movement smaller, slower, and lighter. Movement can be varied in space, time, and weight, and it can show in that way different qualities and meanings.

Improvisation

The teacher inspires the group to play out little movement scenes.

They form a walking circle. One student entering the middle starts with one spontaneous movement or a short sequence and repeats it constantly. Voice accompanies the action. The moment the person leaves the middle, somebody else goes in and takes over the same movement. Somebody notices, "We need to take responsibility to keep the movement going."

Improvisation takes off when the task is expanded. Three persons are entering the circle one after the other, the second person trying to move in a complementing way to the first one and the third one as well. Dancers leaving from the middle are replaced immediately by those from the circle, who develop group awareness and enjoy spontaneity.

Reflecting: Students talk about their favorite moments. Having more actions going on at the same time interests them most. Contrasts in space, time, and dynamics catch the eye. Jumping in for somebody else is a fun challenge. They also recognize that everyday gestures have been a joyful stimulus to free up movement.

Structured improvisation

The following tasks serve as rules for improvisation as a "real-time" composition or spontaneous *Gestaltung.*

- Three dancers enter the circle successively and perform repeatedly a manipulated action. They focus on movement contrasts and relationships. They leave the circle in the same sequence. A new trio starts.
- Mirroring: Anyone can decide to face one of the three dancers and to move as their reflection. The copying dancer moves simultaneously with their chosen partner and reverses the actions.
- Shadowing: One or more persons stand behind and slightly shifted in relation to the leading dancer and copies them.

All movements can happen on the spot or in locomotion. The leading dancers leave with their copying partners in the same sequence they entered the circle. A new trio starts.

Music: Reich, S. (1989). Different trains: America, before the war. On Kronos Quartet 25 years. Nonesuch. https://www.youtube.com/watch?v=9zPrgy-OhFw

Reflecting: Students notice that movement repetition and the minimal style of Reich's music create a machine-like feeling. Would a different type of music inspire other sensations? They learn new artistic terms encouraged by their improvisation, i.e., "abstract" and "representational." The group agrees on the teacher's suggestion to finish the session by just enjoying dancing in a personal and improvised way.

References and Resources

Barthel, G., & Artus, H. G. (2007). *Vom Tanz zur Choreographie. Gestaltungsprozesse in der Tanzpädagogik* [From dance to choreography. Creation processes in dance pedagogy]. Oberhausen: Athena.

Bischof, M., & Lampert, F. (Eds.) (2020). *Sinn und Sinne im Tanz. Perspektiven aus Kunst und Wissenschaft* [Sense and senses in dance. Perspectives from art and science]. Bielefeld: transcript Verlag. https://doi.org/10.1515/9783839453407

Blom, L. A., & Chaplin, L. T. (1989). *The intimate act of choreography* (3rd ed.). London: Dance Books.

Ellfeldt, L. (1988). *A primer for choreographers*. Palo Alto, CA: National Press Books.

Fischer, R. (1998). *Tanzen mit Kindern. Spielformen. Technik. Improvisation. Gestaltung* [Dancing with children. Forms of play. Technique. Improvisation. Creation]. Kassel: Bosse.

Green-Gilbert, A. (2015). *Dance for all ages* (2nd ed.) Champaign, IL: Human Kinetics.

Haselbach, B. (1994). *Improvisation, dance, movement* (M. Murray, Trans.; 2nd ed.). London: Schott. (Original work published in 1976 as Improvisation, Tanz, Bewegung, Stuttgart: Klett)

Hutchinson, A. (1983). *You move. A new approach to the study of movement and dance. Teacher's guide*. London/New York: Gordon and Breach.

Ickstadt, L. (2007). *Dancing heads. A hand- and footbook for creative/contemporary dance with children and young people from 4 to 18 years*. Lockport, NY: iUniverse.

Joyce, M. (1994). *First steps in teaching creative dance to children* (3rd ed.). Mountain View, CA: Mayfield.

Klein, G. (2019). *Choreografischer Baukasten 1* [Choreographic construction kit 1] (2nd ed., print and e-book). Bielefeld: transcript Verlag.

Lampert, F. (2007). *Tanzimprovisation, Geschichte-Theorie-Verfahren-Vermittlung* [Dance improvisation, history-theory-process-transmission]. Bielefeld: transcript Verlag.

Lionni, L. (2017). *Swimmy*. New York: Dragonfly Books. [Published in many languages]

McLear, K. (2012). *Virginia Wolf*. Toronto: Kids Can Press. [Published in many languages]

Meyerholz, U., & Reichle-Ernst, S. (2022). *Januar, Februar, Tanz, April...Tanzspiele und Lieder für jeden Monat* [January, February, Dance, April... dance games and songs for each month]. Innsbruck: Helbling.

Orff, C. (2011). Das Schulwerk—Rückblick und Ausblick/Orff-Schulwerk—Past and Future (M. Murray, Trans.). In B. Haselbach (Ed.), *Studientexte zu Theorie und Praxis des Orff-Schulwerks: Basistexte aus den Jahren 1932–2010/ Texts on theory and practice of Orff-Schulwerk: Basic texts from the years 1932–2010* (pp. 134-159). Mainz: Schott. (Original work published 1964)

Preston-Dunlop, V. (1980). *A handbook for dance in education*. London: MacDonald & Evans.

Steve Reich—Topic. (2018, September 7). *Different trains. America, before the war* [Recording]. YouTube. https://www.youtube.com/watch?v=9zPrgy-OhFw

Švandová, L., & Mojdl, E. (2011). *Tvořivé taneční hry s hudebním doprovodem* [Creative dance games with music accompaniment]. Praha: Nipospos Artama.

Vogel, C. (2010). *Tanz in der Grundschule* [Dance in elementary school]. [Doctoral dissertation, Forum Musikpädagogik. Band 62]. Augsburg: Wißner.

Traditional Dances: Folk, Historical, and Social Dances

Tamara Figueroa (Argentina), Danai Gagné (Greece/USA), Verena Maschat (Austria/Spain)

INTRODUCTION

Traditional Dances and Education
Tamara Figueroa

We are sensitive and social beings. We need the community, and in it the social group lives, grows, and transforms itself through communication. Of all the arts, the so-called dynamic arts—and especially dance—have their particular way of reaching the individual and their communication potential. Experiences in dance instill confidence, knowledge, and security in our bodies, in our relationships with others, in our creative capacities, and in the development of sensitivity as the primary essence of being. We can organize traditional dances in three categories: the traditional dances of one's region and culture, those of universal folklore, and those of the immigrant cultural heritage.

From the point of view of traditional dances of one's region and culture, we are in the presence of symbolic values born in the heart of the community and of oral transmission taught and learned from the shared experiences of a heterogeneous age group and sifted by the passing of generations. This affirms the community identity and the national being and gives evidence of the practices and customs of one's own culture.

If we talk about the traditional dances of universal folklore, we enter into the knowledge of other cultures, nurturing a respect for them framed in their contextualization, developing social skills, and experiencing new sonorities and ways of living and feeling the body in space.

As for the traditional dances of the immigrant cultural heritage, they represent an opportunity to activate the intertwined threads of multiculturalism brought to the classroom by their representatives in changing roles, from a non-vertical model of education.

Traditional dances provide, in the current educational context, a re-functionality of the power to congregate, to communicate, to strengthen socialization in the group, and to generate a sense of belonging. They are also positioned as a multifunctional resource that enables the deployment of different learning content such as the development of motor skills and abilities, music appreciation, instrumental performance, and group singing.

All this leads us to see and perceive traditional dances as living symbolic values, as ancestral culture that returns and envelops, within new contexts. We see the dances re-signified in new social dynamics, such as the classroom, but displaying all their ancestral power, alive, always in movement. Perhaps with a new journey born in the communities they enter the classroom carrying this dialectic value between education and tradition.

Traditional Dances and Orff Schulwerk
Danai Gagné

The sensitivity developed through aesthetic experiences and artistic manifestations puts a particular perspective to our view. It prepares us, predisposes us, and sharpens our perception of areas that tell us about the world.

Traditional dances make it possible to approach knowledge of the world by promoting abilities related to spatial, musical, kinesthetic-corporal, intrapersonal and interpersonal, creative, emotional, and collaborative intelligence. The idea of the development of multiple intelligences and the social value of dance are closely related to the pedagogical concept of Orff Schulwerk, which conceives of music, speech, and movement as a unit of meaning and prioritizes empirical work within the framework of a group that develops communicational relationships and stimuli, enriching individual capacities.

Traditional dances are important elements in movement and dance education with Orff Schulwerk because:

- They are an integral part of a culture, an indispensable part of the folklore of a country.
- Carl Orff's Schulwerk would not have spread so quickly beyond the confines of Germany and Austria if it were not for dances and songs indigenous to other cultures. Orff encouraged all of us to go back to our countries and research our own country's songs and traditional dances.
- Traditional dances frequently play an integral role in stories, legends, myths, and fairytales.
- They contribute to community-building, promoting socialization and great joy to the participants of all ages.
- These types of social events help people network and establish friendships and good professional relationships that not only can last a lifetime, but also can change the course of many people's lives.

Looking at traditional dances from different points of view
Engaging in traditional dances allows students to experience many elements. The dances provide kinesthetic experiences that help to express musical ideas. Kenneth Robinson points out in his book *The Element* (p. 48) that, "dancers use multiple forms of intelligence – kinesthetic, rhythmic, musical and mathematical." Some elements taught through traditional dances include:

- Humanistic: Traditional dance events can teach tolerance and acceptance of all kinds of people regardless of ethnicity, race, political views, or sexual orientation. In other words, they are all inclusive.
- Educational: Children acquire early on a sense of identity and appreciation of their own cultural background through dances and songs of their respective countries. They also learn to respect other children's cultural backgrounds.
- Worldview: Traditional dances related to religious events provide exposure to belief systems of other cultures, teach respect and tolerance, and widen people's horizons that envelop worldviews different from their own. Children and adults become aware that their own worldview is limited and not the only one.
- Health: Traditional dance gatherings generate a joyful feeling among the group members regardless of the various moods and feelings people may bring at the beginning of such events. The body/mind/spirit connection during traditional dance gatherings of people of all

ages helps organize different steps and styles, stimulate the endorphins in the body resulting in healthier and more joyful living.

- Music and movement education: Much can be learned from traditional songs and dances such as beat, rhythm, meter, melody, form; spatial and body awareness; social and emotional capacities; the ethnic background of music and dance from a specific region of a country; or the historical background of a dance from earlier periods.

Two different teaching styles

Two styles of teaching, the didactic and the evocative, are both useful in teaching traditional dances in the Orff Schulwerk approach. The didactic style involves direct verbal and non-verbal instruction of material like the rhythm of steps, spatial development, form, etc., usually by imitation and repetition. Through the didactic style, a dance is taught more expediently by providing information and references. The evocative style allows for input from the students, is less definite, and the outcomes are somewhat unpredictable. This style is used less frequently because it is slower and more open-ended. It is always risky, to quote Robinson again, "to wander in the wilderness of our intuitions" (p. 48).

Yet, within the evocative style of "risky" teaching we find the precious gems of Orff Schulwerk. It is that amazing risk of creation found at the core of improvisation. Students are asked to synthesize what they have been taught, and encouraged to express their own ideas, which leads them to new discoveries. It is this "risky" style that allows teachers to see behind students' eyes as their artistic ideas emerge. This type of risk is a healthy one and sits at the core of the Orff Schulwerk philosophy. We, the teachers, take a leap of faith in the students, giving them the creative power and trust they need to rise to the creative occasion. We become facilitators, traffic directors, the devil's advocate, the questioner on a unique trip never taken before. We give free reign to our students' ideas whether working with melody, movement, speech themes, rhythm, meter, drama, or forms.

Teaching Methods and Traditional Dance Forms
Verena Maschat

Traditional dance forms we use in elemental music and dance education are, on the one hand, folk dances that have been handed down for centuries from old to young by aural tradition, and, on the other hand, historical dances, i.e., social dance forms from the Renaissance to our times, passed on to us through written sources.

In the case of folk dances, there never was the need to develop any special form of didactic because the learning happens naturally by participation and imitation. Historical dances were taught mostly in a courtly setting by dancing masters who in their treaties published only after 1600 gave some indication of their method of teaching, apart from the music, the dance elements, and choreographies.

There are various approaches to traditional dances, all of which are based on the respective music as the main support for learning, remembering, and appreciating them. The complex character of dance requires not only careful listening but also visual capacity, body awareness, coordination, and spatial orientation. Consequently, the teaching methods must be varied and should respond to the different needs of the respective group or occasion, taking into consideration the different types of learners.

Didactic approaches to teaching these dances are predominantly non-verbal, and they include emphasis on the rhythm of steps, spatial concept, variation, improvisation, "dancing with the hands," elemental notation, etc. They may develop from the elements to the final form, from the holistic approach to the details. Participants should not be aware of the didactic procedure, and ideally each person should assimilate the dance through the music instead of counting beats or steps. Any cognitive or analytic process in relation to traditional dance should come out of the joy of movement followed by an interest in knowing and understanding the respective sources.

PRACTICAL EXAMPLES

Overview
1. **Verena Maschat: Historical dance from England – "Rufty tufty"**
   "Rufty tufty" is a country dance found in John Playford's ample collection The Dancing Master, published from 1651 to 1728.
2. **Danai Gagné: "Tsakonikos"–Greece**
   This is a practical example of how a traditional dance is taught using the evocative style.
3. **Tamara Figueroa: "Pala Pala"–Argentina**
   "Pala Pala" is a couple dance with a lively, pantomimic, and playful character.
4. **Verena Maschat: Universal mixers**
   Mixers are a universal social dance form. Though the term was only introduced during the 20th century, social dances where we dance with changing partners or counter-partners have been common as early as the 17th century.

1. Historical Dance from England—"Rufty tufty"
Verena Maschat

There are very few sources for early dance, but those that do exist provide valuable information about the music and the dance forms enjoyed as early as the 15th century. At the end of the 16th century country dances as social dance forms were practiced at the court of Queen Elizabeth I.

One of the most widely known collections of dances published during the 17th century is John Playford's *The English Dancing Master* (1651). These country dances, a social dance form less formal than the court dances, quickly gained popularity, and by 1728 a total of 18 editions had been published. Many dances reappeared in several editions, but new dances were always being added. These dances were soon exported to European countries as well as to America. They are couple dances in several different formations that incorporate interactions with other partners and counter-partners, but in the end the partners always come together again. Beginning with the second edition, the books' title changed to *The Dancing Master*. A clear change in both musical style and dance forms is evident through these nearly 80 years of the publications. Melodies in the earliest editions are clearly Renaissance in style whereas the later editions contain a more elaborated Baroque style.

Basic elements common to many country dances are (no specific indications are given but we recommend always starting with the right foot):

- Sides: 4 steps forward to shoulder-to-shoulder right, 4 steps back into place.
    Same with left shoulder.
- Arms: Link right arms, full turn (8 steps). Same with left arms.
- Set and turn single: Spring lightly to the right onto right foot, step briefly on the left (two quarter notes), quick change of weight back onto the right (half note).

Same to the left.

Full turn to the right with four steps (half notes).

Curiously, "Rufty tufty," the dance chosen for this example, appears only in the first edition.

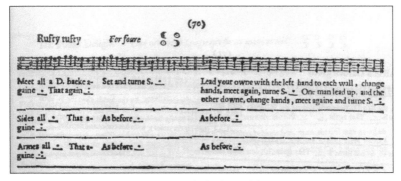

Facsimile from the 1st edition: John Playford, *The English Dancing Master* (1651), p. 70.
Licensed from the Vaughan Williams Memorial Library of the English Folk Dance and Song Society.

Rufty tufty

"Rufty tufty" dance description

Set: two couples facing; lady on the right. Inner hands joined (low).

Three verses. Music: A B CC. Start and finish with a brief informal bow.

Verse I

Part	Bars
A	1–8 4 steps forward and back. Repeat.
B	1–8 Face partner. Set and turn single. Repeat.
C1	1–2 Men lead partners away from the set, change hands on fourth step.
	3–4 Lead back to place.
	5–6 All turn single (away from the set, pathways look like a four-leaf clover).
C2	1–6 Same, but leading opposite lady away and back.

Verse II

    A   1–8 Partners side r/l.

    Parts B

    and C: as before.

Verse III

    A   1-8 Partners arms r/l.

    Parts B

    and C: as before.

Examples of "Rufty tufty"

- Country Dance and Song Society of Pittsburgh:
  https://www.youtube.com/watch?v=JujXHpzNNy8
- At the British Museum (with a little acting):
  https://www.youtube.com/watch?v=ljHAWQyWRxw
- L'Amusette Baroque dance group, Finland. Costumes from the 18th century but correct interpretation:
  https://www.youtube.com/watch?v=5PhNjsejNoU
- Contemporary, danced by the Asheville, North Carolina Morris Dance group:
  https://www.youtube.com/watch?v=MCFa4W3WyqM

Another excellent source of information about the music, dances, and customs of Renaissance France is Thoinot Arbeau's *Orchésographie*, first published in 1588. It contains the melodies and detailed descriptions of many dances from the early 16th century such as Basse-dance, Pavane and Galliarde, La Volte, Courante, Allemande, many Branles, Morisques, Canaries, and Les Bouffons. The clear descriptions of some of the easier dances like Branles or Pavane can be helpful for teachers who want to include a court dance in a scenic play.

2. "Tsakonikos"–Greece
Danai Gagné

This is a practical example of how a traditional dance can be taught using the evocative style.

The students have worked with action words, creating word sentences in the classroom. They have created choreographies based on word sentences. They have also learned about even and uneven meters.

The "action words" could be: Step–Twist (the body)–Hop–Close–Wind–Unwind. Based on this word sentence, students are split into groups of 5 or 6, and they are asked to create a dance. The meter given is 5/4.

The teacher tells the myth of Theseus who led 14 youths to Crete to be eaten by the Minotaur residing in a maze called Labyrinth. The dance needs to portray (in the way the students envision it) the labyrinth, in which the dancer leads the youths into the maze by creating a coil through winding inside it.

When all groups are finished, they will share their dance. It will not look like the "Tsakonikos" dance, *per se*, but will be close to it. At this point, the teacher will say, "You all created great versions of this dance. Now I will play the melody of this dance on my recorder. Listen to it a few times and decide if you will make some changes to your dance or not." Some groups may tweak some of the steps, others may not.

At this point the teacher will show them how this dance is traditionally performed. It will be easy for them to follow the teacher's steps since they have already come close to it in the dances they created. The melody can be orchestrated using Orff instruments.

Many elements of music and dance are learned from this project:

- Form of the piece.
- Uneven meter review.
- An important element of Greek culture, its history, and its myth.
- Kinesthetic memory makes it easier to internalize meters and rhythms of traditional dances.
- Formations of dances that have a meaning or are purely decorative.

Tsakonikos

This is a stately dance from the southern Peloponnesus, winding slowly in and out of the labyrinth. Dancers are close together in a semicircle facing diagonally to the right, arms hooked; steps are small. The leader moves a white handkerchief as a reference for the dancers.

Part A

Bar 1: Four small steps forward r-l-r-l, on the 5th count touch right foot lightly next to the left.

Bar 2–8: repeat seven times.

Part B

Bar 1: Walk livelier r-l-r, gentle hop on r lifting left leg slightly forward (men higher than women), one more step left.

Bar 2–8: repeat seven times.

Video examples of "Tsakonikos":

6th Grade class of Leonidi School (Greece):
https://www.youtube.com/watch?v=mmdztt6YH64
Dora Stratou: https://www.youtube.com/watch?v=PLuZmCPU77M

3. "Pala Pala"–Argentina

Tamara Figueroa

"Pala Pala" is an independent couple dance "of corners" (the dancers' movement originates from the corners of a square), with a playful, lively, pantomimic, and mischievous character. It comes from the central region of Argentina. The poncho is used as an accessory element.

Dance form

Music: 6/8 meter. Introduction and interlude: 8 bars

Dancers start at opposite corners of an imaginary square and move forward and back on the diagonals.

¡Adentro!: Advance and retreat (2+2 bars); *Esquina de medio giro* ("corner" of half turn): Advance, pass back to back and finish with a half turn left in the next corner to the left (4 bars). This sequence of figures is repeated four times.

¡Aura!: Encounter: Advance, half circle to the right and "embrace" (4 bars).

Interlude: Retreat, starting the 2nd verse from the opposite corner from where you started.

Here are links to two examples of "Pala Pala":

    https://youtu.be/k_A_otzCHT4?feature=shared

    https://www.youtube.com/watch?v=oaMEyXJZ2us

This teaching example is done with a mixed group of 20 eight-year-old school children. The dance step and the ways of spontaneous locomotion are appropriate for this age group, and the theme is present in children's games. The choreographic structure uses repetition of a sequence; the story is told through a pantomimic dance; and the Quechua language is part of our cultural heritage.

The theme is introduced with the "Legend of the Pala Pala," which tells the story of the meeting of different animals native to the region.[1]

The characteristics of the flapping movements of different birds (breadth, dynamics, speed) are discussed, and the accessory element (alternative use of scarves) is explored through improvised movements in place and throughout space individually and then, by simultaneous imitation, in duos, trios, etc., using the entire space.

Music: Cacharpaya https://youtu.be/1FcCddWv6HE?si=vrAuKjU3ZVbsMA3r

With the traditional game *Buenos días, su señoría* (Good morning, your honor), the skipping step and the advance and retreat movements are approached, because the game has steps and locomotion similar to the dance. Singing the refrain of the dance, we play "The Nest," which consists of leaving the nest, going back to the nest, and turning within it during 8 bars. The work on the imaginary square is performed with one dancer in each corner, in order to visualize the change of corners. In the *Aura* section, each dancer performs a half turn left advancing to the next corner. This leads to the traditional choreography in pairs. We reflect on the step, figures, locomotion, and expressive movements of the dance. Then we propose to approach, with different music, new routes and ways of group interaction through improvisation, selection, and choreographic creation, as an introduction to the traditional dance.

Group dynamics: In two subgroups of changing roles, simultaneous activities are proposed: one dances the dance and the other sings the traditional song accompanied with body percussion, and later with a collectively created instrumentation.

Conclusions:

In the different stages of the project, it was possible to observe the cooperative work among the children, both in the organization and in the practices and corrections, with enthusiasm from the approach through the games to the final production.

The result of the process was shared within the framework of our Tradition Day[2] with a positive balance of the proposal, from several points of view:

---

1 *El cuento del Pala Pala:* https://youtu.be/lC4-3Sh2o_w?si=Yh3EAlIISs-VVzJ_

2 *Día de la Tradición* (Tradition Day) is celebrated on November 10 in Argentina.

- from the pedagogical point of view, a gradual transition on different music and movement contents, promoting the choreographic and instrumental execution, through improvisation and collective creation;
- from the artistic point of view, the elaboration and presentation of an integral project;
- from the perspective of group dynamics, the autonomy and versatility in the roles of singing, playing, and dancing;
- from the socio-cultural point of view, the reunion of the native families of the dance region with their intangible heritage and the role of the children as cultural disseminators allowing the school community to approach the traditional heritage of the country.

4. Universal Mixers
Verena Maschat

Mixers are a universal social dance form. Though the term was only introduced during the 20th century, social dances in which we dance with changing partners or counter-partners were common as early as the 17th century.

A very well-known traditional example is the Circassian Circle[1] (big circle, couples facing center). Another basic form is the Sicilian Circle[2] (big circle, two couples facing along the circle). Both these mixers are basic formations that can be danced to various AABB dance melodies combining a variety of dance figures according to the respective target group or occasion.

Today it is common practice that a teacher of traditional dance—a choreographer or a "caller"—looks for a suitable piece of music or asks a composer or a group to create one. The most common meter is 4/4, and the structure would be one, two, or four phrases of eight bars. In each repetition there is a change of partner.

The elements frequently used are (each element uses 8+8 steps = 4 bars):
- hand tour right/left,
- both hands around, first clockwise (CW), then counterclockwise (CCW),
- dôs-à-dôs (back-to-back, called "dosido") passing first right shoulder, then left shoulder,
- four-hand star right/left,
- circle of four to the left (CW), then to the right (CCW),
- swing partner,
- pairs promenade (CCW),
- big circle, in and out, circle CW and CCW

Possible formations are:
- couples facing each other, distributed freely in space,
- circle of pairs facing center / facing each other,
- double circle of pairs facing each other (men inside, ladies outside),
- longways of couples facing each other (two couples form a "set"), changing places at the end of each repetition (progression).

A very common formation is the double circle, ladies outside facing their partner. We can use a basic step pattern on which every participant can invent variations.

Basic step pattern for a tune in 4/4 meter:
Bar 1: step-step-step-touch to the left
Bar 2: same to the right

---

1 Circassian Circle description: https://www.libraryofdance.org/dances/circassian-circle/
2 Sicilian Circle description: https://www.libraryofdance.org/dances/sicilian-circle/

Bar 3-4: repeat the above

Bar 5: step-touch left, step-touch right

Bar 6: repeat

Bar 7 + 8: Dosido right shoulder, going backwards diagonally to your right, changing partners.

Possible music example: https://www.youtube.com/watch?v=TiMTBB5ohy8

Variations:

- Instead of "touch": brush, stamp, kick, clap, snip, etc.
- Bar 1–4: second step crossing behind.
- Bar 2 and 4: full turn right.
- Add arm movements.

Trio dances are also common, usually one man with a lady on either side.

- For example, in the Russian "Troika" the man passes forward to join the next two ladies. (https://www.youtube.com/watch?v=WxAiMVJgBpY)
- Another basic form has the inner lady leave and join a new trio. (https://www.youtube.com/watch?v=ymDPiR5bD-o)
- In the Scottish "Dashing White Sergeant," we find groups of three facing each other along the circle. (https://www.youtube.com/watch?v=Wm_5l_bs-6Y)

We can create our own variations to all these basic dance forms for mixers exchanging the elements with easier ones according to the level of the participants, the dance space, and the occasion in order to guarantee an enjoyable experience for all the dancers.

References and Resources

Al Rondó. Ideas en Danza. (2024, January 2). *El cuento del Pala Pala* [The tale of the Pala Pala] [Video]. YouTube. https://youtu.be/lC4-3Sh20_w?si=Yh3EAlIISs-VVzJ_

Al Rondó. Ideas en Danza. (2024, January 2). *El Pala Pala. Coreografía* [Video]. YouTube. https://youtu.be/k_A_ot-zCHT4?feature=shared

Alevizos, S., & Alevizos, T. (1968). *Folk songs from Greece*. Michigan: Oak Publications.

Arbeau T. (1588). *Orchésographie: méthode et théorie en forme de discours et tablature pour apprendre à danser, battre le tambour* [Orchésographie: method and theory in the form of a discourse and tablature for learning to dance and beat the drum]. Facsimile. Geneva: Minkoff Reprint, 1972.

Arbeau, T. (2003). *Orchesography* (Mary Stuart Evans, Trans.; introduction and notes by Julia Sutton; revised edition). New York: Dover. (Original work published in 1588)

Asheville Morris. (2011, October 19). *Rufty Tufty* [Video]. YouTube. https://www.youtube.com/watch?v=MCF4W-3WyqM

BBC Scotland – Comedy. (2015, March 31). *The Dashing White Sergeant—learn the steps with Robbie Shepherd* [Video]. YouTube. https://www.youtube.com/watch?v=Wm_5l_bs-6Y

Dale Adamson. (2016, October 11). *Western Trio Mixer—USA* [Video]. YouTube. https://www.youtube.com/watch?v=ymDPiR5bD-o

Dean-Smith, M. (1957). Playford's English dancing master, 1651. A facsimile reprint with an introduction, bibliography and notes by Margaret Dean-Smith. London: Schott.

Dimotikó Scholeío Leonidíou/Δημοτικό Σχολείο Λεωνιδίου [Primary school of Leonidi]. (2014, June 18). *Tsakonikos dance* [Video]. YouTube. https://www.youtube.com/watch?v=mmdztt6YH64

Ensemble Robby Schmitz. (2019, August 14). Shuffle Mixer. [Recording]. YouTube. https://www.youtube.com/watch?v=TiMTBB5ohy8

Figueroa, T., & Vergara Las Heras, M. (2012). La eternidad es hoy. Tiempo y espacio para el cuerpo en la escuela [Eternity is today. Time and space for the body at school]. Música y Movimiento, 3, 7–9.

FOLKLORAMA Bailes Folklóricos Argentinos. (2022, January 16). LABORDE 2022_Ugarte Campos_PALA PALA [Video]. YouTube. https://www.youtube.com/watch?v=0aMEyXJZ2us

Gloriana Living History. (2016, August 15). C17—Rufty Tufy [sic]—British Museum Dec 2015 [Video]. YouTube. https://www.youtube.com/watch?v=ljHAWQyWRxw

Keetman, G., & Ronnefeld, M. (Arr.) (1991). Alfranzösische Tänze [Old French dances]. London: Schott.

Keetman, G., & Ronnefeld, M. (Arr.) (1991). Country dances from "The English Dancing Master" by John Playford. London: Schott.

L'Amusette Barokkitanssiryhmä. (2013, June 2). Tallipihan kesäkauden avajaiset 2013: Rufty Tufty [The opening of the summer season 2013: Rufty Tufty] [Video]. YouTube. https://www.youtube.com/watch?v=5PhNjsejNoU

Library of Dance. (n.d.). The Circassian Circle. Retrieved November 14, 2023, from https://www.libraryofdance.org/dances/circassian-circle/

Library of Dance. (n.d.). The Sicilian Circle. Retrieved November 14, 2023, from https://www.libraryofdance.org/dances/sicilian-circle/

López-Ibor, S., & Maschat, V. (2006). ¡Quien canta su mal espanta!/Singing drives away sorrow! Songs, games and dances from Latin America (Incl. DVD). New York: Schott.

maroavak. (2011, September 29). ECD at international showcase 2011 005.MOV [Video]. YouTube. https://www.youtube.com/watch?v=JujXHpzNNy8

Maschat, V. (1999). Basic dance forms. The Orff Echo, 31(2), 17–20.

Maschat, V. (2001). Ist es auch Tradierter Tanz, hat er doch Methode [Teaching methods and traditional dance forms]. Orff-Schulwerk Informationen, 67, 46-49. https://www.orff-schulwerk-forum-salzburg.org/magazine-osh

Maschat, V. (2005). Volkstanz und Orff-Schulwerk—wie passt das zusammen? [Folk dance and Orff-Schulwerk – a possible match?]. Orff-Schulwerk Informationen, 74, 31–33. https://www.orff-schulwerk-forum-salzburg.org/magazine-osh

Maschat, V. (2006). El efecto social y emocional de la danza coral [The social and emotional effect of choral dance]. Orff España, 9, 7–9.

Mathéy, P., & Panagopoulos-Slavik, A. (1993). RRRRRO. Poetry, music and dance from Greece. London: Schott.

Playford, J. (1977). The English dancing master. Princeton, NJ: Princeton Book Company (Original work published in 1651)

Raul Olarte – Topic. (2015, January 9). Cacharpaya (original) [Recording]. YouTube. https://youtu.be/1FcCd-dWv6HE?si=vrAuKjU3ZVbsMA3r

Robinson, K. (2009). The element. How finding your passion changes everything (9th ed.). London: Penguin Books.

Sabrina Munck. (2009, July 21). Troika [Video]. YouTube. https://www.youtube.com/watch?v=WxAiMVJgBpY

Stefanos Livanos. (2010, November 9). Tsakonikos—Dora Stratou [Video]. YouTube. https://www.youtube.com/watch?v=PLuZmCPU77M

Van Winkle Keller, K., & Shimer, G. (1990). The Playford ball. 103 early English country dances. London: Dance Books.

Additional resources

Country Dance and Song Society. Easthampton, MA, USA: https://cdss.org/

English Folk Dance and Song Society, London, UK: https://www.efdss.org

Library of Dance: https://www.libraryofdance.org

Movement, Dance, and Elemental Drama

Manuela Widmer (Austria), with Astrid Bosshard (Switzerland),
Katerina Sarropoulou (Greece), Natalya Shestopalova (Russia)

INTRODUCTION

Carl Orff was a theater man. His genre is the music theater. Even his most famous work, *Carmina Burana,* is often staged and designed as dance theater. In the original German version of Orff's and Keetman's *Schulwerk* (1950–1954) there is an abundance of songs and texts that provide the basis for creative play, often in connection with instrumental pieces that function as dances (e.g., "Bärentanz," "Narrentanz"[1]). Also, one can find in the numerous adaptations of the Schulwerk all over the world comparable song and text material from different cultures that allow for creative drama.

In addition, all cultures of the world know play and dance songs as well as poems, fairy tales, and legends, and new stories that are often in the form of picture books. This is rich material from which we can start when we want to work with acted scenes in the Schulwerk. From this, projects of varying scope may be created, which can also be performed for public audiences. In addition to texts (including our own), works of art (pictures, sculptures, etc.), instrumental music, and various other materials, costumes and masks can also be the basis for movement, dance, and music theater productions.

The essence of working with Schulwerk is to offer models. Therefore, one of the main tasks for teachers is to explicitly encourage learners to go their own way. The models are thus modified and supplemented by teachers *and* learners for their specific cultural and linguistic environment. The authors who have exchanged ideas and provided examples here on the subject of "Movement, Dance, and Elemental Drama" draw from the common source of their work in the Schulwerk. Yet, they each have their own creative pedagogical-artistic experiences and have drawn their individual conclusions for a didactic concept of movement and dance with work in theater.

Basic Conceptual Thoughts on Elemental Drama

The work with movement, dance, and drama in the Orff Schulwerk is based on a humanistic orientation: Human beings are at the center of the concept; they are the standard for the pedagogical-artistic forms of work, the selection of a theme, and the technical challenges. The balance between individual development and a creative group process is always kept in mind by the group leader. It is important to consider at the same time the individual, the group, and the common content-related and artistic demands and goals.

---

1   Ed.: "Bärentanz" (p. 39) and "Narrentanz" (p. 82) in C. Orff and G. Keetman (1952) *Musik für Kinder, Vol. II,* Mainz: Schott; also p. 39 and p. 72 in Orff and Keetman (1959) *Music for Children, Vol. II* (M. Murray adaptation). There are many examples of rhymes and songs for creative play in *Musik für Kinder Vol. I* and *Music for Children Vol. I* (English adaptation by M. Murray), Mainz/London: Schott.

The French theater pedagogue Jacques Lecoq (1921–1999) always supported "mixing" in his work, i.e., "crossing borders from one area to the next." He approached all arts in his courses, looking for the "common poetic base" of music, dance, and words. "The 'pure' theaters are dangerous," he writes, assuming that "chaos is indispensable to creation, albeit organized chaos, in which each is able to find its own roots and drives" (Lecoq, 2000, pp. 69, 220).

For the pedagogical-artistic work with movement-dance-drama in the Orff Schulwerk, we also rely on frameworks whose core consists in "mixing," and that are thus open for the multimedia-based integration of all art forms. In such projects, forms of play that create holistic access to music-dance content have proven their worth and involve the following aspects:

- Perception and sensitivity training
- Social interaction
- Self-direction
- Creative self-activity

Because the personal experiences of the group members are central, this means understanding the guidance of the group in a constructivist sense as…

- *an active process*—creating motivation and interest in the participants to become active themselves and to experience music, movement, and play in their own actions.
- *a self-directed process*—the preparation, planning, and execution of a play, or parts of it, are partly in the hands of the group. The leaders will strive to support the self-directed processes, to give impulses if necessary, and to accompany them in a coordinating way.
- *a constructive process*—songs, dances, and movement games are invented in whole or in part by the group with appropriate support; melodies are improvised or composed by singing or playing instruments.
- *a social process*—in creative work in pairs or threes, one stimulates the other, one word gives way to another, one sound leads to something new, one movement triggers the next.
- *a situational process*—in the here and now our games become effective. The current situation of the group connects with the individual possibilities of all participants in all forms of diversity. And, last but not least…
- *an artistic process*—the arts of music, dance, and speech are always at the center of our dramatic creation (Widmer, 2004, p. 249; Dubs, 1995, cited in Widmer).

When we consider the possibilities of using movement in the context of creating elemental music theater traditional as well as contemporary approaches are conceivable.

Movement—mime
- Poses, gestures, gait, and other movements (like specific locomotion) that represent a character, its essence, or a particular state.
- Movements that emphasize the interaction of the characters.
- "Living scenery": poses or movements of actors representing objects or phenomena.[1]
- A stylized pantomimic dance depicting typical sequences and actions.

---

[1] An example: the special use of costumes allows a clear distinction between the functions of the "neutral" and the "active" players. All players are dressed in neutral black clothing. The characters involved in a scene wear a costume element. Other performers can serve as their "living backdrop."

Movement—dance
- A traditional dance that conveys the atmosphere of the time and place of the action and illustrates the corresponding stage situation (e.g., a ball).
- An interactive dance with the audience at the end of the performance, reproducing, for example, the situation of a feast or excitement.
- A freely improvised dance illustrating a particular phenomenon (e.g., the fall of leaves).
- An abstract dance that aims at expressing certain states or ideas through movements.

PRACTICAL EXAMPLES

Projects with Movement, Dance, and Elemental Drama

The four projects presented below give readers the opportunity to position themselves accordingly with their own ideas and to pick up new ideas for their work. By chance, birds play an important role in two of the projects. But the conception and working approaches differ greatly, as does the chosen target group. Although all four projects stand on their own, they are nevertheless related because in all of them one can easily discover the unifying basic conceptual ideas that have been prefaced in this article.

Overview
1. **Manuela Widmer (Austria)** describes a family weekend in which adult amateurs and children of different ages create an elemental drama inspired by a picture book. The leader introduces some play components that are used and designed by the participants in an individual way. In particular, the invitation to play should enable children as well as adults to discover and enjoy their potential for personal expression.
2. **Natalya Shestopalova (Russia)** works for several weeks with a group of young people with previous music and dance experience. She chooses the extremely complex work De temporum fine Comoedia (A Play on the End of Time) by Carl Orff, from which she reshapes excerpts in speech, music, and dance using ideas of the participants. The challenging task brings to life the composer's richly pictorial language.
3. **Katerina Sarropoulou (Greece)** reports on the final project of a three-year advanced training course for music and movement/Orff Schulwerk. A team of teachers supports the work and gives specific impulses. Above all, the group should demonstrate its ability to work independently. The author describes the artistic process from finding a theme, working through improvisation and composition processes, to stage design.
4. **Astrid Bosshard (Switzerland)** gives insight into the joint interdisciplinary project "Platforms" that was developed by all students of the Bachelor of Arts in Music and Movement program at the Basel University of Music. It depicts with diverse scenes what can happen on a platform while waiting for a delayed train.

1. "The Song of the Colorful Birds"–A Fairy Tale and Song from Ghana as a Basis for Elemental Music Theater
Manuela Widmer

The project
The concept of elemental music theater always includes movement, dance, and speech, as in Orff's definition of elemental music. Through the theater-based approach, the visual arts in the broadest sense also play a role for stage design, masks, costumes, and props.

Several families with children from about four years old (some with disabilities) met over a weekend. The group of 20 players was approached with the following intentions:

- *The abilities and wishes of all participants were in the foreground* and were integrated by the leader in the play process.
- *Support and inspiration could be experienced in and through the group.*
- *The togetherness demanded a specific dramaturgy.* Roles were doubled and invented. There were group compositions for voice, speech, instruments, and movement/dance.
- *There was consistent transfer of responsibility to the players,* i.e., the teacher gradually made themself unnecessary as leader and supported the group members during the development process so that they could act more and more independently and on their own responsibility.

The process
- *Initial phase*—familiarizing with the material (the picture book *Das Lied der bunten Vögel*).
- *Development phase*—offer of first structures (scene structure) and introductory games/exercises related to the theme, where the participants had the opportunity to get to know all the roles (birds, animals, farmer).
- *Rehearsal phase*—support in finding roles and tasks, plenty of room for creative design (inventing texts, song melodies, dance forms, etc.). Logging the process of the play. Organization of stage design, costumes, masks, and props.
- *Performance*—for a small circle of friends and family members of the participants.
- *Final stage*—watching the video recording of the performance and sharing personal impressions.

Documentation of the family weekend
About the content: Five birds in the colors red, blue, yellow, white, and green live peacefully together. They visit the farmer in the village every evening, sing and dance for him, and receive food in return. One day each bird flies alone to the farmer: "Then I will get all the food for myself!" But the birds master only one line of the song, and the disappointed farmer chases each away without giving them any food. The next morning, they bashfully confess to each other what they have done. Relieved, they set off together again to visit the farmer, who is pleased that they are back and, after singing and dancing, gives them plenty of food.

Families as a play group: The special heterogeneity of several families with children between the ages of four and twelve proved itself this weekend. There was already a familiarity within the individual family groups, and the older children were sociable and helped to build bridges among the families. Adults who were initially skeptical of the play requirements often received the impetus to take on a task or role from their own children. In turn, the adults supported the children in more complex tasks.

Personnel, space, and time frame: The room and instrumental equipment were appropriate for the size of the group and its multi-age participants. The weekend proved to be a manageable period of time for an intensive experience. The clear structure provided by the leader enabled the participants to "free themselves through play." Varied methods motivated and helped them to overcome low drive phases and entry problems.

Creative possibilities: Carl Orff wrote that in working with amateurs he would start with the drive to play originating from movement because—according to Orff—through the body adult non-professionals can be introduced more naturally and unconsciously to their roles (Orff, 2011/1932, p. 72). Thus, adults as well as children were quickly involved in the play through the characterization of the many different animals and the birds. The song of the colorful birds ("Tsche tsche kule") is structured as a call-and-response. From this, solo-tutti interpretations of the song and a dance form were developed in small groups. The movements of the other animals could be worked out as solo dances or duets with the birds. To frame the story, an "African overture" and an "African epilogue" were created with musical and dance elements using another traditional song from Zimbabwe.

Conclusion

The structure of the story is simple. Recurring parts reduced the amount of material to be created and did not overtax the memory of participants of various ages. Many roles and tasks offered enough incentives for all participants. Movement and dance activities were in the foreground and were open to different abilities. Those who were not so fond of movement could take on vocal-speech and instrumental tasks. The equipment could be limited to the use of many colorful scarves. The teacher provided careful encouragement for the creative processes and ensured at the end that the dramaturgy (overall structure, spatial design, scene transitions) was convincing. Experiencing a performance together in which everyone had an individual as well as a collective share brought joy and strengthened communication within the families.

Tsche tsche kule

Traditional song from Ghana, used by Kobna Anan in his picture book "The Song of the Colorful Birds."

Participants create their birds' dance to the song "Tsche tsche kule."
Photo © Manuela Widmer

2. *De temporum fine Comoedia* (A play on the end of time) by Carl Orff–Part of the Educational Program of the Diaghilev Festival, Perm, 2022
Natalya Shestopalova

The project
A group of nine teenagers aged 13–15 took part in this project, working on the production from 10 a.m. to 1 p.m. every day for nine days. They had previous music and dance training and were very motivated.

The main goal of the project was to bring this work by Carl Orff closer to these teens through direct experience with its key moments in music making and movement. During the sessions, the young people became acquainted with fragments of the mystery play in a form accessible to them: reduced, simplified, translated into Russian, and transformed in the course of independent creative work. Because elemental music is closely connected with movement, one of the most important areas of work was devoted to physical experience. The result of the project was an alternative embodiment of Orff's mystery play in elemental style that was suitable for the stage and corresponded to the abilities and perceptions of the participants. Following the project, the participants attended the Diaghilev Festival performance of *De temporum fine Comoedia* by the musicAeterna Choir and Orchestra with conductor Teodor Currentzis.

The process

Timing—the work on the project took place in two phases:

1. Getting acquainted within the group, with forms of work in the spirit of elemental music drama, and with the material of the performance along with the development of scenes took place over five days.
2. Rehearsals of individual scenes and transitions, precise distribution of roles and functions, compilation of the whole piece, and two performances for an audience occurred over four days.

Creative approach to the content—Carl Orff's mystery play consists of three parts: "Die Sibyllen" (The Sibyls – female oracles), "Die Anachoreten" (The Anchorites – male hermits), and "Dies Illa" (That day). We kept this structure in our production.

1. "Die Sibyllen" is the part dedicated to the proclamation of the coming end, aimed at intimidating the audience. The main means of musical expression is through the voice, both spoken and sung. As for the movement, at first it is static, with the Sibyls arranged on stage in picturesque scenes that follow each other seamlessly. In the last part, "Vae! Ibunt," the Sibyls move in a circle around the audience, pushing the level of intimidation to the extreme.
2. In "Die Anachoreten" the Anchorites anxiously await the end of the world, wondering what will happen. In our production we included only two sections: "Mundus terrenus" and "Ule oneire." Half of the group is involved in the movement and the rest of the participants play musical instruments, distributed across the stage like living scenery.

   In "Mundus terrenus" a fearful, hostile atmosphere is conveyed by careful creeping movements in which all levels of space—especially the lower level—are involved. In contrast, during "Ule oneire," immersion in states of calm is conveyed through the slow, graceful movements of the actors, who now walk upright to their full height.
3. "Dies Illa" is the most dramatic and dynamic part. It contains the main action of the work, depicting the end of the world in its consummation, while the previous two parts are only an anticipation of it.

The artistic images embedded in the music and text suggest intense embodiment through movement. The alternation of sections is rich in contrast, building a line of increasing tension toward the climax. The first section, "Wo irren wir hin, verloren, verlassen," begins in a desperate, heavy, slow walk, with aimless, chaotic movement. In "Vae, Portae Inferi" it develops to a climax in which all the participants are thrown together into a tight heap that ferments like in the maw of a volcano. Different levels of space are used. The piece concludes with measured, purposeful movement of the actors, first each in their own direction, then towards the exit of the hall. Passing through the transparent curtain at the door, the actors seem to enter another world and dissolve into it.

Conclusion

As a result of working on the piece, the young participants deeply understood its musical style, revealed their creative abilities and communication skills, and experienced many beautiful moments. The audience was very impressed by our performance, which conveyed the essence of Carl Orff's mystery play in a clear and accessible way.

A scene from teenagers' performance of *De temporum fine Comoedia*.
Photo: Andrej Chuntomov

3. "Birds and Humans Aboard"—A Journey of Teachers' Self-Awareness and Joy of Life
Katerina Sarropoulou

The project
"Birds and Humans Aboard" is a piece based on a theme of birds and their relationship with humans. The theme was inspired by ancient Greek poet Aristophanes' "The Birds" and the Persian Sufi poet Farid ud-Din Attar's "The Conference of the Birds." A performance was presented in July 2022 by the graduates of the three-year Orff Schulwerk course at the theater of the Moraitis School, as part of the artistic field of their studies.

The process
All students took part as musicians, dancers, and actors, and chose the idea of the play democratically in their plenary session. Working in groups or individually, they invented methods of self-organization and proposed folksongs and literature sources. The scenic transition of the students' ideas into live artistic material became possible by encountering the sounds and movements of different Greek bird species. Each student selected a bird, studied its natural environments, researched its characteristics, named it, and individually prepared verses, poems, musical ideas, or melodies for their own bird story. Bird species formed the characters of a shared narrative: seagull, flamingo, cuckoo, owl, albatross, cormorant, kingfisher, stork, heron, great crested grebe, and eagle.

Movement/dance

Guided or free movement improvisations were the fundamental element of the process, and this enabled the study of birds' dynamics in space. Topics included exploring flight movements, miming nature's elements, designing group choreographies in geometric shapes of a flock. Improvisations gave rise to dance qualities such as bird's gliding or floating to different rhythms in space. Dance forms provided creative impulses for musical ideas and accompaniment on the Orff instruments, interacting with the dynamics of the choreography. During rehearsals, a common poetic ground was created shaping the group's aesthetic choice for the final style of the piece.

Music/sound/speech

Four components formed the musical fabric of the performance:

- Soundscapes with body rhythms, instrumental accompaniment, and melodious birdsongs.
- Leitmotifs: small melodies associated with the characters of the narrative and played each time birds or humans appeared on stage.
- Songs: traditional songs that were integrated into the plot of the performance and original songs inspired by the bird characters.
- Rhythmic language: Students performed texts integrated into the plot. For example, "The Albatross" by Charles Baudelaire, and their own "Sailor's letter to his beloved" and "The sighing and suffering of the bird," a Greek albatross, unable to walk after five years of continuous flight in the air without ever touching land. The two dramatic situations were juxtaposed: the loneliness of the sailor and the powerlessness of the bird's efforts to walk.

A grid of dance and musical forms, soundscapes, words, and songs shaped humorous or melancholic characters and knitted the plot of the final story: humans living in harmony with the world of wild free birds. The birds, by coexisting with humans on the deck of an imaginary ship named Heaven traveled to Cloud Island and "taught" the humans forgotten senses and emotions, joy, empathy, and intimacy. Yet humans, at a given moment, exercised power over free birds by caging them until a sailor freed them. The birds returned traumatized to their habitats, where human intervention had already altered their natural landscape.

Conclusion

"Birds and Humans Aboard" was a pedagogical journey. Being present on stage is an experience of a teacher's self-development that promotes attention to the senses, feelings, and qualities of communication, connecting students' beneficial emotions with joy of life. It is the organic relationship of music to movement/dance, and their creative interaction, that makes students sense the ancient relationship of music *and* dance (*Musikè*). The student-creators rejoiced in the process as a springboard towards self-awareness of the artist-educators. Birds and their encounters with humans are a timeless theme that lends rich material and highlights universal human needs of caring for oneself and of well-being. Giacomo Leopardi in his essay "Panegyric of Birds" (1882, pp. 144–150) concludes his praise of birds with the wish, "so I should like temporarily to be transformed into a bird, in order to experience their contentment and joyfulness of life."

The Moraitis School three-year Orff course performance of *Birds Aboard*. Athens, July 2022.
Photo © Jannis Makropoulos

4. Bahnsteig'n[1] (Train Boarding)–Coming and Going at the Train Station: A Stage Project of the Basel University of Music
Astrid Bosshard

Project
In the Bachelor of Arts in Music and Movement program, the annually developed stage project forms an important pillar in the students' artistic education. This process, which takes place parallel to the daily study program, lasts for two months, involves all B.A. students of the different years, and is officially part of the curriculum. The final performances are open to the public, the target audience being children from 6 years to adults.

The basic guiding principle combines making music, moving, dancing, speaking, singing, and performing. The students contribute with their resources, abilities, and idiosyncrasies. They are to incorporate existing pieces as well as compose and choreograph their own and thus develop a production ready for the stage in a collective, creative process in which personal responsibility is of great importance. Everything will be danced and performed live. The production process and direction are co-produced by the author, Astrid Bosshard, and Amelia Burri (lecturer in rhythmics/dance).

Process
The Swiss-German song of the train stations by Mani Matter ("Ds Lied vo de Bahnhöf"[2])—in which the train has already departed or has not yet arrived—forms the theme for the setting in the microcosm of the station. The platform itself becomes an inspiration and artistic confrontation and represents the metaphorical sense of coming and going—and perhaps never arriving.

---

1 In German the noun *Bahnsteig* (platform) consists of Bahn (train) and *steig* (to climb aboard the train), which can also be used as a verb *steigen* and so the students played with the main word *Bahnsteig* and changed it to the verb *bahnsteigen*.
2 Matter, M. (1996). Ds Lied vo de Bahnhöf. On *I han es Zündhölzli azündt* [Album]. YouTube December 13, 2021. Zytglogge Verlag. https://www.youtube.com/watch?v=OgW3vpCBUJM

In playful interaction, the various facets are explored individually as well as collectively. This turns out to be an almost inexhaustible field for improvisation. Coming and going in different tempi, formations and expressions, motor tics and stereotypes of the passersby, and the motionless waiting in contrast, show an everyday event like a rush hour in a dance-musical realization. It comes to contacts as well as to unrelated passing by of each other.

Individual scenes (see film: https://vimeo.com/306714111)
Waiting for the delayed train, a vibraphone sounds with the typical three-part "jingle" of the Swiss Federal Railways (SBB), then comes the announcement from the loudspeaker. The passersby react immediately with facial expressions and gestures. Depending on where the viewer looks, the perspective changes. A permanent simultaneity of different "worlds" presents itself:

- In one direction a mating pair of bird lovers dances to "Bésame mucho," in the other, someone struggles with his luggage with artistry and humor.
- In the station hall "Bobino Kolo" from Serbia is played and danced to, and at the end of the platform a musician plays her trumpet solo.
- When the Sugarhill Gang with "Rapper's Delight" is barely over, Bach's G Minor Sonata is already playing on the viola of a street musician, and…
- Right after that, the tutti with the "Rock Trap" by William J. Schinstine utilizes dense texture and fast tempo.
- Arriving is not always associated with joy, as the scene with "Ay, triste que vengo vencido d'amor" shows.
- After the second rush hour, the cleaning crew takes over and everyone dances to a pop-style song written by some of the students, and finally,
- The jazz standard "Take the A-Train" by Billy Strayhorn introduces the departure of the last train, and the opening song sounds in unison in the finale.

….just to name a few scenes of the piece (see the link to the video referenced above).

Conclusion
The body is the starting point for movement, sound, and interaction. The playful research, the creative improvisation processes, and finally the intensive and consistent work on a multi-layered embodiment in the sense of a connection between body, mind, and emotion, has paid off. The piece is performed three times to a full auditorium. One is a student performance, and in the evening, it is attended by nearly all adults. The varied reactions of the different audiences and their effect on the play, as well as the interactions between players and audience, were central experiences for all participants, which we reflected on together.

University of Music, Basel, Switzerland: Annual stage project of the Arts in Music and Movement program
Photo: Zoe Wehrmüller https://vimeo.com/306714111

References and Resources

Anan, K., & Amonde, O. (1993). *Das Lied der bunten Vögel* [The song of the colorful birds] (3rd ed.). Münsingen-Bern: Fischer.

Audubon, J. J. (1994). *Adubon's birds of America. The royal octavo edition.* San Diego, CA: Thunder Bay Press. (Original work published 1839)

Baudelaire, C. (1992). *Flowers of evil and other works/Les fleurs du mal et œuvres choisies. A dual-language book* (W. Fowlie, Ed. & Trans.). London: Dover Edition. Publications. (Original work published 1964)

Dubs, R. (1995). *Lehrerverhalten.* Ein Beitrag zur Interaktion von Lehrenden und Lernenden im Unterricht [Teacher behavior. A contribution to the interaction of teachers and learners in the classroom]. Zürich: Verlag des Schweizerischen Kaufmännischen Verbandes.

Hellenic Ornithological Society (Ed.). (1996). *Ola ta Poulia tis Elladas. O protos olokliromenos odigos gia ta poulia tis Elladas* [All the birds of Greece. The first and only complete photograph guide to the birds of Greece]. Press Institution Free Press.

Lecoq, J. (2000). *Der poetische Körper. Eine Lehre vom Theaterschaffen* [The moving body: Teaching creative theater]. Berlin: Alexander Verlag. (Original work published 1997)

Leopardi, G. (2016). Panegyric of birds. In *Essays and dialogues by Giacomo Leopardi* (C. Edwardes, Trans.). Project Gutenberg. Retrieved June 28, 2023, from www.gutenberg.org/ebooks/52356. (Original work published 1882)

Mani Matter—Topic. (2021, December 13). Ds Lied vo de Bahnhöf [recording]. YouTube. https://www.youtube.com/watch?v=OgW3vpCBUJM

Orff, C. (2011). Das Schulwerk: Rückblick und Ausblick/The Schulwerk: Past and future (M. Murray, Trans.). In B. Haselbach (Ed.), *Studientexte zu Theorie und Praxis des Orff-Schulwerks: Basistexte aus den Jahren 1932-2010/ Texts on theory and practice of Orff-Schulwerk: Basic texts from the years 1932–2010* (pp. 134–159). Mainz: Schott. (Original work published 1964)

Orff, C. (2011). Thoughts about music with children and non-professionals (M. Murray, Trans.). In B. Haselbach (Ed.), *Studientexte zu Theorie und Praxis des Orff-Schulwerks: Basistexte aus den Jahren 1932-2010/Texts on theory and practice of Orff-Schulwerk: Basic texts from the years 1932–2010* (pp. 66–76). Mainz: Schott. (Original work published 1932)

Orff, C., & Keetman, G. (1950–1954). Orff-Schulwerk—*Musik für Kinder,* Vols. 1-5. Mainz: Schott.

Schafer, R. M. (1993). *The Soundscape: Our sonic environment and the tuning of the world.* Rochester, VT: Destiny Books.

Widmer, M. (2004). *Spring ins Spiel. Elementares Musiktheater mit schulischen und außerschulischen Gruppen. Ein Handbuch* [Jump into play. Elemental music theater with school and extracurricular groups. A handbook]. Boppard: Fidula.

Movement/Dance and the Fine Arts

Barbara Haselbach (Austria), Sofía López-Ibor (Spain/USA),
Raquel Pastor Prada (Spain), Warangkana Siripachote (Thailand)

INTRODUCTION

Historical Background

Dance and visual arts have developed common paths since antiquity, deeply linked to a series of social values and symbolic-magical functions such as those represented by cave paintings of fertility or hunting ritual dances. Choral or chain dances are known practically all over the world, and paintings, frescoes, sculptures, and reliefs have been preserved since ancient times in art from Greece, Rome, Egypt, India, China, and elsewhere. From the 14th to the 19th century, numerous pictorial representations of court dances and folk dances have survived.

During the 20th century, the historic avant-garde intensified these connections through different artistic movements that explored the possibilities of representing the movement and dynamism of modern life. Taking dance and the performing arts as an important source of inspiration for their works are Futurism, Orphism, Dadaism, the *Ballets Russes*, or the Bauhaus school, where the pedagogical applications of this integrating vision of art were developed.

Since the late 1950s, the theme of the body has aroused enormous interest among the new artistic practices that have emerged under the generic name of action arts. Happenings, performances, body art, fluxus, video-creation, or video-dance encompass a wide variety of procedures that fuse painting or sculpture and dance with other artistic languages such as theater, literature, music, or new audio-visual technologies. Dancers close to and akin to avant-garde art began to absorb these artistic procedures in what is known as contemporary dance.

This interest in the interrelation of different artistic expressions has not only taken place among artists and creators, but also in the educational space. Arts education has been linked to the renewed interdisciplinary practices that occur in avant-garde art, through specific didactics that seek the integration of the arts in the classroom. Within the Orff Schulwerk, Barbara Haselbach has been a pioneer in this work of interrelating dance and visual arts for more than thirty-five years in collaboration with artists and institutions such as art galleries and museums.

Why Integrate the Fine Arts?

- Our anthropological conditions as poly-aesthetic beings include the need to express ourselves. We all experience and learn about the world first and foremost through all our senses. Also, in reaction to this, the creative shaping of our perceptions and impressions happens by using the elements of sounds and tones, colors and shapes, movements and words with growing skill and awareness. Children do not separate these areas (as is often the case with subject teaching in schools), but use all forms of expression, often emphasizing their strongest talent.

- Children are all different. They each have different likes, preferences, versatility, and learning styles, each in their own unique way. We give children the opportunity to expand their special talents in an interdisciplinary, artistically oriented class, to get to know new forms of expression, and to learn not only with but also from each other.

The Orff Schulwerk as a pedagogical concept involves integrating the skills developed in music, dance, speech, and visual arts. The arts have common features, ideas, and parameters that appeal to all the senses. The Schulwerk is a holistic approach that provides an opportunity for wider and deeper understanding of all subject matters while the students are engaged in a multisensorial way.

Dorothee Günther, the director of the School for Dance and Gymnastics in Munich, where the Orff Schulwerk originally started in the 1920s, wrote:

> *A person sensitive to movement, out of their awakened feeling for their body, can also experience movement visually; if we give them a piece of clay to shape with their hands, they will be able with very little practice to create sculptures that are movement-related and spontaneous. It will be the same if we give them a pencil; the movement pictures that are drawn will relatively quickly acquire life.... When one is allowed to do what one wants, patient application to work and with it technique, arise of themselves. And that is the most important consequence. Above all – a sense of one's own security awakens an interest in unfamiliar forms, one sees, hears, feels in other areas and there grows a sincere interest for artistic creation that has not been imposed externally (Günther, 2011/1932, pp. 88–90).*

How to Approach Integrating the Fine Arts

Our concept of combining visual arts, movement/dance, and music is based on the following learning models:

- *Learning from body experience*
  Our body experiences and stores all impressions and can also express them again. For our work this concerns learning about aspects of space such as curved and straight lines, volume, symmetry-asymmetry, width-narrowness, or of music such as tempo, rhythm, crescendo-decrescendo, or of dynamics/energy such as accents, relaxation-tension. This involves all that can be "embodied" and later expressed as well with the body itself or with color, voice, or instruments.
- *Learning from the concept or the work of art*
  This is about building a personal experience and thus a relationship with different forms of artistic expression (e.g., children's books by artists, folk art, examples of art works, graphics, paintings, sculptures) that can lead to a deeper understanding of the inspirational work of art.
- *Learning from the creative process*
  This may lead to individual or group representation of a given theme or a personal idea, which must not be understood as imitation or "translation" from one artistic medium to another, but as an attempt to express perceptions, impressions, and reflections on a theme or model in one's own way.

- Visual arts, dance, music, and language should not be objects of learning so much as paths and stations between the inner world and the outer world, which bring messages and make communications possible.

Approaches/ways of teaching
- Working with the senses (auditory, kinesthetic, visual, tactile) using the parameters of the various media in a perceptive and expressive way (input and output) and—depending on the age of the students—reflecting their perceptions.
- Observing and interpreting works of art through a different artistic medium of expression.
- Planning the flow and development of ideas in the lesson using different media progressively.
- Receiving students' inputs and starting from their ideas and suggestions as well as the teacher's.
- Empowering students through feedback, questions, and discussions. Promoting social-emotional learning (self- and social awareness and relationship skills).

PRACTICAL EXAMPLES

Overview:
1. **Warangkana Siripachote: Project "Home"**
   Starting from a project that revolves around what children hold close to their hearts, it has inspired the idea to create a learning experience for children ages 5-6 years that connects picture books, art, and music and movement together.
2. **Sofía López-Ibor: Richard Serra–Process art**
   This project is based on the principles of "process art," an artistic movement that arose during the 1960s. The approach places its emphasis on the act of creating, and focuses on self-growth, improving the students' cognitive, social, and emotional skills.
3. **Barbara Haselbach: Keith Haring–Dancing figures**
   Experiences take students from self-perception and observation of others to graphic sketching, and from dance graphics by Keith Haring to improvisation and choreography.
4. **Raquel Pastor Prada: Barbara Hepworth–The geometry of nature**
   This project, for ages 9-12, focuses on the sculptures of Barbara Hepworth, which connect organic forms of nature with geometric shapes and volumes. Activities range from body awareness to the creative composition of choreographies and sculptures, connecting body, cognition, and emotion.
5. **Barbara Haselbach: Folk art and ostinati**
   All cultures show repeated motifs in their different crafts (weaving, carving, architecture, pottery, etc.). Here we find inspiration for musical or movement motifs and offer ideas about how to use them for elemental choreographic forms.

1. Project "Home"
Warangkana Siripachote

Introduction
When creating a learning experience for children, one should consider a topic that is meaningful and significant to them. While the topic should be inspiring and able to spark new ideas for the children, teachers also play an important role in creating opportunities for the children to express their ideas and feelings naturally.

Suggestions and ideas for designing a learning experience

Picture books can be very important tools in creating a learning experience. In this project, children are introduced to the concept of "Home" through many picture books, such as *Home* by Carson Ellis (2015). This book is interesting in terms of its content and illustrations because the author has expressed ideas of "home" through various ways, for example: shapes and forms, geographical characteristics imaginary and realistically portrayed, as well as the homes that belong to people of different professions or animals. This picture book can widen and deepen children's perspectives towards the ideas of "home," and it leaves us to ponder what our "homes" look like.

Teachers can use open-ended questions to encourage children to explore different ideas and express their ideas and feelings freely.

- Tools and materials should be taken into consideration as they are significant to encourage the children's skills and areas of development.
- In each process of the learning experience, especially when it comes to creating an artwork, teachers should allow enough time and offer flexibility as appropriate.

Learning process

- We can begin by asking children an open-ended question like, "When speaking of 'home,' what do you think of?"
- The use of a picture book inspires children and takes them into the world of imagination.
- The children create their imaginary homes through various forms of art such as:
  - Creating houses by arranging their bodies: Working by oneself, in pairs, in groups of four
  - Moving along with music or the rhythm, listen and stop.[1]
- Each house could invent its own song that represents them.
- Invite a friend to come and visit or stay inside our house.
- Visitors can choose to bring a musical instrument with them as a present for each house they visit.

Working by oneself.

Working in pairs.

Jittamett Kindergarten, Bangkok
Photos: Krongtong Boonprakong.

---

1 Suggestion for the music to accompany the activity: H. Diederich's (2001) "Der Querenburger" from Ensemble Rossi's album *Djingalla 2*. https://www.youtube.com/watch?v=jTGd1XhGmpM

Working in groups of four
Jittamett Kindergarten, Bangkok
Photo: Krongtong Boonprakong

Jittamett Kindergarten, Bangkok
Creating a big-size house in which children can play
Photo: Warangkana Siripachote

- Create a miniature house using recycled materials such as paper boxes and construction paper.
- Each house can be placed on a piece of land (paper) and can be occupied by characters of their own choice/design.
- Create houses from clay and sticks (learning the concept of construction and the structure of the buildings).
- Always encourage children to tell a story, talk about their feelings or the process of making or working on each project.

Extending the idea of houses into building cities (group work):

- After reading together a picture book like *How far can you go?* By Taro Gomi, start with an open-ended question like, "When speaking of 'city,' what do you think of?"
- Explore the idea of creating a city, using different forms of art, such as drawing, clay making, creating with different materials.
- For example, after creating paper box houses, children can place their houses on the given area to create a city that reflects a society in which we all live together. Afterwards, draw other elements such as roads and bridges to connect oneself with others, engage in discussion and add what we want to have in our community.
- Walk around the city, share our thoughts and reflections in a group.
- Always have time for the children to explore their artwork and play with their cities freely. Encourage role-play interaction (house welcoming and visiting).
- A miniature city can also be a starting point for the children to move and create with their bodies. It can be used as a model structure for exploring the ideas of position and spatial awareness as well as body movements with friends. Music can tell you when to move and pause. Take turns playing the roles of neighbors or visitors.
- Other ideas include holding a celebration or a dance festival together for this city, dance around the villages or along the streets.
- Discuss the process of working together with friends, including our feelings or what we have learned.

Building a city
Jittamett Kindergarten, Bangkok
Photo: Warangkana Siripachote.

A YouTube video of the project "Home" can be viewed here: https://youtu.be/icrCIYlyz_U

2. Richard Serra–Process Art
Sofía López-Ibor

Play is a necessary ingredient in art because there is a kind of wonder that goes on when you play.

—Richard Serra

Introduction
Richard Serra is an American artist known for his large-scale steel sculptures. Born in San Francisco in 1938, he grew up visiting the shipyard and had a fascination for large sheets of metal. He made his first sculptures out of fiberglass and rubber. His huge steel sculptures go through a process of oxidation that creates an interesting texture and color.

The Matter of Time by Richard Serra,
Guggenheim Museum, Bilbao, Spain.
Photo: Alejandra Escalada

Orff Schulwerk teachers often say that the most interesting part of their teaching is the process how you work with the students, which becomes more relevant than the outcome or result. This idea connects with Process Art, which Richard Serra represents. In his Verb List, Richard Serra deals with the idea of weight, balance, density, size, and shape and how they affect the viewer.

Richard Serra, Verb List 1967
Digital Image © The Museum of Modern Art/Licensed by SCALA/Art Resource, NY
Artist: Richard Serra (b. 1938) © ARS, NY used with permission

Suggestions for the classroom

Serra created a list of actions that he could do with different materials, which can lead to creating shapes, three-dimensional sculptures, and music scores. The act of playing with a simple material such as a piece of paper can lead to music and dance creation with students in a process that is based both on experiential and cognitive learning. The students are engaged in exploration while they have opportunities to explain and verbalize what they are learning.

Teaching and learning

The process starts with an **interactive and participatory** activity in which students play and dance with a simple piece of paper. They explore movement with the paper, balancing, turning, floating, and more. They observe and imitate each other.

The San Francisco School students exploring movement and paper shapes inspired by Richard Serra's Verb List
Photos: Sofía López-Ibor

After the exploratory phase we focus on a **learner-centered** activity where the students make a list of actions and verbs they observed in the previous activity. Once the students have collected their list, we show the Verb List by Richard Serra (e.g., "to roll, to crease, to store, to fold"). Students explore the given list to create individual and collective paper sculptures.

The activity that follows is **content-focused.** The teacher presents information for the students to discuss and observe, in the form of a slide presentation or a collection of photographs. When the students have the opportunity to see one of the Serra sculptures, we engage them with inquiry driving and open-ended questions. For example, they can think and problem-solve about how the monumental sculpture was installed inside the museum. They can also engage with their senses and imagine how it feels to walk inside, outside, and around the *Sequence* sculpture.

The final activities in the lesson are also interactive-participative using the Richard Serra Verb List. We can listen to music while drawing our own action words with black crayon. One suggestion is to use "In the Upper Room: Dance No. 9" by Philip Glass (2009), (https://www.youtube.com/watch?v=wPdLu8GQprE). Students can also compose variations on a simple melody inspired by the same Verb List using composition techniques such as augmentation, diminution, repetition, and re-organization of small patterns. Students can also create mini studies in a group.

Practicing Serra's Verb List
Photo: Sofía López-Ibor

Richard Serra. A Drawing in Five Parts. 2005
Image copyright © The Metropolitan Museum of Art. Image source: Art Resource, NY
Artist: Richard Serra (b. 1938) © ARS, NY used with permission

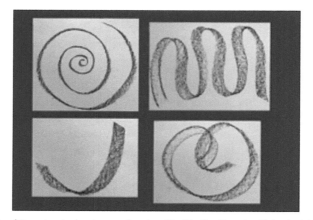

Richard Serra inspired action words painted by The San Francisco School students
Photo: Sofía López-Ibor

The ideal extension and culmination of the project could be to see one of the real "Sequence" sculptures by Serra, where the students can reflect about Serra's vocabulary in a real scenario.

Richard Serra, *Sequence*
Photo: Lorenz Kienzle
The Museum of Modern Art/New York, NY
Digital Image © The Museum of Modern Art/
Licensed by SCALA/Art Resource, NY
Artist: Richard Serra (b. 1938) © ARS, NY used with permission

Reflection

What did the children think about the sculptures and their mini studies? One of the advantages about working with such a clear vocabulary is that the students can make precise statements about what they see or what they have perceived. We normally have groups of students perform for each other to give feedback and suggestions. We also encourage the students to ask questions and clarify doubts, with the goal of really appreciating what each one of them has to offer. An easy way of establishing this kind of conversation with the students is simply asking the question, "Can you tell us about your work?"

3. Keith Haring–Dancing Figures
Barbara Haselbach

Introduction

Keith Haring (1958–1990), American Pop Art artist, lived, among other places, in New York, where he helped shape the alternative art and street art scene. His drawings in the New York underground stations became famous. He often worked with children in workshops on various projects. His art is characterized by his highly political commitment supporting homosexuals, AIDS patients, and oppressed peoples in Africa. When asked what he wanted with his art,

Keith replied, "A more holistic and basic idea of wanting to incorporate [art] into every part of life" (Drenger, 1988, p. 53).

Suggestions for the classroom
Aims
Perceiving and understanding the body in stillness and movement through kinesthetic, visual, and tactile perception (the input) and activities such as creating a dance or pantomime scene as a solo, duet, or group creation to one's own music or, alternatively, to recorded music (the output).

In order to really experience the connections between body awareness and expression in visual, tactile, movement, and musical creation, as well as discussing and reflecting these experiences, enough time should be spent on developing the theme.

The process
Target group: Upper primary level, but also possible with older students and adults.
- Body awareness: free dancing—music stops—with closed eyes feeling one's position and body sculpture. In order to vary and enrich the perception and movement experience, the teacher may give indications such as: How do you feel your feet? Is the upper body bent or straight? Where are the arms? Where is the focus, down or up or where? How can you move on the spot? Can you sink down and rise? Can you move in slow motion? Can you move just your arms and upper body? Can you make angular/round movements?
- During the stops students are asked to see themselves with their inner eye.
- Draw the position of one's own body with fast strokes (e.g., with crayon) on a large sheet of paper on the floor.
- Visual perception: free dancing - music stops - looking around, watching, and imitating, then sketch somebody else's "statue."
- Create dance figures from the sketches with wire or tin foil. In each repetition of the music, a different person's "statue" should be chosen to be sketched and transformed into a wire or foil figure.
- Put the figures on chairs or benches within the dance space like at an exhibition in a gallery.
- Short discussion in the whole group. How could the figures become alive and danced?
- Introduce Keith Haring and some of his drawings from his book *Dance* (1999).
- Scenic-musical interpretation of selected Haring pictures in duos or trios, etc., with possible repetitions to create an ABC, ABA, or ABACA form.
- Every danced sketch is accompanied by another small group of participants.
- Demonstration of the studies, feedback, and reflection.

Students from the San Francisco School looking at Keith Haring's pictures
Photo: Sofía López-Ibor

Resource
https://www.haring.com/!/selected_writing/keiths-kids

4. Barbara Hepworth–The Geometry of Nature
Raquel Pastor Prada

Introduction
Barbara Hepworth (1903–1975) was an English sculptress who worked with simple, organic forms, inspired by the nature of the rural landscapes of her native Yorkshire. Her sculptures express the sensation, the intimacy of being inside the landscape, through the dialog between the concave and the convex, the obverse and the reverse, the interior and the exterior, or the "hole" as an active element in the sculpture. From 1930 onwards, her work became increasingly abstract, with pure, elemental, and geometric forms, but she never lost the reference to nature and its forms.

Suggestions for the classroom
Target group: Ages 9–12 years and adults.

We delve into abstract sculpture and explore with our body simple geometries such as the sphere or the line, to evolve towards more elaborate concepts such as the spiral or the hole. We explore stillness, movement, and the creation of spatial forms and volumes. Sculpture permeates our body and becomes form in movement. We relate abstraction and emotion, due to the understanding through and from the body.

The work process should start from body awareness, looking at photos of the sculptures, careful observation of the sculptures, and the analysis of sizes, proportions, morphologies, and structures, exploring the continuous transformation of form in space, until the creative composition of group choreographies.

The process

- **Dancing** freely in space and performing lines, planes, and spheres with the movement and positions of the body (Laban's "Shapes"; see the article by B. Haselbach and A. Wolf, "Overview of Various Applications of Movement and Dance in the Orff Schulwerk").
- **Getting to know Barbara Hepworth**. Teacher's presentation to answer some questions: Who was she? What did she do? What interested her?
- **Observing** and **analyzing** the sculptures.
- **Exploring** body lines, planes, and spheres found in the works. Also new forms observed like the spiral and the hole.
- **Drawing** partners, quickly capturing the overall shape of their bodies through geometric shapes.
- **Performing** body exploration in pairs.
- **Drawing** partners through quick graphic traces.
- **Observing** and **reflecting** on the drawings.
- **Creating** a composition of movement in small groups. Each group chooses three sculptures to inspire their choreography.
- **Choosing** the preferred drawing to transform it into a plasticine or clay sculpture using volumes and geometric shapes.
- **Verbalizing** and **reflecting** on the process, the choreographies, and the sculptures created.

Hepworth with plaster of *Sphere with Inner Form* in the Palais, 1963
Copyright permission for reproduction granted from barbarahepworth.org.uk

Students in a creative dance lesson exploring the sphere in pairs.
Escuela Municipal de Música y Danza de Ciempozuelos, Madrid, Spain
Photo: Raquel Pastor Prada

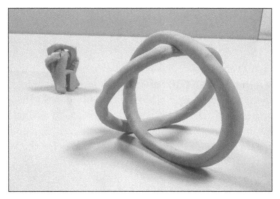

Plasticine sculpture made by an adult student from their favorite drawing
Salud en Movimiento during a weekend encounter in Avilés, Spain
Photo: Raquel Pastor Prada

Students exploring the line form in pairs, while another classmate draws them
CEIP Ciudad de Nejapa, Tres Cantos, Spain.
Photo: Raquel Pastor Prada

Resources

https://barbarahepworth.org.uk/
https://artsandculture.google.com/project/barbara-hepworth

5. Folk Art and Ostinati
Barbara Haselbach

Introduction
For thousands of years, every culture has created ornaments in a wide variety of materials: carved in stone, drawn in the sand, painted on cloth, burnt into bark, later painted on walls, hammered into weapons, woven into clothing, or embroidered. These ornaments are made of simple, straight, or curved lines and dots, small motifs such as circles, crosses, spirals, and similar geometric figures. Often the shapes are typical of a tribe, a country, a culture, for example the meander for the ancient Greeks or the spiral waves for the Maori in New Zealand.

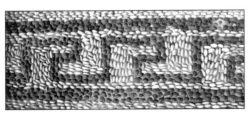

Pattern from ancient Greece

Patterns from New Zealand

From: *Ornamente der Völker* (Ornaments of the people), Wasmuth, 1959
Used with permission from www.wasmuth-verlag.de

The multiple repetitions of a motif are also found in the steps of folk dances. However, movement motifs inspired by such patterns from folk art can of course also be invented by the dancer and combined with several other motifs to form a choreography.

The process
Motivation
The teacher shows several examples, either from books, slides, or on fabrics, ceramics, etc. Students are asked to describe what they see. Variations? Different motifs?

Kelim from Ukraine

Printed fabric, Finnish

From: *Ornamente der Völker* (Ornaments of the people), Wasmuth, 1959
Used with permission from www.wasmuth-verlag.de

Experimentation
• Draw what you see with the fingers in the air. First small, then larger, later also on paper.
• Create similar patterns with movements, with steps or gestures, turns or small jumps.

- Draw your movement with oil pastels or crayons. What changes happen when you "dance" a partner's drawing? Such experiments provide a rich field for experimentation and should be discussed.

Elaboration

Several small groups of three or four participants invent together a motif (consisting of loco-motion, gestures, stillness, clear rhythm, and spatial paths) and repeat it as an ostinato over 8 or 16 bars. Meter signature and tempo are set by the teacher and apply to all groups, so that the various examples can be performed simultaneously.

Jug from Portugal
From: *Ornamente der Völker*
(Ornaments of the people), Wasmuth, 1959
Used with permission from www.wasmuth-verlag.de

Choreographic variations

1. Building a layered ostinato
   The groups find a place in the room that allows them to perform their ostinato without inhibiting another group. One child is the conductor and gives the cues for each group, also showing when to stop. Two or three groups can dance at the same time. A new conductor invents a new sequence. Finally, all the groups are dancing. To keep the tempo, a simple, soft accompaniment in the basic beat is recommended.
2. ABA Form
   After a short rhythmic prelude, several groups dance their ostinati simultaneously for 16 bars, then stop (part A), taking care not to collide with the others. Then the other groups start and perform the B part. A will be repeated. An alternating observer from outside can always give their opinion and make suggestions for improvements. The non-dancing group can add a discreet body percussion accompaniment.
3. Solo over layered ostinato
   The arrangement becomes more interesting when one or two soloists dance freely in the room in relation to the ostinato groups.
4. Choreography according to a specific model
   The starting point can be one of the models shown at the beginning. The dance interpreta-tion can be invented by the students or directed by the teacher.

Reflection

The teacher or the students ask some questions that are discussed together, e.g., Was the task easy or difficult? Was the connection between visual representation and dance realization recognizable? What was interesting? What music could be used or produced?

References and Resources

Bossert, H. T. (1959). *Ornamente der Völker. Volkskunst in Europa und Asien* [Ornaments of the people. Folk art in Europe and Asia]. Tübingen: Wasmuth.

Diederich, H. (2001). Der Querenburger (instrumental). In *Djingalla 2: Tanz- und Bewegungsmusik* [Recorded by Ensemble Rossi]. YouTube. May 13, 2022. https://www.youtube.com/watch?v=jTGd1XhGmpM

Drenger, D. (1988). Art and life: An interview with Keith Haring. *Columbia Art Review*, Spring, 49.

Dubuc, M. (2016). *Here comes Mr. Postmouse*. Bristol, England: Book Island Limited.

Ellis, C. (2015). *Home*. Somerville, MA: Candlewick Press.

Glass, P. (2009). Philip Glass: *In the upper room* [Album]. Orange Mountain Music.

Gomi, T. (2014). *How far can you go?* (どこまでゆくの？). Tokyo: Fukuinkanshoten.

Günther, D. (2011). Der rhythmische Mensch und seine Erziehung / The Rhythmic person and their education (M. Murray, Trans.). In B. Haselbach (Ed.), *Texts on theory and practice of Orff-Schulwerk: Basic texts from the years 1932–2010* (pp. 78–93). Mainz: Schott. (Original work published 1932)

Haring, K. (1999). *Dance*. (Estate of Keith Haring, Ed.). Boston, New York, London: A Bulfinch Press Book.

Haselbach, B. (1991). *Tanz und Bildende Kunst. Modelle zur ästhetischen Erziehung* [Dance and visual arts. Models for aesthetic education]. Stuttgart: Klett.

Haselbach, B. (1999). Sobre la interrelación entre la danza y las artes plásticas [On the interrelation between dance and visual arts]. *Música, Arte y Proceso*, (7), 71–87.

Haselbach, B. (2004). Integrating the arts through body experience. *The Orff Echo*, 36(2), 20–23.

Haselbach, B. (Ed.) (2005). From elemental music and dance pedagogy to modern art. *Orff-Schulwerk Informationen*, 75 (This issue is devoted to this topic).

Haselbach, B., & Salmon, S. (Eds.) (2017). Encounters between Orff-Schulwerk and modern arts. *Orff-Schulwerk Heute*, 97 (This issue is devoted to this topic).

Iwai, T. (2008). *100-storey house* (100かいだてのいえ). Tokyo: Keiseisha.

López-Ibor, S. (2011). *Blue is the sea. Music, dance and visual arts*. San Francisco: Pentatonic Press.

McShine, K., & Cooke, L. (2007). *Richard Serra sculpture: Forty years*. New York: The Museum of Modern Art.

Mitsumasa, A. (1982). *Anno's journey*. London: Bodley Head.

Pastor Prada, R. (2012). *Artes Plásticas y Danza: Propuesta para una didáctica interdisciplinar* [Visual arts and dance: Proposal for interdisciplinary didactics] [Doctoral dissertation, Universidad Complutense de Madrid/Spain]. Repositorio Institucional. https://eprints.ucm.es/16759/

Serra, R., & Shiff, R. (2016). *Richard Serra: Forged steel*. Göttingen: Steidl.

Serra, R., Rose, B., White, M., Garrels, G., & Borden, L. (2011). *Richard Serra drawing: A retrospective*. Houston, TX: Menil Collection.

Serra, R., Schneider, E., Shiff, R., & Lawrence, J. (2008). *Richard Serra—drawings—work comes out of work*. Bregenz: Kunsthaus Bregenz.

Serra, R., Sylvester, D., Reinartz, D., Ferguson, R., McCall, A., & Weyergraf-Serra, C. (1998). *Richard Serra: Sculpture 1985–1998*. Göttingen: Steidl / Los Angeles: The Museum of Contemporary Art.

Tischitz-Winklhofer, B., & Valtiner-Pühringer, D. (2022). *Kunst—Stück—Werk. Malerei—Musik—Sprache—Tanz 1. Eine interaktive Entdeckungsreise für Kleinkindgruppen* [Art—piece—work. Painting—music—speech—dance 1. An interactive journey of discovery for toddler groups]. Salzburg: Tandem.

Movement, Dance, and Speech

Christine Schönherr (Austria), with Françoise Grenier (Canada),
Barbara Haselbach (Austria), Christoph Maubach (Germany/New Zealand)

INTRODUCTION
Christine Schönherr

Written and Spoken Language

Language, a medium we are familiar with, takes on a central role in our everyday lives, and thus it is a role to which we probably do not give much thought. Consequently, in the context of elemental music and movement education we ask ourselves: When do we use language? What does it help us to do? What does it achieve?

Language, in written as well as in spoken form, gives us the possibility for rational understanding, for purpose-oriented information, and also for social exchange, communication, and contact. When we speak, we also show ourselves as a person. Language thus serves human expression and self-expression. Speaking is therefore also called the sound fingerprint of each individual person. It is interesting to note that the word "person" is derived from the Latin verb *personare*, which means "to sound through" and refers to speaking through the mouth of the mask in masquerading. Language, like music and dance, is a medium in which artistic expression can develop and be brought to completion. With this statement we approach the composer Carl Orff and his elemental music and movement pedagogical concerns.

Spoken language is based on sound and thus, based on the musical parameters of volume, pitch, duration, and timbre. It is therefore not surprising that Orff gave speech an important part in his pedagogical concept. For him, the speech exercise stands at the beginning of all musical practice (Orff & Keetman, 1950, n.p.[1]). I can very well share this point of view from my experience in teaching children, adults, and the aged. However, language can do more! I am thinking of the inspiring speech pieces such as those handed down by Orff and Keetman.

In the speech exercises we find single words, sayings, and proverbs. If we speak them, preferably several times in a row, in a "musical-listening" way, upbeats, full beats, rhythmic building blocks (ostinati), even and uneven meters, as well as meter changes arise as if by themselves (see Orff and Keetman, 1950, Vol. I, pp. 68–70).

The following is an example from the speech exercises: "Wie die Pfeife, so der Tanz" ("Let the piper call the tune" in the adaptation of Margaret Murray, or "Like the music, so the dance"), a proverb that Orff notated in 3/8 meter (Orff & Keetman, 1950, p. 69, no. 11; in the 1958 Murray adaptation, p. 51, no. 11).

---

[1] Ed.: Citations that are marked "n.p." (no page number) refer to the notes at the end of *Orff-Schulwerk—Musik für Kinder/Music for Children*, Volume I.

Wie   die   Pfei - fe   so   der   Tanz.

Let's try it out. Speak it several times in a row and the words almost start to dance. But we do not stay with the original, rather we speak the text in different meters, repeat words, rhythmicize them differently, switch between metrically bound and non-metric speech, articulate sometimes legato, sometimes staccato, in different volumes, and varying modes of expression. It is astonishing how much variation is possible with six words.

In terms of content, the proverb calls for dancing, for a dance-like arrangement, in connection with the music (whistle). In our setting, the pipe could also be the spoken proverb, to which we move in dance while speaking. Thus, we are in the middle of the interplay of language and movement and in the interaction between linguistic accompaniment and dancing. The body becomes speech-expression and dance instrument. An extension of the improvisation and effect on the dance movement arises when the speaking dancer also includes body percussion.

Orff's intensive relationship with language as an artistic medium is evident in his speech pieces, for which he chose texts ranging from Sophocles and Hölderlin to Brecht. Here his concern to "bring music into language without abolishing its autonomy" (Thomas, 1977, p. 5) becomes clear. Since the publication of the Orff Schulwerk volumes, the speech models have naturally expanded greatly through other contemporary texts, poems, and speech pieces.

The Origin of Language

In connection with the focus of this publication, a short excursion back into prehistoric times and thus to the origin of language follows. It brings us to a number of approaches and different theories coming from prehistoric linguistics, psychology of language, or biological anthropology. Scientists agree that motor skills played a crucial role in language development. Speech psychologist Friedrich Kainz (1969) tells us that intense motor activity frequently is accompanied by sounds. Thus, during pleasurable activities a kind of whooping sets in, and during strenuous work, groaning. It is this coupling of expressive sounds and gross motor activity that has contributed to the development of language. For example, some years ago in India I observed a group of men trying to pull a heavy ship ashore. Within a short time, movement and a linguistic sequence of sounds were united in a common rhythm, which obviously had a labor-saving effect. Work songs and lullabies have probably also developed from such experiences, the latter promoting falling asleep due to the calm, uniform rhythm in connection with swaying movement.

Speech Disorders

Due to the original connection between speech sounds and motor skills, it is not surprising that speech disorders in childhood are mostly associated with motor problems. This manifests itself in the form of clumsiness or lack of movement coordination. Therefore, it is obvious to combine speech therapy with training of movement functions and movement sequences.

Rhythm, a principle anchored in the entire universe, is also particularly supportive in speech disorders due to its organizing, coordinating effect. That is why speaking rhythmic language, e.g., counting verses or poems that rhyme, is a good way to support speech disorders. It is particularly effective when rhythmic speech is also combined with movement.

Speech and Language

"We are player and instrument in one person." This statement by Horst Coblenzer (personal communication, n.d.), former speech teacher at the Max Reinhardt Seminar Vienna expresses that the speaking person is the instrument that makes the language sound. Every vocal-verbal utterance is anchored in the whole body. And even more, it is accompanied by movement, i.e., the movement of the diaphragm in the breathing process, the movement of the articulation tools such as lips and tongue. This leads to mimic expressions, the movement of the eye area, the forehead, the eyebrows, an important area of body language. We go one step further and include our hands and arms in our speech, for example, in the form of gestures, especially if the content of our words is important to us. This expands our body language. Depending on the linguistic template, this can then develop into a movement-dance design. Our body is both our speech and our dance instrument.

Language, an Artistic Medium

Like music and dance, language stimulates processes in which we explore it in free play, experiment with it, improvise with it, shape it. The design of the improvisation can remain exclusively in the realm of language. But especially in view of the above, it makes sense to feel the connection to movement and to include elements of movement and dance already in the improvisation. The possibilities of text creation are broadened and deepened by this, and the expressive power of dance is also strengthened by the language. Language and dance cross-fertilize each other.

Suggestions for the Selection of Linguistic Templates and their Compositional Possibilities in Relation to Movement/Dance

Linguistic content consists of *Urstoffe* [raw materials] of language (sounds, syllables, word parts), numbers, action verbs (e.g., creep, slide, push, pull), onomatopoeic words, sayings, proverbs, riddles, tongue twisters, nursery rhymes, counting rhymes, nonsense language, language games, word twists, advertisements, poems, newspaper articles, fables, stories.

The following traditional children's rhyme (Enzensberger, 1971, p. 199) is an example of the ways in which we might approach a text, starting with language.

> *Ong drong dreoka*
> *lembo lembo seoka,*
> *seoka di tschipperi*
> *tschipperi di kolibri,*
> *ong drong dreoka.*

The words are not found in any lexicon, they do not exist in everyday language, we have chosen a nonsense text here. It has no content-related statement, the language sound is in the foreground. This opens up possibilities for interpretation and thus for creative development.

What does the text offer in terms of linguistic-sound suggestions?
Let us take a closer look at the words. Speak them, and let the sound have an effect on us. We hear that at the beginning "Ong drong" the "O" dominates in connection with the nasal "ng" and sounds rather dark. The sound brightens a bit via the "e" in "lembo lembo" to the "a" in "seoka," and then rises to the bright "i" in "tschipperi" and "kolibri." The sound of "tschipperi"

is additionally determined by the energetic explosive sounds "tsch" and "p," only to abruptly break off in the last line and return to the opening words. This miniature text offers fine tonal nuances and precisely because it has no content-related statement, it lives for working them out.

How is the dance movement developed?
Let us move our body, our speaking instrument, in various ways, perhaps moving in different levels: at the beginning low, in the second line in middle level, then jumping up at "tschipperi" and "kolibri," to land low again at the end of the verse.

On another pass, gesture-like arm movements develop, in the sense of "gestural speech music making" (Thomas, 1977, p. 5). With gliding legato movements in the first line, we paint the linguistic sound event in the air (air patterns), which inspires choppy staccato movements in the third line.

We speak metrically bound and compare this with a free metric interpretation. Does this change our arm movements and movements in space? Which version seems more coherent to us? Let us postpone this decision for a while until clearer and clearer ideas for a dramatic interpretation develop. Which characters speak the text? In which situation? With which intention? How do we divide the text? Are there only speaking dancers or do we divide one run through between dancers and accompanying speakers? In what ways do we incorporate the space?

From experimenting and improvising, our speech-dance design of the nonsense verse gradually develops. Probably there will be a multiple run-through of the text with different variants, also their order well chosen.

PRACTICAL EXAMPLES

Overview
The following examples give insight into different contents and forms of language and poetry, and also into different methodological approaches.

1. **Barbara Haselbach: Poem by Eugen Gomringer**
   An example of "concrete poetry" that can be used with any age group from about six years old, with various solutions of interpretation.
2. **Christine Schönherr: Speech sounds–exploring, making them audible and visible**
   How to explore the "raw material" of language, starting with primary school age, possibly in connection with learning to write.
3. **Françoise Grenier: Halloween–Language and movement**
   An example of how to develop a short Halloween sketch with speech, movement, and accompaniment for primary school.
4. **Christoph Maubach: Proverb from Aotearoa (New Zealand)**
   The meaning of this proverb in Maori language leads to movement experiments and a final speech composition accompanying a choreography.

1. Poem by Eugen Gomringer
Barbara Haselbach

Eugen Gomringer is a Swiss author, born in South America, considered the founder of concrete poetry. His poems are a treasure trove of ideas for dancing. The selected example (Gomringer,

1969, p. 119) can easily be translated into every language of the world. It inspires various creative interpretations.

> From five
> to four
> from four
> to three
> from three
> to two
> from two
> to one
> from one
> to five

The group
With minor adaptations of the following ideas to suit the experience and ability of the respective group, the text can be used with any age group from about six years on.

1. Hand version (motivation)
This version can be practiced as an introductory game.

The teacher shows the back of their right hand and all five fingers: "How many fingers can you see?" Then only the left with four, and so on until the whole text is performed. It is repeated over and over again with increasing speed and the children also use their hands and repeat the numbers. The speaking will be sometimes fast, sometimes slow, whispered, loud, high, low, crescendo, etc. After a while children may take over the lead; they also might invent their own "jumpy" sequence using all ten fingers (which is a greater challenge, but of course no longer the original poem).

2. Shrinking and growing groups
Groups of five are formed, all (or just one person) speak each line using different expression. With every spoken line one of the five members "disappears" (sinking to the ground, hiding behind another one, making a half turn so facing backwards, moving away, etc.). The final line should be spoken with a short, impressive pause before "...to five"! Then all members suddenly return back again as quickly as possible (like a Jack-in-the-box). Repeat with different movements.

The text also can be varied, a new line invented and started with:

> From zero
> to one... (and so on)

One child after another will have a solo, choosing a special way to speak and join the group, and inventing a final line:

> ...from five
> to zero

everybody disappears like a flash!

3. Changing the beat (version for a more experienced group)

How can one speak the text and dance to a rhythm of 5/4, or 4/4, 3/4, etc.?

The teacher plays for a little while in 5/4, then 4/4, 3/4, etc., choosing different instruments to characterize a striking march in 4/4, a swinging waltz in 3/4, etc.

The group is invited to improvise dancing with forward, backward, sideways steps, with turns and leaps, supported by their own body percussion.

The changing meter also changes the rhythmic way of speaking the text and needs to be worked on beforehand.

After various ways of speaking and dancing in 5/4, 4/4, 3/4, 2/4 and even 1/4 have been practiced and explored by the group, especially appropriate examples will be chosen and joined in a sequence, so that the whole text is performed in changing meters.

4. Choreography/*Gestaltung* with several groups

Small groups are distributed in the room. The central group starts by speaking the first two lines (forte and piano in free meter) and dancing their motif more or less on the spot, repeated by one group after another.

Another group demonstrates its solution for lines three and four and this is repeated by all the groups together at the same time.

Lines five and six could be spoken and performed by two groups far away from each other, exchanging places with swinging waltz steps.

Lines seven and eight may be shown by all together on the spot using a crescendo that leads to line nine (*ff*)—then, after a short general pause in tense silence—on line ten all quickly come together to one big group.

Endless variations are possible and can be invented by the groups themselves.

2. Speech Sounds–Exploring, Making Them Audible and Visible

Christine Schönherr

The following suggestions are intended—with appropriate adaptation—for students of different ages. At primary school age, the topic could be linked to spelling lessons; letters thus also become a sound and movement experience.

Introductory considerations

Carl Orff writes in his notes and comments about the speech exercises in the un-numbered final pages of *Orff-Schulwerk* Volume I (Orff & Keetman, 1950, n.p.): "The way of speaking must, always vividly, emphasize particularly the sonority!" In order to make the sounds of words resonate, it is exciting to explore vowels and consonants for their qualities and to connect them with movement.

The breath—the basis of all phonation—is our starting point
Sensing the movement of the breath

- Attunement: We first get out of breath through free, dance-like movements in the room, or simply through an energetic game of tag.
- Supine position: By placing our hands on different areas of our torso—abdomen, chest, flanks—we feel the inhalation and exhalation movement.
- Sitting: The incoming breath triggers free movements of the arms, which at the end of the exhalation rest back at the starting point.

Exhale on flowing sounds "f," "sh," "s" (unvoiced)

- Movement in space: Exhaling we connect the sound with gliding-flowing movement; inhaling we remain standing in place.

Exploration and improvisation with speech sounds in the sense that "Every sound has magic power" (Schafer, 1972, p. 15)

The consonants include the nasals (m, n, ng), the explosives (p, t, k), voiced streaming sounds (s, sh), and fricatives such as (w, r, l). The vowels are a sound world of their own.

- With hands, arms, legs, gestures, or the whole body in place or in connection with locomotion, we try to make the phonetic characteristics of the vowels and consonants audible and visible. Speech, gesture, body expression, and dance movement form a unity.
- We paint consonants and vowels in the air with different parts of the body. Soundscapes emerge, some full of jags and corners, triggered by fast, short, linear movements (explosive sounds). Others have curves, gentle highs and lows, developing from quiet movements when sounding a, e, i, o, u, m, n, ng, w. Appropriate spatial paths are added.
- We integrate colored ribbons, hear and see the sound and movement effects.
- Exchange of experiences.

Individual sounds combine to form words

"A word is a chain of magical sound crystals" (Schafer, p. 15)

- Everyone creates their "name poem" linguistically and in dance with the sound sequence of their name.
- Group improvisation: The performers agree on a name from members of the group. The phonetic sequence of the name develops in free, vocal, and dance performance. Ideas are taken up, varied, and in connection with each other a dance-sound piece is created.

Creation of a spoken composition: "Machine Shop" (Benker, 1985, p. 6)

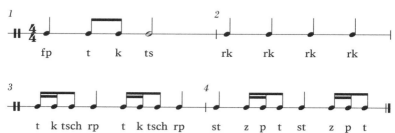

1. *Elaboration*

The machine sounds consist only of consonants, mostly explosive sounds. Each syllable "races" from the diaphragm as it is spoken. This creates an exact way of speaking, which also triggers arm/leg or whole-body movements.

2. *Compositional development considerations*

Which machine starts? How does it start—with movement, with speech, or with both? In a solo or group setting? When and in what way do the next machines start? Should rhythm instruments also be used? Do the machines just stay in place? The choreographic incentive is to relate the machine movements to each other in order to do justice to the title "Machine

Shop." Does a machine lose a few screws? What then? When and how does calm return? Is there, perhaps, another machine shop where differently working machines are active? There are no limits to the possibilities for speech and movement interpretation.

3. Halloween—Language and Movement
Françoise Grenier

Introduction
Here in Canada, the Halloween tradition is one of the unavoidable themes of October. This holiday is celebrated by virtually everyone, in schools, at home, in businesses, and on the streets. Glowing pumpkins, ghosts, and witches are emblematic of the holiday, which culminates in dressing up and collecting candy and other treats door-to-door on the night of the 31st. Each year, this theme is widely exploited in primary schools. Here is an example of how to develop a short Halloween sketch with speech, movement, and accompaniment.

Target group/duration
Eight- and nine-year-olds, three one-hour sessions.

Objectives
Compose a witch's spell and interpret it using the elements of dance influenced by animated vocal expressions of the text using space: high, medium, low levels; directions, pattern, attitude, and forms; energy, and speed; relationships among speaking dancers. Create atmosphere using instruments.

First session
Approach: Context setting and exploration
Talk about Halloween: The season, meaning, presence of all kinds of witches (good, bad, nature, etc.) and ghosts in other world folklore. Protagonists, related feelings, atmosphere, costumes, etc.

- Witch: Give her a name and describe her character and feelings, her activity.
  Each one becomes a witch and explores a way to speak, to move, and show its way to one partner.
- Ghosts: How can we manifest their presence? Sounds? Movements? Colors?
  Explore movement direction, attitude, gait, mimicry. Noises: Swhischhhhh! Hoos!
  Follow the direction of one's own moving hand; trace a path alone, with a partner, make a circle, etc.

Discussion
Are our sounds and movements satisfactory? Why?
We need a text to feature ideas and meaningful movements.

Text composition
Look for significant words, rhymes, onomatopoeia suggesting character, feelings, action, movement.

- It is the witch who speaks, tells her feelings, occupation, etc.
- Discussion and notation of the text to remember.

Second session
Revision and final text of the witch's spell:

On m'appelle Miramala!	They call me Miramala!
On me craint, on me fuit! (Ostinato)	I'm feared and shunned! (Ostinato)
Je mijote, Caramba!	I simmer, Caramba!
Rasptapolin! toute la nuit!	Rasptapolin! all night long!
Sabots de bœuf et queues de rats,	Ox hooves and rat tails,
Corne de poux, poux, poux, poux, poux!	Horn of lice, lice, lice, lice, lice!

Voice exploration

- Chant the text rhythmically and choose a line to become an ostinato.
  - ○ Whispers, high or low voice, crescendo, diminuendo, etc.
- Chanting in two groups:
  - ○ Text/ostinato
  - ○ With different soloists, 2x2, etc.

Movement exploration
(Gathering place: around a cauldron in the middle of the room)
Try postures, gaits, witches' and ghosts' movements following the voiced dynamics.
Work in small groups of four.

- Roles: Witches? Ghosts?
- Find a starting posture, move towards the center while saying the text in a specific way.
- Ways of moving around the cauldron.
- Final body posture.
- Discussion: take notes of the decisions?

Third session
- Text and movement
- Review of second session
- Witch hats? White gloves, etc. from our costume box
- Choice of instruments to set atmosphere (gong, thunder drum, grain shakers)
- Discussion on the course of play: Who? When? How?
- Take notes

Rehearsal of final setting
Intro:
- Gong ring/midnight
- Ghost's movements with white gloves; voices: swhischhhhh, hoos, and variations; thunder drum; stop!
- Whisper ostinato four times, then speak the spell together

Rondo:
- A: Vocal ostinato (4 x crescendo) tutti
- B: Small group performance - spell /voice and movement
- A–C–A–D, etc.

Coda:

- In a circle around the cauldron holding each other's shoulders and bending down: entire text chanted in one chorus (diminuendo)
- Gong ring/sunrise

Review and final performance:
- Time to review parts in small groups
- Review of the entire progression together
- Final production

Discussion
How did you like it? What was easy, difficult? What was beautiful? Why? What would we add or change to present this to other classes? Could this become part of a bigger whole?

4. "With your food basket and my food basket the people will thrive"–Proverb from Aotearoa (New Zealand)
Christoph Maubach

Introduction
Children in New Zealand grow up with a strong awareness of their bicultural environment. Close to 30% of New Zealand children learn *Te Reo Māori* (Māori language). The following example is an elemental speech exercise. New Zealand children learn language and speech by watching and listening, by imitation, and through activities. Playful manipulation of vowels and consonants, varied articulations and changes in musical parameters connected with bodily expression and gestures offer jump-off points for improvisation and speech composition. Engagement with the meaning, connotation, and cultural context can nurture the creative journey.

Nā tō rourou, nā taku rourou, ka ora ai te iwi
Literal translation: With your food basket and my food basket the people will thrive.

Nā tō rourou

Māori whakataukī
Māori proverb
arranged by Christoph Maubach

This notated example has a rhythmical structure and a rhythmical speech accompaniment. But the saying can also be articulated in a free-metric way. Variations in duration, pitch, and tone color can spark off new ideas and develop new creative forms for a speech composition.

Brief cultural context

Language, spoken words, oratory, speech, and sayings play a very important role in education and culture of the people of Aotearoa/New Zealand. It has three official languages, Māori, Sign Language, and English. At the beginning of the 19th century Māori was the predominant language. As more English speakers arrived in the country, the Māori language was increasingly confined to Māori communities. By the mid-20th century, it looked as though *Te Reo Māori* was dying out. Major educational initiatives were launched from the 1980s onwards and they have brought about a revival of *Te Reo Māori*. In recent years many more New Zealanders frequent Māori language classes in adult education settings. Māori is a language that comes to life through its expressive verve, its use in oratory, exclamations, and through its application in song (*waiata*). It is pronounced with emotion, uses variations in dynamics as well as repetition. It includes "body talking" and often shows sincere depth of feeling. For children in particular, speech, song, and music are intertwined. Gesture and movement, naturally integrated in the expression of young children, add further dimensions to speech and song.

Learning intentions

Learning experiences can be provided for different age groups.

a. Participants discuss and explore the meaning of this *whakataukī* (Māori proverb):
   "With your food basket and my food basket the people will thrive."
   The significance of the saying refers to the idea of co-operation and the combining of all manner of resources to make progress in all sorts of ways. The *whakataukī* encapsulates the notion that while working in isolation might result in survival, working together can take people beyond survival and onto prosperity. This metaphor can be explored creatively in movement, speech, and other musical and artistic ways.

b. Concepts such as alone/together, little/much (few/many) are explored in movement.

c. The musical elements of the speech piece are explored and with elemental composition practices participants create a speech composition that could be performed with a simple but expressive dance form.

Activities should be interlinked, a spoken form can be intensified by movement, a dance rondo becomes more dazzling accompanied by a speech composition.

1. Movement and dance

• To recorded music, participants explore their own movement activities and develop an individual movement motif.
• Individuals meet with a partner and share their motifs.
• Together in pairs they develop a new motif, possibly with something used in their previous versions.
• Development of a dance rondo: The teacher provides a dance phrase (A) using the text, Nā tō rourou, nā taku rourou, ka ora ai te iwi (see speech composition)
• Each team of two provides a rondo couplet (B, C, D, etc.).

2. Sound and speech composition

• Explore the sounds of the speech piece.

- Articulate and voice the text in many different ways, changing dynamics, speed, pitch, etc.
- Speak alone (solo), speak in a group (tutti), or in canon.
- Create a vocal (or instrumental) ostinato accompaniment.
- Imitate (or contrast) a partner and their way of speaking.
- Create a speech composition using all or some of these features and choreograph it.

References and Resources

Benker, H. (1985). *Mit Auftakt hebt die Sache an. 22 Sprechstücke für den Schulgebrauch.* [Things start off with an upbeat. 22 speech pieces for the classroom]. Munich: Max Hieber.

Enzensberger, H. M. (ed.). (1971). *Allerleirauh. Viele schöne Kinderreime* [Many beautiful children's rhymes]. Frankfurt am Main: Suhrkamp.

Gomringer, E. (1969). *Worte sind Schatten* [Words are shadows]. Hamburg: Rowohlt.

Grey, E. (2018). The music of spoken language in the 21st century Orff classroom. *The Orff Echo,* 50(2), 60–67.

Handerer, H., & Schönherr, C. (1994). *Körpersprache und Stimme* [Body language and voice]. Munich: Oldenbourgh.

Haselbach, B. (1994). Language as a stimulus to improvisation. In *Improvisation, Dance, Movement* (pp. 98–102; M. Murray, Trans.). London: Schott. (Original work published in 1976 as Sprache als Improvisationsanregung, in Improvisation, Tanz, Bewegung. Stuttgart: Klett)

Kainz F. (1969). *Psychologie der Sprache* [Psychology of language] (3rd ed.). Stutgartt: Ferdinand Enke.

Keller, W. (1973). *Ludi musici 3. Sprachspiele für die Früh- bis Späterziehung in der Vor-, Zwischen- und Nachschulzeit* [Speech games for early to late education in before, between, and after school time]. Boppard/Rhein: Fidula.

Orff, C., & Keetman, G. (1950). *Orff-Schulwerk—Musik für Kinder* [Orff-Schulwerk - Music for children] (Vol. 1, Hinweise und Anmerkungen/Instructions and notes). Mainz: Schott.

Orff, C., & Keetman, G. (1950). *Orff-Schulwerk—Musik für Kinder: Im Fünftonraum* (Bd.1). Mainz: Schott.

Schafer, R. M. (1972). *...wenn Wörter Klingen.* Vienna: Universal. (Original work published in 1970 as When words sing. Toronto: Arcana; Berandol.)

Schönherr, C. (1979). Erfahrungen mit dem Fach Spracherziehung [Experience with the subject of speech education]. *Orff-Schulwerk Informationen,* 24, pp. 11-15. https://www.orff-schulwerk-forum-salzburg.org/magazine-osh

Schönherr, C. (2001). "Sprich, damit ich Dich sehe" (Sokrates). Einblick in den Fachbereich Sprache am Institut für Musik- und Tanzpädagogik "Orff-Institut" ["Speak so that I may see you" (Socrates). Insight into the area of speech at the Orff Institute]. *Orff-Schulwerk Informationen,* 66, pp. 35–41. https://www.orff-schulwerk-forum-salzburg.org/magazine-osh

Schönherr, C. (2007). Stimme und Sprache im Fachbereich Bewegungsbegleitung [Voice and speech in the area of movement accompaniment]. *Orff-Schulwerk Informationen,* 78, pp. 34–38. https://www.orff-schulwerk-forum-salzburg.org/magazine-osh

Thomas, W. (1977). Introduction. In: C. Orff, *Sprechstücke für Sprecher, Sprechchor und Schlagwerk* [Speech pieces for speaker, speech choir and percussion; Musical score]. Mainz: Schott.

PART III
Target Groups

The Importance of Creative Music and Movement in the Early Stages of Life

Bethany Elsworth (Australia/Canada), Nadja Kraft (Austria/UK),
Wakako Nagaoka (Japan), Soili Perkiö (Finland)

Dance is an essential part of every person because people are dance. The body is a tool for communication. People express themselves through movement. (Gilbert, 2015, p. 7)

INTRODUCTION

This collaborative article looks at the link between music and movement as a way of accompanying and guiding a young child through the early years of life. Four teachers from different countries considered each other's experiences and describe here their individual ways of using the Orff Schulwerk approach with children from before birth up to entrance into school. The outcome of this reflective practice reveals a common link among these Schulwerk teachers that highlights the humanistic nature of this approach. Through thoughtful inquiry, they focus their attention on the impact that creative work with music and movement has upon the development of the child.

While the first part of this article focuses on the developmental stages of movement and the connections that encompass our work with the very young children, the second part reflects on the lived experiences of the authors, who are practitioners.

Before Birth

The biggest changes in any human body happen during their prenatal life inside a mother's womb and the months immediately following birth. Brain and body do not develop without some form of stimulation. For instance, in the beginning the fetus moves freely inside the womb. As it grows, the space it has to move within becomes smaller and smaller. Over time it is able to touch the walls of the uterus. The sensation of physically connecting with the mother offers stimulus for the development of the nervous system. Before birth, the world is a sound, a heartbeat, a hum, the movement of water, feeling the movements of the mother. Hearing is the first sense to develop. The womb is acoustically special, because in its anechoic chamber, the high and harsh sounds of the world are filtered out.

Inside the sound environment of the unborn child is the world of music. It sounds soft. Outside it remains the noise of the environment. From three months before birth, the baby's brain processes sounds, remembering and learning them. Fathers in Nepal tell stories to their unborn child, and mothers all around the world sing lullabies during their pregnancies. Babies begin to learn their musical language before birth.

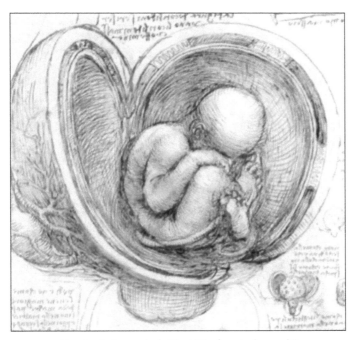

Drawing by Leonardo da Vinci "The fetus in the womb"
from Sketches and Notes c. 1511

Creating a circadian rhythm

The fetus needs to know whether it is night or day. Especially with the firstborn, it is worth creating musical rituals through which the fetus can learn the daily rhythm. It could be, for example, a morning song and later an evening lullaby that sends a clear indicator that nighttime is about to start.

A mother should not listen to music she does not like. The fetus cannot be fooled and can feel through the hormones circulating in the blood the effect a piece of music has on the mother. Loud background noise should be avoided because it is stressful for the body.

The fetus lives in the heartbeat of the mother, senses her movements, and moves with the mother's body. If the mother is well and happy, it is also reflected in the well-being of the fetus.

After birth, the baby's brain is programmed to work in such a way that he or she learns to calm down, eat well, and fall into good quality sleep when familiar sounds from the fetal period are repeated in the new environment. Following a musically enriched period before birth, an individual may have developed a melodic preference for their own cultural music by the time they are born.

Movement Development from Before Birth to About Four Years

Following is a short description showing just how much a young child's body and movement ability change within a very short period.

Prenatal to six months

Already inside the womb, from about 26 weeks onwards, fetuses respond with movement following stimulation. They can move their head, limbs, and mouth. The movement quality becomes smoother and more complex as the fetus grows, and by the time a baby is born, they have figured out how to breathe and are able to move all their body parts outside the womb. These movements are uncontrolled at first, but they practice muscle movement so much that by six weeks most babies can lift their heads while lying on their stomachs.

Children first discover the space in front, then above and beside, and finally behind them. The experience of the expansion of space runs parallel to physical development, which brings with it an expansion of their range of movement. Grasping, stretching, reaching, waving, pushing, pulling, etc., are all ways of experiencing body and space.

Two-month-old babies can hold onto small objects if you place them directly in their hands, and they will try to bring these objects to their mouths to investigate. This grasp is not secure initially and will take a few weeks to mature before babies can hold a shaker and play along to music.

By three months, most babies can lift their chests using their arms for support, and shortly after that the average baby can roll over from back to stomach, followed soon by the other way round. Every child, of course, develops differently, but the average baby can sit up unsupported by approximately six months.

Six to 12 months

Around eight months babies start to crawl, not always on their hands and knees but sometimes using different techniques like bum-shuffling or moving forward on their tummies. However, they are determined to move around the room independently. Around this time, they are also able to catch and hold moving objects like rolling balls, as well as starting to hold a spoon and trying to feed themselves.

Babies find their balance around 10 months of age, when they manage to pull themselves up and practice tirelessly to stand up for short periods of time. Around their first birthday they try to take their first steps, are able to hold objects with more control, and can start to draw.

Toddlers and children up to four years

By two years, the typical child can run, kick a ball, do small jumps, sway, turn around, walk up some stairs with the help of an adult, climb on a small climbing frame, and many more movements related to dance if an adult is doing this with them. They are starting to hold hands in small groups and turn around together with others.

By three years, they should be able to jump with both feet confidently in place, climb up and go down toddler slides, pedal on a tricycle, walk up and down stairs independently, stand briefly on one foot, and walk backwards. They can move their fingers independently, using them in more complex tasks, for example making more complex drawings. They start to skip, can tiptoe for a short while, swing different body parts, attempt to do side steps. From about three years they are usually able to attend music and movement lessons independently and in small groups, and they are starting to understand the concept of making and being in a circle with the help of an adult. Easy partner dances are now possible with clapping and patting hands together with a partner and turning around with them, as well as walking in a circle (still with the help of an adult to keep the shape), walking to the center and back, keeping their balance in different positions for short period of times.

Connection with Music

As mentioned, music as well as movement is passed to the child during the prenatal stages, and the fetus responds in multiple ways. The rhythmic heartbeat and the motion of their mother support growth. The initial encounters a baby experiences include soundwaves and movement. Babies dance inside the mother in a sea of sounds. The melodic and rhythmic sounds produced by the mother and the surrounding environment all influence the growing fetus. They relax to familiar sounds and are aroused by new.

In the same way, babies are emotionally and physically moved by the sounds of music. They react to the stimulus, becoming energized or calmed, or they may convey a variety of responses through the body. Infants are fascinated by musical sounds and are naturally invited to move in time with it. They listen, move towards or with the music, display emotional reactions, and interact with it through the body, the voice, or the playing of instruments.

Connection with Self

Music as a sensory stimulus promotes a response through movement. Music is a natural and enjoyable part of childhood. Play and action songs encourage the child to engage in specific movement. This rhythmic interplay alerts the child to their body and the abundance of movements that they can produce. Music awakens the body into awareness and supports the development of rhythmic motion necessary to walk, run, leap, and dance.

Children experience the design and shape of their bodies through connecting, moving, and touching specific areas. The brain feels the sensation and the child becomes aware of their physical attributes. This awareness allows them to form an understanding of how to present themselves as a physical being in space.

Connection with the Mother and Others

A life growing inside a mother is full of motion. Each stage of the pregnancy process builds with turns, kicks, pushes, and stretches, from the baby to the mother. In turn, the mother soothes the baby with hand strokes and swaying hips. These aspects form a bridge or a link between life inside the womb and the outside world.

According to Karin Schumacher (1994, p. 28), all early mother-child games can be considered elemental music, movement, and language games, as they connect to prenatal experiences. They offer multisensory emotional stimulation and have an effect on the child through the mother's emotional participation, which forms the basis for the child to establish a relationship to the mother, and later to significant others and the environment.

This connection can be strengthened through the joyful experience of musical motion and dance, through knee bouncers and action songs. The musical dialogue of movement responses, synchronized motion, and the joy of dancing in their parents' arms, bring forth an understanding between the baby and the special people in their lives.

PRACTICAL EXAMPLES

The Lived Experiences of Four Music and Movement Teachers with the Early Childhood Sector

Overview

1. **Soili Perkiö: Music and movement with unborn babies and their families**
   The experiences of working in Finland with the beginning stages of life before birth.
2. **Nadja Kraft: Working with children from three months to four years without their parents in kindergarten and preschool settings**
   Teaching very young children in kindergarten and preschool from age zero to four.
3. **Bethany Elsworth: Hearing the call and growing in dance**
   Experiences of working in an early childhood play-based music center in Australia.
4. **Wakako Nagaoka: Children's movement expression activities in kindergarten: A focus on the collaborative work between a guest teacher, children, and teachers of the kindergarten**
   The expressions of children during activities that took place at a kindergarten in Japan.

1. Music and Movement with Unborn Babies and Their Families

Being the oldest of eight cousins **Soili Perkiö** was the one to lead the activities of playing together: drama, singing, playing, and dancing. That was the start of being a music teacher.

Example of a session in a maternity group

The session with the waiting families is about to begin. Warm-up movements are done together with a heartbeat recording.

The group moves around singing, and during the break the group members greet each other, happy chatter filling the space. The baby in the womb wakes up and makes a kick. Mother smiles.

A couple expecting a baby dance together to soft music. Mother asks her partner to touch her belly. They feel several kicks. Baby dances inside the mother in a sea of sounds.

The group sings long vowels together, and the bodies of the mothers-to-be resonate. The partner touches the mother's back and hums along. The fetus calms down and falls asleep.

Hiljaa, hiljaa

Lullaby from Finland

Hiljaa = softly

The primary goals in the maternity groups are to build community through music and movement by

- **strengthening the connection** to the unborn baby and supporting the relationships within the family.
- **fostering relaxation** for the mother: breathing exercises, singing in a relaxed way, dancing, contact with her own body, contact with her expressions, feelings, and experiences through arts.
- **developing repertoire** for musical communication: songs, rhymes, poems, dances, building a musical sequence for a day.
- **experiencing the arts** as a nurturing ground, giving tools to observe and react to the needs of the baby.

> *Long before you were born*
> *I listened to the murmur of your voice,*
> *A bouncing bow in a constellation of stars,*
> *music flowing from your fingertips,*
> *where someone had blown a swell of waves.*
>
> *I see your nails now, like small crescents,*
> *a breath of mist above a lake,*
> *clouds on the soles of your feet;*
> *my eyes gently stroke the hills and dales*
> *   of a small world*
> *your downy earlobes shine in the light*
> *And we are surrounded by a mighty living*
> *   silence.*

"Mother's poem" by Hannele Huovi, original Finnish translated by David Hackston published with permission (Huovi & Perkiö, 2014)

Drawing by Artist Kristiina Louhi, published with permission (Huovi & Perkiö, 2014)

2. Working with Children from Three Months to Four Years Without Their Parents in Kindergarten and Preschool Settings

Nadja Kraft grew up in the Austrian mountains and because of her playful nature soon babysat many of her village's little ones, discovering the power of play songs from a young age. As a mother of three young children herself she has a very gentle yet stimulating approach to working within early years settings.

The experiences are drawn from weekly music and movement sessions at a local preschool. **Ducklings** refer to a baby group with children from three months to about 15 months, **Robins** are between 16 months and three years old, and **Owls** are between three and four years old. The lyrics below are from a song that is part of our welcome ritual and is sung every week. This song is used as an example to describe how children's music and movement abilities develop during the first few years. Its original source is unknown.

Clap your hands, everyone together,
Clap your hands as the music goes around.
Clap your hands, everyone together,
Clap your hands go up (reach up high) *and down* (tap on the carpet).

Ducklings (three months to 15 months)

The challenge here—compared to parent and toddler groups in external settings—is that the babies share a kindergarten teacher among three or four of them. Not everyone can have a turn being rocked or bounced up and down on an adult's lap. Some sit by themselves, some need support to sit up with a special support cushion, some sit in a bouncer, and a few are crawling around on the carpet. As the ukulele gently begins to play, the babies immediately react and show facial expressions and their little bodies begin to move in excitement. After a few initial weeks, some babies join in with clapping as well as reaching up high and some wait for the part to tap the carpet. We change the beat actions to tap your tummy, tap your knees, tap your head, but their little arms are so small they can just about reach the side of it.

One boy, about 10 months old, always sits in front of me. Whenever I did not play the ukulele to show a beat action, he would put my hand back on the ukulele to show me what I have to do. A little girl, aged 11 months, would look at me with a smile throughout the song and would sing on the right pitch the one high note on "go up" every time. Even though they cannot actively sing a song yet, they know the song well, along with the order of the actions, and they join in where they can.

Some general aspects for music and movement sessions with this age group

I never expect the children to sit still because babies "absorb" the music while moving. Songs that are repeated weekly should always be sung in the same key. Babies and toddlers have relative pitch up to 24 months old, and if the pitch is changed it feels like a different piece of music to them. Too many words are unnecessary, so jump straight into the play. I use a range of small handheld instruments that are safe to hold and chew and make a gentle sound, but also bigger instruments like hand drums, an ocean drum, chime bars, steel tongue drum, etc., to introduce them to different sounds and timbres from an early age. Colorful scarves are an all-time favorite, as well as big stretchy lycra material or a fluffy white sheet of garden plant fleece (hardware store, about 3 x 5 m) to gently wave above their heads while singing or playing music.

Robins (16 months to three years)

The children are more independent and sit in a circle, though the younger ones (Soili calls them, "The walkers of the world.") have still a much bigger urge to move about that I do not stop. We are singing the song described above.

The children are now able to tap their knees, tummies, heads (which is now a favorite), nose, etc. Very few children are starting to tap along in time to the beat, others match it occasionally. Their heartbeat is still faster than that of an adult, and their pulse in music is therefore faster too.

The older children like choosing different body parts or movement actions. Everyone joins in on the "up and down," as the children learn to distinguish between high, medium, and low sounds. Some children start to sing along.

Simple children's dances are now possible with the help of the kindergarten teachers, and together they sway, walk in a circle, walk towards the circle center and carefully backwards. They attempt to jump and tap and clap hands. All songs we do are accompanied with movement, whether we sit down and do movement on the spot with our upper bodies and hands, or we stand up and jump, bounce, sway, walk, stomp, tiptoe like a mouse, sneak quietly, use big giant steps, etc.

Owls (three-four years)

The children are completely independent now and have one kindergarten teacher with them for about 15 children. They like sitting on their carpet tiles around the circle. After our welcome ritual, we sing the above song.

The children choose their beat actions independently and have developed a wide variety of ideas. The play song can now be done completely child led, with my role being to accompany with the ukulele and say the name of the child who will decide next. More children can now move their body in time to the beat, and almost all of them sing the song fluently. Our song is now a colorful play that the children master without help.

Simple children's dances are possible with only two adults in the circle, and the children are starting to use their whole bodies in more imaginative ways, enjoying improvising movements to music, dancing freely as well as incorporating more complex movement qualities.

3. Hearing the Call and Growing in Dance

As a young mother entering the world of teaching, **Bethany Elsworth** started to work in the early childhood sector to become familiar with the initial stages of musical life for the child.

When parents or guardians arrive with their special little one, they commence play on a colorful obstacle course. The room is filled with ecstasy as children are guided to explore and challenge themselves in movement play around the room, stretching, balancing, going under and over, through, and extending beyond their known comfort zone. They are supported by a watchful parent and guided by the teacher in ways to attend to each aspect of the obstacle to refine or explore new ways to move. Once their bodies are awake and all have arrived, a small tambourine sounds and the room calms.

> *Bells are ringing, hear them chime. Calling all the babies/children, it's music time.*
> (sung to the tune of "Frère Jacques")

All stop and listen, eyes widen, heads turn, bodies twist towards the sound, and they make their way to the communal area, drawn by the musical cue to join in the music making. In a circle, various play and action songs occur in an effort to understand our bodies.

The following rhyme could be adapted for any aged child. The parent uses their baby's hand or tummy like a garden to lightly tap on seeds, swirl on sunshine, and sprinkle on rain until they complete the rhyme by lifting their little one off the ground. In a circle, older children draw on each other's backs and then they independently grow into a variety of unique shapes. Instruments are used to describe the motion of raking the soil, planting seeds, and the glow of sunlight. These sounds can further inspire the child to dance their garden throughout the room. Collecting the group's ideas can transform a simple children's rhyme into an artistic piece with movement and instrument play.

> *Here is my garden.*
> *I'll rake it with care,*
> *And then some seeds I plant in there.*
> *The sun will shine and the rain will fall,*
> *And then my garden grows big and tall.*
> *(Preschool rhyme, origin unknown)*

This is a time of growing awareness of self as we sing body songs, activate the body in sound, and sense the body in space. The parent or significant other supports the journey as they interact and attune to the musical movement together until the day the child is independently in musical motion.

Musical play is a time of imagery where stories and ideas carry the group through exploration of sounds, movements, instruments, and games. Imagery can invite stretching motions upward to touch the sky and greet the birds, in contrast to the gentle motion of moving between flowers on the ground. Play allows the child to explore the movements of others and bring forth their own creative dance ideas. With support from an adult, music evokes movement as babies are lifted into musical steps, infants are taken for dances on parents' laps, and older children join hands to step into the groove. Sensory opportunities are given through the use of scarves, parachutes, puppets, balls, and bubbles, calling to the child's sense of wonderment to connect to the world around them. The act of playing with music and movement supports the understanding of self within a social setting.

This Australian play center for children aged six-months to five years, where I formerly taught, focused on the connection of music and movement to support the child to develop physically, emotionally, intellectually, and socially. The parent often came to establish a stronger bond with their loved one, seek connections with others, and build confidence to offer meaningful experiences for their child. All came to support growth through musical play. The program provided a sequential offering of songs and movement games to encourage engagement appropriate to the child's development. A fundamental aim for the teacher was to adapt delivery of activities for each group and invite creative contributions from the child and parent throughout each session.

A few students left a lasting memory in my heart. A young girl with muscular dystrophy, much older in her group, determined to achieve the movement in her way and time, overcoming any obstacle with squeals of laughter. Mother and daughter beaming with every success. A father with his newly adopted two-year-old daughter from India, tied up like a pretzel and settled high on his chest, happy in her perch as she had never touched the ground. Musical stimulus coaxed her towards the ground until one day she met the earth. Then musical interplay encouraged her body to begin to uncurl in playful dance. Such experiences confirm that music arouses personalized movements in each individual.

With the signal of a known goodbye song the session would close but the play never ended. The child is empowered to continue in musical motion long after the class finishes. Experience teaching in the early childhood sector grounded my understanding that we are musical beings. Music naturally supports human development through the way we relate to it, respond to it, manipulate it, and are enlightened by it. Musical movement and dance in the early years supports connection with self, others, and the world around.

4. Children's Movement Expression Activities in Kindergarten: A focus on the collaborative work between a guest teacher, children, and teachers of the kindergarten

Fascinated by the activities of the Orff Schulwerk, **Wakako Nagaoka** has been working in the Early Childhood Education Department of a junior college to research and practice Orff Schulwerk and share the ideas with students.

Movement activities for five-year-olds at Hiyoshidai Hikari Kindergarten

I am always fascinated by the children's expression in music and movement when I visit the Hiyoshidai Hikari Kindergarten in Yokohama, where I did research during my doctoral studies. The teachers of this kindergarten have also been invited by the Orff Schulwerk Association Japan to give practical demonstrations at several seminars. Yoko Iwamoto (Director of the kindergarten) and Kunihiko Iwamoto (Deputy Director) had participated in Orff Schulwerk workshops in Germany and Austria. These experiences are incorporated into their activities at the kindergarten. Approximately six times a year the kindergarten introduces special movement activities with Aki Kawashita (a guest dance teacher). Regardless of their position or gender, the director and deputy director also participate in these activities.

"The magic mallet"

During a session in 2022, the children of the class of five-year-olds sat in their usual places in the hall. By imitating the movements of the guest teacher, they sensed their whole body and its movement possibilities. You could say they were guided through a warm-up. This also was an extension of a previous activity for the class. A variety of expressions began to emerge including the children's overwhelming desire to move with their friends, the kindergarten teachers, and the guest teacher. After a few moments she rolled a mallet onto the floor, took it into her hand again, and began to touch each child's head gently with the mallet. Then she told the children that she was going to cast a spell on the kindergarten teacher with this mallet. Mystical music began to play, and the kindergarten teacher began to improvise movements that were suggested by the waving of the mallet. The children, fascinated by this interplay, applauded loudly. The children were drawn into the magic of the mallet and began to improvise their own movements. Music and movement influenced each other. Any distinction between the child and the teacher—between the enchanter and the enchanted—disappeared. At the conclusion of the movement activity the guest teacher asked the children, "Who can say what was interesting?" Many hands were raised, and among the responses were statements like, "I felt as if I were under a spell, and I loved it." "I was amazed how magical it was." These experiences deepened the children's "physical-emotional-cognitive learning process" (Haselbach, 2003, p. 77).

Impact of the guest teacher

The principles of the activity are important for the realization of such practices. When we consider the background, the following two points emerge. The first is how the kindergarten integrates and relates this movement activity into the kindergarten life of the children. These movement activities are incorporated into the kindergarten day by taking into account the children's natural progression from one activity to the next. This daily plan is displayed on the whiteboards in the classrooms. The guest teacher advises the kindergarten teachers about the activities for the next month's event. This allows the kindergarten teachers to further support the children's movement experience by connecting them to other activities.

The second point is concerned with the training of the kindergarten teachers so they can initiate these movement activities effectively in kindergarten. The director of the kindergarten told me that she organizes teacher training on the same day, and that they all participate, regardless of their position in the workplace or gender. The deputy director of the kindergarten said, "Ms. Kawashita's workshops have greatly influenced not only my life as a kindergarten teacher, but also as a person." Opening the kindergarten to the outside and its comprehensive development creates a positive cycle for children's movement activities. In this way, the movement activities of the Orff Schulwerk offer a space where people can connect with others in expressive play, and this gives human fulfillment for all. Music and movement have an important role to play in the development of the kindergarten child.

References and Resources

Davis, W. B., Gfeller, K. E., & Thaut, M. H., (2008). *An introduction to music therapy: theory and practice* (3rd ed.). Silver Spring, MD: American Music Therapy Association, Inc.

Ensslin, C., & Widmer, M. (2012). *Bim und Bam—Musik und Tanz für Kinder: Unterrichtswerk für Eltern-Kind-Kurse* [Bim and Bam - music and dance for children: Teaching resource for parent-child courses]. Mainz: Schott.

Gilbert, A. G. (2015). *Creative dance for all ages* (2nd ed.) Reston, VA: SHAPE America.

Gruhn, W. (2003). *Kinder brauchen Musik. Musikalität bei kleinen Kindern entfalten und fördern* [Children need music. Developing and promoting musicality in young children]. Weinheim: Beltz.

Haselbach, B. (1978). *Dance education: Basic principles and models for nursery and primary school* (M. Murray, Trans.). Mainz: Schott. (Original work published in 1971 as Tanzerziehung. Grundlagen und Modelle für Kindergarten, Vor- und Grundschule, Stuttgart: Klett)

Haselbach, B. (1994). *Improvisation, dance, movement* (M. Murray, Trans.; 2nd ed.). London: Schott. (Original work published in 1976 as Improvisation, Tanz, Bewegung, Stuttgart: Klett)

Hirler, S. (2006). *Musik und Spiel für Kleinkinder. Ein Praxisbuch für die musikalische Früherziehung in Krippe, Tagespflege und Eltern-Kind-Gruppen* [Music and games for toddlers. A practical book for early musical education in nurseries, day care, and parent-child groups]. Weinheim: Beltz.

Huhtinen-Hildén, L., & Pitt, J. (2018). *Taking a learner-centred approach to music education*. Pedagogical Pathways. London: Routledge.

Huovi, H., & Perkiö, S. (2014). *Vauvan Vaaka*. Helsinki: Tammi.

Keetman, G. (1974). *Elementaria: First acquaintance with Orff-Schulwerk* (M. Murray, Trans.). London: Schott. (Original work published in 1970 as Elementaria. Erster Umgang mit dem Orff-Schulwerk, Stuttgart: Klett)

Marjanen, K. (2009). *The belly-button chord: Connections of pre- and postnatal music education with early mother-child interaction* [Doctoral dissertation, University of Jyväskylä, Finland]. https://soundhealingresearchfoundation.org/wp-content/uploads/2022/02/The_Belly_Button_Chord_Connections_of_pr.pdf

Nykrin, R., Grüner, M., & Widmer, M. (Eds.) (2007-2008). *Musik und Tanz für Kinder: Unterrichtswerk zur Früherziehung 1–2* [Music and dance for children: Teaching resource for early childhood education]. Mainz: Schott.

Salmon, S. (2008). The importance of play-songs in inclusive teaching. In S. Salmon (Ed.), *Hearing, feeling, playing: Music and movement with hard-of-hearing and deaf children* (pp. 243–262). Wiesbaden: Reichert.

Seeliger, M., & Oswald, C. (2003). *Das Musikschiff. Kinder und Eltern erleben Musik. Von der pränatalen Zeit bis ins vierte Lebensjahr* [The music ship. Children and parents experience music. From the prenatal period to the fourth year of life]. Regensburg: ConBrio.

Schumacher, K. (1994). *Musiktherapie mit autistischen Kindern* [Music therapy with autistic children]. Stuttgart: Gustav Fischer.

Widmer, M. (1997). *Alles, was klingt. Elementares Musizieren im Kindergarten* [Everything that sounds. Elemental music making in kindergarten]. Freiburg: Herder.

Young, S. (2003). *Music with the under-fours*. London: Routledge.

Moving Forward: Looking into the Primary Classroom

Michele Ellis (Australia/Netherlands), İlkay Nişanci (Turkey),
Victoria Redfearn Cave (USA), Michaela Reif-Schnaidt (Germany)

INTRODUCTION

For the purposes of our article, we define the primary level to include ages six to twelve. This time of development is characterized by the growth of the intellect and by the interest in peer relationships. With that comes practice in collaboration and connection. We feel that movement is a critical subject for these ages as it deepens opportunities for self-expression and communication. From movement inspired by music, pattern, a speech piece, a theme, or a piece of visual art, we (who are all practitioners) give a window into four different cultures and classroom contexts. In addition to providing lesson examples, the article addresses the following topics relevant to movement pedagogy in the primary classroom: how to sustain a culture of movement in the classroom; how to shape the qualities of student movement; and how to handle obstacles and opportunities for movement that might exist in a school or classroom. Ultimately, studying movement and dance has value in itself as well as being a vehicle to enhance other areas of study and life.

Reflections on the Subject

The authors answer two important questions about the classroom situation individually.

1. How do you create and sustain a culture that inspires movement in your classroom?

Michele Ellis
Classroom culture is the result of student needs and teacher aspirations. Therefore, a culture that inspires movement must involve input and responses from both the students and the teacher. Before commencing any movement activity, I observe what the children do naturally (such as walk and stop), then I use these motions to form simple structures. From this initial neutral starting point movements can be investigated and extended with the nurturing and encouraging eye of the teacher. The continual exchange of student offerings and teacher guidance helps to create an inspiring learning space.

İlkay Nişanci
The way to ensure a person's participation in movement starts with their feeling of acceptance within the classroom environment. Valuing children's ideas is the beginning for them to start learning from each other. The ability of the class to become a well-functioning organism is related to the influence of students on each other. That is how a class that resonates with its togetherness can create a culture.

Michaela Reif-Schnaidt

Movement can take place in all phases of teaching. Whether at the beginning of the day or the lesson, as motivation in the introductory phase, as explanation in an elaboration phase, as a formative element in a deepening and consolidating phase, or for visualization in the reflection phase, movement is always relevant. Thus, teaching is always in motion, and movement is impression and expression at the same time. When movement is used as a medium for learning other topics this type of movement should not be considered as "second class."

Victoria Redfearn Cave

Environment is key. Does your room have enough space? Is creative play at the center of the movement activity? Does the aesthetic of the room invite movement? Those magic moments during the beginning of the year establish the culture where you can say, "we move here." Singing and movement games can help set the tone and build vocabulary that can eventually lead to students creating their own dances. It is also helpful if the movement experience can have multiple entry points such as observing, using speech, using movement accompaniment, sketching, or performing body percussion.

2. How can we increase the quality of movement that students offer us?

Michele Ellis

The elements of dance (body, action, space, time, and energy) provide an extensive palate of exploration material to guide, shape, and stimulate student movements. An instruction such as, "move in pairs," may at first elicit the response of moving side by side. A teacher can then provide alternatives such as moving back-to-back, in reverse, using one body part, showing flowing or jagged gestures, or applying different weights and gesture sizes. The teacher may then ask if there is another way thereby giving students choice and voice in their learning. The range of movements will come from giving students agency.

Victoria Redfearn Cave

After a safe space has been established for movement and students have a familiarity with vocabulary for movement, it is up to the teacher to facilitate a culture of reflection and conversation. How can you observe a movement piece that a student creates and give feedback? You can establish norms in a classroom that make dialogue safe, give guidance on collaborative work, and empower young creators. You can suggest this by using phrases like, "what do you notice?" or "what do you wonder?" Ask the group that created the piece to self-reflect on what could be improved. The teacher is the facilitator, the keeper of the culture, and is there to help all learners.

Michaela Reif-Schnaidt

To increase a quality, the same applies to movement as to other elements. There must be something to build upon and work with. The more intensive this basis is, the better it can be played with, expanded upon, and dealt with. The more confident the students feel with their movement material, the more freely they will continue to work with it. My own method as a teacher is largely listening and commenting on the observations of the onlookers. Wherever there are spectators among the students, they are the ones who can highlight particularly successful aspects and thus focus on them.

İlkay Nişanci

Pointing out examples of movement quality to the class is important in the process of learning from each other and in terms of the quality affecting the whole class. I have experienced that the image of an object the children have in their minds while presenting movement will also affect the quality and dynamic of their movement (e.g., hugging the trunk of a tree). In this sense, I think that the transfer of the image to the body affects the natural movement quality.

PRACTICAL EXAMPLES

Overview

1. **İlkay Nişanci: Greeting dance and song, ages six to eight years**
   Variations of everyday movements of greetings including improvised variations and body percussion lead to the development of a movement form combined with a song. This example is especially helpful for beginners and new teachers.
2. **Michaela Reif-Schnaidt: *The Sorcerer's Apprentice*, ages nine to eleven years**
   In a teaching sequence over several weeks, students create movement scenes and accompaniment starting with *The Sorcerer's Apprentice* (ballade by Johann Wolfgang von Goethe and musical work by Paul Dukas).
3. **Victoria Redfearn Cave: Dancing with Charley Harper, ages nine and ten years**
   Visual art from American artist Charley Harper is used as inspiration for choreographies and compositions by the students, aiming to facilitate artistic conversation and to provide safe spaces for creation.
4. **Michele Ellis: Pattern perception, ages ten and eleven years**
   This teaching sequence demonstrates interdisciplinary learning and teaching using patterns that are explored, developed, and demonstrated through the subject areas of mathematics, art, and movement.

1. Greeting Dance and Song
İlkay Nişanci

Group
Six- to eight-year-olds who are reluctant to move their bodies in a class setting.

Idea
This sequence of classes is an exploration of hands and body sounds in connection with movement using the theme of greetings.

Objectives
Students will develop:

- imitation and improvisation skills using the body,
- body and spatial awareness, and
- ensemble movement.

Warmup
Standing in a circle, students copy movements of the teacher: patting, rubbing, and stroking the body all over including arms, hands, tummy, feet, legs, and head to awaken the body. This is followed by touching and drumming softly on the neighbor's back, changing intensity, levels, speed, and flowing actions. Finally, they move together into the center of the circle and out

again to prepare the song. Repeat this a few times varying the speed or actions and return to neutral with your breath and posture.

Exploration

Teacher says, "Observe your neighbors, say hello, and introduce yourself. Then create a special greeting with your hands and body (not shaking hands - find another way)." Teacher shows ideas for movements with the hands. The students greet several people, these friends can be in many places throughout the space.

Teacher walks to the center of the circle and the children follow, stand close to each other in a circle in the middle, and wave. Walking backwards, the circle expands again. Now all the children wave to a friend from a distance. Repeat using different body gestures instead of waving.

Teacher says, "All day we use our hands; just now we have used them to pat and stroke our own bodies, and we have used them to say 'hello.' Now can you make some sounds with your hands?" Teacher repeats ideas from students for everyone to try, then says, "Now find some sounds your hands can make on your body." Repeat the sharing.

Teacher says, "Follow me, shak, shak, shak," while clapping; students imitate. Repeat with "pat, pat, pat" on the knees.

Teacher sings the song "Hands," and the children simultaneously do the teacher's actions following the lyrics (measures 1–8).

Hands

Michele Ellis
İlkay Nişanci

Elaboration

Teacher gives ideas for new sounds for "shak" and "pat" using ideas from the exploration. During the repetition of the song the children invent their own actions for "shak" and "pat."

Variation: Add locomotion in measures 5-8, using the directions of the lyrics. Students can choose their own pathways but must finish by returning to their own spot at the end.

Improvisation: In measures 9-12, children invent their own body percussion that occurs in the space between the singing.

Demonstration

Students and teacher choose a final form together. Choices could be movement alone, gestures for waving and greeting, moving in and out, other locomotor movements, body percussion alone or with a friend. Choices could also include the song with set motions, or improvised sections of movement, or adding small percussion instruments to accompany the song or movements.

Reflection

The class performs with the teacher's support (accompaniment or beat support). Children are invited to reflect on the following: What did you notice? What did you like? If you had to do it again, would you change something? etc.

2. *The Sorcerer's Apprentice*
Michaela Reif-Schnaidt

Group

24 students (nine to eleven years old) who have various previous experiences with music and movement. The cross-curricular teaching idea combines poetry, music, and movement in a teaching sequence over several sessions.

Objectives

Based on the ballad *The Sorcerer's Apprentice* by Johann Wolfgang von Goethe (1797) and continuing with the musical composition of the same name by Paul Dukas (1897), the students are to
- explore the content in a playful way and present it in movement,
- find an accompaniment to the dance with their own elemental instruments,
- rediscover the content in Dukas' composition; adapt their movements to its musical expression; experience the connection between the arts, and
- develop a differentiated perception of movement qualities and creative skills in dance.

Teaching sequence

This lesson occurs in several phases with different numbers of sessions. Each phase covers the elements of motivation, exploration, reflection, elaboration, and demonstration.

1st phase: Introduction of the ballad and first attempts at its representation through movement
- Presentation of Goethe's ballad by the teacher; the children express their impressions.
- Division of the class into reciting and movement groups with distribution of roles (sorcerer's apprentice, water, broom).
- Movement and free dance are based on the content, rhythm, and melody of speech of the ballad that is recited simultaneously by the speakers (still including the teacher).

- Everyone with the same role acts at the same time; simultaneous action motivates and gives security.
- Division into groups of six with three speakers and three movers.
  - ○ The roles (sorcerer's apprentice, water, broom) are presented individually, even less experienced children try their own solutions.
  - ○ Differentiating movement qualities, gestures, and facial expressions. Acting and reacting are partly still improvisational, according to the known content.
  - ○ Spoken text recedes into the background until it is completely dispensed with (during the next phase speakers become musicians); recognizing each other's movement impulses is enough to develop the dance.
  - ○ The phase ends with presentations of the groups.

2nd phase: Movement accompaniment—choreography
- Staying in the same groups: Speakers become musicians.
- The dance becomes accompanied with different instruments. Assignment of instruments to roles/emergence of leitmotifs.
- Choreography leads to own compositions (which are notated verbally or graphically).

3rd phase: Movement improvisation to Paul Dukas' composition
- This is an activity with the whole class.
- First listening to *The Sorcerer's Apprentice* by Paul Dukas without knowing the title, the assignment is to move to it in a free-associative way.
- Recognition of the content as similar to the ballad and the roles; understanding musical leitmotifs.
- More precise adaptation of the movements to the work.
- Choreography is created. Up to this point, all students may make suggestions.
- Distribution of roles. Everybody moves to the music. Not all students are happy with the situation.
- While the others continue to work on the choreography, the "unhappy" ones can improvise their own music for the thematic idea of the ballad and notate it graphically.

4th phase: Rehearsal and performance
The students perform their work. The decisions needed to determine who participates in which role are also an important factor of social learning. The results of all phases are brought together and rehearsed for the presentation, including the reciting of the ballad, which is performed in front of parents, teachers, and students from other classes.

English and German resources for *Der Zauberlehrling/The Sorcerer's Apprentice*

Oxford International Song Festival. (n.d.). *Der Zauberlehrling*. Retrieved November 20, 2022, from https://www.oxfordlieder.co.uk/song/4163

Wikipedia. (n.d.) *The Sorcerer's Apprentice*. Retrieved November 20, 2022, from https://en.wikipedia.org/wiki/The_Sorcerer%27s_Apprentice

Gesprochene Deutsche Lyrik. (n.d.). *Der Zauberlehrling* [audio recording]. Retrieved November 20, 2022, from https://www.deutschelyrik.de/der-zauberlehrling.673.html

3. Dancing with Charley Harper
Victoria Redfearn Cave

Group
Students are ages nine and ten, many of them have not had creative experiences in a music and movement classroom and are hesitant to participate. However, some students who have been in the school for several years have had practice creating movement and its vocabulary.

Aim
The overall goal of the lesson sequence is:

- to inspire students to move and create using many entry points, and
- to facilitate students learning new techniques that assist them in creating their own music and dances.

Note: In preparation for this project, students have been playing movement and singing games. In addition to community building and connection, the purpose of these games is to help build basic technical skills for the creative project.

Inspiration
Using the artwork of American artist Charley Harper, students begin to explore connections between movement and visual art. Charley Harper was an artist who developed a style that focused on the use of lines and curves to illustrate scenes in nature. His whimsical titles and overall composition, his unique perspective of mirroring images or drawing a part of nature from a different perspective inspires movement possibilities. This particular teaching sequence is inspired by one theme, and it takes place over several weeks.

Phase one: Inspiration and exploration
The teacher introduces the artist through examples of his work along with a video of an interview with him (Designtex, 2014). Then students will participate in a group movement exploration using the painting *Serengeti Spaghetti* (Caras, 1994, p. 64), showing shapes and lines intertwined. They explore the words "tangle" and "untangle" for the warmup. If there is time, they could choose a different painting and brainstorm what movement words they would like to try based on the image.

Phase two: Creation
- Students choose one painting from a curated selection of Charley Harper's work.
- They begin to move using action words. After moving, the teacher might begin asking questions, for example: Where in space will they move? How fast or how slow? What is the quality of movement that they feel best represents the painting?
- As students begin to answer these questions, they will start to create a form, a beginning, middle, and end that they can repeat.

Phase three: Elaboration and reflection
- After reviewing their choreography, they discuss what they notice and what they wonder, asking such questions as: Do the art and movement have to match? Why did we make that choice?
- Some students will choose to add music that might be improvised at first. They usually enjoy making choices about timbre, mode, drone type, ostinati, other color instruments, and whether or not a melody is improvised or set.

- The teacher is simply a facilitator, but can ask questions such as: Does the piece challenge you as a mover? Do the movements feel comfortable and are you excited to share it? What would happen if you performed the dance changing your tempo, your space, your weight, or your energy?
- The teacher also watches for collaborative work and helps to set up classroom norms for interacting, perhaps giving examples and modeling a safe environment for students working creatively.

Phase four: Demonstration and reflection

- The students present their choreographies and accompaniment to each other or to a larger audience (parents and others). One student introduces the piece and shares a part of the artistic process or perhaps an artistic statement with the audience.
- Afterwards, the audience can express their impressions and observations. The performers could reflect on what they would do to continue or deepen their piece if they had more time. The teacher offers the performers a protected space but also invites them to talk.

Children getting ready to try some movements about flocking

Children discussing "Last Aphid"

Photos: Victoria Redfearn Cave

4. Pattern Perception
Michele Ellis

This lesson sequence is an example of interdisciplinary learning and teaching to reinforce student understandings about pattern. The students' abilities to perceive and manipulate patterns is explored, developed, and demonstrated through differing subject areas including mathematics, art, and movement.

Context

A primary class, ages ten and eleven, in an international school. English is the language of instruction, fluency ranges from beginner to native speaker. The school uses an inquiry approach that fosters learning through exploration, problem solving, and experiential learning of a topic or concept across all curriculum areas. This allows for interdisciplinary experiences.

The focus of this teaching sequence is to support mathematical understanding of pattern recognition through movement, music, and art, which serves as a precursor to algebra. Patterns feature in most subject areas such as writing and rhyming structures in literacy and repetition and variation found in art forms.

Aims

- Experience an abstract pattern through the body.
- Assist students to interpret, explore, create, and manipulate a pattern.

Inspiration

A mathematics task. Draw the mirror image of the following:

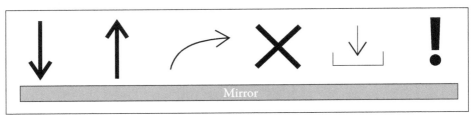

How will students interpret this task? How can their thinking process be made known and communicated?

Motivation

Seated in the circle with the students, the teacher begins to chant **Up** * **Down** * **Right** * **Pass** * (* = rest) repeatedly and students join. Once fluent, the students continue, the teacher adds the following body percussion (BP) accompaniment.

Students add gestures by exploring ways to show the text. Teacher suggests body parts (e.g., eyebrow, knee, shoulder) and space (e.g., diagonal, behind, levels). The exploration begins in a circle and as confidence grows the students stand and move around.

Experimentation

Each student devises a four-movement sequence and finds a natural flow of their gestures. The word "pass" requires a clear gesture so it will show which student is to perform the next sequence.

Game: Reinstate the beat/BP and repeat the chant with all students. One student performs their pattern passing the role of performer to another student. The challenge is to not skip a beat and maintain the chant pattern.

Reflection

What did you see? What did you enjoy? What worked well? What would you change? How can we change the game? Try the suggestions of the class with further reflection and refinement.

Elaboration

In groups of three, combine individual ideas to form a new four-movement sequence. Perform the new pattern three times followed by eight beats rest. Rehearse with teacher accompaniment. During the eight-beat break the teacher models a "fill" with BP/voice. Each group performs in turn. All improvise during the break.

New task: Show the opposite (mirror in space, inversion, retrograde, etc.) of your group's pattern.

Demonstration

New structure: three times the original group pattern, one time the "opposite" pattern. Rehearse and refine. Each group performs with the accompaniment (the fill/break accompanies the opposite pattern) and the other students analyze. How did the group interpret opposite? How did the groups differ?

Perform in a rondo with the spoken chant and body percussion being section A and the group performances between.

There are many elements that can be combined for a longer class choreography, for example:

- the chant
- the body percussion and fill or break
- individual patterns
- group patterns in original form and the opposite form
- passing or the pass gesture
- eight beats of silence or eight beats of improvisation

Students discuss the combination of these elements to create a piece that has a beginning, a middle/complication/climax, and an end or resolution, i.e., a typical narrative writing structure. Accompany with BP, instruments, or recorded music.

Reflection II and feedback from peers and teacher

How were the choreographies structured and performed? In what way were they different? Where else do you find patterns?

Further experiences

This sequence was woven through several curriculum areas including personal identity and art. The students found three symbols that represented them (or their culture) and crafted homemade stamps from cardboard that they used to create three small art works:

1. a pattern with the symbols,
2. the reverse of #1, and
3. a random formation of their symbols.

These works then became scores for choreography. The students devised movements to represent the three symbols and created a short choreography following the cardboard print images as their score.

Opportunities and Obstacles for Movement and Dance in the Elementary Classroom

This section takes an honest look into the opportunities for and obstacles to movement in the primary classroom. From culture setting at home and in the school, to peer influence and space concerns, this section gives a window into daily challenges and potential moments of light that can create positive movement experiences for students. Not only is the Orff Schulwerk teacher a facilitator in the classroom, but they are also a culture setter for the school. The teacher often takes on the role of translator for the parent and school community, offering windows into the classroom and showing with joy the benefits of movement and arts education. Of course, the best ambassadors for the program are the children, with their enthusiasm and passion for creating. In order for the teacher to be in the magical role of facilitator and culture setter for creative expression, they need a network of support. Ultimately, Orff Schulwerk can provide a global community working together to overcome obstacles to movement in the primary classroom, always asking more questions and exploring solutions.

Teacher confidence/training and physical space
Victoria Redfearn Cave

One potential obstacle for movement in the primary classroom can be teacher confidence. What if an educator comes to the music and movement classroom as a musician first? Their training has been focused on a particular instrument and in pedagogy, but they have not personally experienced movement education, nor do they identify as movers themselves. The first thing to consider is how your classroom can benefit from movement. Children thrive in arts environments where movement occurs. Behavior management becomes easier as children at ages six to twelve do not function well if static and still for long periods of time. Movement can also become another tool for self-expression and communication that is quite natural to a child, providing yet another way to differentiate for all learners in your classroom. The options for creativity, a critical skill in the modern classroom, open up when movement becomes a choice on the arts palette.

Once a need is established for movement, the teacher can seek out training, and give themselves permission to try something new for the sake of their students. Finding a supportive environment that can give positive beginning experiences to the educator as a mover is critical. Perhaps there are workshops, or even online professional development opportunities for those new to movement education. Adding movement to everyday life can be joyful and exciting. Perhaps your local town has opportunities for a beginning movement or dance class, yoga, or other movement forms. Seeking out Orff Schulwerk organizations in your home country that provide movement ideas for the classroom and supportive peers is essential to starting on this journey. Often, teachers who are building their confidence will try first steps like giving their room a movement make-over. Removing desks and other furniture, adjusting the lighting, wearing comfortable clothing that allows you to move during class, and inviting students to move are just some entry points. Whether the teacher is trying a folk dance, facilitating a body percussion pattern, or attempting a creative movement warmup, the students are typically wonderful collaborators, and they will respond positively to the teacher who is clearly trying to meet their needs and establish a culture that respects their interests as children. Try telling your students that you are attempting something new and that you need their help. Watch the magic of those primary students as they become your teachers and the classroom begins to transform with the partnership that is the hallmark of the Schulwerk experience.

Connecting movement and dance to core subjects
Michaela Reif-Schnaidt

Schools, as well as teachers and parents, often give the impression that education takes place primarily in the core subjects of mother tongue, mathematics, and science. This is also confirmed by the fact that these three subjects are decisive for transfer to secondary school. Thus, not only is the number of hours in these subjects significantly higher than in music and movement/sports, but also the merit of these subjects in the eyes of the students is different due to the importance of grades and performance measurement in the core subjects. It is therefore an important and understandable approach that teachers take the opportunity to connect these core subjects to music and movement in their lessons. In doing so, they can at least introduce students to the importance of music and movement in all facets and subjects and at different stages of learning and experience. Two of our lesson examples demonstrate such possibilities.

Time and technology
Michele Ellis

Time in teaching is scarce and facing an already crowded curriculum as well as the other non-teaching duties can be a deterrent for teachers to introduce movement into the classroom. Finding time to learn about, facilitate, and evaluate movement is daunting, however the benefits may enhance learning overall and assist the engagement of learners. Incorporating movement into learning or providing movement breaks can assist the learner by integrating learning across the two brain hemispheres, assisting the memory, strengthening focus, and avoiding overload of both information and emotions. Personally, I have found movement to be a neutral place in which to engage all learners immediately, providing that the students experience choice, fun, and purpose with the activities. Movement is an avenue to assess understanding, competency, and confidence without having to use traditional assessment methods.

Technology has provided students with unprecedented access to information. In a survey by the UK website Education Quizzes (https://www.educationquizzes.com/surveys/school-children-screen-time), 33% of school aged children revealed they spent more than four hours per day, at home, looking at a screen. Excessive screen time may have negative effects on sleep patterns, behavior, weight management, academic performance, and leave less time for free and creative play. The same medium has given rise to a social interest in movement. Dance styles that have gone viral include the Jerusalema, Shuffle, and Wellerman dances. These dance crazes have been recreated in schools, rural areas, prisons, workplaces, and with online communities especially during the Covid pandemic. Tik Tok is an influential platform where individuals create and present choreography, and intern, the response is the recreation of those moves from global followers including primary aged children. Further to this, there are infinite hours of movement tutorials and performances from both amateurs to professionals. In his frequently repeated quote, Bill Gates says "Technology is just a tool. In terms of getting the kids working together and motivating them, the teacher is the most important." Using technology to bring student interests into the classroom and connecting it to their learning can forge positive connections, enhance the classroom culture, and provide an avenue for creative self-expression. Further to this, technology allows students to present their work beyond the classroom by utilizing the ever-growing programs and platforms that allow them to film, record, edit, and share their work.

Social and cultural differences
İlkay Nişanci

Orff Schulwerk pedagogy brings educators and students together in a circle in the classroom. The circle has magical ingenuity. It gathers all the energies in the middle. It brings our eyes together. Initiates connections. It leads to learning from each other. It brings equality. Thus, the hierarchy is removed.

As teachers, we work in classes where student groups from different ethnic origins, religions, and socio-economic identities come together. In classes where these differences are evident, students from time to time have difficulty expressing themselves, they are hesitant to show their opinions, and they worry. This situation creates difficulties and obstacles for the environment that we, the teachers, try to establish in our movement lessons. Here, the solution must be sought at the origin of the problem.

Orff Schulwerk pedagogy focuses on the human being and naturally on differences. We carry the dynamics that make up our differences to our social environment. These differences may appear in the form of students comparing and competing. Here, an emotional and therefore a worrisome obstacle arises in a person's ability to reveal their own nature, their freedom of expression. The basis of this is the concern about whether the person will be accepted in the environment because of their differences.

Every artistic movement idea is a sprout waiting to be born from within the human being. This sprout cannot wait to emerge from the soil above it. It wants to emerge, meet the light, and create itself over the ground. It also needs a suitable environment for this meeting.

Humans need an environment in which they are accepted in order to be artistically free, to be able to express themselves, and to present their opinions. We are the educators for schools and classes that provide this environment. As the guide and companion of the class, we can highlight the student's idea so that the student can become self-accepted. We can ask the student who decides to express themself or move in any way, to show their idea to their friends in the class. We can ask the whole class to repeat the same movement. The child whose idea is repeated will know that their opinion is valued for the next time and will try again. On the other hand, the student repeating the idea will also think, "if they can do it, so can I."

What does having differences in the classroom actually offer us? It is basically at the center of our quest as teachers. All people who are accepted into their environments and think their ideas are valued feed on the same basic feeling: confidence. Thus, this feeling creates a new environment and beginning for students and the classroom. I'm thinking of doing, I do, I did, I can.

To End
Victoria Redfearn Cave

What ultimately leads to empowerment for both educator and student? What encourages a teacher to become a lifelong ambassador for culture-setting in their communities? We think that the answer lies somewhere in the support of the teacher network of Orff Schulwerk. In writing this article together, the authors were able to come together virtually and connect. Even though our native languages are different, our home countries and schools are worlds apart, we found laughter, shared vision, camaraderie, and support. Those fruitful conversations and connections inspired us to continue our work in our classrooms, knowing that we are not alone in our quest. Are you looking for a good first step in your journey? We recommend finding a network of fellow Orff Schulwerk educators, have a conversation, and get inspired. It can lead to a lifetime of happiness for you and your students.

References and Resources

Caras, R. (1994). *Beguiled by the wild. The art of Charley Harper.* Gaithersburg, MD: Flower Valley Press.

Green Gilbert, A. (2015). *Creative dance for all ages.* Reston, VA: SHAPE America.

Haselbach, B. (1994). *Improvisation, dance, movement* (M. Murray, Trans.; 2nd ed.). London: Schott. (Original work published in 1976 as Improvisation, Tanz, Bewegung, Stuttgart: Klett)

Joyce, M. (1993). *First steps in teaching creative dance.* New York, NY: McGraw-Hill Education.

López-Ibor, S. (2011). *Blue is the sea: Music, dance, and visual arts.* San Francisco: Pentatonic Press.

Mettler, B. (1975). *Group dance improvisations.* Tucson, AZ: Mettler Studios.

Eibl, K. (Ed.). (1992). *Johann Wolfgang von Goethe, Friedrich Schiller: Sämtliche Balladen und Romanzen in zeitlicher Folge* [Johann Wolfgang von Goethe, Friedrich Schiller: Complete ballads and romances in chronological order]. Berlin: Insel.

Designtex. (2014, January 29). *Designtex stories: At home with Charley Harper* [Video]. https://vimeo.com/85360946

Movement and Dance with Teenagers in Schools and Recreational Settings

Peta Harper (Australia), Judith Thompson-Barthwell (USA),
Doris Valtiner-Pühringer (Austria), Michel Widmer (Austria)

INTRODUCTION

Dance classes with adolescents present a multi-layered challenge because of the contrast between their enthusiasm for dance and their refusal to dance due to insecurities they experience during adolescent development. This does not necessarily refer to dancing itself, but rather to dancing in community with or in front of others. Dance work with boys and girls together may be problematic due to religious or cultural backgrounds and conditioning. Nevertheless, most young people have a strong need to move, to express themselves, and to create.

If movement and dance classes are offered at all in schools with this age group, they usually focus either on folk dances or on current forms from the pop scene. In this article, however, the emphasis is on creative processes developed through movement and dance in a group.

For the teacher this is a great pedagogical challenge because the young individual with his or her abilities and skills, as well as hesitation and shyness, must be at the center of interest, and our teaching is to a large extent about personality development. Our goal here is to offer as many creative and communication-enhancing topics and experiences as possible.

The Influence of Culture

Culture affects how students move and behave. Typical movement patterns related to gender, family, ethnicity, social class, and religion affect their behaviors. In many countries city schools have greater diversity than rural schools. This diversity in cities provides a rich palette of movement repertoire. For example, in Australia students from such communities as Indigenous, Asian, European, Middle Eastern, African, and Pacific Island, where cultural identity is strong and practiced, will often have experience with dance and movement from their culture that can be shared. Yet, the teaching of an Indigenous dance is frequently not allowed unless by permission or in the presence of a culture bearer. Therefore, creative movement experiences not tied directly to specific cultural/ethnic dances can work well.

Dance may not be allowed to be taught or realized in schools in some Islamic cultures, while movement might be possible for these same students when it is considered a health-supporting activity. In addition, the culture of a school environment and the curriculum may dictate what can and cannot be taught.

Students may respond differently depending on the ratio of girls to boys or majority to minority cultures in the classroom. It can sometimes be difficult to ask boys and girls to dance together. This may be partly due to different interests in certain topics, or due to different movement behavior caused by their earlier or later entry into adolescence. Therefore, they should always have the choice to work together in a mixed group or separately in a gender specific group. Sometimes it may be necessary to separate boys and girls for religious or other traditional reasons. There may also be a small number of students who attend certain types of classes outside of school where boys and girls are dancing together, e.g., classical ballet, jazz, tap, and modern dance and perhaps some who study cultural/folk dance.

With students who have dance possibilities in more homogeneous cultures, creative experiences often work well by starting with something familiar from their culture. Students can relate to any aspect of music or dance such as rhythm, song, harmonic structure, or dance moves that can be followed later by expanded learning to other concepts. For example, African Americans often feel safer starting creative expression with syncopated rhythms from their culture.

Some cultural backgrounds can be opposites. There are cultures where supporting the members of the group is more important than individual acknowledgement, and there are cultures where learning through listening, speaking, and moving is emphasized more than reading and writing. Some cultures encourage creativity while others stress following instructions. For cultures that reward learning by listening, writing, and replicating information, engaging in discussion can be very confrontational. Improvisation with the voice, body, and instruments may be confusing for them, while other students may have been encouraged to think critically, challenge ideas, and speak up in discussion. The teacher's challenge is to lead the students to a common place, encouraging them to take risks and engage in active learning.

Creating Dance Projects for Teenagers

Different cultural behaviors of teenagers are shown in sound and vision through cinema, television, and social media. Today, youth are very engaged in media experiences. However, these are not real experiences, but rather second-hand impressions given through the media. This is where lively, action-oriented music and dance lessons that are tailored to individual needs and the possibilities of the group can offer real first-hand experience. Here, self-knowledge and self-efficacy can be experienced as the teacher encourages risk taking through active and creative learning.

Consider the following when designing movement/dance lessons for teenagers.

Goals:

- Strive for clearly identifiable and realistic goals for the group.
- Design lessons so that progress is recognizable.
- Create opportunities for independent action and make creation an essential part of the music and dance work.

Behavior:

- Think through rules for behavior and fairness.
- Make group work inclusive of all group members.
- Use relaxation exercises as necessary.
- Allow for humorous characteristics.

Materials:

- Include tasks to develop body awareness.
- Incorporate coordination exercises.
- Include physically challenging movements and ideas.

- Integrate group preferred recognizable movements and forms.
- Apply rhythmic elements.
- Dance with objects if appropriate.
- Make sure the material is stimulating.

Themes:

- Choose topics of interest that can be developed.
- Give stimulating models and tasks.
- Allow students to develop their own ideas and look for their own solutions.
- Use action-oriented music and dance lessons.
- Tailor lessons to individual needs and to the possibilities of the group.
- Create opportunities for self-knowledge discovery and where self-efficacy can be experienced.
- Encourage students to take risks and engage in active, creative learning.
- Include opportunities related to music-movement elements.

Often it comes to a selection of topics from their lives. This could be: What happens at school break? What happens in public traffic on the way to school? What happens when you pass from boredom to excitement? The use of familiar topics gives security but also generates curiosity.

Below is a short list of suggested themes with titles and brief descriptions. These impulses for dance and movement can also be used for creating live music.

Theme 1–Maps (direction)
Using a map as a stimulus, participants move in different directions around the room. Once comfortable with the space, explore various ways of moving along these pathways e.g., fast/slow, large/small steps, crawling/sliding/rolling/jumping. Train maps can be used to encourage ways of moving through space and interconnecting with class members at a "station." Stations also give a moment for stillness.

Theme 2–Magnets
Participants move in their space as magnets; they can either attract each other or repel. Try choosing one body part that is attracted to someone/somewhere else, and another body part that repels. Explore acceleration, tension, stillness.

Theme 3–Kitchen (space, levels, locomotion)
The proposition for the students is this given scene: You are in a kitchen cooking for someone very special (could be your boss, best friend, someone you fell in love with, etc.); as you are in a hurry you always need to look at the clock, which is in another room.

Theme 4–Architecture
What famous buildings do you know? How can you organize yourselves in the group to show a building and its specific aesthetic with your bodies? Further tasks could be trying different ways of getting into position (slow, fast, all at the same time, one after another, approach in circular movements).

Theme 5–Elements

Fire, earth, wind, and water have different qualities, energy, and characters that can motivate movement/dance. For instance, explore different types of fire, from small flickering flames to a big, outreaching fire that finally diminishes.

Dance in Schools and Recreational Settings

Working with dance and movement can be carried out in schools as well as in recreational settings. Our project reports in the practical examples described below were all carried out in schools. However, the rich repertoire of ideas and didactic processes can also be used in other settings enjoyed by teenagers. Outside of the school day, group work with dance and movement may occur in such places as youth clubs, after-school programs, theater groups, and art schools. In these settings the work does not have curricular pressures and tight time frames that one finds in schools and therefore allows for more autonomy, self-determination, and participation by the young dancers.

When working with dance, it is important in all settings that dance can be understood on the one hand as a technique, as a specific style of movement, and a social tradition, and on the other hand as a creative medium that promotes the individual and social potential of young people. This work is often project-oriented, and the pedagogical staff meets the target group at eye level, and, depending on the group's level of experience, it primarily has an inspiring, advising, and moderating function. The goal of a performance at the end of a project could be very motivating for the participants.

PRACTICAL EXAMPLES

Overview

Following are four examples of creative dance projects designed for secondary school students. Each example comes from a distinct part of the world, from different school situations, and shows a varied approach to movement/dance.

1. **Judith Thompson-Barthwell: Creativity within cultural dance, ages 11–13**
   This lesson explores popular dances of students and their families. Students are asked, "Who influenced the music and dance of the artists you like?" and challenged to find favorite dances and music from their grandparents' and parents' youth.

2. **Michel Widmer: Working out a song in dance and music, ages 11–13**
   This teaching sequence takes a multidisciplinary approach to encourage instrument playing, singing, and dancing, starting from a song. Special attention is given to the development of creative dance.

3. **Peta Harper: The idea of motif—an interdisciplinary experience, ages 15 and 16**
   This series of lessons uses a multidisciplinary approach to explore the idea of motif. Visual art is used as a stimulus from which students create a motif. This is explored and developed into longer phrases and structures using music, movement, and dance.

4. **Doris Valtiner-Pühringer: Mary Wigman's Witch Dance (1926), age 15**
   Using Mary Wigman's famous Witch Dance (Hexentanz) as an example, the period of German expressive dance and its dance style are introduced, and students are encouraged to try their own creations (including live music).

1. Creativity Within Cultural Dance
Judith Thompson-Barthwell

Group
Middle School students ages eleven to thirteen from Romulus Middle School in Michigan, USA, chose to join this general music class for one semester in the fall or the spring. This class evolved into more general music, dance, and drama experiences depending on the group and their interests. The class maintained a former choral focus to perform at festivals during a large portion of the semester and met every day for 40 minutes during a semester.

During this unit of study, the majority of students were African American. There were twice as many girls as boys. They came to class with many popular sounds and dances in their personal repertoire. Some African American students came from religious backgrounds where Black gospel music was played in their homes. Others enjoyed the pop music of rap and hip-hop. Still other Caucasian families listened to country music, White gospel, and cross-over pop music. Over the years, this school district has turned from primarily inhabitants of Caucasian descent to more than 60% people of color, mostly African American.

Goals
- To explore some roots of American culture through music and dance.
- To recognize and appreciate the creativity of the African American culture in dance and music.

Motivation
I asked questions like, "Where did the music you listen to come from?" or "From whom did these artists learn?" along with questions about the music their grandparents listened to, and I challenged them to interview their grandparents and parents.

Exploration
The students:
- explored locomotor and non-locomotor movements to drum rhythms with vocabulary.
- shared popular dances and moves while I used vocabulary to describe their movements.
- labeled some moves using their own vocabulary.
- listened to music of their grandparents and shared what was said about what grandparents did as teenagers and young adults.
- learned steps and handholds of swing dance.
- performed different moves with gestures, drama, and breakaway movements that depart from the basic form to allow for individual movements.
- listened to the music of their parents and shared the dances their parents taught them.
- labeled the steps and noted how some of the same steps were included in swing dance but the configurations were different, i.e., partner versus individual or group formations.

Reflection
The students:
- looked again at movements that were popular to them. They discovered that their popular dances did not travel in space as much yet involved a larger amount of body isolation movements.
- were surprised that their grandparents may have enjoyed dancing like they do.
- recognized that the break-away steps resulted in many ways to be creative.

- enjoyed composing break-away moves in pairs.
- talked about how dances spread and became popular.
- recounted how they learned their popular dances realizing all dancers and musicians listen and watch and learn from those whom they like.
- generalized that in the African American culture once something is learned it is normal to add one's own ideas.
- questioned if other cultures also add one's ideas to what is learned.
- decided to create a presentation piece.

Elaboration
The Charleston was taught, which gave more ideas for breakaway steps. Students arrived at sequences of dances to show dance through the ages. They decided which dances would use live music and which would use recorded sounds.

Demonstration and reflection
The final product was shared with parents. Students later discussed how rhythms (beats) go together with the dances and how those new styles came from older ones. They also noted that creativity in music and dance could be large or small and either was fine.

2. Working Out a Song in Dance and Music
Michel Widmer

Group
This sixth-grade class of an integrative Montessori middle school in Salzburg, Austria, has about 24 students (11 to 13 years old), including four persons with disabilities. The focus of the Montessori school is on the individual support of children with and without disabilities. As a guest teacher I gave a weekly music and movement lesson over the year as a supplement to the general music classes.

Specific aims
- Introduce students to the relationship between music, movement, and speech.
- Enable them to use body percussion, percussion, and mallet instruments as well as various movement and dance activities.
- Support them to create songs, accompaniments, and dance forms themselves.

The process
Sometimes a particular topic is dealt with over several weeks. It includes motivating warmups, working on technique, exploring creative tasks (alone, in pairs, or in small groups), and finally demonstrating the results and reflecting on the process.

Building up motivation
Students are often shy when it comes to dancing. This is usually more evident in boys than in girls. Many young people are intensely involved with dances from music videos. The movement vocabulary learned mostly through imitation can also be used for creative tasks.

Through simple movement tasks we try to intensify their joy in dancing by:
- walking/running/hopping around to drum rhythms, alone or following a leader.
- making sudden stops and changes of direction.
- changing between slow motion, normal tempo, and double tempo.

- making sudden accents or repeated motifs in the accompaniment to give ideas for improvisation in the movement.
- using improvised body percussion while moving in space.

Previously, during their weekly meeting the students suggested songs that I had to evaluate to determine how well these songs could be covered with the existing musical tools and to rate the text content (no violence and no sex). This was then shared with the class. Departing from this usual routine, in the example described here we started differently and decided on a simple chord structure chosen from examples suggested by the teacher, used the friendship idea of one of the songs, wrote our own lyrics, and created our own musical arrangements.

Exploration
Over a period of three sessions, a new text was written:

Freunde gibt es nicht wie Sand am Meer,	Friends do not exist like sand on the beach,
für dich geben sie ihr letztes Hemd her.	But for you they are always to reach.
Wenn's bei dir brennt, sind sie die Feuerwehr,	When you're on fire they are the fire brigade,
Nie wieder allein und keine Angst mehr.	You're not alone, don't be afraid.

The music was worked out (body percussion, mallets, Boomwhackers, and voice), and everyone played all types of instruments in turn. Dance ideas were tried out by all teenagers in pairs or small groups, starting with walking at different tempi combined with the task to "freeze" (stop) for a few seconds or four beats. The freeze should represent a moment of friendship. This also left them time to observe the positions of other students. The various solutions were then looked at for their meaningfulness. The task was repeated to find new positions or to improve the previous ones. Finally, the students worked in pairs, learning shapes from each other, and combining them with their own locomotor movements in order to create a short dance sequence showing their meaning of friendship through dance. The pairs were then asked to present their results, and these were accompanied by the teacher on the *cajón*. In this way, everyone could try out and show their own ideas and gain some new dance experience.

Reflection
In the next lesson, we discussed the process of the theme so far. I suggested some questions to reflect on, e.g., What did you really enjoy? Was there anything you didn't dare to do, but might want to give it a try later? What did you like from the other students' input?

Elaboration
In the following two lessons the work was deepened in small groups (band, choir, dance). The dancers went back to the classroom. Band and choir worked in the music room. The music teacher and I went around to give tips, to resolve conflicts and play with the band. The dance group showed new ideas and I helped to shape them. Finally, we put everything together: dance, music, and song. For the dance we invented an extra instrumental accompaniment. Final form: Prelude/song (with band accompaniment) - dance (instrumental accompaniment) - song (band accompaniment)—final dance with ending.

Demonstration and reflection
At the end all were invited to share comments about the common work. The young people were unanimous in their opinion that the social climate and the ability to make open contact with classmates had grown. We decided to give a presentation for other classes. There was a desire

to repeat a similar creative process, so in the next semester we had a new experience with the famous song "Happy."

3. The Idea of Motif – An Interdisciplinary Experience
Peta Harper

The group
This unit of work was done with an elective music class (students 15 and 16 years old) at an academically selective school in Sydney, Australia. Students had prior musical experience and were motivated musically, but most were reluctant to move/dance and had not much dance before. We worked together for three hours per week. The split of males/females was even. Cultural backgrounds varied with 60% Asian (mostly Chinese and Korean), at least 50% of the class born overseas.

Objectives
- Develop composition skills and phantasy; specifically, how to develop an idea/motif.
- Experience the concept of motif concretely through movement, music, and visual arts.
- Develop understanding of the transference of the concept of motif across the various art forms.
- Learn how to develop a motif beyond just repetition.
- Increase the understanding of and approach to movement and dance.

The use of movement and dance in this setting was in an interdisciplinary approach to serve an educational goal. Students were to experience a composition tool (motif) across several art forms to lead to an understanding of how it can be used in music, dance, and fine arts. Particularly, the use of movement and dance was so students could experience these structures through their bodies, work in a social setting, and experience it as an art form in itself. Increasing experience in working with the motif idea gradually led the students from small to larger movements, using their space more consciously and moving freely with each other.

Motivation
Students were led to movement and dance through using everyday movements as our warm-up, e.g., writing, hailing a bus, brushing teeth, typing, putting shoes on. These movements were then explored and developed in time, space, dynamic, and form (e.g., stretching, slow/fast, large/small, soft-powerful, inversion, retrograde).

Exploration
Students drew the shape of the main five-note descending motif from Chick Corea's *Children's Song No. 3*, as it was played on piano. As they became familiar with it, they sang it as well.

Via direction, students explored other ways of "drawing" the motif, i.e., with different body parts, large/small, etc. They were asked to find their favorite way of showing the musical motif with their body and keep it as their personal movement motif to be developed.

Listening to the recording, students identified how many times the main musical motif occurred, then performed their motif with the recording. They were instructed to adapt their movement to reflect any musical changes.

The class then discussed how the musical motif changed and demonstrated it with their bodies.

As a next step, students formed small groups, and were directed to refine their movements to show as much information about the music as possible. This meant that they needed to identify musical features such as ostinato, rests, tempo changes, inversion, decoration and then find a way as a group to show these features through movement. They performed the result to the class with the recording.

Reflection
To show their observation and understanding, students individually drew a sketch of the musical motif and its development. The class shared their sketches, discussed what they had observed and how the motif and the rest of the music had been represented visually.

Elaboration
A selection of art works (Australian Indigenous art and works by Kandinsky, Escher, and Andy Goldsworthy) was shown to the class. Working in small groups, students selected one artwork for their group and identified the motifs in it, explored and found a way to perform the motif and its developments in three ways: First, musically (vocally and with their instruments), second, only with movement, and finally, including both music and movement, but it was up to the students how they achieved this.

Demonstration and reflection
The groups performed their dance and music sequences to the class first without, then with the artwork. The class audience had to try and match the music and movement to the motif(s) in the artwork. From here, students discussed what they now understood about how to take a motif and develop it to create a cohesive musical work.

4. Mary Wigman's Witch Dance (1926)
Doris Valtiner-Pühringer

The group
These dance lessons take place in the fifth grade (fifteen-year-olds) of the Kunst-Oberstufen Realgymnasium St. Ursula in Salzburg (a private high school focusing on music, visual arts, drama, dance, and rhetoric) once a week for two consecutive 50-minute classes over the course of one semester. There is prior knowledge of music, but not necessarily of dance. The percentage of girls per class is much higher. Most of the students are very motivated and interested in learning and trying out different dance styles.

In general, students in this type of private high school are rather achievement oriented. It is very important for them to know what the goal is to be able to see clearly what they should have achieved at the end of the lesson. They especially love those parts of the class where they are allowed to be creative and explore and compose given movement material in small groups in a freer, more relaxed, and playful way. However, it is quite important for them that the result of their composition is what they consider "beautiful." Therefore, poses and symmetrical parts are often included in their creations and movement compositions.

Content
- Insights into different dance styles from different historical periods.
- Information about different aesthetic forms in dance.
- Practice: Trying out dance styles and learning to experience their special features in meaning, quality, rhythm, and execution, as well as finding an accompaniment.

Objectives
- Sensitization of body awareness (kinesthetic, visual, tactile, auditory, balance).

- Differentiation of motor skills: variations of basic movements in space (floor patterns as well as gestures), dynamics (conscious differences in tension), and time (tempo and rhythm).
- Aesthetic education: focus on all kinds of qualities that determine how we perceive and render an artistic performance.

Motivation

The class is offered various dance styles from different periods, also considering what students can see and hear in everyday life, see in films, and possibly observe in dance performances on stage. Short video examples and photos of costumes of the respective period serve as illustrative material.

The topic of *Ausdruckstanz* (expressive dance) was chosen, using Mary Wigman's *Hexentanz* (Witch Dance) from 1926 as an example. A short theoretical introduction (origins, chronology, characteristics, and representatives of expressive dance, as well as trends in Germany and America) is followed by a video of the Witch Dance.

Reflection

The students describe what was new for them, how they feel about the dance language, what effect it had on them. They also talk about the music, reflect on its effect, and answer questions. Are there musical cues? What is the structure in dance and music? Why is a mask used?

Elaboration

In terms of dance, the material is now developed together in phases. The students sit in a semicircle opposite the teacher and imitate her movements from the Witch Dance. To reinforce the expression, meaningless speech accompaniment is used, amplified by a large gong, the playing technique of which is shown to the students and which they are allowed to try out. With each repetition, the music and dance develop more intensively into a unity in which the musicians and dancers react sensitively to each other.

Demonstration

Once the sequence has been roughly learned, the students take turns demonstrating and observing the dance in two groups. In this way, the movements and the gong accompaniment are deepened and memorized through observation. Because the sequence is first performed in the large group, there is no shame in being different, but rather amazement at the great effect of this dance language. However, it is also possible to perform the dance in pairs (dance and accompaniment) in front of the group.

Summary

The students are enthusiastic about the strong expression and the individuality of the choreography.

References and Resources

Adshead, A., & Layton, J. (1983). *Dance history: A methodology for study*. London: Dance Books.

Art Gallery of NSW (n.d.). *Works in the Australian art/Aboriginal & Torres Strait Islander art collection area*. https://www.artgallery.nsw.gov.au/collection/works/?area=australian-art.aboriginal-torres-strait-islander-art

Black Pepper Swing. (2020, January 4). *Hellzapoppin' in full color*. [Video]. YouTube. https://www.youtube.com/watch?v=qzc7vY9VTnk (lindy hop begins about 2:30)

Burrows J. (2010). *A choreographer's handbook*. London: Routledge.

Chujoy, A., & Manchester, P. W. (1967). *The dance encyclopedia*. New York: Simon and Schuster.

Corea, C. (1984). Children's song no. 3 [Album recorded by Chick Corea]. *Children's Songs*. ECM Records.

Corea, C. (1994). *Children's songs: 20 pieces for keyboard*. Mainz: Schott.

Esquivel, E. (2015, April 6). *Jazz roots 2015—teachers battle outro*. [Video]. YouTube. https://www.youtube.com/watch?v=zpeUnWrteQM&t=54s

Free Step Italia Official. (2017, July 7). *African American jazz dance* (Minns and Leon James). [Video]. YouTube. https://www.youtube.com/watch?v=mK8s3-1A1Oc

Guarino, L., & Oliver, W. (2014). *Jazz dance: A history of the roots and branches*. Gainesville: University Press of Florida.

Hartmann, W. (2021). *Looking at the roots: A guide to understanding Orff Schulwerk*. San Francisco: Pentatonic Press.

Hartogh, T., & Wickel, H. H. (2019). *Handbuch Musik in der Sozialen Arbeit* [Handbook of music in social work]. Weinheim/Basel: Beltz.

Harvey Dobbs. (2015, May 25). *Mike & Theresa bop COTDF champions of the dance floor 2015* [Video]. YouTube. https://www.youtube.com/watch?v=NeEwbjD6IsQ

Hoffmann, B., Martini, U., Martini, H., Rebel, G., Wickel, H. H., & Wilhelm, E. (2004). *Gestaltungspädagoik in der Sozialen Arbeit* [Gestaltung pedagogy in social work]. Paderborn: Schöningh.

Ickstadt, L. (2007). *Dancing heads: A hand- and footbook for creative/contemporary dance with children and young people from 4–18 years*. New York: iUniverse.

Kandinsky (n.d.). *Pictures at an exhibition*. https://www.wassilykandinsky.net/pictures.php

Kohm, H. (2017). *Die emotionale Entwicklung von Jugendlichen und Heranwachsenden* [The emotional development of adolescents and young adults]. Munich: GRIN Verlag.

Legg, J. (2011). *Introduction to modern dance techniques*. Hightstown, NJ: Princeton Book Company.

Malone, J. (1996). *Steppin' on the blues: The visible rhythms of African American dance*. Champaign: University of Illinois Press.

Mooiman, M. (2014, June 23). *Mary Wigman, Hexentanz* [Video]. YouTube. https://www.youtube.com/watch?v=At-LSSuFlJ5c

Orff, C. (1978). *The Schulwerk* (M. Murray, Trans.). New York: Schott. (Original work published in 1976 as *Carl Orff und sein Werk: Dokumentation, Vol. 3, Schulwerk—Elementare Musik, Tutzing:* Hans Schneider)

Shimsham, F. (2013, December 30). *Shorty's vs Whitey's / The 1st air step*. [Video]. YouTube. https://www.youtube.com/watch?v=o1kl69NCH_E

Smith-Autard, J. M. (2002). *The art of dance in education* (2nd ed.). London: Bloomsbury Publishing.

Sorell, W. (1986). *Mary Wigman, ein Vermächtnis* [Mary Wigman, a legacy]. Wilhelmshaven: Noetzel.

Spinks, S. (Writer, Producer, & Director). (2002, January 31). Inside the teenage brain (Season 2002, Episode 11) [TV series episode]. In Aronson-Rath, R. (Editor-in-Chief & Executive Director), *Frontline*. Spin Free Productions; WGBH Boston. https://www.pbs.org/wgbh/frontline/documentary/inside-the-teenage-brain/

Spurgeon, D. (2001). *Dance moves: From improvisation to dance.* Sidney: Harcourt Brace Jovanovich. (Original work published in 1991)

Stearns, M. W., & Stearns, J. (1994). *Jazz dance: The story of American vernacular dance.* Boston: Da Capo Press. (Original work published in 1968)

The M.C. Escher Company B.V. (n.d.). *Selected works by M.C. Escher.* https://mcescher.com/gallery/

University of Glasgow, Crichton Campus (n.d.). *Andy Goldsworthy digital catalogue.* https://goldsworthy.cc.gla. ac.uk/browse/

Wigman, M. (1986). *Die Sprache des Tanzes* [The language of dance]. München: Battenberg.

Movement and Dance with Adults and Seniors

Greacian Goeke (USA), Sister M. Johannita Kweon (South Korea), Insuk Lee
(South Korea/ Germany), Andrea Ostertag (Austria), Christine Schönherr (Austria)

INTRODUCTION
Christine Schönherr

Rising life expectancy and a simultaneous decline in birth rates are leading to demographic changes. This is accompanied by understandable wishes to grow old in good health, to remain mentally and physically fit, not to be pushed into retirement, and to spend the extended period of life in a meaningful way.

Since the 1950s, various theories of old age have developed. The first (1950) was the *deficit model*. This was followed ten years later by the *disengagement theory*, which describes old age as a general process of decline, with voluntary withdrawal from social relationships. The *competence theory*, which emerged in 1987, and the model of *successful aging*, which is to be understood in the sense of fulfilled aging, form an alternative concept. Understandably, this model has not lost its validity to this day because contented aging and individual fulfilment of meaning are connected.

It is therefore not surprising that the most current theory appearing in the headings of the contributions and chapters in the new gerontological publication *Diversität und Altersbildung* (Schramek, Steinfort-Diedenhofen, & Kricheldorff, 2022) is successful aging.[1] It is becoming apparent that the pluralization of lifestyles is slowly breaking down the often-dark role models of old age. It is recognized that there is no such thing as a homogeneous group of the elderly, but that people age differently and the calendar age by no means always corresponds to the biological age.

Offerings for this age group at the Orff Institute - a look into the past
Offerings for senior citizens have a long tradition at the Orff Institute. Verena Maschat started a group for student teaching practice in an old people's home in 1988, which, after three years, was briefly continued by Orietta Mattio. In 1998, Christiane Wieblitz led a group for senior citizens; Peter Cubasch instructed an adult group (age range 18–78) that was continued by Insuk Lee, then Christine Schönherr, and is now directed by Ari Glage. In 2003, Christine Schönherr started a group in a home for the elderly. The experiences and insights gained from these offerings led to the publication in 2013 of a double DVD in German/English with a detailed booklet (Schönherr, 2013). Andrea Ostertag led a dance group for adults (age range 40–65) for seven years.

---

1 T. Hartogh, personal communication to C. Schönherr, July 7, 2022.

General Considerations for Movement/Dance with Adults and Elderly People (all authors)

Terminology
The name for the 65+ age group has changed frequently in recent years and varies from country to country. A respectful, individual designation, culturally adapted to the understanding of the respective country should be considered. We suggest referring to members of such a group not as students but as participants and our role not as teacher but simply as leader of the group.

Intentions for movement and dance programs with adults and elderly people
- Create a safe, joyful space and use a sense of humor.
- Get to know the special expertise and interests of participants.
- Use a non-judgmental perspective regarding self and others.
- Witness and validate each other.
- Break isolation and create community.
- Stimulate senses and imagination.
- Employ open-ended playful exploration, improvisation to creation.
- Highlight pleasure in movement for overall health: "use it or lose it."
- Maintain power and resilience physically and mentally.
- Expand physical and energy presence.
- Build confidence and fluency in movement as artistic expression.
- Accept one's aging body, seeing beauty in its movement.
- Connect to life through creative self.
- Incorporate memories, life experiences, and reflection.
- Learn new things, unfolding hidden talents.
- Offer times for reflection.

Descriptions of the Different Age Groups Led by the Authors

Adults and active older female dancers ages 35–65 at the Orff Institute
Andrea Ostertag

Reasons for founding and participating in this specialized group
This group was founded out of a very personal need: where does a middle-aged woman go to be able to move freely in dance, not bound to any style or partner? Where can you express yourself in dance without feeling too old, without having to prove anything to anyone, without prejudice and self-doubt?

    This dance group consists of women who think and feel the same way and have asked themselves these same questions but have not found a corresponding group in Salzburg. They are women who are still working as well as women who are retired but still very active. The content of the lessons is based on the biographies of the participating women and considers their respective life situations.

Themes
The most important starting point for creative tasks is exploration and improvisation. The participants should be allowed to try out their ideas on certain themes spontaneously. Work with the breath and voice is integrated here, as well as use of musical instruments. Recorded music is an important motivating factor and should be chosen very carefully for each specific

improvisational task. In the sense of the Orff Schulwerk, cross-disciplinary creation takes place: literature, visual arts, and music inspire dancing and stimulate new connections among art forms.

Special for this group is a shared attitude of not wanting to work towards a performance. One does it only for oneself and the dance community. In this age group, one finds many women who are still firmly established in life, but who now have more time for their private interests. Nevertheless, aging also brings with it worries about the future, health limitations, and dwindling self-confidence. To build and strengthen this self-confidence, to feel oneself attractive, elegant, expressive, and interesting is another aim of this class.

Impromptu No Tutu: Active women ages 55–90
Greacian Goeke

Impromptu No Tutu grew out of personal need: When I turned 50, I dreamed of bringing together older women to show what dance in later life can be. No Tutu began as a pilot exercise class but became much more. Over 15 years it has evolved into a loving and creative community of support that carries us through grief, loss, political crises, and reckoning with our own mortality.

Approach
Improvisation is the primary approach to movement. It is an invitation to take risks, move into the unknown and remain flexible at a challenging time of life.

Themes and special features
A theme for each class emerges from our outdoor environment, the seasons, current events, artwork, or poetry suggested by members. Collective poems often arise from the opening warm up. Some members have found their voice as poets through the class.

Props such as poles, elastic bands, and hoops inspire us to extend our movements and enlarge the kinesphere. Hand drums and body percussion conduct and accompany movement. We improvise with anything at hand.

We work with a wide range of classical and world music for exploring patterns and themes. Playlists have developed on the color blue, birds, water, the moon and sun, cars and driving.

The group is very attuned to color and its effect on mood and enjoys costuming, masks, scarves, and dressing in bright tones for each season.

Engaging with the public
We are committed to sharing the joy of movement with all ages, particularly bringing improvisation to reluctant teenagers. We visit elder residences, schools, libraries, museums, and gardens and invite the public to move with us. We have participated in worldwide Dance Anywhere Day and continue the tradition informally.

A valuable reflection resource is the photo archive that has grown over the years. Members comment how seeing themselves helps to build confidence and open a greater variety of ways to move.

Groups of residents in homes for the elderly: Houses of life-stories
Christine Schönherr, Insuk Lee, Sister M. Johannita Kweon

Designing and providing musical and dance activities
Aging is accompanied by physical and mental changes. Therefore, the composition of our groups is characterized by fluctuation: participants die, new residents join. The ability to move decreases. Human needs such as contact, appreciation, recognition, and self-fulfillment are shrinking. But active music-making and movement can help to counteract.

Our offerings should be:
- participant-oriented, including and developing their experiences in music and dance,
- in an atmosphere based on empathy, acceptance, without pressure to reach certain goals,
- with a low threshold in terms of musical and dance demands, so that these activities can be mastered well and give a feeling of success.

Because of poor hearing, speaking with appropriate volume, good articulation, and in short sentences with a slower tempo is very important. The obvious need for contact inspires the offering of activities in teams.

One resident's remark: *I needed something uplifting today and that's why I came, and I got it.* That is enough of a goal.

Content focused on movement/dance
The movement phases offer the opportunity to counteract body-hostile tendencies. Perspectives change from "I have a body that I reject because of its decay" to "I am my body as it is now."

Dance movements only take place sitting in a circle. Arms, legs, the upper body act as representatives of locomotion in space. The leader's alert observation is important so that the physical performance limitations are not exceeded. Small resting points should be offered, feeling the movement reaction in breath and body.

A seated dance around the maypole   Peacock feathers ballet
Photos: Willy Minden, with kind permission

The use of objects such as peacock feathers, balls of different sizes, scarves, ribbons, colored gloves, finger puppets, sticks, fans, balloons, even colored fly swatters or flowers always proves to be motivating. Also, texts, sculptures, paintings, own painting on paper or in the air (air patterns) can trigger dance designs.

Essential movement/dance impulses arise through active music listening with the inclusion of pieces of music that are carefully selected to be appropriate for the group in terms of tempo, length, clarity of form, and emotional impact.

The dance design contributes to the participants *"sentire la musica* experience, i.e., hearing, understanding, feeling the music" (Frigor & Röbke, 2008, p. 95) and translating music into physicality.

Body percussion
Body percussion can be done while sitting. It activates movement, stimulates the circulation and the coordination of arms and legs. The connection of sound and movement can be experienced, especially when instruments are included with the movement.

Interplay of music, movement, and language
The triumvirate also proves to be very effective in this age group as movement is only possible to a limited extend.

Exploration, improvisation, creation
Phases of exploration, improvisation, and creation prove to be particularly valuable for our groups. They offer the freedom for the participants to adapt their movements to the physical possibilities.

The use of live instrumental or vocal accompaniment by the leader is always inspiring and helpful.

Producing something new contrasts with the widespread age-related illness of physical and mental rigidity. It reactivates the joy of living and creating.

Target perspectives
Our offerings are an attempt to contribute to the following experiences:
- That unknown talents in music and dance can be discovered and developed even in old age. "We are not yet too old" (comment of a participant).
- That it is possible to recall songs, instrumental pieces, or dances from times long past, even in the state of dementia.
- That memories of certain life situations arise through music or movement, spreading happiness, helping to manage old age as "the masterpiece of life."
- That learning is still possible on an emotional, motor, and cognitive level in the sense of neuroplasticity, and it has an invigorating effect on mood, state of mind, and fulfilment of meaning.

PRACTICAL EXAMPLES

The following examples show approaches to and content for our topic from different cultures (Austria, USA, South Korea) and with groups differing in age and mobility.

Overview
1. Andrea Ostertag: Skin and touch
Our skin, the largest organ of the body, connects the body's inside with the outside. Especially in the second half of life it goes through changes that are not all positive. Attention through the tactile sense brings us more in touch with ourselves again, increases self-acceptance and leads our movements to a sensual and pleasurable dance.
2. Greacian Goeke and Impromptu No Tutu Movement Ensemble: Ikebana dance
Inspired by *ikebana*, the Japanese art of flower arranging, this improvisational exploration emerged from participants' ideas, and has become an important tradition of our group. Movement is guided by the three-dimensional visual design elements of each arrangement.

3. **Christine Schönherr: Dancing hands**
   Only seated dancing is possible, with hands and feet representing the whole body. Exploring, improvising, creating, and dressing our hands with colored gloves, hands dance in duos or small groups. Finally, "hand fishes" interpret Camille Saint-Saëns' "Aquarium" from *The Carnival of the Animals.*

4. **Sister M. Johannita Kweon: Spring**
   The "lovely" women of a residential home of the Notre Dame congregation enjoy creating movement in an imaginative way, and with the help of props and music from Vivaldi's *The Four Seasons* they develop their impression of spring.

1. Skin and Touch
Andrea Ostertag

Arrive
Walk attentively through the room, notice objects and furnishings, other participants, etc. Find a place in the room and stand still, close your eyes, and imagine the room and the other participants once again in your mind. Breathe in and out deeply, feeling the breath.
   This is accompanied by calm, atmospheric music.

Getting into the mood for the topic
The participants sit or lie on the floor, the leader reads excerpts from the chapter "Skin" in A Widening Field. Journeys in Body and Imagination (Tufnell & Crickmay, 2004, pp.122-123).

Exercises to sensitize the body: Inside and outside
Move only one hand or arm while dancing in place. Sensing inside (bones, tendons, muscles, blood, etc.). Thinking outside (stretching, moving into space, relating to other participants). Integrate other body parts into the movements until the whole body is moving.

Text as inspiration
Leader reads another text from "Skin" (p. 125). Participants listen to the words or move to them at the same time, as it feels right for them in the moment. The text is very imaginative and metrically free. The leader's presentation is structured by pauses between the text segments and repetition of some passages. The text encourages touching oneself and sensually experiencing the skin through the hands or touching different parts of the body.

Reflection
The participants share their experiences.

Dance improvisation and creation
The participants create a short dance sequence that starts "inside," finds a transition to the "outside" and ends with an expansion in space. In pairs they show each other the movement sequences they have created. In the duo improvisation that follows, both dancers start at the same time with their own sequence, vary it and let themselves be inspired by their partner's ideas. The reference to the partner is constantly attentive and it enriches the joint improvisation. Music can be supportive but should not significantly influence the dance.

On the theme
The theme "skin and touch" evokes emotional moments. Especially after nearly three years of social distancing during the pandemic this theme takes on great significance. Touching others had become nearly impossible. Decades later, one will still feel the effects of what it meant

to not be able to touch another. This class was a return to something buried and accordingly emotional. In the reflection, many feelings, tears, stories, and longings emerged.

But it is not only the pandemic that makes this topic an emotional one. Especially at a more mature age—and especially for women—the topic of skin is strongly connected with fading beauty, aging, (supposedly) waning attractiveness. Every woman deals with this differently and some struggle with it, some take it in their stride, some accept these changes and radiate their very own beauty.

Dealing with ourselves, self-acceptance, and self-love also has a lot to do with our skin. The participants should be strengthened internally by focusing on this body organ along with their own and others' touch and be able to express this in dance.

2. Impromptu No Tutu Movement Ensemble: Ikebana Dance
Greacian Goeke

> *We dance together. We are together.*
> —Twyla Tharp

Ikebana Dance
Inspired by *ikebana*, the Japanese art of flower arranging, this dance exploration emerged from participants' ideas, and has become an important ongoing tradition of our group.

Origin
Before No Tutu class one day, Alice was telling Louise about ikebana, using her hands to show how she creates contrasts with the carefully chosen natural materials. She has studied ikebana for more than 20 years since the sudden death of her husband. It is the creative wellspring in her life as a widow.

Louise watched the play of Alice's arms and exclaimed, "It's a dance!" By the time they came into class they had a plan: We would improvise to one of Alice's ikebana, using it as a kind of notation. It was exciting to discover that the design elements of ikebana are present in dance and music and vice versa: symmetry/asymmetry; straight/curved; near/far; weight, levels, directions; staccato/legato; positive/negative space.

Opening
The ikebana class begins as do all our classes by shedding burdens through movement and sound, then silently dedicating our work to a person or idea. I chose koto and flute music to alternate with silence as we responded to the arrangement that I had placed in the center of the room.

Explorations
We might start by walking around and viewing the arrangement up close from all angles, reflecting the smallest details of shape, line, and texture. As we move farther back, duets arise as the dancers reflect juxtapositions of materials. These transforming shapes alternate with stillness. It is valuable to have half the group watch at various points. The group also values following a changing single leader to acknowledge each person's presence and unique movement vocabulary. Members are well versed in Rudolf Laban's Eight Effort Action Drives and archetypal shapes (arrow, wall, ball, and spiral[1]) and enjoy analyzing ikebana through these lenses to expand their movement responses (see the article by B. Haselbach and A. Wolf,

---

1   Ed.: Rudolf von Laban described the body shapes as pin-like or elongated, wall-like or spread, ball-like or round, and screw-like or twisted. Sometimes in translation other, similar terms are used (See: Preston-Dunlop, 1980).

"Overview of Various Applications of Movement and Dance in the Orff Schulwerk" for more about Rudolf Laban).

Later, groups of dancers reflect a particular view of the arrangement, moving into an interconnected shape. We also play with the dancers as ikebana elements with one designer who creates a large group tableau.

Dancing the idea of ikebana
Photo: Greacian Goeke

Reverberations

We have held Ikebana Dance twice a year, when indoors, and now, since the pandemic, we meet in a large botanical garden that inspires us in new ways. Like haiku poetry, ikebana responds to the seasons and allows us to immerse in the passage of time in an aesthetic and emotional way. Class members reflect that dancing to ikebana has sharpened their attention to the forms of plants and trees in the garden and has brought them closer to nature and the cycles of life.

It is very meaningful to our group that Alice shares her creative passion with us. The group knows that if anyone has an inspiration, they are welcome to bring it to class for us to explore. When working with older adults there is always long-life experience to draw from, and these personal contributions deepen the content of the class and strengthen bonds among members.

3. Dancing Hands
Christine Schönherr

Start of the program music and dance
In 2003, my mother moved into a retirement home. My insights into the lives of the residents gave me the idea to offer a weekly one-hour program with the theme "Joy through music and movement." This session was very popular from the very beginning—my oldest participant at the time was 101 years old—and students from the Orff Institute also came regularly. Now being retired, I still offer this program every week.

The group
Usually, ten to fifteen residents come to our class with a walking aid or in a wheelchair. Movement in the room is not possible, we sit in a circle of chairs. Feet, legs, also arms, hands and fingers become representatives for the whole body, and after facial expressions, their movement possibilities are the strongest means of body language expression. It is not for nothing that one

speaks of "eloquent hands." Through exploration, improvisation, and creating, guiding ideas of the Orff Schulwerk, the hands become a new means of expression.

Warmup
We start with movements of the shoulder, elbow, and finger joints—important joint care in old age. At the same time, it is a warmup that flows into movements of the whole arms with hands and fingers such as the change between spreading the fingers and forming a fist. This is followed by independent experimentation.

Exploration
With movement accompaniment
In this phase, mostly imaginative-creative movement motifs emerge, which are observed by the leader and picked up individually, then imitated by everyone. Movement accompaniment by the leader or some participants by means of voice or instrument intensifies the movement and increases the sense of achievement of the "inventors." For participants who are confronted with physical decline and deficits such experiences of appreciation are particularly significant.

With recorded music
The use of non-Western music (e.g., Indian or Chinese) can also stimulate the movement repertoire so that an individual choreography for "two arms and ten fingers" may emerge.

With the use of an object
We disguise, "costume" our hands with different colored gloves, and participants contact and play around each other, thus creating non-verbal movement stories. Without the protection of the hands through disguise, touching would hardly happen. But the desire for contact and mutual attention is obviously there.

From improvisation to a repeatable design
The improvisations in the glove duos can expand into trios or quartets and lead to scenic dance sequences, such as "the group flower awakes in the morning and closes in the evening."

Active listening to music in connection with dance composition
Deepening the theme of hands leads to the inclusion of a composition such as "Aquarium" from *The Carnival of the Animals* by Camille Saint-Saëns. The title and compositional progression stimulate the imagination. Now "hand fishes" dance in lively activity, sometimes ascending, sometimes descending, depending on the course of the melody. Active listening to music and a dance-like, physical, musical experience take place, which in the sense of Carl Orff, we are no longer onlookers but have become actors.

Music penetrates the inner realms, "music opens the doors easily and without violence to the soul" (attributed to political activist Sophie Scholl). The dance performance deepens the musical experience without using words, to the advantage of people with dementia.

Afterwards there are expressions to be heard such as "I feel that I am alive" or "my breath is taken away, it was so beautiful." Memories can also arise that bring joy, strengthen self-identity, and lead to expressions such as "I have become young again."

Continuing the theme
Looking at paintings with expressive hand positions inspires imitation, improvisation and opens up cross-connections to linguistic composition of texts, combined with body language expression.

4. Spring
Sister M. Johannita Kweon

The group
The congregation of Notre Dame in Seoul, South Korea takes care of two retirement homes for elderly women, the so called "Lovelyhouses." I have worked with them since 2008. Here I shall describe my work with a group of nine women aged between 80 and 90, who are still amazingly mobile. These Notre Dame Lovelyhouse women indeed show a strong passion for music and dance/movement.

Step by step their experiences grow, they become motivated to express their feelings and their thoughts, they are obviously happy to connect to others, and they also react intensely to my vocal or instrumental accompaniment to their movements. Some are interested in trying to accompany themselves.

Aim
Some studies show that for elderly people like these, regular meetings are the best for their mental care as well as for their social openness and contacts. Even those with dementia in the other home where I work come to the meetings with some kind of recognizable commitment. In our meetings we sing songs that they can remember, and that remind them of their life before being in the residents' home. Sometimes we try new ones. They are still learning and enjoying it. Looking forward to next week's meeting and their contacts with others with shared memories and new impressions keeps alive their interest in their own lives.

How it starts
The session takes place every week. They come out of their rooms and wait for me with happy smiles on their faces. After joining them, we say greetings with our hands in rhythmic patterns like a game. They love this beginning and use their hands very well.

Warmup for this topic
After the greeting, we start very carefully using small parts of the body like fingers, hands, toes, feet, then the whole body, accompanied with sounds and breath. During this warmup, using some words—like a tree, like a bird, like a waterfall—gives their movement a different dynamic and expression. For this, they take turns as leader to show a movement for the rest of them.

Inspiration
In a way of approaching Orff Schulwerk, using imagination is a wonderful key for creative movement. When they hear a phrase like, "a seed under the earth," or "a stream under the ice," I ask them what it means. Then they bring up all the meanings of that special scene that is a very interesting way to start. After exchanging a few words, I show them some movement. They imitate what they see and individually express freely. Later two people join together to take a turn to be the leader for the movement. Despite their age they try to move very dynamically quick/slow, big/small, sudden/sustained, also with facial expression. This is the first way of creating their movement in an imaginative way.

They love using movement accompaniment (voice and/or instrument), it gives them such pleasant satisfaction. Then we try to create a simple choreography together; just two or three ostinati will be enough. We try out the choreographies together a few times and later perform them with music.

Theme: Spring

With some artificial flowers, scarves, and untuned percussion, we create a scene of spring. Each one shows an aspect with a movement ostinato, using what they had previously explored in very simple ways, such as just raising or folding their arms, opening their eyes wide looking here and there, adding a few steps. Their voices and/or percussion accompanied their simple movement, and a modest performance is created based on what they had previously experienced.

Using recorded music: "Spring" from *The Four Seasons* by Antonio Vivaldi

These women have no education with this kind of music. However, they love to dance with music even though they do not understand it well. The use of this music stimulates the quality of the movement they previously invented and turns it into a modest and enjoyable choreography that they love to perform for themselves, and which gives them a clear memory of spring. Continuing the theme through painting while listening to Vivaldi's "Spring" then writing a poem about the spring are the last activities related to this topic.

To end

Finally, they conduct approximately three minutes of a sort of performance with their simple choreography and this is long enough for them. One might say it is not really a dance performance, but they express what they imagined, imitated, and explored by themselves and most important of all, they enjoy the process and the result.

References and Resources

Barthel, G. (2008). *Vom Tanz zur Choreographie. Gestaltungsprozesse in der Tanzpädagogik* [From dance to choreography. Composition processes in dance pedagogy]. Oberhausen: Athena.

Beal, R., & Berryman-Miller, S. (Eds.). (1988). *Dance for the older adult*. Reston, VA: American Alliance for Health.

Buckwalter, M. (2010). *Composing while dancing. An improviser's companion*. Madison: The University of Wisconsin Press.

Creative Aging International (UK) (2023, March). https://www.creativeageinginternational.com

Frigor, H., & Röbke, P. (2008). *Das Musizieren und die Gefühle: Instrumentalpädagogik und Psychoanalyse im Dialog* [Making music and the emotions: Instrumental pedagogy and psychoanalysis in dialogue]. Mainz: Schott.

Fung, C. V., & Lehmberg, L. J. (2016). *Music for life. Music participation and quality of life of senior citizens*. New York: Oxford University Press.

Girod-Perrot, R. (2017). *Bewegungsimprovisation* [Movement improvisation]. Sankt Augustin: Academia-Verlag.

Goeke, G. (2009). Releasing the dancer within. *The Orff Echo*, 41(4), 9–11.

Goeke, G., & Weingarten, K. (2018, December). SPEAK: To witness and re-member: Movement practices with elders. *In Dance*. http://dancersgroup.org/2018/12/speak-witness-re-member-movement-practices-elders/

Harms, H., & Dreischulte, G. (2007). *Musik erleben und gestalten mit alten Menschen* (3rd ed.) [Experiencing and creating music with elderly people]. München: Urban & Fischer.

Hartogh, T. (2005). *Musikgeragogik—ein bildungstheoretischer Entwurf. Musikalische Altenbildung im Schnittfeld von Musikpädagogik und Geragogik* [Music geragogy—an educational theory draft. Music education for the elderly at the intersection of music pedagogy and geragogy]. Augsburg: Wißner.

Hartogh, T. (2016). Music geragogy, elemental music pedagogy and community music: didactic approaches for making music in old age. *International Journal of Community Music 9*(1), 35–48.

Hartogh, T., Kehrer, E. M., & Wickel, H. H. (2014). Music geragogics: Making music with the elderly. In D. Sagrillo & D. Ferring (Eds.), *Music (education) from the cradle to the grave* (pp. 69–84). Weikersheim: Margraf.

Jekić, A., & Henrich, I. (2013). *Musik tut gut. Musizieren mit Senioren* [Music is good for you. Making music with seniors]. Kassel: Bosse.

Lerman, L. (1984). *Teaching dance to senior adults.* Springfield, IL: C. C. Thomas.

Lifetime Arts (USA) (2023, March). National leaders in creative aging program development. https://www.lifetimearts.org

Marchand, M. (2012). *"Gib mir mal die große Pauke …" Musikalische Gruppenarbeit im Altenwohn- und Pflegeheim; ein Praxisbuch* ["Give me the big kettledrum …" Musical group work in old people's residential and nursing homes; a practice book]. Münster: Waxmann.

Metz, J. (2011). *Wort Klang Bewegung. Elementare musikalische Bildung im späten Erwachsenenalter* [Word sound movement. Elemental musical education in late adulthood]. Wiesbaden: Breitkopf & Härtel.

National Institute on Aging (USA) (2023, March). Participating in the arts creates paths to healthy aging. https://www.nia.nih.gov/news/participating-arts-creates-paths-healthy-aging

Preston-Dunlop, V. (1980). *A handbook for modern educational dance* (Rev. ed.). London: Macdonald & Evans.

Preston-Dunlop, V. (1998). *Looking at dances. A choreological persepective on choreography.* London: Verve.

Schönherr, C. (2004). "Ich bin wieder jung geworden." Reflexionen über elementaren Musik- und Bewegungsunterricht in einem Seniorenheim / "I am young again!"—Reflections about elemental music and movement classes in a home for seniors. *Orff Schulwerk Informationen, 73,* 44–52. https://www.orff-schulwerk-forum-salzburg.org/magazine-osh

Schönherr, C. (2011). Erwachsenengruppe im Orff-Institut – Hochbetagtengruppe im Seniorenheim / Adult group at the Orff Institute – geriatric group in a home for seniors. *Orff Schulwerk Informationen, 85,* 240–244. https://www.orff-schulwerk-forum-salzburg.org/magazine-osh

Schönherr, C. (2011). Wir sind noch nicht zu alt! Angebote aus der elementaren Musik -und Tanzpädagogik für hochbetagte Menschen [We are not too old yet! Offerings from elemental music and dance pedagogy for very old people]. In H. H. Wickel & T. Hartogh (Eds.), *Praxishandbuch Musizieren im Alter. Projekte und Initiativen* (pp. 108–126). Mainz: Schott.

Schönherr, C. (2013). Ich bin wieder jung geworden. Künstlerisch-pädagogische Angebote für Menschen in hohem Alter / I have become young again. Artistic-pedagogical offerings for people in old age [Film; DVD]. Salzburg: Universität Mozarteum.

Schönherr, C. (2020). "Man spürt, dass man lebt." Musik, Sprache, Bewegung/Tanz. Künstlerisch-geragogische Angebote für Menschen in hohem Alter ["You feel that you are alive." Music, language, movement/dance. Artistic-geragogic offerings for people in old age]. In H. Henning (Ed.) *All inclusive?! Aspekte einer inklusiven Musik- und Tanzpädagogik* (pp. 233–243). Münster: Waxmann.

Schramek, R., Steinfort-Diedenhofen, J., & Kricheldorff, C. (2022). Diversität und Altersbildung [Diversity and education for the elderly]. Stuttgart: Kohlhammer

Smilde, R., & Bisschop Boele, E. (2016). Lifelong learning and healthy aging: The significance of music as an agent of change. In A. Fricke & T. Hartogh (Eds.), *Forschungsfeld Kulturgeragogik—Research in Cultural Geragogy* (pp. 205–220). Munich: Kopaed.

Tuffnell, M., & Crickmay, C. (2004). *A widening field. Journeys in body and imagination.* Alton, UK: Dance Books.

Ueba-Nguyen, S. (2023, March). *Third age theory.* https://thirdagecommunity.weebly.com

Dance in Music Schools

Anida Chan, Maggie Ho (Hong Kong), Isabel Galeza (Germany),
Miriam Gurbanov (Argentina), Fátima Moreno González (Spain)

INTRODUCTION

In many countries it is possible to study music and movement/dance in schools that are independent of elementary and secondary public and private schools. In some cases, such schools may be the only source for music and movement/dance instruction available to children and adults, because arts education may not be included in formal educational settings. Funding for these schools comes from various sources that include local, regional, or national governments, foundations, individual donors, individual student tuition, among others. Throughout the world, the availability of schools that offer education in music, dance, and other arts varies from country to country and city to city.

Many children and adults living in Europe have access to some type of music school. The European Music School Union (EMU), founded in 1973, is the umbrella organization of national music school associations in Europe. At present, national music school associations from 26 European countries are members of the EMU, representing more than 6,000 music and art schools. Music and movement classes for children from four to eight years is very common, but there are not many schools that offer education through dance.

National member associations of the EMU are officially acknowledged to work for the public interest and, as a rule, they receive public funding, covering a percentage of the fees that vary greatly among countries. Their task is to guarantee nation-wide standards and to develop infrastructures for the work of their members, such as: curriculum development, organizational assistance, and further training.

These music schools form an integral part of the European educational system and are specially devoted to music education through active music making. That means public responsibility and public funding, quality standards in structure and curricula, a wide range of subjects, qualifications of teaching staff, public performances, and so on. Music schools are generally attended by children and teenagers but are also open to adults up to senior age. They enable people to participate in music making on every level including preparation for professional music studies. Some descriptions and examples in this article are written by authors who work in member schools of the EMU.

The Schools of Music and Dance in Spain
Fátima Moreno González

The *Escuelas Municipales de Música y Danza* (Municipal Schools of Music and Dance) in Spain began their journey in 1990, providing a new vision of artistic education, and an important advance, thanks to Elisa Roche, her pedagogical contributions and her global vision of elemental music and movement education. These centers represent an educational innovation and

216

a new space of quality for non-professional artistic education (education that does not lead to an official degree), approaching the educational ideals of the Orff Schulwerk. The general purpose of these music and dance schools is "to offer practical training in music, dance or, jointly, in both disciplines, aimed at amateurs of any age, without prejudice to their function of orientation to professional studies for those who demonstrate a special vocation and aptitude" (Gobierno de España, n.d.).

The legislation (Gobierno de España) structures these centers by levels (usually by age and by subject/instrument).

- Basic education (for both music and dance):
    - "Music and movement" for children between the ages of four and eight years.
- Musical training:
    - "Instrumental practice" without age limit.
    - "Musical training" complementary to instrumental practice.
    - "Instrumental and vocal ensemble activities."
- Dance training:
    - "Dance," which may refer to the different forms of professional and non-professional dance.
    - Each center can provide offerings according to the needs of its municipality, i.e., being able to extend the age ranges, admitting students from 18 months, including new subjects, and in some cases providing training from six years old exclusively in "Initiation into Dance."

Music and movement in the Municipal Schools of Music and Dance and their relationship with Orff Schulwerk

In Orff Schulwerk, "Music and Movement" is conceived as a binomial in which both disciplines function together in practice. In this global and inclusive approach, student learning is more meaningful if both subjects are implemented together and conceived as a whole. While the students sing, move, interact with the peer group and the teacher, they develop at a psychomotor level that includes such concepts as the recognition of the body scheme, laterality, spatial trajectories, etc.

The incorporation of a suitable repertoire of play-dances and traditional dances, as well as songs with percussion instruments, alternating with activities for the development of creativity (focused on each level), provide improvement at a psychomotor level, developing at the same time both cerebral hemispheres, providing enjoyment and sensitivity towards the arts.

In these schools we speak of dance/movement from an educational/creative perspective being a discipline that—for its adaptability as well as for the capacities that develop in the students—can and should be included at any educational level, but mainly in this type of artistic education center. On the one hand, movement can be understood as an "instrument" to help develop other skills. On the other hand, the incorporation of dance for its own value as an independent subject is respected for the multiple competences it can develop in students.

The body is an essential element for all activities in life. Based on this premise, in this approach the whole body is engaged in the creative process. Thus, it is necessary to prepare the body for creative development. In dance, the performer is the "instrument" interacting with the music, the material, and the environment.

How can dance and movement be implemented in these centers?

The profile of the teacher is a fundamental aspect in putting Orff Schulwerk into educational practice. Teachers must be sensitive to the objectives and goals of each age and to the type of center in which they will develop their activities. They should be adequately trained in the Orff Schulwerk approach, planning and/or sequencing of content, the essential steps in the creative process (exploration-improvisation-composition). They should also have repertoire (suitable for each age group) of play-dances and traditional dances, as well as simple songs with percussion accompaniment, and knowledge of psychology/pedagogy. It is essential that they are trained in the field of movement and its relationship to musical aspects, concerned about being updated and willing to train continuously, as well as being flexible and sensitive to the different realities that may arise on a daily basis in the course of the sessions. The teacher needs to find again the pleasure of spontaneous play, of experimentation without fear of being judged, in short, to regain the capacity for wonder.

The proposed activities should be appropriate for heterogeneous groups and the psycho-evolutionary characteristics of each age group, as well as the socio-cultural reality of the environment, the students' concerns and previous experience, in order for learning to be stimulating and effective. The way to approach expressive movement and music is through experience, offering educational activities sequenced in a logical way, giving students the necessary guidelines and stimuli to motivate them so that they can progressively build their own learning through discovery.

The repertoire of play-dances, traditional dances, and popular songs intrinsically provides a wealth of essential content for students' development at a psychomotor level (e.g., laterality, coordination, or spatial perception), in memory (to master the repertoire of steps and spatial designs), at an affective/social/cooperative level (group work, empathy, collaboration, etc.), and at an emotional level (joy and enjoyment), therefore, embracing the development of all the dimensions of the human being.

Creative activities stimulate the development of the right hemisphere of the brain. The proposed activities are implemented in a sequential manner allowing students to explore and learn about new content and/or materials, to become familiar with them, and begin to deploy the infinite possibilities of movement, providing self-knowledge and the ability to solve possible situations or problems that may be introduced by the teacher. The creative process will begin with the game, extend through exploration, improvisation and—according to age—will culminate with a composition.

It is necessary for the teacher to generate a space for personal and group exploration, with a climate of trust in which each member of the group can experiment and share their creation with the others. This is done by facilitating this energy, guiding group reflection, and motivating constructive criticism. In other words, the observation of the other's creation becomes a new starting point to deepen the experience, also enriching one's own work.

The interrelation of the arts (music, dance, language-literature, visual arts) in practice offers a more complete and holistic formation. The thematic units of work, as well as the materials and starting points that stimulate the development of the students, can be based on speech, a text, a story and/or a plastic artwork, a sculpture, among others. Students can also be motivated to create their own musical, visual, or text "work of art," linking it to creative movement.

The role of dance/movement from the perspective of dance education/creative dance in traditional music schools is forward looking improvement, a vision of global artistic education, more complete because in addition to the multiple capacities that musical practice develops, it will contribute to the development of psychological, corporal, and emotional capacities. In practice, both brain hemispheres are put into operation, providing knowledge, enjoyment, as well as an approach to culture and awareness of the arts.

Introducing educational/creative dance in the training of music students provides a greater understanding of the musical content itself, because the body in movement supports the internalization of the meter and rhythm in a more natural way. In addition, a foundation in dance/movement provides more resources for creative development, a better postural positioning for working with any instrument, the development of coordination, and a more complete enjoyment of the activity.

In these centers the interaction between music and dance is or should be bi-directional and enriching. Even if it is at a very elemental level such as "dancing while other students make music," proposing an exchange of roles favors concentration, motivation, being stimulating for the auditory/perceptual development and a form of cooperative work that is beneficial in multiple aspects to the student's development.

Collegium Musicum de Buenos Aires
Miriam Gurbanov

The *Collegium Musicum de Buenos Aires*, a non-profit association founded in 1946, is an innovative institution because what was experienced there in its beginnings, both artistically and pedagogically, did not occur in other areas. Throughout its 78-year history, with the conviction that every human being has a natural disposition for music, the Collegium offers children, teenagers, and adults the opportunity to engage in a musical activity independent of their musical abilities, contributing to the general culture of society and favoring the development of the sensitivity of individuals.

The Children's Department of the institution offers the following activities that are developed according to each age group:

• Making Music as a Family is an activity for two- and three-year-olds accompanied by an adult.
• Children from four to six years old may participate in two activities: Movement and Music and Musical Initiation.
• For those from seven to twelve years of age, there are six levels of Music Theory and Praxis that correspond to primary school grades.
• Vocal-Instrumental Ensemble I, II, and III, where boys and girls of different ages and levels of knowledge collaborate with the sole purpose of making music.
• Optional workshops are offered in the subjects of recorder, guitar, keyboard, singing, ukulele, musical theater, and movement.

Movement and music at the Collegium
The area of movement has always been present. During these 78 years of music education different proposals involving movement have been implemented, first were optional activities such as Rhythmic Gymnastics and Dalcroze Rhythmics. A turning point came in 1960 when Corporal Expression, created by Argentinean dancer and pedagogue Patricia Stokoe, was incorporated into the pedagogical program. Since 2003 and as a result of several teacher education courses led by Verena Maschat, this subject was replaced with Movement and Music.

The Movement and Music program has its own space and a specific curriculum for groups of children from four to six years old. It also includes a movement workshop and a musical theater workshop where choreographic compositions are created individually or by the entire group. The groups are taught by teachers trained specifically in the area of movement.

Dance in a Music School in Germany
Isabel Galeza

As part of my work as director of the music and art school DOrff-Werkstatt, Andechs, I was able to gain various insights into the field of dance and its place in music schools. I learned that, on the one hand the area of children's dance may be classical in nature, and on the other hand one may find it to be practically applied in early childhood music education. For many parents only the musical development of their children is in the foreground. However, some parents are aware that dance has great importance in discovering music, in learning new content, and in understanding music through the whole body.

The core questions for me are:

- How can dance/movement be incorporated in early music education in the context of a classical music school?
- Why is dance important for musical development in early music education, and what are the benefits of movement/dance later for a music student in their instrumental lessons?
- What possibilities does a music school have to integrate dance—and especially the connections between music and dance—quite naturally into the daily music school activities?

PRACTICAL EXAMPLES

Overview
1. **Fátima Moreno González: Dancing with an object**
   An activity with plates of three different colors is for children who are eight years old and older in a music school in Spain.
2. **Miriam Gurbanov: Movement / Stillness - Sound / Silence**
   In an Argentinian music school, these experiences lead nine-year-old children to create a choreography.
3. **Isabel Galeza: Movement inspiration through different objects**
   Children ages six to nine develop movements using objects of different characteristics to create duos with live accompaniment in a German music school.
4. **Anida Chan and Maggie Ho: First encounter with Cantonese Opera**
   In a special summer program in Hong Kong, children ages six to nine participate in a project that exposes them to Cantonese Opera.

1. Dancing with an Object
Fátima Moreno González

Group description
This activity is aimed at groups of children who are eight years old and older, with or without previous experience with movement/dance and its connection with music and other arts.

Overall objective
To develop students' creativity with the help of an object.

Objectives
- Explore the different possibilities of movement individually through use of an object.
- Work in pairs, trios, and in groups introducing the concepts of "mirror," "shadow," and "active listening" with the help of an object.
- Create short improvisations with the object.
- Perform a group choreography with the object as an essential element of the composition.
- Incorporate elements that expand the students' choreographic repertoire.

Content
- Individual and group work with an object (plate).
- Creative development using an object (plate).
- Shadowing, mirroring, spatial levels, paths.

Resources
- Plastic plates (or polystyrene trays) in three colors.
- Different types of music.
- Small percussion instruments (for the teacher).

Procedure
Phase 1
- "We present the object." After a guided or free body warm-up, the objects are distributed (plates in three different colors). For the distribution, the students will be seated on the floor in a circle and the colors will be passed alternately, with an ostinato of sounds and gestures.
- "Free exploration" (calm music). With our plate we explore its possibilities of movement, starting in place and then moving through space.
- "We observe colors" (energetic music). The free exploration continues as we ask them to sit down to observe the exploration of those who have the plate of the color the teacher indicates.
- "We are looking for the same color." Students continue moving freely in space and look for someone with the same color to interact briefly (non-verbal communication). They change partners when they hear a signal from an instrument played by the teacher.
- "We are looking for a different color" (music with varied tempi). Moving freely, students look for someone with the object in a color different from theirs. Facing each other they improvise in mirror, changing the leader at a movement or stillness signal previously agreed by them.

Phase 2
- "5, 4, 3, 2, 1." Scattered throughout space, students work on balance, concentration, and creativity. They balance their plate upside down on their fingertips, first on five (greater security) down to only one (calm music).
- "Shall we add up?" In pairs they invent a short sequence of movements with the object, and they alternate leadership, change hands, and decide with how many fingers they hold the plate at each moment of the sequence (accompanied by sounds created by themselves).
- "We observe." They share their improvisation with the rest of the group.

Phase 3
- "Choreographic composition." Students create a choreography with the object in groups of approximately five, using aspects previously worked on to enrich their compositions (mirrors, pairs, "fingers," sounds, colors) and using a motivating music with a clear structure.

- "Let's go to the theater." The choreographic compositions are performed for the rest of the group. A brief reflection/constructive criticism on what has been observed will be encouraged, emphasizing aspects of aesthetic education.

Suggestion
"Let's dance." Teach a traditional folk dance where an object is used (e.g., La Botella/Mexico), so that students can internalize the content and observe it in other contexts. This can be incorporated in any phase of this sequence.

Further ideas with our object
- Mime/theater scene "transforming" it into another object (fan, frisbee, serving tray, etc.).
- Create a rhythmic piece with sounds produced using two plates.
- Create a graphic score on the floor with the plates (duration, pitch, etc.) and interpret it (sound and movement).

2. Movement / Stillness–Sound / Silence
Miriam Gurbanov

This theme is developed in three sessions aimed at students from nine years of age, with or without previous experience in body work and its link with musical content and other arts.

Objectives
- To experience individual and group movement, acquire knowledge of and incorporate subject material from other arts.
- To become aware of the opposition between movement and stillness (sound and silence).
- To encourage creativity through conscious work and sharing.
- To perceive and raise awareness that sound and silence are fundamental elements in life.
- To experience sound and its absence through movement.
- To develop group work activities, favoring attention and creativity.
- To continue development of the roles of both musician and dancer.

Session 1—Preparation
Content
- Peripheral vision. Use of the entire space. Spatial levels. Spatial and body design.
- Body awareness. Breathing. Movement and stillness (as part of the movement).
- Sound and silence. Tempo.

Procedure
- Spread freely in the space, each participant begins to walk at their own pace (no accompaniment), exercising peripheral vision and being aware of the group.
- They are asked to unify their speed without focusing their gaze on any point, "feeling" the group.
- When a student stops, everyone must stop (the nearest person can serve as a reference).
- Another student starts at a different speed to which everyone has to adapt.
- It is repeated, but the stop will be by making a shape with the body, in this case there will be a short stop with that chosen pose.
- Add to the previous activity variations of speed and spatial levels proposed by the teacher and/or by the students.

Adding sound
Placed in pairs, one performs the movement and the other will improvise what they perceive using percussion or melodic instruments. Change roles.

New pairs might be formed to further enrich the work. The dancing member must design a route until reaching a shape. This short design will be memorized to be repeated as an "ostinato." The other member will create the music that accompanies the route.

Composition, observation, and analysis
Once it has been secured, it will be shown to the group. A moment of stillness should be included in the pattern. The duration of each one will be determined by the pair. A brief discussion will follow.

Session 2—Elaboration
Space: Personal space. Locomotion in the entire space.
Content: Hearing. Sound/silence expressed in movement.
Resources: Rain stick. Triangle.

Procedure
- Body awareness. Lying on the floor without contact with another participant. Eyes closed. Perception of the duration when inhaling and exhaling.
- They perform a continuous movement during inhalation and a different one during exhalation.
- Still with their eyes closed, they listen to the duration of the sound of a rain stick (triangle or another suitable instrument) played by the teacher. They raise an arm as soon as they perceive that the sound has stopped.
- Do the same while standing, performing a continuous movement in place during the sound and a bodily form during the silence.
- It is repeated, but during the sound each one moves through the space and during the silence movement stops.

Composition, observation, and analysis
Divided into groups, students will develop a short composition with the elements worked on and show it to the others, followed by a brief discussion.

Session 3—Choreographic creation
Objectives
- To create a composition taking into account the content worked on.
- To observe and reflect.

Resources
Percussion instruments and everyday sound materials.

- We begin by recalling the elements of movement worked on (locomotion, stillness and body shapes, levels, speed, duration, continuous and discontinuous movement).
- The teacher presents different percussion instruments and everyday materials with which they can make a sound accompaniment to the choreographies (e.g., claves, temple blocks, guiro, cymbals, newspaper, corrugated cardboard, bunch of keys, etc.).
- The class is divided into groups (minimum of four members in each group).
- Each group will create a sequence by contributing movement motifs from the sequence worked on in previous sessions.

- Roles are switched so that all students explore both creative experiences: dance and musical accompaniment.
- Each group has the opportunity to show their work to the whole class.
- The teacher proposes a reflection on what has been observed.

Other suggestions
Experience the movement/stillness only with the sound of the paper generated by the performers. Integrate the material into the movement respecting the original pattern. Create drawings generated by movement/stillness on large pieces of paper spread on the floor using markers or pencils. Then use the drawings as paths for a choreographic sequence.

3. Movement Inspiration Through Different Objects
Isabel Galeza

Theme
Develop new movements using objects that have different characteristics to create duos with live accompaniment.

Group description
Sixteen students aged six to nine with diverse experience in music and dance. The sessions take place in the music theater workshop in the music school. Once a week the students meet for 90 minutes in the afternoon to develop together text, music, and movement for their own music theater piece.

Goals
- Experience physically opposing states using material in motion.
- Transfer movements derived from the material to the body.
- Together with a partner create a duo with or without material.
- Work on an instrumental movement accompaniment with another duo partner.

Motivation/introduction to the topic
In order to develop one's own dance personality, the human individual must face a wide range of opposing states, for example, limp—tense; high-spirited—despondent; narrow—wide; hard—soft. These physical states can be very far apart in one's own experience. Through the approach with the material, however, movements can be playfully opened up, explored, and transferred from the material to the body and to movement.

Exploration of the material
Warm-up: For the preparatory improvisation, students imagine four points in space that they connect in different ways, for example with a body part, a great tension, a sweeping movement, etc.

Improvisation: The room is divided into four imagined squares. Contrasting objects are placed in each one of the squares. The students move freely from field to field and playfully move with the objects, e.g., elastic bands, folding rulers, scarves, bean bags. Over time, they move in the fields without picking up the objects and only reflect the quality of the object, e.g., the elastic band with long, drawn-out movements; the folding ruler with pointed, stretched movements; the scarf with light, sweeping movements; and the bean bag with heavy, grounded movements.

Composition

Two students choose an object as a duo and work out a short sequence of movements, first with the objects, then without. The sequence of movements should be fixed and repeatable.

Demonstration

The duo groups demonstrate their work to the other students. The group discusses which instruments might suit which duo group and which quality of movement. The students can use their voices, body percussion, instruments they can play (piano, recorder, violin, etc.), as well as all percussion instruments from small percussion to barred instruments, marimba, and vibraphone. Together with another duo group, an accompaniment to the movement sequence is developed. The focus is on the quality of movement and its musical realization.

Reflection

The students express how much their otherwise often stereotype movements have changed through the experiences with the objects. The younger children in particular found the movements with the elastic band to be the most intense. As a result, the movements were executed with more intensity, higher quality, and awareness.

4. First Encounter with Cantonese Opera
Anida Chan, Maggie Ho

Idea

Hong Kong has always been a vibrant city with mixed culture, deeply influenced by Western culture. However, we feel that it is important to help our children to get to know, love, and appreciate their own cultural traditions. Cantonese opera is one of the great heritages of Chinese culture, and it is especially relevant to our children because of the use of Cantonese as the language. However, the number of people appreciating this performing art has been declining. It is often perceived as entertainment for our grandparents, not for children or young adults. We think that it is essential to introduce this valuable cultural tradition to our children and would like to give the children in our music school a playful approach with the help of a competent specialist in this area.

Group

There were five children (aged six to nine) who participated in this summer course that included ten sessions of three hours each, with a stage performance at the end of the summer. It was a relatively small group, but we could take care of each child and they had their own chance to shine on stage.

Process

The *Sifu* (teacher) of Cantonese opera is well known to be very strict and harsh on the students. But luckily, we met one teacher who was open-minded and funny, and willing to co-operate with us, teaching together using the Orff Schulwerk approach. She was also a professional Cantonese opera actress and singer.

At first, she showed the children videos of Cantonese opera, introducing the actors, movements, stage settings, costumes, objects, and music, which are all very unique and different from what the children are familiar with.

Then, the teacher taught them some basic skills of specific movements such as leg kicking, cloud hands, walks, and jumps, etc. We added percussion instruments as accompaniment to make it more musical and memorable for the children.

We went on to explore the different objects used in Cantonese opera, such as spears, flags, and ribbons. With these objects and the movements that developed to operate them, we went on to create some short scenes. For example, the movement of very long ribbons (resembling the traditional "water sleeves") made the children think of a fairy goddess under the sea. The spears and flags were great for fighting scenes, and the children all became imaginary shrimp and crab soldiers. With movements as stimulators, they were having great fun creating.

Singing is essential in Cantonese opera. We learned about the "solfège" in Chinese music, which has a similar concept in Western music but different representations. The teacher sang in a female vocal style about the breakfast she had, which was hilarious to all of us. The children then went on imitating this singing style, while improvising lyrics about what they had for breakfast.

We then worked on a famous Cantonese opera scene, which was about a princess from the Dong-ting Lake, being rescued by a young man, and expressing her gratitude towards him. The children worked very hard to learn the lyrics and movements. They also made their own costumes. It was really a challenging yet memorable experience for them.

Outcome

On the day of the performance, the children started by Chinese style rapping what they had composed. Then, in rondo form, they performed a short well-known Chinese piece with Orff ensemble as section A, then *Liangxiang* (make an entrance on stage) with different objects and movement as section B. Next was the flags and spears fighting scene with carefully designed movements that looked exciting. Finally, it was the famous Cantonese opera scene with singing. The performance was accompanied by the music teachers playing percussion instruments such as gong, rhythm blocks, and drum, along with the Chinese instrument *Guzheng* (a type of zither).

Feedback

The children had an unforgettable experience and became interested in Cantonese opera. A parent appreciated that we made a great effort introducing this cultural tradition to children in an innovative and fun way. We hope to do more projects like this in the future.

References and Resources

Collegium Musicum de Buenos Aires. (n.d.). *Collegium Musicum, Home*. Retrieved August 26, 2023, from https://www.collegiummusicum.org.ar

European Music School Union. (n.d.). *What we do*. Retrieved August 26, 2023, from https://www.musicschoolunion.eu

Gobierno de España Agencia Estatal Boletín Oficial del Estado. (n.d.). *Orden de 30 de julio de 1992 por la que se regulan las condiciones de creación y funcionamiento de las Escuelas de Música y Danza* [Order of July 30, 1992, regulating the conditions for the creation and functioning of the schools of music and dance]. Retrieved August 26, 2023, from https://www.boe.es/eli/es/o/1992/07/30/(5)

Haselbach, B. (1977). Tanzerziehung in der Musikschule [Dance education in music schools]. *Orff-Schulwerk Informationen, 19*, 27–31. https://www.orff-schulwerk-forum salzburg.org/magazine-osh

Orff-Schulwerk Informationen number 19 is dedicated exclusively to dance in music schools with articles about a five-day course on the topic and several articles by different authors (only in German). https://www.orff-schulwerk-forum-salzburg.org/magazine-osh

Stokoe, P. (1978). *Expresión Corporal, Guía didáctica para el docente* [Body expression. Didactic guide for teachers]. Buenos Aires: Ricordi Americana.

Stokoe, P. (1990). *Expresión Corporal: Arte, Salud y Educación* [Body expression: Art, health and education]. Buenos Aires: Humanitas. Instituto de Ciencias Sociales Aplicadas.

Movement and Dance with Inclusive/Mixed-abled Groups in the Context of Orff Schulwerk

Tetiana Chernous (Ukraine), Angelika Holzer (Austria),
Evelyne Walser-Wohlfarter (Austria)

INTRODUCTION

We are all different. When we stop talking about inclusion, then inclusion happens.

In this article we focus on principles and methods to empower inclusion in movement and dance, which is a central form of expression in Orff Schulwerk. The practical examples in the second part give insights into different projects, some of which are already inclusive and some that are steps towards inclusion.

Orff's concept follows the idea "of allowing the common ground of rhythmical-based forms of expression to become practical and personal experiences through creative processes that are achievable by all" (Haselbach, 2011/1984, p. 196). Wilhelm Keller (1962) left a rich heritage to open elemental music making for all people that still inspires us. It can be said that from an educational perspective Orff Schulwerk is an inclusive approach (Sangiorgio, 2018; Salmon, 2010). So how do we ensure that every learner matters equally?

About inclusion

"Every learner matters and matters equally." This definition from the UNESCO *Guide for ensuring inclusion and equity in education* (2017, p. 12) reveals the meaning of the process we call inclusion.

When we investigate the history of societies, we see developments from exclusion ("others" locked away) to separation (certain institutions for the "others") towards integration (the "others" are in the same group and are given special treatment). The actual goal in different countries and regions is to enable inclusion. The 2020 Global Education Monitoring Report *All means all* (UNESCO) argues for thinking of inclusion as a process: actions that embrace diversity and build a sense of belonging, rooted in the belief that every person has value and potential, and should be respected, regardless of their background, ability, or identity (p. 20). As various current crises (caused by the pandemic, international conflicts, climate change, economic problems, etc.) can be very individually stressful, settings that include people with psychological stress will become even more important.

When we think even further ahead, our goal for the future is to no longer be needing the term inclusion, i.e., it will be self-evident that everyone matters. The concept of inclusion is revealed in general educational methodology, and Lamproulis (2017, p. 25) postulates that, "In an era where our 'inclusive' society fails to engage its members, inclusiveness in the arts is not a choice but a necessity." There is a broad interest in practicing inclusion in art, music, and dance education.

There are different terms used for the concept of collaborative dancing among people with differing abilities and backgrounds. We find "community dance," "diverse dance," "integrated dance," "mixed-abilities dance," or "inclusive dance" (Quinten & Schwiertz, 2014). The term mixed-ability dance is used in this article to make clear that dance for people with and without disabilities is spoken about. When we use inclusive dance in this article, we speak about a group where all people are welcome, where a process is aimed to "overcome barriers limiting the presence, participation and achievement of learners" (UNESCO, 2017, p. 7).

Principles of inclusive dance

Working on the principles of inclusive dance allows us to see that these go hand in hand with the principles of the Orff Schulwerk (Hartmann & Haselbach, 2017) and beyond. An open human view and the related attitude is the basis for working with inclusive groups. Attitude comes before method.

The individual is in the center

One fundamental methodological principle is the focus on the human being. Regardless of physical characteristics, mental condition, origin, age, gender, religion, sexual orientation, etc., the individual is at the center. An inclusive group is characterized by welcoming all the differences that make us human. All participants are included and valued with their individual abilities, interests, and needs (Salmon, 2010, n. p.).

The concept of diversity

Inclusive dance practice is not concerned with perfection, nor with dichotomies of healthy vs. disabled, young vs. old, trained vs. untrained, but with plurality. Beyond compassion, inclusive dance means to create forms of dance that do not exclude, but enable, so that every given physicality requires something new, something that has not existed before (Walser-Wohlfarter & Richarz, 2020).

Creativity in improvisation and composition

In inclusive dance, improvisation is an essential process in which the diverse participants can explore their own movement possibilities. As the work progresses, an individual and collective repertoire of movements develops. "Improvisation is suitable for a class that includes (…) disabled people because it does not require fixed, uniform movement, but in it the different ways of moving are of equal value" (Walser-Wohlfarter & Richarz, 2022, p. 29). According to Hartmann & Haselbach (2017, p. 25), the students should be able to "experience creative activity from the beginning. A teaching practice that does not demand and support the creativity of the students can hardly be called Orff Schulwerk."

For some students with cognitive disabilities the spontaneous form of direct expression of feeling, authentic self-expression, experimentation, exploration, and improvisation, may be their only possibility. For others, creative processing of impressions can lead to artistically created expression where invention, composition, and rehearsal lead to a finished piece (Salmon, 2010, n. p.).

The concept of time

The concept of time expands in diverse settings. A diversity of people also means that different needs regarding time on tasks are to be considered. When for example a blind professional dancer, a wheelchair user, a dancer with spastic cerebral palsy, and two amateur dancers (one with and one without a mental disability) meet in class they can all learn a great deal from each other. All five perceive the world through different channels and need individual periods of time to process information. It requires openness, curiosity, and courage from everyone and sensitivity on the part of the teacher. For example, each of the five dancers would need a different amount of time to cross the room diagonally. For various reasons, people often need a longer amount of time to become involved, to break down their barriers, their fears. This aspect of time requires that the teacher should pay more attention to the participants.

The social dimension and the concept of connection

When the teacher manages to get people to connect with each other the ground is prepared for artistic work. Wolfgang Stange mentions that a wide variety of fears can break down the connection, and that the teacher is always working in the background to rebuild and maintain this connection again and again (E. Walser-Wohlfarter & A. Holzer, personal communication, July 27, 2022). "If it is possible to find diverse solutions for the diverse bodies that come together in the studio, the elemental aspect of dance is fulfilled: the encounter" (Walser-Wohlfarter & Richarz, 2022, p. 29).

Different levels of the encounter are enabled in inclusive dance settings:

1. Encounter with yourself takes place on a deeply personal level of self-interaction and with one's individual creativity (I am my body, I am my sound, I am my creativity). It happens in awareness of one's own needs, possibilities, feelings, and emotions. The feelings of safety, trust, and joy of mutual creativity provide the preconditions for such self-meetings. It opens the door to exploring one's own uniqueness, meaningfulness, and value.
2. Encounter with someone else happens through interaction with another person on a body/dance-dialogue level. In order to establish a true contact between people with very different movement repertoire, certain conditions to enable the dialogue must be created. A deep feeling and understanding of the meaning and essence of the partner's movement should be here. Curiosity, interest, and willingness to hear, feel, and understand the partner should be included.
3. Encounter with the group enables joint creativity and social processes. An inclusive group should encourage interaction while considering the capabilities of every person. This meets our natural need to belong to a social group.

Stange adds that dance itself must be a passion, as does the desire to help others grow (E. Walser-Wohlfarter & A. Holzer, personal communication, July 27, 2022).

The idea of passion and the artistic dimension

The teacher must bring passion for dance. No matter what they want to convey. According to Stange, they must do it with great dedication and conviction in order to be able to inspire others. That passion becomes common ground, because "working with different physicalities, facing sensory challenges, expanding on classic art forms and breaking out of the familiar environment requires more effort, more time and a lot of personal involvement and trust" (Lamproulis, 2017, p. 25). "The entrance of disabled people into dance studies creates vital openings for new experience, for confusion, for connection, and most importantly, for dialogue about what that art of dance can signify" (Benjamin, 2002, p. 8). Stange, referring to inclusive dance, says: "We can be grateful that in this work we experience moments in which honesty becomes visible."

The role of the teacher

A teacher of creative dance opens doors to new experiences. This requires a skilled facilitator who is experienced with the content (movement and dance) and who can provide a wide range of teaching and learning methods.

Working with inclusive groups, we value and celebrate differences and have a participatory attitude. We want all people to participate and co-create, therefore we need to provide an atmosphere of openness and safety for all students. We have a passion for dance and curiosity as well as warmth and affection for people as they are in the moment. There is a need to individualize by identifying students' abilities and reactions, and by choosing modifications if needed (Kaufmann, 2006).

The following questions can be helpful for teaching mixed-abled or inclusive groups:

- Do I value and celebrate differences?
- Do I love to improvise and am I open for new ideas arising from the process?
- Do I know methods for adapting instructions to meet the needs of all learners?
- Am I able to present/invent variations on the theme?
- Am I open to inform myself about different disabilities?
- How open am I to work in a multidisciplinary team and to collaborate with different specialists (in the field of special needs, therapy, physical education, etc.)?
- Do I use respectful and simple language?
- Do I express myself through non-verbal communication?
- Do I have access to barrier-free, accessible spaces, or can I find/organize them?

PRACTICAL EXAMPLES

Overview

1. Tetiana Chernous: Dance project with child-parent groups
This example describes the process of working with a child-parent inclusive group whose focus is on movement within the Orff Schulwerk.

2. Angelika Holzer: Dance project with teacher education students and children with special needs
The general design of dance classes in a mixed-abled setting and important findings are described.

3. Evelyne Walser-Wohlfarter: How disabilities influence my artistic work
Using a production by the ensemble "tanzfähig," insights into the choreographic approach are described.

1. Dance Project with Child-Parent Groups
Tetiana Chernous

The target group
Child-parent groups, families with two-and-one-half to six-year-old children with special care needs and different types of disorders, as well as their neurotypical siblings (Lu et al., 2021) are involved.

What are the peculiarities of the combination of two such different worlds as children and their parents? They should be easily combined, but in a practical way we can notice many challenges. Modern life separates families more and more, and this is a big issue that becomes an obstacle to a child's development. The problems of a modern family, in particular a family raising a child with special needs, normally relate to such challenges as emotional distancing in relationships, focusing on functional care, lack of creativity in everyday communication. This was the reason for creating this group according to inclusion principles. The Orff Schulwerk concept with its powerful tools of movement and dance was a guide for the group work. Effective non-verbal mechanisms of interaction were activated that gave a chance to direct the work of this inclusive group towards creative exploration, reduce the level of authoritarianism, and improve relationships, which had a positive effect on the development of the children. The presence of siblings in the group also extended the opportunities for inclusive interaction.

Meeting ritual, warmup, and a search for your own topics

The main goal in this step is to break the ice and enliven participants sensually, emotionally, physically, and mentally. At the beginning of a process, space and environment are very important. The participants come into the room filled with instruments and appealing materials, and there is also a good amount of space for movement. Children adapt naturally, moving freely in a new space. Sometimes they are attracted to the instruments and different objects; sometimes they are involved in the common movement and then a spontaneous interaction in the movement happens. Clear instructions for parents, who also need to adjust to the new space that they and their child are interacting in and adjust to the other members of the group, help them make this process more understandable.

The music accompanying this process reflects the main theme of the lesson (e.g., seasons, travelling, autumn, zoo). Most often I use my own improvisation, however, recorded music might be used as well. This step is concluded by the meeting ritual when the participants gather in a circle and greet each other by introducing themselves through their own movement.

As a basis for the meeting ritual, I usually use one greeting song, which is easily put in the main context of the topic, e.g., we meet in autumn, at the zoo, in the rain, on a train. Each participant shows their movement, which reflects the images that are important to them and related to the topic.

Interaction and focusing on communication

All group members focus on some aspect of the main topic and share their ideas through movement. For example, if we talk about autumn, it might be rain. As a rule, the whole group repeats with pleasure, and in this way not only movement, but also a psycho-emotional experience is shared. It is important that each participant has a chance to show their ideas. Behind this pleasant exchange there is a natural need to be seen and accepted by the group and of course the creativity is growing with every shared idea.

Enrichment or broadening of thinking

According to Yatchmenoff et al. (1998), there are many possible variants to enrich the main idea. For instance, introducing additional materials for the creative process, such as musical instruments, art elements, and other objects. Movement can be accompanied by musical instruments. The group process also involves the gradual transition from single to pair work and to larger groups.

Creating and fixing of a sequence

All participants develop a single music and movement pattern (beginning, main part, and end). If the group is divided into segments, it can be two or three images, creating a common story or using several sequences to build a larger form.

The process of visualization of an enriched idea contributes to the creation of a holistic image. It helps to display both movement and sound ideas, while being the product of co-creation as well. Sometimes it can be a common drawing done by the whole group, sometimes a sculpture or craft made from natural materials.

A drawing or other form of visualization will be used later to remind participants of their emotions, circumstances, and impressions of the process. We keep such visuals as a link that provides access to an emotional resource and a new motor experience.

Closing stage: gathering experience, gratitude, farewell ritual
Using a certain ritual is also quite crucial for the completion of the process. It can include a traditional song or dance. Normally, we use a song in which—as in the greeting song—there is room for movement improvisation by each participant. Like the greeting ritual, the participants share their movements, reflecting their experience of the meeting, which means what they did or did not like.

All participants—but especially parents—need help in initiating their own creativity. Clear instructions should be given to guide their actions and imagination.

The idea of involvement and adaptation into the creative process at all stages is important. It is important to make them think wider, to broaden their outlook, activate participants physically, mentally, and socially, and encourage them to be interested in their own ideas as well as those of the group.

2. Dance Project with Teacher Education Students and Children with Special Needs
Angelika Holzer

This project focuses on joint experiences of two very diverse groups of students. It provides steps towards a more inclusive society by preparing future teachers for their work with heterogeneous groups. In the project, schoolchildren with severe disabilities and my teacher education students danced together. In addition to "learning by doing," reflection, metacognition, and ongoing self-assessment (Sangiorgio, 2018) were central to build skills and knowledge for the education students. We danced together five times for two hours in the sports hall of the school.

There was a wide range of abilities and disabilities in the room, so the focus was on improvisational skills and variation on the theme, on the possibilities of communication and interaction through movement, and on valuing time together.

Design of the class
Each class started with the education students. We talked about the focus of today's class and did a dance warmup. Being prepared on a body level turned out to be very rich for encountering the children. Most children communicated with their bodies and not with spoken words.

- **Orientation—arriving in the room and in the circle:** When the children entered, my "screening process" as a teacher started. I welcomed each child and observed how they reacted in that moment and what they were able to understand. I could already find common movement abilities. The teacher education students observed this process and welcomed the children.
- **Ritual—name and movement:** In the beginning, each person said their name (or an assistant said the name for a non-speaking child) and made one movement. Then everybody in the room answered with one individual movement. It was all about answering and not about imitation, because not everyone can imitate every movement. This ritual ensures that at least in the beginning everybody was noticed by the whole group. It also was to warm up the body physically. Desired forms of interaction could be shared. For example, we are dancing with the person, not with the wheelchair. Everybody could notice different communication and

movement possibilities. For example, when Heike points her finger upward it means "yes," when she puckers up her mouth she is saying "no."

- **Exercises to explore a theme:** Each exercise was demonstrated with a partner/small group and verbally explained (e.g., exploring fast and slow movements and stillness).
- **Work on the theme:** In duets, small groups, and the whole group the exercises were danced, variations on the theme were presented.
- **Design, practice, and finally present a group dance.** This is in front of the whole class (e.g., we move fast from one corner to the next, then on a low level towards the center, find a stillness, and then move backwards into the first corner).
- **Final reflection and closing ritual in the circle:** Each person could offer feedback (verbally or danced). As a closing we inhaled and brought our hands towards the sky, exhaling we brought them down towards the earth (three times) at the end we touched our heart or belly. The rituals at the beginning and at the ending of each class provided a secure surrounding.

Before and after the lessons, the education students had time to discuss the individual experiences and reflect on the different behaviors of all involved. The following principles and methods supported an inclusive learning environment: secure surrounding, focus on competences, work with common movement abilities, free choice, improvisation, a shared theme.

The dance project in a mixed-abled group offered many individual experiences. Each participant made their own journey. One enjoyed, learned, was in contact, struggled, or had fun. To be sure, it invited us to open our hearts and helped us to connect (Holzer, 2018).

3. How Disabilities Influence My Artistic Work
Evelyne Walser-Wohlfarter

When I work with a group on an artistic idea or theme, it is in the foreground as well as the access of the people participating in the theme. The physical, mental, or intellectual limitations that the participants bring to the studio recede into the background on the one hand, because the artistic work goes beyond that. And on the other hand, the limitations remain present, but if we include them in the process, we can also take the person in their entirety on the path of an artistic exploration.

The subject itself must not be hindered. What is exciting is that the method of working out the theme can be more diverse because of the participants' disabilities. This means that the topic can go into even more depth and breadth. From my experience, this is precisely why inclusive dance contains further potential that is available to a choreographer.

Interestingly, it is often expected that dance work will be limited if people with disabilities are involved. However, it only becomes so if the choreographer does not manage to get out of their usual ideas of what dance should be and refuses to get involved with the unexpected again and again. It requires great flexibility and openness towards people in their diversity.

Furthermore, the question must be asked as to how disability is incorporated into a production. Should it be placed at the center of the dance piece or is it simply one of many characteristics of the dancer? And how essential is this disability for individual expression? Is it at all? If, on the part of the audience, the disability fades into the background in the course of a dance piece, does the person as such become more visible? And is it not about what happens between people? And this in-between is free of any restriction. If the choreographer succeeds in making this in-between visible and tangible, inclusive dance has freed itself from all the external restrictions.

When the Lilacs Bloomed[1] is a duet between an older, tall, male dancer with a walking disability and a small, professional female dancer. It arose from my preoccupation with what is still present from the post-war period in Berlin. I was interested in how people who knew each other very well before the war, then suffered different and drastic experiences during that time, met again after the war, and what that has to do with us today. The announcement of the piece was: *All the stories our bodies hold come alive again when we meet each other. By telling them to each other, our memories begin to flow. The feelings we have for each other change. Afterwards, nothing is ever the same as before—even if we may repeat the same thing. If you want, you can feel how the time we share opens the space we have in common.*

For me, the dancer's disability was not an issue. However, I was aware of the unusual aesthetics of his walking for the stage. But it was not emphasized. It was simply there. Anna Volkmann (2013) noted in her review, "then at some point you discover the one leg that looks and functions differently from the other."

I am much more interested in how the male dancer, himself a child of the post-war period, and the female dancer can connect with the vulnerability inherent in this subject matter. How can encounter and non-encounter be expressed? How does vulnerability feel, how does it emanate from us individually? Where is the "I" and where is the "we"?

If I had worked with people with other physicalities, different images would certainly have emerged, but I would have followed the thread that the theme set out for me. Thus, I would like to state that disability is not in the foreground of my artistic work. It is a small part of many things. As a dance maker, I am interested in getting to the essence of a theme and finding something that connects us. Capturing what is revealed to us in the dance studio and opening spaces to share this with the audience is my great joy.

An audience member wrote some words about the piece. These make clear that it is less about the performer's disability and more about what is allowed to develop between the dancers and the audience. She wrote the following: "A dance without narration, without history, without the past. A dance that opens its own associative spaces in its abstractness. A dance that does not lecture, that does not want anything, but invites you to open to what you see, to let yourself be touched, to get involved in a world beyond words. A dance, carefully choreographed with sparse means of expression, which reaches all the more deeply and places a non-intentional understanding of the all-too-human search for closeness, for connection, in the space."

References and Resources

Benjamin, A. (2002). *Making an entrance. Theory and practice for disabled and non-disabled dancers.* London: Rutledge.

Hartmann, W., with Haselbach, B. (2017). Die Prinzipien des Orff-Schulwerks/The principals of Orff-Schulwerk (V. Maschat, Trans.). *Orff-Schulwerk Heute, 97,* 23–26. https://www.orff-schulwerk-forum-salzburg.org/magazine-osh

Haselbach, B. (2011). Reflections on the dance educational aspects of Orff-Schulwerk (M. Murray, Trans.). In B. Haselbach (Ed.), *Texts on theory and practice of Orff-Schulwerk, Vol. 1: Basic texts from the years 1932–2010* (pp. 196–219). Mainz: Schott. (Originally work published in 1984)

Holzer, A. (2018). Let's dance together! Students and children in a mixed-abled project. In T. Haugen & K. Skjerdingstad (eds.), *Children and young people, aesthetics and special needs. An interdisciplinary approach* (pp. 223–240). Oslo: Vidarforlaget.

Kaufmann, K. (2006). *Inclusive creative movement and dance.* Champaign, IL: Human Kinetics.

---

1 *Als der Flieder blühte* is a 26-minute dance piece produced by the initiative *tanzfähig*. Concept and choreography: Evelyne Walser-Wohlfarter; dance: Alessandra Lola Agostini and Bernhard Richarz; music: Pyotr Ilyich Tchaikovsky.

Keller, W. (2011). *Elemental music—an attempt to define it* (M. Murray, Trans.). In B. Haselbach (Ed.), Texts on theory and practice of Orff-Schulwerk, Vol 1: Basic texts from the years 1932-2010 (pp. 118-133). Mainz: Schott. (Original work published in 1962 as Elementare Musik. Versuch einer Begriffsbestimmung)

Lamproulis, C. (2017). Hinter den Kulissen von Un-Label [Behind the scenes of Un-Label]. In Sommertheater Pusteblume e.V. (Ed.), *Un-Label. Innovation Vielfalt. Neue Wege in den darstellenden Künsten Europas. Ein Handbuch zur inklusiven Kunst- und Kulturarbeit* (p. 23–26). https://un-label.eu/project/handbuch/

Lu, Y., Douglas, S. N., Bagawan, A., & Hauck, J. L. (2021). Using neurotypical siblings as intervention agents to guide individuals with autism spectrum disorders: A systematic review. *Research in Autism Spectrum Disorders, 89* (article 1018568). https://doi.org/10.1016/j.rasd.2021.101868

Quinten, S., & Schwiertz, H. (2015). Fähigkeitsgemischter Tanz—Der aktuelle Forschungsstand. *Zeitschrift für Inklusion* (4). https://www.inklusion-online.net/index.php/inklusion-online/article/view/254

Salmon, S. (2010) Inclusion and Orff-Schulwerk. *Musicworks, 15*(1), 27-33. http://bidok.uibk.ac.at/library/salmon-orff-e.html

Sangiorgio, A. (2018). Das Potential des Orff-Schulwerks für die Arbeit mit besonderen Zielgruppen/Working with special populations: The potential of the Orff-Schulwerk approach. *Orff-Schulwerk Heute 99*, 13–21. https://www.orff-schulwerk-forum-salzburg.org/magazine-osh

UNESCO (2017). *A guide for ensuring inclusion and equity in education*. Paris: UNESCO. https://unesdoc.unesco.org/ark:/48223/pf0000248254

UNESCO (2020). *Global education monitoring (GEM) report summary. Inclusion and education all means all*. Paris: UNESCO. https://unesdoc.unesco.org/ark:/48223/pf0000373718

Volkland, A. (2013, August 24). *II Das Nichtperfekte als Herausforderung—zwei Performer nehmen sie an und eine Solistin ist noch unentschieden (tanzfähig und Elena Walter)* [The imperfect as a challenge – two performers accept it and one soloist is still undecided (tanzfähig und Elena Walter)]. ada-Studio und Bühne für zeitgenössischen Tanz. https://ada-studio.jimdofree.com/studioschreiber-texte/studioschreiber-texte-2013-14/text-1-2013-14/

Walser-Wohlfarter, E., & Richarz, B. (2020). Zeitgenössisch in Vielfalt unterrichten—Aus der Praxis einer Tanzinitiative [Contemporary teaching in diversity—from the practice of a dance initiative]. In H. Henning (Ed.), All inclusive?! *Aspekte einer inklusiven Musik- und Tanzpädagogik, Innsbrucker Perspektiven zur Musikpädagogik*, pp. 147–168. Münster: Waxmann Verlag. https://elibrary.utb.de/doi/pdf/10.31244/9783830992769

Walser-Wohlfarter, E., & Richarz, B. (2022). Vulnerable disability. Dance with an inclusive group – a video is created. *Orff Arts and Education 1/22*, 26–29. https://magazin.orff.de/en/profiles/aad8ce2cb493/editions/2c-65b6470e548c49474b/pages/page/14

Yatchmenoff, D. K., Koren, P. E., Friesen, B. J., Gordon, L. J., & Kinney, R. F. (1998). Enrichment and stress in families caring for a child with a serious emotional disorder. *Journal of Child and Family Studies, 7*, 129–145. https://doi.org/10.1023/A:1022935014502

Movement/Dance Projects with Diverse Target Groups

Insuk Lee (South Korea/Germany), Annabell Opelt (Germany), Sonja Pfennigbauer &
Vivi Tanzmeister (Austria), Paul Scheer (Austria), Manuela Widmer (Austria)

INTRODUCTION

Teachers who are trained in Orff Schulwerk, especially graduates of the Orff Institute, are by no means active only in kindergartens, schools, music schools, or teacher training institutions. Especially those who work as freelancers often initiate independent projects or are invited to do so. These very often arise in the free time sector. Due to their subject matter, such projects interest a certain group of people and may be a short-term activity for a special occasion. Sometimes they result in groups that continue to work together for a longer period, or they may be organized events that repeat.

The content, goals, and organization often differ significantly from any curricular-determined instruction at public or private educational or social institutions. Participation is voluntary and, of course, participants are not formally evaluated or graded. Those who are interested in the project's topic, feel comfortable in the group and under its leadership to get involved, contribute ideas, and, to a certain extent, may also assume co-responsibility.

Typical examples are events at special festivities (see Insuk Lee's report on a St. Nicholas festival that brings together kindergarten children with seniors from an old people's home on an intergenerational basis), or gatherings of committed parents, grandparents, or godparents that have been taking place for years and have become a tradition. Families may come together with their children for the annual weekend of a family course (see Annabell Opelt's example), or a community music drama can bring together children with amateurs and professionals (see Manuela Widmer's project description).

The establishment of performance groups for the purpose of preparing a dance and music program for public performance represents such a special project (see the contribution about the Flitz Company from Sonja Pfennnigbauer and Vivi Tanzmeister). And there is the idea of a children's circus, in which children learn a different way that rhythm helps them to learn difficult movements through juggling and other artistic techniques. These are joyful projects for children, prepared in a playful way (see the description of this work by Paul Scheer).

As different as these and many other examples of special projects may be, they all have essential features of Orff Schulwerk pedagogy in common: the appreciation and importance of each individual group member and their particular talents; playful, creative learning in a holistic way of perception; and expression of movement and dance experiences as an embodied form of music in a communicative way.

PRACTICAL EXAMPLES

Overview

1. **Annabell Opelt: The Family Course of the Orff-Schulwerk Gesellschaft Deutschland [German Orff-Schulwerk Association]–a cross-generational course concept**
   The annual Family Course involves different family constellations with children from the age of six. The intergenerational approach runs through the entire course concept.

2. **Insuk Lee: Intergenerational St. Nicholas celebration with kindergarten children and senior citizens**
   Although children and seniors at St. Josefs Home in Munich live under one roof, they generally keep to themselves. The St. Nicholas celebration brought together the generations.

3. **Paul Scheer: Movement and rhythm as part of a new circus pedagogy**
   Circus pedagogy involves educators working with laypersons with the aim of having fun while learning and exploring new things rather than gaining difficult skills. It is a new pedagogy that uses a combination of theater, movement, balance, dance, and music.

4. **Sonja Pfennigbauer and Vivi Tanzmeister: Mixed-abled dance ensemble Flitz**
   In a safe space, where all dancers can move freely and without judgment, dancers focus on art, human connection, and the quality of the experience independent of each individual dancer's level.

5. **Manuela Widmer: *The Conference of the Animals*–for children and other artists**
   A community music drama based on the novel by Erich Kästner. Libretto: Manuela Widmer, composition: Jakob Gruchmann. © Publishing House for Children's Theater, Hamburg/Germany.

1. The Family Course of the Orff-Schulwerk Gesellschaft Deutschland [German Orff-Schulwerk Association]–A Cross-Generational Course Concept
Annabell Opelt

Idea
The Family Course of the German Orff-Schulwerk Association was founded in 1985 by Christiane Wieblitz. It takes place annually from Palm Sunday to Maundy Thursday. Every year between 30 and 35 families take part. There are different family constellations with children from the age of six. The intergenerational approach runs through the entire course concept.

Group
Parents come with their children, grandparents with their grandchildren, or godparents with their godchild. In this context, exciting heterogeneous group constellations develop that differ in age as well as in previous music and dance experience, yet still allow for common creative activities. During the mornings, classes are held in age-matched groups, while the afternoon program offers targeted and intergenerational music, theater, dance, and drumming projects. Only the teen project works as a closed group under the guidance of instructors.

Theme and Content: Example with folding lanterns
The dance project takes place on three afternoons (2.5 hours each). The content of the workshop and the didactic structure of a topic depends on the leadership team and the composition

of the groups, and that can vary. The focus is on social interaction and creative work in the family social structure. The process-oriented and open character often leads to a performance on the last day.

Various topics can be mentioned as examples:

- Exploration of a specific object (e.g., large foldable lanterns) and development of a movement composition.
- Exploring movement impulses initiated by spatial relationship variations (e.g., exploring closeness and distance).
- *La Chapelloise*, a French folk dance, initially explored in movement sequences and its original form, expanded, and finally transformed.
- Visual arts as inspiration for movement impulses.

Introductory phase

This serves as the playful contact, the physical warmup, and the opening for the further creative process. The tasks are not differentiated according to age. Instead, they are formulated in such a way that they can be implemented by everyone or that there is support within intergenerational pair and group formations.

Exploration of ideas and material

Often the exploration phase starts as individual work. The goal is either to move the material or to be moved by the material. Well-chosen music supports this phase. All participants have a lantern, and the leader gives supporting ideas as impulses that refer to the size, the level, or the locomotion with the material. In this way, it is possible to try out initial ideas as well as to work together with partners. Each partner can keep their own lantern, or each pair may use only one.

Short reflection

The reflection usually takes place in a seated circle or—depending on the objective—through a questionnaire. The aim is to enable an initial exchange. There can be room for observations as well as for questions or challenges.

Elaboration

Because there should be room for intergenerational work in particular, emphasis is placed on partner and small group work in the elaboration and during the further creative design process. However, a solo can also find its place should it arise in the process and be desired by the group. In this phase, movement ideas are increasingly tested (e.g., tempo, dynamics, or character) and their execution is fixed.

Demonstration, feedback, reflection

Results are shown and discussed. Depending on the process and project planning, writing on a flipchart or "moderation cards" can be useful at this point. In terms of content, the reflection focuses on one's own experience, the perception and effect of what was observed, or the joint conception of the piece.

Final thoughts

This linear description of the didactic steps cannot completely depict the process-oriented work. Depending on the objectives and the course of the process, rounds of reflection are added and the elaboration of the material goes through different stages.

Due to the frequently repeated participation of some course participants, the concept of family refers not only to the biological family, but also to "course families" that are created annually.

Anne Frey, a psychologist and course participant for many years, described this quality in her article "Strengthening Relationships and Growing Together," "When each generation gets a part, and this is brought together so that something common emerges in which everyone is present and the whole is more than the sum of the parts—what could be better?" (Frey, 2019, p. 35).

2. Intergenerational St. Nicholas Celebration with Kindergarten Children and Senior Citizens
Insuk Lee

An intergenerational project was launched on the initiative of the social pedagogue at the St. Josefs Home in Munich. Although children and seniors lived under one roof, they largely kept to themselves, separated from those in different phases of life. The upcoming St. Nicholas celebration was to be a joint celebration of young and old, bringing together the generations.

Participants
The participating seniors, aged 70-100, are residents of the nursing care area and have various age-related impairments; about 20% were wheelchair-bound and 50-70% used walkers. They were already participating in the weekly music and dance classes and were enthusiastic about the idea of the St. Nicholas celebration.

The kindergarten children, who live in the same building, have their own rooms and a separate entrance so they have little opportunity to interact with the seniors, except for chance encounters in the common courtyard.

Student observers
The students of the Richard Strauss Conservatory in Munich, who enrolled in the course Elemental Music Education with Seniors, were involved in the concept development and documentation. The project took place under the author's supervision as part of their studies. They recorded and photographed the entire process. They took over the procurement of costumes and equipment, while the children made the hat and cape for St. Nicholas.

Preparation and approach of the two age groups
The preparation lessons for the kindergarten children began four weeks prior to the celebration. On three Tuesdays, they learned songs and dances for the joint session with the seniors on Wednesday.

There was no extra session for the seniors at that time, but in the fifteen minutes after the children left, they felt a great need to talk about their impressions. (Children have 45 minutes, seniors have 60 minutes).

In the first lesson together there was, among other activities, a game with balloons to the tune of "a bird comes flying," which became "a balloon comes flying." The balloon flew back and forth between seniors and children, a game with loose contact at intervals. In the second session, a small cloth flew back and forth between a child and an elderly person, both grasping its ends and swinging back and forth. The third time, hands came flying as little birds, and direct contact with hands had become possible.

St. Nicholas celebration
Finally, in the fourth session on St. Nicholas Day, seniors, dressed up with hats, scarves, and costumes from Lapland, India, China, America, and Africa and ready for a scenic play, awaited the children to help St. Nicholas find his bishop's hat. Everyone sang and danced together

during the long journey around the world with St. Nicholas until he found his hat again in Africa. Children who were dressed as reindeer sang a song and pulled a 75-year-old resident behind them so fast that he was completely out of breath.

At the end, everyone was happy and fulfilled by what they had experienced together. There was excitement in their reddened faces. Afterwards, old and young together set the tables for lunch and sat happily in a colorful mixture.

The greatest benefit from the project was probably derived by the seniors, and this was visible because, since the beginning of the joint music lesson of young and old, even seniors who were otherwise difficult to motivate came willingly to the music lesson and greeted the children with joyful smiles. Children were now a conversation starter outside of the joint lesson and they spoke about their own great-grandchildren.

And what did the children get out of it? One child is reported to have said, "I think it's great that I can pick a grandma to play with, because my grandma already died." It was a one-time project, but it grew into a group of children who had weekly classes and visited the seniors once a month.

3. Movement and Rhythm as Part of a New Circus Pedagogy
Paul Scheer

Introduction
When we hear the word circus, we mostly think about a big tent, animals, and people who are skilled in difficult physical movements. These thoughts still fit to the traditional circus, but nowadays more circus artists are doing contemporary circus in which a story or theme is conveyed through traditional circus skills. There is also circus pedagogy, which involves educators working with laypersons with the aim of having fun while learning and exploring new things rather than gaining difficult skills. It is a new pedagogy that uses a combination of theater, movement, balance, dance, and music. Much of what I experienced and learned during my studies at the Orff Institute finds its transfer and application in my circus work with children.

Circus summer courses for young people
The *zirkus kollektiv kaudawelsch* is a circus collective based in Vienna that every summer presents a youth circus project in Drosendorf, Lower Austria where children learn about circus. In the team there are nine pedagogues who distribute the weeks amongst them covering different areas evenly, so that the participants all receive the same circus pedagogy education. The following descriptions are from the weeks taught by Paul, Tobi, and Markus.

The entire project is about having fun and trying out new things. The children stay for one week, sleeping in circus wagons, practicing in a circus tent, and sharing what they learn with friends and family in a show at the end of the week. They are eight to sixteen years old and most of them come for several years in a row. There are two to three circus pedagogues teaching during each week and they each do six hours per day of circus with the children. The rest of the time two different people take care of the children. They eat, play, and swim with them and put them to bed.

During the circus time—both mornings and afternoons—we start with a full body warmup to music with dance and coordination movements. There are up to six workshops a day where the children become familiar with new props. The fundamentals that are proposed during the week are ball, club, and scarf juggling; diabolo; kickstick; objectbalance; plate spinning;

unicycle; walking globe; stilts; acrobatics; poi; trapeze; hula hoop; and theater. The props that always need a safety person are trapeze and walking globe because the children are in the air.

At the end of every day, they do a group relaxation accompanied by the sound of a sansula. It is fascinating how children who are running around all day, are really listening and relaxing at this point. Live music shows its power there.

Between the workshops they play group games or have free time when the children can decide on their own what they want to do. During the free time the circus pedagogues walk around and give input or correct some movements if needed and are there for safety reasons for the risky activities. Each child is better at something different so many different skills come together. The children teach and learn from each other. After the workshop hours, the materials can be used in free practice. At the beginning of the week, there is only a small selection of objects the children can use, and as the week progresses, more and more are added. After this concept of self-activity is established, the children love it and keep asking for it. It is a magical moment when all the children focus on their thing, either alone or in groups. In these moments, the educators just watch and only give small impulses when needed.

During this time music is played in the background. This music is also important to set this specific atmosphere for individual practice and focus. We play all different kinds of music depending on the energy level and the need, but it is always music that the children do not know or associate with. The music helps them to focus and enjoy what they are doing.

The theater workshop

A special session is the theater workshop where they do theater games and exercises. A focus is on where to stand on the stage, stage presence, and how loud one should speak so that everybody in the tent can hear you. Because the audience will be sitting on three sides of the round stage, this is a big challenge for the performers.

Preparing the show

On Wednesday before the training ends the pedagogues speak for the first time about Friday's performance, and the children must decide what props they want to use in the performance. It is not about what they are best at, but what they enjoy the most. In the show it is all about having fun. The children can also let us know if they want to talk on stage.

Following Wednesday's discussion with the children the pedagogues plan the show, trying to include all the suggestions and wishes of the children. They build a story around the show and try to give a different meaning to the props used in it. This kind of show is called *cirque nouveau*, where there is a storyline between the acts, while the acts themselves are more traditional, showing one trick after another in any order.

On Thursday, the pedagogues create the performance together with the children. Each prop has its own time slot in the show. After the sequence is decided, they choose the music that fits the acts, the theme, and the show.

Sometimes after the show there is an opportunity for family and friends to try out the props and the children can show how they work. They find out that most of them are harder than they look.

Circus pedagogy is different from sports that force people to do specific things. It aims to create playful spaces for children where they can acquire skills and abilities, and they can develop into self-confident people while they are always able to ask for guidance when they need it. Every circus prop needs a different focus and practice. This is the reason that everybody finds their thing that they are good at. Some like to play more theater; others love to juggle the diabolo. Even though they are completely different things the children function as a group.

It is also possible for school classes to come to the *Circusluft Drosendorf* during weeks before or after the summer project sessions. Groups can book three, four, or five days. Therefore, the program and the planning for the show depends on how long each group has practiced together. The biggest difference is that the participants in these groups already know each other, and they come with an established group dynamic that the pedagogues have to deal with. Through playing group games and helping each other with spotting or skill sharing, the group members get to know each other from a different perspective. The circus offers a place for everybody and the ones who are outsiders in the class sometimes gain respect by managing a prop faster than others in the class.

Rhythm supports the technique
There is a lot of rhythm in circus technique. Without the right timing and rhythm, many sequences will not work. The most visible is in juggling where you can see the pattern in the air. If the rhythm is off or not stable the pattern does not work. The rhythm is created through different throwing heights, the point where you catch, and the dwell time (the time you hold an object in your hand before you throw it again). In changing those three parameters you can juggle any rhythm.

Inclusive juggling
Craig Quat is an American juggler who was one of the first to apply the term *inclusive juggling*, which makes juggling possible for people by using tools that enable them to do things that otherwise they would not be able to do. He invented many different tools but the most common is the juggleboard where you play in duos. The juggleboard is a tool to make juggling patterns more visible and done with musicality. It is a board where you have five lanes to roll balls. One person is leading and sets the rhythm. The other one is following the patterns that are coming. The goal of this tool is to combine left and right hands together in lateral and bilateral movements to improve the coordination, make new brain connections, and most importantly have fun doing it. When you make notches into the wood and use hard balls to hear the ball rolling, blind people can juggle with it.

4. Mixed-Abled Dance Ensemble Flitz
Sonja Pfennigbauer and Vivi Tanzmeister

Who we are
Openminded, outspoken, and colorful are words that come up trying to describe Company Flitz, the mixed-abled dance ensemble, founded in 2018 by us: Sonja Pfennigbauer and Viviane Tanzmeister. We both studied Elemental Music and Dance Education at the Orff Institute, Mozarteum University in Salzburg, Austria. That is where the project Company Flitz started, is based, and still works in strong collaboration within the University and its students.

Our background in contemporary dance and street and club styles is the foundation for our practice and artistic point of view. Our goals are to encourage our dancers to embrace their artistic expression, broaden their horizons, and practice mindfulness individually and in relation to others. Our classes and workshops are welcoming and open to anybody who wants to participate and learn more about themselves and society. We provide weekly classes, performances, and workshops for dancers with and without disabilities. Within this format we also include our dancers as assistants and teachers for our workshops in schools and artistic projects as well as for lecture demonstrations about inclusion and dance in our space.

We try to create a safe space, where all dancers can move freely and without judgment and we do not tolerate disrespectful speech or offending behavior. We focus on art, human connection, and the quality of the experience independent of each individual dancer's level.

Our working guidelines

From the beginning, we wanted to create a diverse group, open to everybody. However, this happened only partly. We mostly teach people with learning difficulties now, which led us to question the term "inclusive" because of the homogeneity of the group. The term mixed-abled, implying the diverse abilities within a group, feels the most suitable for now.

In the beginning of the ensemble, it was a time to try out ideas, find our teaching style and our values, and gain experience in creating performances with the dancers. After two years of exploration, we know that each dancer and person is important, meaningful, and valuable in developing a diverse and creative society that is also reflected in arts and culture. We realized that we do not have to create a specific kind of method to teach our dancers. We share values with Orff Schulwerk principles and Alito Alessi's Danceability, and we are influenced by our mentors from our dance education at the Orff Institute.

The Flitz dancers face the same struggles, and they have the same goals and needs as ourselves when we attend a dance class. We see individual differences as opportunities for enriched learning. To sum it up, we developed skills like finding the appropriate wording, feeling the atmosphere in the room, discovering and applying what is needed to learn, and offering different varieties of explanation and execution. One key factor for a successful class is always to find the common denominator within the group. From this place of common understanding, we offer variations and options to develop certain tasks and experiences.

The main goal of our practice with the dancers ranges from body awareness, verbal and artistic expression to personality development and manifesting self-esteem.

The structure and thoughts behind our classes

The general structure of classes varies but is always framed by familiar rituals that we established in the very first classes during 2018. These rituals include exercises for mindful body warmup, spatial awareness, and group dynamics (e.g., developing a feeling for distance and closeness and how much is comfortable).

These exercises prepare the dancers physically and mentally for some technical input like floor work, step patterns, and sequences. At the heart of the work are improvisational concepts that revolve around specific topics or philosophical concepts like "connected-separated," "relationships," and of course the topic of "disDANCING" during the pandemic.

We work on ideas from different points of view over several weeks to gain a deeper and long-term understanding of certain concepts. We offer the same exercises within different group settings, for example, with a partner, with the whole group, trying out for oneself, showing your ideas to the other dancers.

Dancing under trees
Photo by Hector Palacios, with kind permission from Verein Umami

Some key questions

We ask ourselves before and after teaching:

- How do we choose to communicate with our students?
- How do we adapt the teaching to personal learning styles of any student?
- Are we creative and flexible to change our plans on the spot if needed?

For the end of the class, we always provide a reflection circle where the dancers verbally share their impressions and observations of the class. We strongly encourage the dancers to learn to speak about art, their experiences, and their wishes, and to widen their range of expression and understand their different perceptions of the exercises.

About the music

To provide the dancers with the right atmosphere and the possibilities to experience music connected to the dance, we include live music in specific parts of the class like the warmup ritual, explorations through the room, or improvisational tasks. We choose the instruments based on their sound or the intention of the movement. We vary between guitar, vibraphone, piano, and the Orff instrumentarium as well as different forms of drums. For our very first performance we also had the chance to perform with live marimba and percussion music by Martina Weninger during a performance for the *Inklusionstag* (inclusion day) at the University Mozarteum.

When we use recorded music, we always try to widen the range of listening habits of the dancers. Most of the dancers enjoy popular music with a lot of lyrics and strong beats. We frequently try to utilize instrumental music from different genres. Another extremely important point for us is to use only music that is anti-racist, feminist, and does not glorify drug abuse or the patriarchy. We created different playlists based on atmosphere or movement ideas like calm, strong energy, or lightness, or based on artists that represent our values. These playlists are shared with the dancers so they can implement the new listening experiences to their everyday life. The theme song of the Flitzis would be "Instrumental" by José González.

How we create a performance

When we prepare for a performance, we mostly use the improvisational concepts that we worked on and developed in class. The concepts, movement quality, and music are based on the subject we choose to explore with the group. Mostly the topics are based on the questions that appear within the classes or include political issues like social justice, ableism, or human rights. To make choices and connections to the topics clearer we also include texts written and spoken by the dancers. One example would be a text from Michi, one of our dancers about the topic "Connected-Disconnected":

> *Are we connected? Or are we already separated again? What is that actually, connected? Cables connect, cords connect, thoughts connect, movement connects, music connects. So much connects, and yet we are so often separate. What is it that separates us?*

To give more insight about the movement, we work for a long time on the quality, feeling, and creative challenge based on an improvisational concept that suits the subject we want to explore more deeply. For the performance we create a specific score and order in which the different concepts appear. That is how we make sure the dancers can rely on their body memory, stick to the agreed score, and still have freedom to express themselves freely.

We also include some fixed choreographed parts (tutti). With regard to music, we always strive for live music. Until now we have only had the chance to experience live music one time, but we would love to work in a more interdisciplinary way in the future.

We have performed with shows in the framework of events like *Lange Nacht der Forschung* in Salzburg, *Fest der Vielfalt* in Saalfelden, *Inklusionstag* at the Mozarteum Salzburg, and several internal shows for family and friends in the Gunild Keetman Saal at the Orff Institute. For the advertisement of the performance, we create images from the dancers in which other dancers and artists with disabilities could feel represented and that would interest them in seeing the performance.

Accessibility—hints for the practice

Access to information is the key to participation. For our dance ensemble we needed to learn how to remove the barriers that prevent someone from accessing it. This means we learned to make the information and service available to as many people as possible. Here we want to share our two main tips to make a class accessible.

The place and space: The foundation for accessibility is making sure that spaces like studios, institutions, or classrooms are accessible through public transportation, do not contain insurmountable obstacles (e.g., stairs), and have easy access to sanitary facilities. How to get to the place independently is especially important for our dancers who want to be independent from parents and caretakers. This information must be placed within the description of your course, making it clear that the space is safe for as many people as possible.

The style of writing: We use communication via email or social media like WhatsApp to spread general information about classes or performances. We try to use *Leichte Sprache* (literally: easy language), a version of the German language directed to people who have low competences in German or in reading in general. It uses short sentences, clear information, and the avoidance of negation. The use of colors to highlight the essence is also very helpful. We learned that addressing an email to the dancers themselves and also sending the information to parents makes clear communication and participation possible. For informal communication like the sharing of photos and videos of the class we use WhatsApp groups. To avoid a flood of text messages there is an option that enables only certain administrators (like the teachers) to write and share content in the group.

Reaching the target group and having active access to the community is often done through more direct contact than only through advertising via social media, flyers, or posters. Due to more dependence on the parents, some of our participants were first reached through their parents' interest in our program. It can be a door opener for potential participants if you go to events where the community comes together, and they get to know you and your artistic and pedagogical work in person. Easily accessible information will automatically diversify and enrich your group and the people who want to join.

Visions for the future

What we envision for the future is a dance company free from the labels "disabled," "different," or "special." We want to push the personal, physical, and cognitive boundaries of our dancers. We want to open new horizons for our dancers to experience the world and people around them and to support opportunities for them to get in touch with areas of life that would normally not be accessible. Our aim is not only a socio-political one but also a high level of artistic and aesthetic expression that we want to encourage and foster through not only our classes but also our community-building projects and performances.

Photos: Verein Umami.

5. *The Conference of the Animals*–for Children and Other Artists
Manuela Widmer

A community music drama based on the novel by Erich Kästner. Libretto: Manuela Widmer, composition: Jakob Gruchmann, © Publishing House for Children's Theater, Hamburg/ Germany.

What is a community music drama?

Different communities—children and adults at different levels of musical education—meet on stage. They experience and marvel at each other and learn from each other. The children listen to the musicians and singers; the adults admire the children's agility, strength, and stamina, and their memory and ability to concentrate. The motivation of all participants increases because no routine creeps in, and the cheerfulness with which the children rush into the theater, even during repeated performances, immediately dispels fatigue. If one child is absent due to illness, another immediately takes over their role; this flexibility is contagious and the adult choir proceeds just as successfully the next day.

What is *Conference of the Animals* about?

Erich Kästner wrote the book in 1949 with the subtitle "A book for children and connoisseurs." After the news goes around the world that once again an international peace conference has failed, it becomes too senseless and irresponsible for the animals. Elephant Oskar announces a conference of the animals to wrest an everlasting peace treaty from the humans. But the way there is full of surprises....

Who is playing?

The libretto is written in such a way that it can be performed by about 50 children, professionals, and amateurs. The composition includes tercets for professional singers, instrumental music for professional musicians, spoken pieces, polyphonic vocal parts, and songs for adult as well as child singers (6 to 12 years old).

What do we need?

The music drama takes place in a performance space or on a stage (with a lighting system if possible). We deliberately do without an elaborate stage set because the movement and musically varied action on stage creates an intense effect for all the senses. Masks and costumes can be made professionally but can also be created with simple means (depending on the financial situation).

How do we prepare?

The adult professionals (singers and instrumental musicians) receive a basic introduction and prepare their parts independently. At guided rehearsals, hints are given that are important for the scenic realization, e.g., on the tempo of musical pieces to which movement and dance take place; ways and positions for the soloists.

The adult amateur choir needs several scenic rehearsals after preparing the pieces because they move, dance, and act theatrically. The choir members choose their roles and solo parts. No one should feel over- or underchallenged.

The same is true for the children. Working with them involves the longest period of time. The children learn rhythmic speech texts, small dialogues, and songs, and act as animals moving and dancing. They get to know the play scene by scene and understand how the scenes intertwine.

At the joint rehearsal weekend, all the individual parts are put together. The intensive rehearsal work is crowned with the performance.

Last but not least

A community music drama project can be performed in any community. It can be a composed work, or one developed with the group. What is needed is a dedicated music, movement/

dance educator with an interest (or additional training) in drama, who contacts local schools, independent groups (such as amateur theaters, choirs), as well as some instrumentalists (e.g., from a music school, conservatory, college), seeks support from the community, the state, and interested sponsors, and - boldly goes for it!

Photo: © Hubert Auer, Hallein

References and Resources

Barthel, G., & Artus, H.-G. (2013). *Vom Tanz zur Choreographie. Gestaltungsprozesse in der Tanzpädagogik* [From dance to choreography. Composition processes in dance pedagogy]. Oberhausen: Athena.

Frey, A. (2019). Beziehung stärken und miteinander wachsen. Der Familienkurs aus seiner persönlichen und einer wissenschaftlichen Perspektive/Strengthening relationships and growing together. The Orff Schulwerk Society's family course from a personal and a scientific perspective. *Orff-Schulwerk Heute, 100,* 34–39. https://www.orff-schulwerk-forum-salzburg.org/magazine-osh

Gilbert, A. (2015). Creative dance for all ages. Reston, VA: SHAPE America.

Günther, D. (2011). Der rhythmische Mensch und seine Erziehung/The rhythmic person and their education (M. Murray, Trans.). In B. Haselbach (Ed.), *Studientexte zu Theorie und Praxis des Orff-Schulwerks, Bd. 1: Basistexte aus den Jahren 1932-2010/Texts on theory and practice of Orff-Schulwerk, Vol. 1: Basic texts from the years 1932-2010* (pp. 79–93). Mainz: Schott. (Original work published in 1932)

Kästner, E. (1949). *Die Konferenz der Tiere* (W. Trier, Illus.). München: K. Desch.

Kästner, E. (1949). *The animals' conference: A story for children and other understanding people* (W. Trier, Illus.; Z. de Schauensee, Trans.). New York: D. McKay. Note: This book is available in many translations.

Reitinger, R. (2018). Musik erfinden mit Kindern im Vor- und Grundschulalter. Umriss eines methodisch-didaktischen Konzeptes [Creating music with children of preschool and primary school age. Outline of a methodical-didactical concept]. In: *Handreichungen zur Kompositionspädagogik.* https://www.kompaed.de/fileadmin/files/Artikel/KOMPAED-Reitinger_31.1.18.pdf

Tsakalidis, K. (2011). *Choreographie—Handwerk und Vision* (2nd ed.)/Choreography: craft and vision. Developing and structuring dance for solo, duet and groups. Konstanz: Stage Verlag. (English version published in 2020)

Widmer, M. (2023, February 20). Film *"Die Konferenz der Tiere"* (n. Erich Kästner). März 2022. © *Verlag für Kindertheater, Hamburg* [Video]. YouTube. https://youtu.be/ySc1K-Pcg3s

Appendix
Selected Bibliography

Here you will find a select list of books and articles about Orff Schulwerk as well as books and articles about movement and dance that relate especially to work in elemental music and movement/dance education.

Abraham, A., & Hanft, K. (1986). *Maja Lex: Ein Portrait der Tänzerin, Choreographin und Pädagogin* [Maja Lex: A portrait of the dancer, choreographer, and teacher]. Düsseldorf: Grafische Werkstatt.

Boorman, J. (1971). *Creative dance in grades four to six*. Don Mills (ON): Longman Canada.

Coogan, C. (2011). Elemental composition and its didactics—Dance. *Orff-Schulwerk Informationen, 85* (special edition: 50 Jahre Orff-Institut), 171-173. https://www.orff-schulwerk-forum-salzburg.org/magazine-osh

Coogan, C. (2014). Orff-Schulwerk: Fundamentals of creative/elemental dance for children in elementary school age. *JaSeSoi ry Journal, 2*, 9–10.

Davies, M. (2003). *Movement and dance in early childhood* (2nd ed.). London: Paul Chapman Publishing.

de Quadros, A. (Ed.). (2000). *Many seeds, different flowers: The music education legacy of Carl Orff*. Perth: Callaway International Resource Centre for Music Education.

Erion, C., & O'Hehir, M. (Coordinators). (2005, Spring). Keetman Centenary [Special issue]. *The Orff Echo, 37*(3).

Fischer, C. (2009). *Gunild Keetman und das Orff-Schulwerk. Elementare Musik zwischen künstlerischem und didaktischem Anspruch* [Gunild Keetman and the Orff-Schulwerk. Elemental music between artistic and didactic demands]. Mainz: Schott.

Frazee, J. (1998). *Discovering Keetman*. New York: Schott.

Frazee, J. (2006). *Orff Schulwerk today: Nurturing musical expression and understanding*. New York: Schott.

Fritsch, U. (Ed.). (1994). *Tanzen—Ausdruck und Gestaltung* [Dancing–expression and creation] (2nd ed.). Butzbach: Afra.

Gersdorf, L. (1986). *Carl Orff*. Reinbek bei Hamburg: Rowohlt.

Goodkin, D. (2002). *Play, sing and dance: An introduction to Orff Schulwerk*. New York: Schott.

Gray, E. (2002). Trying out a new way of teaching music: The origins of Carl Orff's Schulwerk. *The Orff Echo, 34*(4), 12-21.

Grüner, M. (2016). *Orff instruments and how to play them* (Y. Douthat Hartinger, Trans.). Mainz: Schott. (Original work published in 2011 as *Orff-Instrumente und wie man sie spielt*, Mainz: Schott)

Grüner, M., & Haselbach, B. (Eds.). (2011). *50 Jahre Orff-Institut / 50 Years Orff Institute 1961–2011* [Special edition]. *Orff-Schulwerk Informationen, 85*. https://www.orff-schulwerk-forum-salzburg.org/magazine-osh

Günther, D. (1964). Die Bewegungserziehung innerhalb des Orff-Schulwerks [Movement education within the Orff Schulwerk]. In W. Thomas & W. Götze (Eds.) *Orff-Institut Jahrbuch 1963* (pp. 61–66). Mainz: Schott.

Günther, D. (2011). Elemental dance (M. Murray, Trans.). In B. Haselbach (Ed.), *Texts on theory and practice of Orff-Schulwerk: Basic texts from the years 1932–2010* (pp. 118–133). Mainz: Schott. (Original work published in 1962)

Günther, D. (2011). The Rhythmic person and their education (M. Murray, Trans.). In B. Haselbach (Ed.), *Texts on theory and practice of Orff-Schulwerk: Basic texts from the years 1932–2010* (pp. 78–93). Mainz: Schott. (Original work published in 1932)

Hartmann, W. (2021). *Looking at the roots: A guide to understanding Orff Schulwerk*. San Francisco: Pentatonic Press.

Hartmann, W., Maschat, V., & Regner, H. (2000). Orff-Schulwerk im Bayerischen Rundfunk [Orff-Schulwerk in the Bavarian Broadcasting Company]. *Orff-Schulwerk Informationen, 64,* 24–28. https://www.orff-schulwerk-forum-salzburg.org/magazine-osh

Hartmann, W., with Haselbach, B. (2017). Die Prinzipien des Orff-Schulwerks/The principals of Orff-Schulwerk (V. Maschat, Trans.). *Orff-Schulwerk Heute, 97,* 23–26. https://www.orff-schulwerk-forum-salzburg.org/magazine-osh

Haselbach, B. (1978). The role of music in dance education. *Orff-Schulwerk Informationen, 22,* 5–13. https://www.orff-schulwerk-forum-salzburg.org/magazine-osh

Haselbach, B. (1979). *Dance education: Basic principles and models for nursery and primary school* (M. Murray, Trans.). London: Schott. (Original work published in 1971)

Haselbach, B. (1991). *Tanz und Bildende Kunst. Modelle zur ästhetischen Erziehung* [Dance and visual arts. Models for aesthetic education]. Stuttgart: Klett.

Haselbach, B. (1994). *Improvisation, dance, movement* (M. Murray, Trans.; 2nd ed.). London: Schott. (Original work published in 1976 as Improvisation, Tanz, Bewegung, Stuttgart: Klett)

Haselbach, B. (1999). Sobre la interrelación entre la danza y las artes plásticas [On the interrelation between dance and visual arts]. *Música, Arte y Proceso, (7),* 71–87.

Haselbach, B. (2011). Das Element Bewegung/Tanz—The element movement/dance. *Orff-Schulwerk Informationen: 50 Jahre Orff-Institut, 85,* 164–168. www.orff-schulwerk-forum-salzburg.org/magazine-osh

Haselbach, B. (2011). Reflections on the dance educational aspects of Orff-Schulwerk (M. Murray, Trans.). In B. Haselbach (Ed.), *Texts on theory and practice of Orff-Schulwerk, Vol. 1: Basic texts from the years 1932–2010* (pp. 196–219). Mainz: Schott. (Revision of the original work published in 1984)

Haselbach, B. (2013). Dorothee Günther (M. Murray, Trans.). In M. Kugler (Ed.), *Elemental dance—Elemental music: The Munich Günther-Schule, 1924–1944* (pp. 42–55). Mainz: Schott. (German edition published in 2002).

Haselbach, B. (Ed.) (2005). From elemental music and dance pedagogy to modern art. *Orff-Schulwerk Informationen, 75* (This issue is devoted to this topic).

Haselbach, B. (Ed.). (2011). *Studientexte zu Theorie und Praxis des Orff-Schulwerks, Bd. 1: Basistexte aus den Jahren 1932–2010 / Texts on theory and practice of Orff-Schulwerk, Vol. 1: Basic texts from the years 1932–2010.* Mainz: Schott.

Haselbach, B., & Bacher, E. (Eds.). (2010, February). Index (1961–2009) Orff-Schulwerk Informationen, Yearbooks of the Orff Institute, Documentation of Orff-Schulwerk Symposia [Special Edition]. *Orff-Schulwerk Informationen.* https://www.orff-schulwerk-forum-salzburg.org/magazine-osh

Haselbach, B., & Salmon, S. (Eds.) (2017). Encounters between Orff-Schulwerk and modern arts. *Orff-Schulwerk Heute, 97* (This issue is devoted to this topic).

Haselbach, B., & Stewart, C. (Eds.) (2021). *Texts on theory and practice of Orff Schulwerk, Vol. 2: Orff Schulwerk in diverse cultures—An idea that went round the world.* San Francisco: Pentatonic Press.

Haselbach, B., Grüner, M., & Salmon, S. (Eds.). (2007). *Im Dialog. Elementare Musik- und Tanzerziehung im Interdisziplinären Kontext / In dialogue. Elemental music and dance education in interdisciplinary contexts.* Mainz: Schott.

Jungmair, U. (1992). *Das Elementare. Zur Musik- und Bewegungserziehung im Sinne Carl Orffs. Theorie und Praxis* [The Elemental: On music and movement education in the spirit of Carl Orff. Theory and practice.]. Mainz: Schott.

Kallos, C. (2021, March 12). *Hermann Regner (1928–2008) "Ein Leben für die Musik"* [Film]. YouTube. https://www.youtube.com/watch?v=KoLg4blHQX4

Keetman, G. (1974) *Elementaria. First acquaintance with Orff-Schulwerk* (M. Murray, Trans.). London: Schott. (Original work published in 1970 as *Elementaria. Erster Umgang mit dem Orff-Schulwerk*, Stuttgart: Klett)

Keetman, G. (2011). Memories of the Günther-Schule (M. Murray, Trans.). In B. Haselbach (Ed.), *Texts on theory and practice of Orff-Schulwerk*, Vol. 1: Basic texts from the years 1932-2010 (pp. 44–65). Mainz: Schott. (Original work published in 1978)

Keller, W. (1970-1990). *Ludi Musici, Vols. 1–5*. Boppard/Rhein: Fidula Verlag.

Keller, W. (1974). *Introduction to Music for Children* (S. Kennedy, Trans.). Mainz: Schott. (Original work published in 1954 as *Einführung in Musik für Kinder*, Mainz: Schott)

Keller, W. (1996). *Musikalische Lebenshilfe. Ausgewählte Berichte über sozial-und heilpädagogische Versuche mit dem Orff-Schulwerk* [Musical help in life. Selected reports on social and curative educational experiments with the Orff-Schulwerk]. Mainz: Schott.

Keller, W. (2011). Elemental music – an attempt to define it (M. Murray, Trans.). In B. Haselbach (Ed.), *Texts on theory and practice of Orff-Schulwerk: Basic texts from the years 1932–2010* (pp. 118–133). Mainz: Schott. (Original work published in 1962 as *Elementare Musik. Versuch einer Begriffsbestimmung*)

Klein, G. (Ed.). (2015). *Choreografischer Baukasten. Das Buch* [Choreographic construction kit. The book] (2nd ed.). Bielefeld: transcript Verlag.

Kotzian, R. (2018). *Orff-Schulwerk rediscovered: Music and teaching models*. Mainz: Schott.

Kugler, M. (1989). Körperarbeit und Tanz in der Günther-Schule [Bodywork and dance at the Günther-Schule]. *Orff-Schulwerk Informationen 43*, 6–11. www.orff-schulwerk-forum-salzburg.org/magazine-osh

Kugler, M. (2000). *Die Methode Jaques-Dalcroze und das Orff-Schulwerk "Elementare Musikübung." Bewegungsorientierte Konzeptionen der Musikpädagogik* [The Jaques-Dalcroze method and the Orff-Schulwerk "elemental music practice." Movement-oriented conceptions of music education]. Frankfurt am Main: Lang.

Kugler, M. (2019). *Online-Lexicon der Orff-Schulwerk Gesellschaft Deutschland e.V. [Online lexicon of the German Orff Schulwerk Association] www.orff-schulwerk.de/lexikon* [Publication of an English translation on the IOSFS website is forthcoming.]

Kugler, M. (Ed.). (2013). *Elemental dance—elemental music: The Munich Günther School 1924–1944* (M. Murray, Trans.). New York: Schott. (Original work published in 2002 as *Elementarer Tanz – Elementare Musik. Die Günther-Schule München 1924–1944*, Mainz: Schott)

Laban, R. von. (1975). *Modern educational dance* (3rd ed.). London: Macdonald & Evans.

Lex, M., & Padilla, G. (1988). *Elementarer Tanz: Bände 1–3* [Elemental Dance: Volumes 1–3]. Wilhelmshaven: Noetzel.

Maschat, V. (2005). Volkstanz und Orff-Schulwerk – wie passt das zusammen? [Folk dance and Orff-Schulwerk – a possible match?]. *Orff-Schulwerk Informationen, 74*, 31–33. https://www.orff-schulwerk-forum-salzburg.org/magazine-osh

Maschat, V. (2006). El efecto social y emocional de la danza coral [The social and emotional effect of choral dance]. *Orff España, 9*, 7–9.

Maschat, V. (2010). Dance as an expression of personal freedom. *Orff-Schulwerk Informationen, 83*, 62–65. https://www.orff-schulwerk-forum-salzburg.org/magazine-osh

Newlove, J., & Dalby, J. (2004) *Laban for all*. New York: Routledge.

Nykrin, R., Grüner, M., & Widmer, M. (Eds.) (2007–2008). *Musik und Tanz für Kinder: Unterrichtswerk zur Früherziehung 1–2* [Music and dance for children: Teaching resource for early childhood education]. Mainz: Schott.

Orff-Schulwerk Heute. Semi-annual publication issued by the Orff Institute and the International Orff-Schulwerk Forum Salzburg. Volumes 90-100 cover years 2014–2019. https://www.orff-schulwerk-forum-salzburg.org/magazine-osh

Orff-Schulwerk Informationen. Semi-annual publication issued by the Orff Institute and the International Orff-Schulwerk Forum Salzburg. Volumes 1–89 cover years 1964–2013. https://www.orff-schulwerk-forum-salzburg.org/magazine-osh

Orff-Schulwerk International. Online publication issued semi-annually by the International Orff-Schulwerk Forum Salzburg, beginning Spring, 2022. https://www.orff-schulwerk-forum-salzburg.org/magazine-osh

Orff, C. (1931). Bewegungs- und Musikerziehung als Einheit [Movement and music education as a unit]. *Die Musik, 23*(4), 732–734.

Orff, C. (1978). *The Schulwerk* (M. Murray, Trans.). New York: Schott. (Original work published in 1976 as *Carl Orff und sein Werk: Dokumentation, Vol. 3, Schulwerk - Elementare Musik*, Tutzing: Hans Schneider)

Orff, C. (2011). Music out of movement (M. Murray, Trans.). In B. Haselbach (Ed.), *Texts on theory and practice of Orff-Schulwerk: Basic texts from the years 1932–2010* (pp. 94–103). Mainz: Schott. (Original work published in 1932)

Orff, C. (2011). Orff-Schulwerk – Past and Future (M. Murray, Trans.). In B. Haselbach (Ed.), *Texts on theory and practice of Orff-Schulwerk: Basic texts from the years 1932–2010* (pp. 134–159). Mainz: Schott. (Original work published in 1964)

Orff, C. (2011). Thoughts about music with children and non-professionals (M. Murray, Trans.). In B. Haselbach (Ed.), *Texts on theory and practice of Orff-Schulwerk: Basic texts from the years 1932–2010* (pp. 66–77). Mainz: Schott. (Original work published in 1932)

Orff, C., & Keetman, G. (1995-1996). Orff-Schulwerk: Vol. 1: Musica Poetica [Album: CD 13104-2]; Orff-Schulwerk: Vol. 2: Musik für Kinder [Album: CD 13105-2]; Orff-Schulwerk: Vol. 3: Piano Music [Album: CD 13106-2]. Tucson, Arizona: Celestial Harmonies.

Orff, C., & Keetman, G. (1950–1954). *Orff-Schulwerk. Musik für Kinder* (Vols. 1-5). Mainz: Schott.

Orff, C., & Keetman, G. (1957–1966). *Orff-Schulwerk. Music for children* (Vols. 1-5) (English adaptation by M. Murray). Mainz: Schott.

Orff, C., & Keetman, G. (1990). *Orff-Schulwerk: Music for children* [Album: CD]. London: Schott (ED 12380).

Orff, C., & Keetman, G. (1994). *Musica Poetica. Orff-Schulwerk* [Album: 6 CDs]. Berlin: BMG.

Orff®– Arts and Education. Since 2020, the digital magazine of the Carl Orff Stiftung [Foundation]. https://www.orff.de/en/publications/magazine/

Padilla, G. (1990). Inhalte und Lehre des Elementaren Tanzes [Contents and teaching of elemental dance]. In E. Bannmüller & P. Röthig (Eds.), *Grundlagen und Perspektiven ästhetischer und rhythmischer Bewegungserziehung* [Foundations and perspectives of aesthetic and rhythmic movement education] (pp. 245–271). Stuttgart: Klett.

Preston-Dunlop, V. (1980). *A handbook for modern educational dance* (Rev. ed.). London: Macdonald & Evans.

Pruett, D. B. (2003). Orff before Orff: The Güntherschule (1924-1945). *Journal of Historical Research in Music Education, 24*(2), 178–196.

Regner, H. (1977, 1980, 1982). *Music for children—Orff-Schulwerk—American edition*, Vols. 1, 2, and 3. New York: Schott Music Corp.

Regner, H. (2002). *Musik lieben lernen* [Learning to love music] (4th Ed.). Zürich: Atlantis Musikbuch-Verlag. (Original work published in 1988)

Regner, H. (2011). Carl Orff's educational ideas – Utopia and reality (M. Murray, Trans.). In B. Haselbach (Ed.), *Texts on theory and practice of Orff-Schulwerk: Basic texts from the years 1932–2010* (pp. 168–195). Mainz: Schott. (Original work published in 1975)

Regner, H., & Ronnefeld, M. (Eds.). (2004). *Gunild Keetman. Ein Leben für Musik und Bewegung /A life given to music and movement* (M. Murray, Trans.). Mainz: Schott.

Salmon, S. (2010) Inclusion and Orff-Schulwerk. *Musicworks, 15*(1), 27–33. http://bidok.uibk.ac.at/library/salmon-orff-e.html

Salmon, S. (2012, Winter). Musica humana—Thoughts on humanistic aspects of Orff-Schulwerk. *Orff-Schulwerk Informationen, 87*, 13–22. https://www.orff-schulwerk-forum-salzburg.org/magazine-osh

Sangiorgio, A. (2018). Das Potential des Orff-Schulwerks für die Arbeit mit besonderen Zielgruppen/Working with special populations: The potential of the Orff-Schulwerk approach. *Orff-Schulwerk Heute 99*, 13–21. https://www.orff-schulwerk-forum-salzburg.org/magazine-osh

Schönherr, C. (2001). "Sprich, damit ich Dich sehe" (Sokrates). Einblick in den Fachbereich Sprache am Institut für Musik- und Tanzpädagogik "Orff-Institut" ["Speak so that I may see you" (Socrates). Insight into the area of speech at the Orff Institute]. *Orff-Schulwerk Informationen, 66*, pp. 35–41. https://www.orff-schulwerk-forum-salzburg.org/magazine-osh

Schönherr, C. (2004). "Ich bin wieder jung geworden." Reflexionen über elementaren Musik- und Bewegungsunterricht in einem Seniorenheim ["I am young again!"—Reflections about elemental music and movement classes in a home for seniors]. *Orff Schulwerk Informationen, 73*, 44–52. https://www.orff-schulwerk-forum-salzburg.org/magazine-osh

Schönherr, C. (2007). Stimme und Sprache im Fachbereich Bewegungsbegleitung [Speech and language in the subject area of movement accompaniment]. *Orff-Schulwerk Informationen, 78*, 34–38. https://www.orff-schulwerk-forum-salzburg.org/magazine-osh

Schönherr, C. (2011). Wir sind noch nicht zu alt! Angebote aus der elementaren Musik -und Tanzpädagogik für hochbetagte Menschen [We are not too old yet! Offerings from elemental music and dance pedagogy for very old people]. In H. H. Wickel & T. Hartogh (Eds.), *Praxishandbuch Musizieren im Alter. Projekte und Initiativen* (pp. 108–126). Mainz: Schott.

Schönherr, C. (2013). Ich bin wieder jung geworden, Künstlerisch-pädagogische Angebote für Menschen in hohem Alter / I have become young again, artistic-pedagogical offerings for people in old age [Film; DVD]. Salzburg: Universität Mozarteum.

Thomas, W. (1988). *Carl Orff: A concise biography* (V. Maschat, Trans.). London: Schott.

Thomas, W. (2011). "In the beginning was the word…"—on the significance of the spoken word in Orff-Schulwerk (M. Murray, Trans.). In B. Haselbach (Ed.), *Texts on theory and practice of Orff-Schulwerk: Basic texts from the years 1932–2010* (pp. 160–167). Mainz: Schott. (Original work published in 1969)

Widmer, M. (1997). *Alles, was klingt. Elementares Musizieren im Kindergarten* [Everything that sounds. Elemental music making in kindergarten]. Freiburg: Herder.

Widmer, M. (2011). *Die Pädagogik des Orff-Instituts in Salzburg. Entwicklung und Bedeutung einer einzigartigen kunstpädagogischen Ausbildung als Impuls für eine allgemeinpädagogische Diskussion* [The pedagogy of the Orff Institute in Salzburg. Development and significance of a unique education through the arts as an impulse for a general pedagogical discussion]. Mainz: Schott.

Periodicals

In addition to the periodical of the Carl Orff Foundation and the three periodicals of the International Orff-Schulwerk Forum Salzburg listed above, you may learn about periodicals of Orff Schulwerk Associations by going to the International Orff-Schulwerk Forum Salzburg website. There you can follow links to individual OSAs and information about their national publications. https://www.orff-schulwerk-forum-salzburg.org/members

Authors

Barthwell-Thompson, Judith (USA). Graduate of the Orff Institute Special Course in 1988; taught movement and music to children from pre-school to adults; after retiring, volunteers in several educational settings and runs a teacher education course in Detroit, Michigan.

Böhm, Franziska (Germany). BA, MFA in Laban; lecturer in the Department of Music Pedagogy, University of Potsdam; PhD student and visiting lecturer Trinity Laban Conservatory of Music/Dance; international presenter; OSA Germany.

Bosshard, Astrid (Switzerland). Graduate of the Orff Institute, master's degree in TaKeTiNa® Rhythm Pedagogy; many years of teaching children; professor of music and movement pedagogy, Basel University of Music; deputy director of studies and lecturer.

Chan, Anida (Macao). BA in Social Science (Psychology), the Chinese University of Hong Kong; European Mentorship Program in Orff-Schulwerk Pedagogy 2020-2021; music director for "Orff 4 Kids" music studio in Hong Kong; composes children's songs in her native Cantonese language.

Chernous, Tetiana (Ukraine). Music teacher and therapist; lecturer at the Department of Psychology and Pedagogy (National University of Ostroh); vice president of the OSA Ukraine; founding member of the Association of Music Therapists of Ukraine.

Coogan, Christa (USA/Germany). BA in Dance, The Juilliard School, MA in Dance Studies, University of Salzburg; lecturer at the University for Music and Theater, Munich; international presenter in the area of improvisation-creative dance; faculty at San Francisco International Orff Schulwerk course; International Mentorship Program; member of the IOSFS board.

Ellis, Michele (Australia/Netherlands). Orff Institute Special Course graduate and San Francisco School intern (2017); music and general teacher working in international education; teaches Orff Schulwerk in classrooms, teacher education courses, and workshops.

Elsworth, Bethany Ellen (Australia/Canada). MM in Music Therapy; graduate of the Orff Institute Special Course, board member of Carl Orff Canada; committee member of the IOSFS; music educator; author.

Figueroa, Tamara (Argentina). Postgraduate degree in Dalcroze; teacher of native dance and folklore; dancer; music and dance teacher for children and adults; teacher educator at the Escuela de Maestros and the Collegium Musicum Buenos Aires; board member of the OSA Argentina.

Gagné, Danai (Greece/USA). Diplomas from the Hellenic Conservatory, the Orff Institute, and the de Kiriko Modern Dance School; well-known clinician in USA and abroad; author of several books; director of the Orff Schulwerk certification program at the Trevor Institute, New York.

García del Fresno, Ana Rosa (Spain). Degree in Primary Education, with specialization in music education; music and movement teacher according to Orff Schulwerk principles in public kindergartens and primary schools including students with special needs.

Goeke, Greacian (USA). MFA; Orff Schulwerk level 3; movement and music educator for all ages since 1990 in California schools and senior centers; past president of Northern California chapter/AOSA; PlayNotes editor; founder of Impromptu No Tutu.

Goodkin, Doug (USA). Orff Schulwerk music educator for preschool/primary/middle school/adults/elders; created and developed the music program at The San Francisco School (45 years); director of San Francisco International Orff Schulwerk Course; author of many publications.

Gray, Esther (USA). Three levels of Orff Schulwerk teacher education from Denver, CO; studied Orff Schulwerk pedagogy with Michael Kugler in Munich, Germany; retired professor, Western Michigan University; former elementary school music teacher.

Grenier, Françoise (Canada). Master's degree in Music Education, graduate of the Orff Institute in Salzburg; director of the teacher education courses for the Québec chapter of Carl Orff Canada and COC Francophone liaison.

Gurbanov, Miriam (Argentina). Teacher, dancer, choreographer; coordinator of Movement and Music, Collegium Musicum, Buenos Aires; lecturer in dance at the *Escuela Superior de Educación Artística Buenos Aires;* theater director graduated from the *Escuela Metropolitana de Arte Dramático, Buenos Aires.*

Harding, James (USA). Teaches music and movement to children ages 3 to 14 years old at the San Francisco School; author of *From Wibbleton to Wobbleton* (Pentatonic Press 2013), a book of music and movement lessons with the theme of creative play.

Harper, Peta (Australia). Bachelor of Music Education from Sydney Conservatorium of Music; graduate of the Orff Institute Special Course; music educator for more than 25 years; president of Australian National Council of Orff Schulwerk; vice president of OSA New South Wales.

Haselbach, Barbara (Austria). Dance teacher, choreographer; former director of the Orff Institute and its Special Course; past president of the IOSFS; editor of *Orff-Schulwerk Informationen/Heute;* Orff Schulwerk teacher educator worldwide; author and editor of several books.

Holzer, Angelika (Austria). MA in Elemental Music and Dance Education (Orff Institute); DanceAbility teacher; Life/Art Process graduate; university lecturer; teacher education instructor; inclusion expert; dancer.

Isabel Galeza (Germany). MA in Elemental Music and Dance Education (Orff Institute); teacher for all age groups in Munich; lecturer for and board member of OSA Germany; director of the music and art school *DOrff-Werkstatt Andechs.*

Kennedy, Susan (USA). MA in Dance Performance, Film and Ethnology, UCLA; Orff Schulwerk certification levels 1-3, Mills College; movement teacher for levels 1-3, San Francisco Orff Schulwerk Course; workshop presenter in USA, Canada, and China; Orff Schulwerk specialist, ages 4–14.

Kraft-Köllich, Nadja (Austria/UK). Graduated from the Orff Institute in Salzburg, Austria; further studies at the Sibelius Academy in Helsinki; lives in the UK teaching children from ages 0–11; committee member of OSA UK.

Kweon, Sr. M. Johannita (South Korea). MA in Integrated Art Therapy, specialized in music; since 2008 teacher for elemental music and movement in various schools; teaches workshops in Korea.

Lee, Insuk (South Korea/Germany). Graduate of the Orff Institute (Elemental Music and Dance Education) and the *Musikhochschule München* (percussion); taught at music schools, conservatory, and *Musikhochschule* in Munich.

López-Ibor Aliño, Sofía (Spain/USA). Graduate of and teacher at the Orff Institute; music educator, researcher, and performer; presenter of Orff Schulwerk workshops around the world; teacher at The San Francisco School and its International Orff Schulwerk teacher education program; author.

Maschat, Verena (Austria/Spain). Assistant professor at the Orff Institute 1977-1993; international lecturer of music and dance education; lecturer in the Education through Dance master's degree program at *Universidad Autónoma Madrid;* board member IOSFS.

Mastrogiannopoulou, Kalliopi (Greece). Orff Institute Special Course and the three-year Orff Schulwerk program at the Moraitis School, Athens; studied guitar, music theory, and pedagogy; music teacher in pre-school education and a conservatory in Athens.

Maubach, Christoph (Germany/New Zealand). M.Ed., Melbourne, AUS; Graduate Diploma in Teaching, Waikato University, NZ; DIPT, Orff Institute, Salzburg; senior lecturer emeritus, Waikato University; teaches in-person and hybrid courses for participants of all ages; consults and presents in Europe, Taiwan, New Zealand, and Australasia.

Moreno González, Fátima (Spain). PhD in Dance Education; master's degree in Performing Arts and in Bullying and Mediation; licentiate in dance pedagogy; teacher, collaborator in educational/inclusive institutions and independent researcher.

Nagaoka, Wakako (Japan). PhD; MA from the Orff-Institute, Mozarteum University Salzburg; professor of early childhood education at Hamamatsu Gakuin University, Junior College; deputy representative of OSA Japan.

Nişancı, İlkay (Turkey). Graduate of the Turkish "Train the Trainer" program 2015 and the Orff Institute Special Course 2017; music pedagogue; since 2010 teaches Orff Schulwerk and percussion for students of different ages as well as seminars and workshops for different professional groups.

Novotná, Hana (Czech Republic). Graduate of the Orff Institute Special Course and the San Francisco School internship program; assistant professor at Janáček Academy, Brno; music and dance educator; vice-president of OSA Czech Republic.

Opelt, Annabell (Germany). Studied Orff Schulwerk as well as recorder performance at the University Mozarteum, Salzburg and University of Music and Performing Arts, Vienna; founding member of the ensemble Cembaless; works at the Starnberg Music School and as an academic assistant at the University of Potsdam.

Ostertag, Andrea (Austria). MA in Musicology and Dance Studies; since 1991 lecturer for Elemental Music and Dance Pedagogy at the Orff Institute; teaches workshops worldwide; specialized in dance; clown doctor.

Özbay, Sencer (Turkey). BA and MA in Music Performance; graduate of the Orff Institute Special Course in 2016; lecturer at the Kocaeli University Fine Arts Faculty, Music Department in Istanbul; works with children at his private music school.

Pastor Prada, Raquel (Spain). PhD from the *Universidad Complutense de Madrid*, graduated in fine arts and qualified in Spanish dance; professor at the Faculty of Education and direc-tor of the master's degree in Education through Dance, *Universidad Autónoma Madrid;* vice president of OSA Spain.

Perkiö, Soili (Finland). MM; lecturer at the Sibelius Academy, Helsinki; music educator, com-poser, author of educational books, performer in children's concerts, TV and radio programs.

Pfennigbauer, Sonja Marlis (Austria). Graduate of the Orff Institute, BA in Music and Dance Education; works as a dancer, dance teacher, art facilitator, and lecturer.

Redfearn Cave, Victoria (USA). Graduate of the Orff Institute Special Course; teaching for more than 28 years; faculty member at the George Mason University Orff Schulwerk program; authored pieces for *The Orff Echo;* currently artistic director of the Mosaic Children's Choir.

Reif-Schnaidt, Michaela (Germany). MA Orff Institute; studies in historical instruments, University of Music Würzburg; teaching degree in Elementary School Didactics; head of further education for primary school teachers.

Sangiorgio, Andrea (Italy/Germany). PhD; professor of Elemental Music Education at the University of Music and Theater in Munich, Germany, with focus areas: elemental music and movement education, group improvisation and musical creativity, cognitive aspects of music learning.

Sarropoulou, Katerina (Greece). Studied philosophy, theater, and mime; since 1986 teaching speech, movement, theater improvisation, drama, neutral and expressive masks; since 2009 directing the Orff Schulwerk Course at the Moraitis School, Athens; theater director, chore-ographer, poet.

Scheer, Paul (Austria). BA graduate of the Orff Institute; member of the circus *kollektiv kaudawelsch;* works as circus pedagogue, artist, musician, and dancer.

Schönherr, Christine (Austria). Studied music, eurhythmics, recorder in Hamburg, Orff Schulwerk in Salzburg; lecturer for 35 years at the Orff Institute; since 2003 focus on music and dance activities for senior citizens, also in residential homes.

Shestopalova, Natalya (Russia). MA in Musicology, Saint-Petersburg Conservatory; 2015 BA, Orff-Institute, Mozarteum, Salzburg; since 2015 music teacher in Wyborg, Russia.

Siripachote, Warangkana (Thailand). Early childhood art teacher (teaching children ages 3 to 6 years) at Jittamett Kindergarten, Bangkok, Thailand.

Staveley, Robin (Australia). PhD research in the area of embodiment and cognitive neurosci-ence in pedagogy; teacher of music and movement for more than 40 years in universities and schools; currently she has an honorary appointment to the University of Technology in Sydney.

Stewart, Carolee (USA). PhD, graduate of the Orff Institute Special Course; retired dean of the Peabody Preparatory at Johns Hopkins University; middle and high school teacher; teacher educator; conference chair, past president of OSA USA; editor of several Schott American Edition supplements.

Tanzmeister, Viviane (Austria). Graduate of the Orff Institute 2021; founder of Companie Flitz; freelance dancer, choreographer, and dance teacher.

Valtiner-Pühringer, Doris (Austria). MA; graduated from and teaches dance subjects at the Orff Institute; conceives and directs children's concerts; co-author of *Kinder Konzerte für alle Sinne;* international Orff Schulwerk teacher.

Walser-Wohlfarter, Evelyne (Austria). BA and MA from the Orff Institute; lecturer, teacher educator; co-leader of the *initiative tanzfähig;* inclusion expert; dancer; choreographer; international dance projects collaborator.

Ware, Patrick (USA). Completed Orff Schulwerk certification levels 1-3; AOSA Approved Teacher Educator for movement, recorder, and basic pedagogy; OSA USA vice president for diversity, equity, inclusion, and accessibility; OSA USA president elect; K-5 public school teacher.

Widmer, Manuela (Austria). PhD; elemental music and dance teacher at the Orff Institute (1984–2012); educational scientist; teacher education courses worldwide; author; director of numerous elemental music theater productions.

Widmer, Michel (Austria). Works with children, youth, adults, families, and people with special needs, in and out of schools and in teacher education in many countries; lectured at the Orff Institute for more than 30 years (social work and inclusion), also works as a theater maker and clown.

Wolf, Angelika (Austria/UK). Studied at the Orff Institute, further training in Laban-Bartenieff Movement Studies, Hatha-Yoga, and Franklin-Method; teaches dance, movement, and music in various pedagogical universities.

Information about the International Orff-Schulwerk Forum Salzburg

International
Orff-Schulwerk Forum
Salzburg

History

The Seminar and Information Center for Orff-Schulwerk "Orff-Institut" was founded in 1961 at the then Mozarteum Academy in Salzburg by Carl Orff and Dr. Eberhard Preussner with the support from the Austrian Ministry of Education. In 1983, the Information Center was renamed Orff-Schulwerk Center Salzburg by Dr. Hermann Regner and became an independent institution. In 1984 it was registered as an independent non-profit association in Austria. When the Orff Center Munich was created in 1988, the name was changed to Orff-Schulwerk Forum Salzburg. Finally, in 2014 the organization's name changed to International Orff-Schulwerk Forum Salzburg, assuming an increased area of responsibility.

The directors of the organization were Wilhelm Keller (1966–1982), Hermann Regner (1983–1994), Barbara Haselbach (1994–2018), and Shirley Salmon (2018–present).

The Forum

(Latin: market, marketplace) was placed in the city center in ancient times. It was a place where people could meet, gain information, execute business, listen to, and be heard by others. Today "forum" also means a meeting place for specialist discussion, for the exchange of experiences and opinions.

Structure

The IOSFS is a network of national Orff-Schulwerk Associations, Associated Schools and Institutions, and individual members around the world. Its mission is to collect, to document and to publish international information about the work with Orff-Schulwerk, to further communication between institutions or individuals, to be an advisor for pedagogical questions, and to initiate events or support them.

Forms of membership
- Orff-Schulwerk Association (OSA)
- Associated School or Institution (ASI)
- Individual member
- Honorary member

Tasks

As the center of an international network, it is the task of the International Orff-Schulwerk Forum Salzburg to collect and make available information about working with Orff-Schulwerk and to encourage exchange of information. In fulfilling this function, it works in close contact with the Orff Institute, the Orff Center in Munich, and all international Orff-Schulwerk Associations.

The activities of the International Orff-Schulwerk Forum Salzburg include:

I Contact and Exchange
- with and among national Orff-Schulwerk Associations
- with and among Associated Schools and Institutions
- with graduates with advanced studies in Orff-Schulwerk
- with interested teachers, researchers, artists, and institutions

II Information
- about Orff-Schulwerk in the past and present
- about projects and developments in different countries
- about courses and publications
- about current themes with regard to contents and organizational questions

III Publications
- Magazine: *Orff-Schulwerk Informationen / Orff-Schulwerk Heute* (OSH) Issues 1–100 (https://www.orff-schulwerk-forum-salzburg.org/magazine-osh); since 2022, *Orff-Schulwerk International* (online at iosfsjournal.com)
- *Texts on Theory and Practice of Orff-Schulwerk*
- Reports about international Orff-Schulwerk work
- Documentations of symposia (Book/DVD)
- Other publications

IV Advice
- on publications of new adaptations of the Schulwerk
- on academic work, publications, new editions
- on syllabi, curricula, and for lecturers in various educational and social institutions
- on future projects
- on the introduction of Orff-Schulwerk to an institution or country
- on the founding of a new Orff-Schulwerk Association or Associated School/Institution

V Events
- Annual conventions for IOSFS members and guests
- Meetings with editors of Orff-Schulwerk Association newsletters and magazines
- Orff-Schulwerk symposia and other events

VI Recommendations and Guidelines of the International Orff-Schulwerk Forum Salzburg
- Recommendations and guidelines for organizing teacher education courses
- Recommendations for the founding of a national Orff-Schulwerk Association
- Recommendations for the founding of an Associated School/Institution

Contact:
www.orff-schulwerk-forum-salzburg.org
info.iosfs@gmail.com

Orff-Schulwerk Associations Around the World

Country	Association	Founded
ARGENTINA	Asociación Orff-Schulwerk Argentina (AAOrff) http://www.aaorff.com	2009
AUSTRALIA	Australian National Council of Orff Schulwerk (ANCOS) http://www.ancos.org.au	1976
AUSTRALIA	New South Wales Orff-Schulwerk Association Inc. (NSWOSA) http://www.orffnsw.org.au	1972
AUSTRALIA	Orff-Schulwerk Association of South Australia Inc. (OSASA) http://www.osasa.net	1984
AUSTRALIA	Queensland Orff-Schulwerk Association (QOSA) http://qosa.org.au	1967
AUSTRALIA	Tasmanian Orff-Schulwerk Association (TOSA) http://www.ancos.org.au/pages/state-associations/tasmania	1983
AUSTRALIA	Victorian Orff-Schulwerk Association (VOSA) http://www.vosa.org	1977
AUSTRALIA	West Australian Orff-Schulwerk Association (WAOSA) http://www.waosa.org.au	1994
AUSTRIA	Orff-Schulwerk Gesellschaft Österreich https://orff-schulwerk.at/	1961
BRAZIL	Associação ORFF Brasil - "Música e Movimento na Educação" (ABRAORFF) http://www.abraorff.org.br	2004
BULGARIA	Bulgarische Assoziation Orff-Schulwerk	2004
CANADA	Carl Orff Canada - Music for Children / Musique pour Enfants https://www.orffcanada.ca/	1974
CHINA	China Orff Schulwerk Association (COSA)	1991
COLOMBIA	Asociación Orff Colombia (ACOLORFF) http://www.acolorff.org	2014
CROATIA	Croatian Orff Schulwerk Association - CROSA Hrvatska Orff Schulwerk Udruga – HOSU http://www.hosu.hr/	2002
CZECH REPUBLIC	Česká Orffova společnost (COS) http://www.orff.cz/	1995
ESTONIA	Estonian Society for Music Education (EMÕL) http://www.emol.ee	1992
FINLAND	JaSeSoi ry, Orff-Schulwerk Association of Finland http://www.jasesoi.com	1985
FRANCE	Association Carl Orff France http://orff.fr/	2001
GEORGIA	Georgian Orff-Schulwerk Association (Georff)	2015
GERMANY	Orff-Schulwerk Gesellschaft Deutschland e.V., Musik+Tanz+Erziehung http://www.orff-schulwerk.de	1962

Country	Association	Founded
GREECE	Hellenic Association of Music & Movement Education (ESMA) http://www.orffesma.gr	1990
HONG KONG	Hong Kong Orff-Schulwerk Association http://www.hosa.org.hk	2016
ICELAND	Samtök Orff Tónmennta Íslandi (SOTI)	2007
IRAN	Association Orff-Schulwerk Iran (ADAMAK) http://www.iranorff.com	2015
ITALY	Orff-Schulwerk Italiano (OSI) http://www.orffitaliano.com	2001
ITALY	Società Italiana di Musica Elementare Orff-Schulwerk (SIMEOS) http://www.simeos.it	1978
JAPAN	Japanese Orff-Schulwerk Association http://www.orff-schulwerk-japan.com	1988
MACAO	Macau Orff Schulwerk Association (MOSA) https://www.macauorff.org	2018
NEW ZEALAND	Orff New Zealand Aotearoa (ONZA) http://www.orffnz.org	2005
POLAND	Polskie Towarzystwo Carla Orffa (PTCO) http://www.orff.pl	1994
RUSSIA	Orff-Schulwerk Association Russia (ROSA) http://rusorff.ru	1988
SCOTLAND	Scottish Orff-Schulwerk Association (SOSA) http://www.orffscotland.org	2010
SINGAPORE	Orff-Schulwerk Association Singapore https://www.singorff.com	2002
SLOVENIA	Slovensko Društvo Carla Orffa (SDCO) http://slorff.weebly.com	2001
SOUTH AFRICA	Orff-Schulwerk Society of South Africa http://www.orff.co.za	1972
SOUTH KOREA	Korean Orff Schulwerk Association (KOSA) http://www.korff.or.kr	2004
SPAIN	Asociación Orff España (AOE) http://www.orff-spain.org	1996
SPAIN	Associació Orff Catalunya https://www.orff.cat/	2020
SWITZERLAND	Orff-Schulwerk Schweiz - Gesellschaft für Musik- und Tanzerziehung http://www.orff-schulwerk.ch	1979
TAIWAN	Taiwan Orff-Schulwerk Association (TOSA)	1992
THAILAND	Thai Orff-Schulwerk Association (THOSA) http://www.thaiorff.org	2008
TURKEY	Orff-Schulwerk Egitim ve Danismanlik Merkezi Türkiye - Orff Merkezi http://www.orffmerkezi.org	2001

Country	Association	Founded
TURKEY	ORFFDER—Anadolu Orff-Schulwerk Derneği (Anatolian Orff-Schulwerk Association) http://www.orffder.org	2021
UKRAINE	Orff Association Ukraine https://orff-ua.com	2018
UNITED KINGDOM	Orff Society UK http://www.orff.org.uk	1964
USA	American Orff-Schulwerk Association (AOSA) http://www.aosa.org	1968
VIETNAM	Carl Orff Vietnam	2024

Network of Associated Schools and Institutions

Country	Name of School or Institution
ARGENTINA	Escuela de Artes Pestalozzi http://www.pestalozzi.edu.ar
AUSTRALIA	Eton Farm Primary School http://www.etonfarmps.wa.edu.au
CHINA	IMMEA—Institute for Music and Movement Education Advancement http://www.immeachina.cn
CZECH REPUBLIC	Grundschule der deutsch-tschechischen Verständigung http://www.gtmskola.cz
GERMANY	Carl-Orff-Grundschule Traunwalchen https://www.carl-orff-gs-traunwalchen.de
GERMANY	Carl-Orff-Grundschule Andechs https://carlorffschule.de
GERMANY	DOrff-Werkstatt e.V. http://www.dorffwerkstatt.de
GERMANY	Carl Orff-Grundschule Altenerding http://www.carl-orff-gs-altenerding.de
GERMANY	Elementare Musikpädagogik. Künstlerisch-pädagogischer Studiengang innerhalb der Hochschule für Musik und Theater München http://emp.hmtm.de/
GREECE	The Moraitis School http://www.orff.gr
GREECE	National and Kapodistrian University of Athens, School of Education, Department of Early Childhood Education https://www.ecd.uoa.gr/language/en/
ITALY	CDM Centro Didattico Musicale http://www.centrodidatticomusicale.it
ITALY	Musicanto–Centro per la Ricerca e la Didattica Musicale http://www.musicanto.org
ITALY	Scuola Popolare di Musica Donna Olimpia http://www.donnaolimpia.it
ITALY	International School of Bergamo http://www.isbergamo.com
SOUTH KOREA	Notre Dame Kindergarten, Osan https://cafe.naver.com/ndosan
SOUTH KOREA	Notre Dame Orff-Music Institute (NOMI) http://cafe.daum.net/notredameorff
THAILAND	Jittamett Kindergarten http://www.jittamett.ac.th/jittamett.ac.th_public_html/About.html
TURKEY	ALEV Schule https://alev.k12.tr
USA	San Francisco School http://www.sfschool.org

Country	Name of School or Institution
USA	Alliance for Active Music Making (AAMM) http://www.allianceamm.org
USA	American Center for Elemental Music and Movement (ACEMM) http://www.acemm.us

Studientexte zu Theorie und Praxis des Orff-Schulwerks/
Texts on Theory and Practice of Orff-Schulwerk

edited by Barbara Haselbach

*Band I/*Volume I
Basistexte aus den Jahren 1932–2010/
Basic Texts from the Years 1932–2010

edited by Barbara Haselbach
bilingual edition with English translations by Margaret Murray 2011

The authors of Orff Schulwerk and their closest co-operators describe the basics of what has become unquestionable common knowledge of Elemental Music and Dance Pedagogy. The selected texts present a necessary theoretical completion of the experiences of practical work. They give foundation and justification of it.

Preface: Barbara Haselbach
Introduction: Michael Kugler

Articles

Erinnerungen an die Günther-Schule (1978)
Memories of the Günther-Schule (1978)
> Gunild Keetman

Gedanken über Musik mit Kindern und Laien (1932)
Thoughts about Music with Children and Non-professionals (1932)
> Carl Orff

Der rhythmische Mensch und seine Erziehung (1932)
The Rhythmic Person and Their Education (1932)
> Dorothee Günther

Musik aus der Bewegung (1932)
Music out of Movement (1932)
> Carl Orff

Elementarer Tanz (1962)
Elemental Dance (1962)
> Dorothee Günther

Elementare Musik—Versuch einer Begriffsbestimmung (1962)
Elemental Music—an Attempt to Define It (1962)
> Wilhelm Keller

Das Schulwerk—Rückblick und Ausblick (1963)
Orff-Schulwerk: Past & Future (1963)
> Carl Orff

"Am Anfang war das Wort ..."—Zur Bedeutung der Sprache im Orff-Schulwerk (1969)
"In the Beginning was the Word ..."—on the Significance of the Spoken Word in Orff-Schulwerk (1969)
>   Werner Thomas

Carl Orffs pädagogische Ideen—Utopie und Wirklichkeit (1975)
Carl Orff's Educational Ideas—Utopia and Reality (1975)
>   Hermann Regner

Reflexionen über die tanzpädagogischen Aspekte des Orff-Schulwerks (1984/2010)
Reflections on the Dance Educational Aspects of Orff-Schulwerk (1984/2010)
>   Barbara Haselbach

"Musik für Kinder – Music for Children – Musique pour Enfants"
Anmerkungen zur Rezeption und Adaption des Orff-Schulwerks in andern Ländern (1984)
Comments on the Adoption and Adaptation of Orff-Schulwerk in other Countries (1984)
>   Hermann Regner

Elementare Musik-und Bewegungserziehung. Fundamente und anthropologische Aspekte (1997/2010)
Elemental Music and Movement Education. Focus on Fundamentals and Anthropological Aspects (1997/2010)
>   Ulrike E. Jungmair

50 Jahre "Musik für Kinder—Orff-Schulwerk." Gedanken zum aktuellen Status eines musikpädagogischen Klassikers (2000/2010)
50 Years "Music for Children—Orff-Schulwerk": Thoughts about the Present Status of a Music Educational Classic (2000/2010)
>   Rudolf Nykrin

Volume II
Orff Schulwerk in Diverse Cultures—
An Idea That Went Round the World

edited by Barbara Haselbach and Carolee Stewart

2021

This book is a commentary on the phenomenon of the rapid and worldwide dissemination of Orff Schulwerk, which has been in continuous process for more than 80 years since its origins in Central Europe. A selection of articles on the topic of adapting and adopting Orff Schulwerk is followed with contributions from countries in Asia, Africa, North and South America and Oceania, supplemented by some European countries that have a special feature. In documenting the various adaptations of Orff Schulwerk, the authors describe characteristics and differences that result from the integration with each country's cultural traditions and educational systems.

Foreword: Shirley Salmon
Introduction: Barbara Haselbach, Carolee Stewart

Part I: Texts on Theory of Orff Schulwerk

Musik für Kinder–Music for Children–Musique pour Enfants:
Comments on the Adoption and Adaptation of Orff Schulwerk in Other Countries
    Hermann Regner

A Consideration of Cross-Cultural Adaptation of the Schulwerk Pedagogical Model
    Mary Shamrock

Intercultural Aspects of the Orff Schulwerk
    Michael Kugler

The Principles of Orff Schulwerk
    Wolfgang Hartmann

Something Old, Something New - Orff Schulwerk and World Music
    Doug Goodkin

Part II: Texts on Practice of Orff Schulwerk Around the World

Africa

The World to My Village, My Village to the World: Orff Schulwerk in Ghana
    Kofi Gbolonyo interviewed by Doug Goodkin

Orff Schulwerk in South Africa
    Compiled and edited by Janice Klette Evans

America: North and South

The Development of Orff Schulwerk in Argentina
    Compiled and edited by Nacho Propato

The Orff Approach in the Brazilian Creative Environment

Maristela Mosca, Magda Pucci, Lucilene Silva

Voyage of Discovery: Orff Schulwerk in Canada 1954–2021
James Jackson, Catherine West, Françoise Grenier, Julie Mongeon-Ferré

Orff Schulwerk in Colombia
Catherine Correa Lopera, Beatriz Serna Mejía

Orff Schulwerk in the United States: Always Developing
Carolee Stewart

Asia

Orff Schulwerk in China
Compiled and edited by Xu Mai and Sarah Brooke

Orff Schulwerk in Iran: A New Beginning
Kamran Ghabrai, Nastaran Kimiavi, Mastaneh Hakimi, Farzan Farnia, Shahrzad Beheshtian

Adaptation of Orff Schulwerk in Japan
Masayuki Nakaji, Tohru Iguchi, Junko Hosoda, Junko Kawaguchi, Wakako Nagaoka

Orff Schulwerk in Singapore
Paul Grosse

Orff Schulwerk in South Korea
Hye-Young Kim, Sung-Sil An, Hyeon-Kyeong Kweon (Sr. Johannita), Young-Bae Yun, Oh-Sun Kwon, Yeni Kim, In-Hye Rosensteiner

Orff Schulwerk in Taiwan
Fang-Ling Kuo

Orff Schulwerk in Thailand
Krongtong Boonprakong, Wittaya Laithong, Amanut Jantarawirote, Geeta Purmpul, Sakrapee Raktaprajit

Europe

The Czech Orff Schulwerk
Jiřina Jiřičková

Orff Schulwerk in Greece: Past and Present
Maria Filianou

Orff Schulwerk in the Nordic Countries
Kristín Valsdóttir

Orff Schulwerk in Russia
Inna Akhremenko, Elena Filimonova, Galina Khokhryakova, Irina Shestopalova, Natalya Valchenko, Vyacheslav Zhilin

Orff Schulwek in Spain
Sofía López-Ibor, Ester Bonal
Orff Schulwerk in Turkey

Orff Merkezi–Orff Schulwerk Education Center Turkey
  Banu Özevin, Bilgehan Eren, Fatoş Cümbüş Auernig, Işık Sabırlı
The Pekinel Project to Improve Musical Education in Anatolia
  Güher and Süher Pekinel
ORFFDER - Anatolian Orff Schulwerk Association
  Ali Öztürk, Atilla Coşkun Toksoy, Didem Karşıyakalı Doğan, Evrim Onay,
  Senem Özyoğurtcu, Emine Yaprak Kotzian

Orff Schulwerk in Ukraine: Traditions and Innovations
  Svetlana Fir, Tatiana Chernous

The Orff Approach in the UK
  Kate Buchanan, Sarah Hennessy, Caroline McCluskey

Oceania

Orff Schulwerk in Australia
  Compiled and edited by Peta Harper and Sarah Powell

Orff Schulwerk in Aotearoa New Zealand
  Linda M. Locke

The Orff Institute at the University Mozarteum Salzburg

The Orff Institute was founded in 1961 by the composer and pedagogue Carl Orff as a training and further education center for Elemental Music and Movement Education and center for Orff-Schulwerk. Today, the Department of Elemental Music and Dance Education-Orff Institute of the Mozarteum University is characterized by a contemporary art practice and a pedagogy emphasizing creativity. Music, dance, and speech are designed and taught in an inter- and transdisciplinary way. In science and research, contributions to the theorization of Elemental Music and Dance Education as well as related disciplines are generated.

Studies at the Department of Elemental Music and Dance Education—Orff Institute Salzburg

Bachelor's Degree
"BA Elemental Music and Dance Education"
   8 semesters

Master's Studies
"MA Elemental Music and Dance Education"
   building on the bachelor's degree in Elemental Music and Dance Education
   or related studies
   4 semesters
"MA Elemental Music and Movement Education"
   building on pedagogical or artistic studies
   4 semesters

University Courses
Advanced Studies in Music and Dance Education - Orff-Schulwerk
   in English language, one academic year, biennially
Music and Dance in Social Work and Inclusive Pedagogy
   part-time 8 weekends per academic year
Elemental Music and Movement Pedagogy
   part-time 8 weekends per academic year

International Summer Courses
https://www.moz.ac.at/en/orff-institute